THE
WOMAN
WHO
NAMED
GOD

Also by Charlotte Gordon

POETRY

Two Girls on a Raft
When the Grateful Dead Came to St. Louis

NONFICTION

Mistress Bradstreet

THE WOMAN WHO NAMED GOD

ABRAHAM'S DILEMMA AND
THE BIRTH OF THREE FAITHS

CHARLOTTE GORDON

LITTLE, BROWN AND COMPANY

NEW YORK   BOSTON   LONDON

Little, Brown and Company
Hachette Book Group
237 Park Avenue, New York, NY 10017
Visit our website at www.HachetteBookGroup.com

First Edition: July 2009

Little, Brown and Company is a division of Hachette Book Group, Inc.
The Little, Brown name and logo are trademarks of
Hachette Book Group, Inc.

The author gratefully acknowledges use of the following previously copyrighted material: Excerpts from *The Discovery of God: Abraham and the Birth of Monotheism* by David Klinghoffer, copyright © 2003 by David Klinghoffer. Used by permission of Doubleday, a division of Random House, Inc. Excerpts from *Understanding Genesis, The Heritage of Biblical Israel*, vol. 1, 5th ed., by Nahum Sarna. New York: Schocken Books, 1978; New York: Jewish Theological Seminary of America, 1966. Excerpts from *The Death and Resurrection of the Beloved Son* by Jon Levenson. New Haven: Yale University Press, 1993. Excerpts from *Legends of the Jews*, © 1966 by Louis Ginzberg, published by The Jewish Publication Society, with the permission of the publisher.

Library of Congress Cataloging-in-Publication Data
Gordon, Charlotte.
   The woman who named God : Abraham's dilemma and the birth of three faiths / Charlotte Gordon. — 1st ed.
      p. cm.
   Includes bibliographical references.
   ISBN 978-0-316-11474-5
   1. Bible. O.T. Genesis — Criticism, Narrative.   2. Narration in the Bible.
3. Abraham (Biblical patriarch)   4. Sarah (Biblical matriarch)   5. Hagar (Biblical figure)   I. Title.
   BS1235.52.G67 2009
   222'.110922 — dc22   2009010539

10 9 8 7 6 5 4 3 2 1

RRD-IN

Printed in the United States of America

For Paul

Sh'ma Israel Adonai: Eloheinu Adonai echad.
Hear, O Israel, the Lord is our God, the Lord is One.
(Deuteronomy 6:4)

Credo in unum Deum.
I believe in one God.
(Apostles' Creed)

Lā ilāha illa'Llāh
There is no god but God.
(Koran 2:255)

CONTENTS

INTRODUCTION

A heartbroken man stands at the threshold of his tent, watching the desert unfold. It is daybreak, and golden hills ripple gently across the horizon. He knows how dangerous the sands can be. Giant dunes shift in the wind. The nearest well is at least a day's journey away. By the time the sun has reached its peak the heat will be unbearable.

The man's name is Abraham, and it is into this wilderness that he has banished two members of his camp, his second wife and the teenage son he loves. He watches them now as they fill sacks with lentils and water. He helps the woman strap on her pack but says nothing to her—there is nothing left to say. He knows she and the boy have little chance of survival. They will face suffocating heat, dust storms, and paralyzing despair. He's certain he'll never see them again.

The woman's name is Hagar, and Abraham's relationship with her has nearly ruined his life. The young man beside her is Abraham's firstborn son, Ishmael. Standing behind Abraham is his first wife, Sarah, a woman whose legendary beauty has made Pharaohs and kings desperate for her love. In her arms Sarah holds a little boy, Isaac, born after decades of prayer and aggravation. Sarah can't help but feel triumphant now, confident in both her husband's fidelity and the belief that her son will become Abraham's only heir.

When Sarah turns away, Abraham stares after Hagar, memorizing her shape, listening for Ishmael's voice. He watches until their shadows grow fainter. As soon as the figures have disappeared into the desert, he, Sarah, and Isaac go together into their tent. Abraham has obeyed his wife's demands to reject Hagar and Ishmael, just as God had commanded him to do, but it is less clear that he has adhered to the second part of God's command: "Do not be distressed over the boy or [the woman]" (Gen. 21:12). How can he stop thinking about them? How can he stop worrying about their fate?

ABRAHAM IS TRADITIONALLY known as the father of three religions. For centuries his story has been at the center of a generalized cultural anxiety about religious identity. Not only does it prefigure the ongoing enmity among the Jewish, Christian, and Islamic worlds, it also concerns the fate of three very famous parents and the estranged half-brothers they produced. Regardless of whether one chooses to believe that any of these events actually happened, this story's impact on the shape of history is immeasurable. It is what anthropologists call a myth of origin and its implications are inescapable, even for those who would like to think they are untouched by its aftershocks.

Perhaps another reason this story is so compelling is that Abraham, Sarah, and Hagar are Biblical characters who behave like real human beings. With their jealousies and passions, doubts and anxieties, they are among the first in the western assemblage of cultural icons to be racked by such modern ailments as self-doubt and inner turmoil. In this way, their heirs are not only Jacob, Jesus, and Mohammed, but also Hamlet and Ahab, the Reverend Dimmesdale and Isabel Archer, Anna Karenina, Mrs. Dalloway, and Jane Eyre. This is especially true of Abraham, who seems more like an Updike character than an ancient as he stands at his tent, torn between duty and desire, his love for one woman and his responsibility to another, and tormented by faith in a god whose motivations he doesn't always understand.

The eviction of Hagar and Ishmael from the campsite of Abraham and Sarah is arguably the pivotal moment in one of the Bible's most troubling love stories, and it is easy to picture the characters as if they were actors in a movie. We watch Hagar weep. We hear Sarah rant. We witness Abraham's grief. The story brims with potent details. Indeed, it is as though Scripture wants us to *feel* the story as powerfully as possible. And it is easy to understand why.

Even those who have only a dim recollection of the tale of Abraham, Sarah, and Hagar are still awash in its cultural wake. In fact, it is a common staple of modern life to be married to one person and longing for another or living with one person and raising another's children. Abraham's family life is our family life. He has passed his ambivalences down to the modern era, and, of course, this internal division has larger consequences than twenty-first-century domestic life. Rockets fired at civilians in Sderot, the settlers' aggression in the West Bank, a president's reference to Islamic countries as "the axis of evil," and Osama bin Laden's stated hatred of the West are just a few examples of how this myth lives on, how Hagar's children and Sarah's children struggle against each other, just as their mothers once did.

So how did this ancient tale, a creation story as important as the Garden of Eden, become one of the most frequently misinterpreted of all western stories? Perhaps it's because it has been trumped by the Christian emphasis on the New Testament, or by the horrific tale of Abraham's near slaying of his son on Mount Moriah, or else it has been obscured by secular modernity's overweening contempt for Scripture. There is also the troubling fact that so many church fathers, rabbis, and Islamic scholars have traditionally downplayed the importance of women and the love between men and women in the shaping of each of their religions.

As a result, those artists and writers who have been fascinated by the story, including Victorian moralists, Renaissance painters, and religious leaders, both liberal and conservative, have tended to use its characters to support their own agendas. Hagar is seen as a victim, a lascivious sinner, an abused slave, or as the strong, nurturing mother of Ishmael. Sarah is painted either as a jealous wife, a Jewish prophet, or the mother of all true Christians. Abraham is generally regarded as the obedient servant of God, the embodiment of a one-dimensional faith, rather than as a complicated, many-layered individual who suffers greatly during this episode in his life.

Of course, this kind of appropriation happens to all Bible stories. But in this case, when integral pieces are missing from interpretations, it is difficult to appreciate the fact that some of the most crucial western ideas about freedom come from Hagar, or that modern attitudes about rightful inheritance and family obligation can be traced directly back to Sarah. As for Abraham, he is a man who often felt uncertain and could be cruel to the women he loved. If one overlooks the complexities of these characters, the story's most powerful themes are greatly diminished and the eternal human struggle with what it means to be faithful, not only to God but to each other, becomes hidden behind simplified cardboard cutouts.

Ultimately, then, the terrible split that Abraham experiences between the two women he loves, and between their eventual offspring, is one of the most important stories about relationships in our culture. The fallout from this ancient family quarrel continues to affect us both personally and politically. With soaring divorce rates, the disputed ethics of sexual encounters, and conflicting definitions of what makes a family, we need only look back to this tale to understand where at least some of our complicated attitudes come from. Millions of people have been taught to believe that Hagar's son, Ishmael, survives his desert exile and becomes the father of the Arabs; Sarah's son, Isaac, marries Rebecca and sires the Jews. Warring nations rise from one father's divided loyalties. Four thousand years later, gunshots ring across Gaza, the twin towers fall in

New York, troops march into Baghdad, and Iranian president Mahmoud Ahmadinejad denounces the Israeli government as "the flag of Satan."[1]

In the gloomy light of the modern era, I'm sure I'm not alone in wishing it had all happened differently: What if Abraham had changed his mind, defying God's commandment and his wife's demands? What if he had chased after his mistress and firstborn son, begged Sarah to forget his betrayal, and urged Hagar to forgive Sarah's jealousy, so that they might raise their sons together? Would we be any better at living in peace?

Fortunately, there are possibilities in this story that lie hidden in its shadows, gaps, and silences.[2] Here, we can find strange revelatory moments that might strain our preconceptions but also offer hope. What is left unsaid is sometimes as important as what is said, particularly when we are curious about the lives of women. Perhaps God chose the wife, not the husband. Perhaps the husband did rebel against God. And, perhaps, the victim was not a victim, after all, but was a prophet and a nation founder in her own right.

My Approach

That Abraham, Sarah, Hagar, and, for that matter, any other Biblical figure actually existed depends on what you believe about religion in general and the books of the Bible in particular. But whatever position you take regarding faith and the veracity of Scripture, for thousands of years these men and women have been camped in the imagination of the West, trekking through the desert, watering their donkeys, marrying, squabbling, and sometimes speaking to God and hearing His voice in return. In other words, whether we like it or not, the world has been populated by these characters for millennia, and their flaws, desires, and pieties have become part of how we measure ourselves.

Some may say: These are just stories. What about facts? What really happened back then? Did Abraham, Sarah, and Hagar truly exist? But this desire for hard evidence is based on modern attitudes, ones that misunderstand the Bible more profoundly than any credulity of the past ever did. In our secular age, when we use the word "myth" as a synonym for falsehood, we forget that stories can have enormous weight. Cultures pass down crucial tales about how they came to be, and about why they are the way they are. Even if the stories themselves get lost, the ideas stick. If we want to understand who we are, why we aspire to certain dreams, or why we hate some things about ourselves more than others, then we need to grapple with these stories.

The Bible is a thickly twisted braid of documented record, legend, law, and fable and it is this unwieldy collection that we have inherited. I do not seek to uncover the historical Abraham, Sarah, or Hagar. They are figures who straddle the realms of mythology and history and are a strange mixture of supernatural and realistic elements. Each one lives for more than 120 years; each one has a unique relationship with God.

A historian might guide you on a search for the "real" Abraham, Sarah, and Hagar and help you explore the actualities (the socioeconomics, diet, customs, marriage practices, etc.) of the people of the second millennium B.C.E., the period when these figures are thought to have lived. A theologian could help you uncover many of the religious meanings of this story, its impact on your faith and your view of God. With an archaeologist, you might get to go on a tour of ancient sites and look for evidence that these people, or people like them, existed. Finally, a Bible scholar could help you understand when this story might have been written down and the politics and historical stratagems that helped shape the narrative.

But this book explores the stories that have been passed down to us as *stories*. Although I will draw on the findings of theologians, scholars, archaeologists, and historians, the questions that drive this book are not: Is it true and what does it mean? or How did these people pitch their tents and make a living? Rather, I ask: Who were these characters as individuals? Why did they do what they did? Did they change over time? What do the Bible and the legends of all three faiths suggest about their personalities, strengths, and flaws?

Unlike the Koran and other religious documents, the Bible has always been seen as both literary and religious in nature. In fact, originally, it made no sense to separate the two: religion was literature and literature was religion. Early commentators sat in their houses of prayer and studied each word of each tale and asked questions that sound remarkably literary or "modern" to our secular ears. Why does Abraham ask Sarah to lie to Pharaoh? Why does Sarah offer Hagar to Abraham? Why does Hagar mock Sarah? All these questions and their answers were meant to illuminate a divinely sponsored work, and such analysis was intended not only to shed additional light on these texts, and on the nature of God, but was also seen as a religious activity in itself.

I do not claim to be engaging in such an exalted activity. Nor do I seek to challenge or even address whether the Bible is the Word of God, written by divine inspiration or the divine hand itself. But I do attempt to draw nearer to these men and women in Genesis through careful study of the text and by combing through the findings of historical, theological, linguistic, and archaeological research.

Not surprisingly, when one immerses oneself in the drama of Abraham, Sarah, and Hagar, a fourth personage emerges, one who plays a crucial role in each character's life. In this book I will refer to Him with a capital *G*, as this is how He has been known for thousands of years. I will also use the pronoun "He," as this has also long been our cultural convention. The Abraham, Sarah, and Hagar story raises the problem of fidelity not only in marriage but also in relation to God. The two are strangely linked in each of the tales that form the novella of Abraham and the women he loved.

It is striking how rarely the tools of literary interpreters have been used in studying this story.[3] At first it would seem that this is because of the theological roadblocks that have been in place throughout the centuries. But really the problem seems to have been that scholars who have been trained to analyze literature are held back by their lack of knowledge of Biblical languages. Thus, the study of the Bible has remained largely in the hands of those well versed in the languages in which the Bible was written down: Aramaic, Hebrew, and Greek. Generally speaking, these individuals have been those whose job descriptions are very different from that of the literary scholar.

But Biblical interpretation can be a far more democratic process than it has been. Modern interpreters can learn Hebrew and Greek. They can rely on a variety of translations and experts. They can turn to the work of the important pioneers in the field—Jack Miles, Phyllis Trible, Elie Wiesel, Arthur Waskow, and many more. It is our responsibility to seek out this book and reevaluate who we are in relationship to the past. Otherwise, we are left with an inert document of apparently contradictory messages that antagonists can deploy, mining the text for one new weapon after another, defending arguments of hate.

A Note on Sources

I use the Hebrew Bible, the Jewish Publication Society (JPS) version, for the text of the story itself. When I have relied on my own translations, I make note of this in the citations. For passages from Christian Scripture, I consult the New Revised Standard Version. I also rely heavily on the legends that have sprung up around these three characters and will draw from the Midrash (the collection of rabbinical writings that attempt to elucidate the Bible); the Koran and the hadith (the collection of writings, similar to the Midrash, that comment on the Koran); the Christian Scripture, particularly the writings of Paul; and the writings of early church fathers, especially Augustine. I also refer to the work of the first-century Jewish historian Josephus, and noncanonical works, such as the Book of

Jubilees, a retelling of Genesis from the second century B.C.E., and the Apocalypse of Abraham, a collection of legends about Abraham from the late first century C.E. (For more information on these sources, see the section called "Some Definitions.")

When it comes to Hebrew Scripture, however, it is no surprise that there is an enormous amount of commentary from the Jewish sources, and I make reference to these throughout the book. These sources — what they are, where they came from, and why and when they were written — may be confusing to the layman, so I will try to explain them briefly here.

After the Romans destroyed the Temple in 70 C.E., the rabbis of the first and second centuries C.E. faced the fact that their religion, based as it was on sacrificial offerings at the sacred altar, was in danger of dying. When the last Jewish rebellion against the Romans failed (the Bar Kokhba rebellion in 135 C.E.), the Jews were driven from the land, and the Romans attempted to wipe out their memory, even renaming their land Palestine so that the name Judea would be lost in history. Of course, it is ironic that it would be the Roman Empire that would ultimately vanish, while strangely, the defeated rebels, the Jews, continue to thrive. Why is this?

In a word: the Bible.

After their defeat, the surviving Jewish leaders began to shape a new culture and a new way to worship. Study of the Bible would have to replace the sacrificial cult of the Temple. The synagogue would provide the social context for this study. Thus, the words of the Jewish holy book assumed an extraordinary importance. They were all that was left of a people.

Now that there was closer focus on the text, however, its ambiguities and seeming inconsistencies became more apparent. So it was fortunate that the rabbis had another sacred source to rely upon besides the written Bible. According to traditional Jewish belief, God actually gave Moses two Torahs at Sinai: the written Torah, known to the world as the first five books of Hebrew Scripture, and the Oral Torah, a collection of legends and law that had been passed down from generation to generation but had never been written down. These tales and legal formulations were considered as legitimate and as sacred as written Scripture, and so, in the midst of the chaos of this time in Jewish history and no doubt in fear that the traditions might vanish in the diaspora, the rabbis took it upon themselves to record this Oral Torah.

The stories they wrote down are called *Midrash*, from a Hebrew word that comes from the root *drsh*, which means "to seek out." Thus, the Midrash about Abraham attempt to "seek out" or solve many of the questions left unanswered by the written Torah. In addition, the rabbis also ferreted out clues from inside the written Bible and wove together tales based on strange grammatical points, redundancies, and other oddities they discovered. Despite the enormous effort their work entailed, these early commentators did not believe the Midrash were their own creation. Instead, they conceived of themselves as recording or explaining the cryptic words of God, who had delivered the Midrash to them.

In addition to this careful scrutiny of the stories of the Bible, the rabbis were also intent on recording the traditions and law ("halakhah") of their people: How should one observe the Sabbath? What kind of food was acceptable to eat? What kind of prayers should be said and when? By the sixth century, the final results of these labors were compiled into the Talmud.

Although there are examples of Midrash, or interpretive exegeses, inside the Talmud, most of these are based on legal practices and are called Midrash halakhah. In the interest of organizing the Talmud and keeping it to a manageable size, the rabbis decided to collect the rest of the Midrash—the parables, homilies, and stories that were not primarily based on law or legal proceedings—into separate collections. For my book, the collection that has been most helpful is called *Genesis Rabbah*. This book, which offers a running commentary on almost every word of Genesis, is one of the oldest examples of Midrash and contains passages that were probably recorded as early as the third century.

The exegetical techniques that mark both the Talmud and the Midrash have been refined over the centuries and passed down through the generations, becoming hallmarks of Jewish thought as well as an inspiration to early Christians and Muslims. Interestingly, the Koran and hadith record many of the same stories as the Midrash, lending even more weight to the importance of these legends. Even early Christians take the writings of the rabbis into account. In fact, some might say that the church father Paul was actually performing Midrash, or rabbinical exegesis, in his interpretation of both Scripture and the words of Jesus.

The tradition of Midrash and legal commentary continued into the Middle Ages. In fact, it continues to this day. However, some of the most comprehensive analyses of both the Torah and Talmud were written in the eleventh and twelfth centuries. I have particularly relied on the explanations and interpretations of Rabbi Shlomo Yitzhaki, known by his acronym, Rashi. I also refer to Rabbi Moses ben Maimon, better known as Maimonides or by his acronym, Rambam; Rabbi Abraham Ibn Ezra; and Rabbi Moses ben Nachman, also known as Nachmanides or Ramban.

While any interpretation of Genesis must take into account the work of the rabbis, the observations and teachings of Christian and Muslim commentators are also essential, as they give different perspectives on all four characters. This is particularly true of Islam, since Hagar and Ishmael, rather than Sarah and Isaac, are seen as the heroes of the Arabic world. I have also relied on contemporary feminist scholars from all three traditions, as well as feminist literary theory, to develop and discuss questions about the women in the story.

One of the challenges of this book is that, in the many stories from different traditions, there are a myriad of Abrahams, Sarahs, and Hagars. Over the centuries each Jewish, Christian, and Muslim scholar has "discovered" new facets of their personalities and of God's as well. These tales and interpretations have merged with the original Biblical stories in confusing and often contradictory ways. Abraham did not cast Hagar out into the desert, the Muslims say; he took her by the hand and led her to Mecca. Abraham's son Isaac is a prototype for Jesus, the Christians declare, a holy man whose tale is not finished until the coming of the Christ. As for the Jews, the early rabbis dedicated themselves to making Abraham and Sarah into a hero and a heroine befitting their status as the founding father and mother of the Israelites.

These legends sometimes tell us more about the people who invented them than about the characters themselves. Commentators point out elements in the story they find bewildering, even though these points may seem straightforward to us. Others add details to support a political or theological agenda. Still others elucidate the text with their knowledge of language and history, introducing ideas that would never have occurred to those readers who do not know Hebrew, Aramaic, or Greek.

However, there is one central question that none of these commentators can answer, and which certainly cannot be resolved in this book: Who wrote the Bible? The most traditional point of view is that God is the author of the Bible and that every word has been divinely inspired. Another theory, known as the Documentary Hypothesis, holds that a redactor or a team of redactors put together the different documents during some period of time, probably beginning in the sixth century B.C.E., during the exile in Babylon. Naturally, there are many other arguments that fall in between these two.

From the perspective of a literary interpreter, though, what is most important is the body of work as a whole, as it exists now, regardless of who was responsible for its creation. Like the faithful, the literary interpreter can say that there are no coincidences in the Torah, or perhaps more accurately, that if there are instances of chance, they are still available for interpretation, as is true of any work of art. A repetition can be seen as an aesthetic strategy, a pattern of meaning, a motif, rather than the redundancy of a sloppy redactor. Whether or not these motifs are of divine authorship is, for my purposes, beside the point.

By reading the story of Abraham, Sarah, and Hagar with respect and attention to its layers and complexities, we—believers and nonbelievers alike—can begin to understand a legacy that has shaped human culture and much of the modern world, and, in doing so, perhaps we can begin to understand one another. As the Jewish theologian Abraham Heschel wrote, "No religion is an island. . . . We must choose between interfaith and internihilism. Should religions insist upon the illusion of complete isolation? Should we refuse to be on speaking terms with one another and hope for each other's failure? Or should we pray for each other's health and help one another in preserving one's respective legacy, in preserving a common legacy."[5]

THE
WOMAN
WHO
NAMED
GOD

CHAPTER ONE

BEGINNINGS

O city, your name exists but you have been destroyed.
— *Lamentation of Ur* (64–71)[1]

Nasiriyah. The name of this Iraqi city seems bewilderingly obscure to most Americans, although it was the location of one of the earliest battles in the U.S. coalition force's invasion of Iraq. For those who were watching this battle on television, the exploding RPGs made it difficult to see the city clearly, clouding the streets in smoke and obscuring most of the buildings, including the huge, mysterious temple that stands just outside the city limits.

On the ground, however, there is no avoiding the temple's presence. The U.S. army even established an air base at the foot of the ancient, flat-topped structure, known as the Great Ziggurat. Tradition says that it was here that the Biblical father of Islam, Christianity, and Judaism was born. This man's conflicted relationships with two women would give rise to the religious hatreds that prompted the bloody struggle in Iraq, as well as the centuries of mistrust and suspicion among Jews, Muslims, and Christians.

His name was Abram, or Abraham, as we know him today, and back then, the city that crouched at the temple's feet was known as

Ur, not Nasiriyah. The ancient settlement was located about ten miles southwest of the modern city, not far from where Highway 7 joins with Route 7/8. When Abraham walked out of Mesopotamia and headed toward the Promised Land at God's behest, it is likely that it was this temple, or one very like it, that he left behind, initiating a journey that would inspire the faithful but would also give rise to centuries of conflicts and contested legacies.[2]

The land in which Abraham lived sometime around 1900 B.C.E. was very different from the countryside of modern-day Iraq. The smell of the sea hung in the air, as the gulf waters used to wash ashore at Ur, making the city an important trading post.[3] Pilgrims flooded the alleyways that led to the ziggurat to pay anxious tribute to the city's patron deity, the moon god, Nanna. An imposing figure, Nanna had a blue beard, rode a bull through the sky, and was responsible for the cycle of days and nights that constituted a lunar month, about twenty-eight days, or the span of a woman's menstrual cycle. Not coincidentally, women were important in this city, and a high priestess, not a priest, presided over the temple and its rituals.[4]

Ur's lavish marketplace was filled with lemons, mangoes, cinnamon, goats, salted trout, precious oils, dried skins, weavings, yarn, jewels, incense, and pottery. The city's steep embankments protected it from the seasonal floods of the Euphrates. In turn, the river ensured the city's prosperity through trade and bountiful fresh water.

Whether Abraham reaped any benefits from the wealth of his native land is unclear, as the Bible does not tell us anything about his early years. All we know is that when we first meet him, Abraham is simply called Abram, son of Terah. The Bible also tells us the names of his brothers, Haran and Nahor, and his wife, Sarai. In fact, we learn more about Sarai than Abram. She was barren, the Bible asserts, mentioning this fact twice, while neglecting any details about Abram (Gen. 11:30).

This omission is strange since Abram plays such an important role in the Bible. One might think there would be omens heralding his arrival, or tales of precocious brilliance. But no comets blazed across the sky the day he was born. No wise man recognized him as a prophet. He did not float down the river in a basket of rushes. Angels did not announce his birth. At first he is a blank, an everyman. His only notable characteristic is that his wife cannot have children.

But even if we do not know anything about the boy Abram, we do know that in the days of his youth, the temple cast a long shadow on the city in which he lived. Each level was painted a different color—blue, red, and yellow—and the sacred building on top was coated with gold, so that in the sun the pillars and rooftop glittered with an unearthly sheen.[5] If you stood at the bottom gazing up, the priests and priestesses sweeping up the mighty stairways to the temple's entrance must have seemed more like creatures of the sky than ordinary mortals.

As for the gods, Nanna was everywhere, and he was not alone. He had sisters, brothers, and parents who represented the other forces of nature: Anu ruled the heavens, Enlil controlled the earth, and Enki held sway over the sea. Marduk ruled as overlord of all gods and men. According to Mesopotamian teachings, there were hundreds of these divines and they could be anywhere, in the Euphrates, among the stars, in the ditches that lined the fields, or on the throne of the land, as many of the kings were themselves considered gods.[6]

From time to time, these deities descended the ziggurat's staircase and walked on the earth, spreading destruction or good fortune, depending on their mood, which was often foul. With the line between mortals and divines so blurry, most people assumed that the only way to survive in this world was to keep the deities happy. Since the gods were like human beings, they needed to be fed and flattered. They also needed gifts, because if they became angry or felt ignored, catastrophes might result.[7]

Immersed as they were in Mesopotamian culture, Abram and

Sarai would have understood that Nanna and the other gods were neither caretakers nor deities who "loved" humanity, but were ravening beings that often required human blood to survive. In those days, no one had ever heard of a god who paid personal attention to his followers or who believed that all he had created, including human beings, was "very good" (1:31). Rather, the inhabitants of Ur described creation as a violent battle between the gods. Human beings came from the blood spattered on the battlefield to provide the victorious gods with a continual supply of slaves.[8]

Indeed, human blood seems to have been an essential staple of Mesopotamian religion. In 1924 the famous archaeologist Sir Leonard Woolley discovered a skeleton in full ceremonial splendor at the bottom of a sandy pit not far from Nasiriyah. Mounds of gold, silver, and lapis lazuli surrounded it, and on top of the skull rested an elaborate golden headdress. Piles of human bones lay near the central skeleton, representing all that was left of fifty-four attendants. These skeletons lay in orderly rows, indicating that they had died in an anticipated fashion—most likely victims of ritual suicide. The bony fingers of one female attendant still clutched a hair ribbon she did not have time to fasten before the poison she had consumed took effect. The skeletons of six soldiers bearing spears and wearing copper helmets stood guard at the entrance. In Woolley's mind, these were the remnants of a culture that required human deaths to appease the angry gods. He imagined monstrous feasts where royal attendants drank their last drugged drinks and nibbled their final tidbits before being buried alive.[9]

Whether or not Woolley's descriptions of Mesopotamian religious practices are completely accurate, the sheer number of gravesites uncovered at Ur, as well as their elaborate nature, meant that Abram and Sarai could not have avoided knowing about Mesopotamian death rites. The daily religious practices of the people would also have been familiar to them, as they lived in a crowded city that was devoted to the worship of the deities. Everyone they brushed shoulders with—the shopkeepers, the little children playing in the street, their neighbors and friends—feared this pantheon of divine slave masters.

Still, various religious thinkers claim that Abram somehow managed to shun his neighbors' habits. To these commentators, it is unthinkable—even sacrilegious—to imagine that the patriarch of monotheism could have started life as a pagan. However, Karen Armstrong, an expert on the history of religion, argues that at this stage in his life the great man would "certainly have believed in the existence of such deities as Nanna's father, Marduk."[10] Despite its controversial nature, this argument makes sense since Mesopotamian culture was the only one Abram and his family had ever known. Even the Bible declares that Abram's father, Terah, was a worshipper of strange gods (Josh. 24:2). For any citizen of Ur, it would have been difficult not to participate in the local rituals, since religion was not separated from city life; it *was* city life.

Records tell us that each month secret rites were enacted in the temple on top of the ziggurat. A procession of priests and priestesses traveled the winding path to the enormous structure, and twice a year the priests brought forth an enormous statue of Marduk and marched through the city. People lined the streets and rushed to kiss the stone face and feet in hope of deflecting the god's wrath. The priests themselves studied the statue's face for any changes, most of which predicted doom for the city. One priestly teaching declared:

> When Marduk . . . has an open mouth—[he] will raise his
> voice in anger against the land.
> When Marduk has his eyes closed—the land's inhabitants
> will feel sadness.
> When Marduk has a somber face—famine will take hold of
> the countries.[11]

Those Mesopotamians who witnessed such parades believed that they were actually watching Marduk pass by. They thought of idols as small deities who were "born in heaven" and who could see, hear, speak, and, most important, protect their owners. People buried their statues at the threshold of their houses or propped them up outside their doors to protect themselves from evil. It would have been considered foolhardy not to set them up on altars inside your home, offer them food, and dress them in clothes. Even the dead required idols; no one, except perhaps the poorest beggar, was buried without their protection.[12]

Even if one did not march in the monthly processions or ignored the citywide festivals, the red and black clay faces of the idols stared from booths in the marketplace and on the street corner. Some were huge; some were tiny. Most were human figures, although some were animals. The workmen who fashioned them underwent complicated rituals to disconnect them from their labor. A priest would take a wooden sword and symbolically cut off the workers' hands. After this emblematic amputation, the worker had to repeat an oath, swearing, "I did not make him." The idol had come from the gods and was a god.[13]

Yet this proximity to idolatry and pagan deities need not tarnish Abraham's reputation as a faithful Biblical patriarch, according to one early Jewish source.[14] This text interpreted the Biblical lines about Abram's father and the strange gods to mean that, although Abram's family worshipped idols, Abram himself had never succumbed to this temptation. In other words, there was a sharp contrast between father and son. Otherwise, why would God have selected Abram? Early church fathers took a different tack. Instead of arguing that Abram held different beliefs from his forefathers, Augustine wrote that Terah must have secretly taught the principle of monotheism to his son. [15]

To the Jewish commentators who set down the earliest Midrash, writings that sought to explain Biblical mysteries and fill in gaps of the narrative, it was even more urgent that Abraham's credentials of faith be unquestioned. They lived in the chaotic period after the Temple in Jerusalem had been destroyed by the Romans in 70 C.E., when Jews had been forced out of Palestine and were in danger of extinction. These early leaders needed Abraham to be an inspirational founding father, not a man with an unknown past, since the Scriptural silence about his early years rendered him vulnerable to those who might want to tarnish his good name.

After careful study of the scrolls, they were relieved to conclude that Abraham had never been a pagan, but had been a pillar of faith in God from the moment he was born.[16] One set of tales, recorded by Louis Ginzberg in his magisterial collection of Jewish legends, features Abraham as a godly baby boy, who had faced danger from the beginning of his life, just like those other famous religious figures Moses and Jesus. Interestingly, the Koran records many of these same stories, lending them even more importance.

When Abraham's mother was pregnant, the Midrash says, the king of the land, Nimrod, was told by his advisers that a man would soon be born who would rise up against him. Immediately, Nimrod ordered his soldiers to kill all the new male babies in the land, but when her time came, Abram's mother, Amatlai, stole from her home and wandered in the desert until she found a cave. Here she gave birth to her baby, and "the whole cave was filled with the light of the child's countenance as with the splendor of the sun, and the mother rejoiced exceedingly."[17]

This cave has become so fixed in the lore of Abraham that the faithful still search for its location. Turkish Muslims suggest that it was nowhere near Ur but was in fact situated in present-day Sanliurfa, a Turkish city near the Syrian border. The locals sell tickets to enter what they call the birthplace of Ibrahim.[18]

After the baby was born, Abraham's mother knew that she could not stay and nurse him, and so she declared, "Better thou shouldst perish here in this cave than my eye should behold thee dead at my breast." She wrapped the baby in her cloak and left him wailing in the cave.[19] The tales diverge at this point. One famous version says that Abraham remained alone in the cave for thirteen years and emerged speaking Hebrew, proclaiming his knowledge of God.[20] Others were dissatisfied with this idea. How could a baby survive without food or drink? What else happened during this early period of the great man's life? He could not have been idle for thirteen years.

According to this set of storytellers, God heard Abraham crying and sent the angel Gabriel down to earth to care for him. Gabriel made milk flow "from the little finger of the baby's right hand," and this miraculous drink was so nutritious that after ten days Abraham was able to walk and talk like an adult. He left the cave and gazed out at the evening sky. When the stars came out he said, "These are the gods!" But when the morning came, the stars disappeared, and so he declared, "I will not worship these, for they are no gods." When the sun cast its warmth over the land, he exclaimed, "This is my god, him will I extol." However, when the sun disappeared below the rim of the horizon, Abraham knew that he had made another mistake. The sun was not a god; it too came and went. When the moon rose, once again Abraham was sure that he had found god, until it too faded from view. At last, Abraham had his great insight: none of these extraordinary objects were divine. There must be a god who had created the stars, the sun, and the moon. He exclaimed, "There is One who sets them all in motion."[21]

In these stories, Abraham was able to look beyond the grandeur of the planets to see the invisible hand that made them. Karen Armstrong quotes Jean-Paul Sartre to express the immensity of Abraham's discovery: "Imagination is being able to see something that isn't there."[22] In other words, Abraham could "see" the God that was not tangible, and one day he would help make Him known to others. But not yet.

Before he could preach his discovery of the one true God, Abraham had to undergo many tests. In the Midrash, Abraham is not only a wise theologian but someone who can withstand political pressure and even torture. One famous story reports that the young man was summoned to Nimrod's court, where he faced the king's questions about his beliefs:

"Do you believe in fire, water, or the planets as gods?" Nimrod asked.

"No," said Abraham. "There is only one true God."

"Bow down to our gods." Nimrod commanded, enraged that this man was challenging his own status as a god among men. But Abraham refused to bend his knees, and so Nimrod's soldiers threw him into a fiery furnace. Although the flames engulfed him and he felt the pain of being burned, he stepped unscathed from the flames. His miraculous escape not only terrified the court but also symbolized Abraham's rebirth as a hero.[23]

This tale was embellished over the centuries to include many different versions of the anguish Abraham endured. In addition, the flames would reappear in other Biblical tales, such as Daniel's escape from Nebuchadnezzar's furnace (Dan. 3:1–30). For most of the faithful, especially those Jews who faced torture because of their refusal to abandon their religion, the most important point was that Abraham adhered to his faith and asserted the truth of God's existence despite the threats of a tyrant and despite physical suffering. Courageous and strong, Abraham could see through the false teachings of his day and was also a rebel against tyranny, remaining firm in his beliefs when pushed to the brink.

The Midrash emphasizes this point by claiming that not only did Abraham have to fight against the ruler of the land, he also had to do battle with his father. According to these stories, as well as the Koran, Terah was actually an idol maker and Abraham watched with horror as his father chiseled and sold them to his customers. The boy resisted any temptation to worship the statues his father made and instead lectured Terah about the dangers of idolatry. Terah, however, remained unconverted.

One story says that Abraham smashed all of the idols in the shop, but even this desperate measure did not work. Terah simply picked up his chisel and started chipping out another statue. In another version, Abraham does not bother with his father's idols but destroys the royal collection, shattering Nimrod's most prized possessions. Clearly, Abraham was fearless in the face of established authority.[24]

Abraham also reached out to the common people. If anyone approached the young man to buy an idol Abraham would prove the folly of such a purchase by asking the would-be buyer how old he was. For example, if the person said that he was fifty years old, Abraham would reply, "Why would a person of your age and experience bow down to a statue that was made today?"[25]

In one story an old woman tried to buy an idol in Terah's shop to replace one that had been stolen from her home. Her desire was understandable. It would have felt as risky for a woman of the ancient world to lack an idol as for a contemporary woman to have no lock on her door. But legend has it that Abraham barraged the old lady with a series of questions: "How can you say that the image you worship is a god? If it is a god, why did it not save itself out of the hands of those thieves?" The old woman was startled and in distress pleaded with Abraham to tell her what god she should worship instead. Abraham replied, "Serve the God of all Gods." Immediately convinced, she joined Abraham in missionary work and converted many of her neighbors and friends.[26]

Thus, according to these stories, by the time Abraham was called to leave Mesopotamia, he had already experienced many trials. He had had the courage to confront his father, the king, and the people of Ur about their idol worship. It was no wonder, then, that the Lord would turn to Abraham when He decided to found a nation in the Promised Land. Here was a man who had proven his loyalty since the day he was born.

———◆———

CHAPTER TWO

LEKH LEKHA

The courage to break his cultural and familial ties and aban-
don the gods of his ancestors . . . out of allegiance to a God of all
families and cultures was the original Abrahamic revolution.
        —Miroslav Volf, *Exclusion and Embrace*[1]

The voice came from nowhere. We do not know if it was a whisper or a roar, whether it was masculine or feminine. All we
know is that Abram was seventy-five years old when he heard a
mysterious presence speak. The Bible does not tell us if it was night
or day, whether he was in the market or at home, if he was eating
lunch or sleeping. It does not even disclose whether Abram understood that the speaker was the Lord, and if he did, how he intuited
this. All we know is what the voice said and how it changed everything, from the contours of Abram's life to the shape of human history. And yet they were surprisingly simple words:

> The Lord said to Abram, "Go forth from your native land and
> from your father's house to the land that I will show you. I will
> make of you a great nation and I will bless you" (Gen. 12:1–2).

God's directive meant that it was time for Abram to shed the dirt of the city from his sandals and strike out on his own into the desert—a daunting prospect, even if a trifle exhilarating. To emphasize the sacrifice Abram would have to make, God listed the losses he would have to face—his country and his family. If Abram obeyed God, however, he would gain his own land and found a nation.[2]

The literal translation of God's first words, *lekh lekha,* is "go yourself," and one ancient interpretation suggests that this means "go forth to find your authentic self, to learn who you are meant to be."[3] For Abram, the second word was just as important as the first, as it introduced the idea of autonomous selfhood, an idea that modern people take for granted but that was not an assumption held by the ancient world. As Joseph Campbell, an authority on world mythology, declared, "In such a world there was no such thing as an individual life, but only one great cosmic law by which all things are governed."[4] The ties of family and occupation were all-important. Those who had authority over you—your father, your uncles, your master, the elders of your community, and, of course, the gods—made decisions on your behalf. No beneficent principle held that each individual had the freedom to determine his or her own life.

So, when God uttered the word "yourself," Abram could hear an implication that is almost inaudible to our ears: he had the right to direct the course of his life. He could break away from his father and reject the customs of his city. Although the prospect of such an endeavor was terrifying, God was clear that if Abram listened to His words, all limitations would disappear; he would be blessed.

One only has to think of the towering ziggurats and the Mesopotamian pantheon of angry gods to understand God's logic. Nothing new could flourish in such an ancient civilization.[5] But even though God must have realized it would be difficult to make such a shattering departure, He did not utter any comforting words such as "You can trust Me" or "I will take care of you." Nor did He offer any explanation of how He would render the compound blessings of children and a homeland.

Without such divine reassurance, most people would have refused to obey God's words or believe His predictions. But Abram established his difference from ordinary mortals by listening to God. He may not have had the driving curiosity of a Gilgamesh, nor the physical prowess of an Achilles, two of the other great heroes from this time period, but he had something neither of these legendary men possessed, the ability to suspend his incredulity and believe in the impossible. This tremendous feat of the imagination was heroic in its own light. In fact, after the decadent behavior of preceding Biblical generations—Adam's descendants had been so evil that God had wiped them out with the Flood, and Noah's descendants had proven even more sinfully disobedient—Abram's response is singular. God commands and Abram packs his bags. Divine purposes and human ones are, for once, in harmony.

ABRAM AND SARAI were actually no longer in Ur when God issued His commandment. Abram's father, Terah, had moved the family to Haran, a settlement about six hundred miles northwest of Ur. Cryptically, the Bible says that Terah had meant to go all the way to Canaan, the long, narrow country that lay along the Mediterranean and that would one day be revealed as the Promised Land. But for some mysterious reason Terah had stopped far short of his goal.

Crowded and unappealing, Haran was less than halfway to the coastal settlement of Terah's dreams. In the rainy season, the earth turned into a thick yellowish bog. In the summer, the heat was appalling. The land was not particularly fertile. Neither citrus nor olive trees could grow. Why did he halt here?

Situated on the left bank of the Balikh River with the modern-day Syrian-Turkish border only ten miles to the south, Haran is now small and somewhat desolate; only a few abandoned mud huts are scattered along the riverside. The modern settlement is about two kilometers away, an easy walk for the visitors who come here hoping to glimpse what life was really like in the ancient world.

But no matter how powerful one's capacity to imagine the past, it is almost impossible to picture what Haran was really like four thousand years ago. In Abram's time, close to twenty thousand people lived in this city, a central way station for the east/west trade routes that ran between the Mediterranean and Mesopotamia.[6] The steady flow of traffic caused the city as a whole to prosper, offering commercial opportunities for entrepreneurial citizens. Perhaps this is why Terah gave up on his dream of Canaan. If he stayed in Haran, he could become rich. God had not spoken to him, and so he could not know that he had failed to complete a journey of crucial importance, leaving an opening for his son to become a hero while he would emerge as the also-ran.

The family's journey to Haran was typical of the time period, as was Terah's ambition to move farther west to Canaan. For reasons that are unclear, a huge migration was occurring in the ancient world; entire tribes slowly filed from east to west.[7] Thus, when Terah took his clan up the Euphrates, the path was well traveled by other migrating families, as well as traders and merchants. Marsh dwellers poled their rafts, and peddlers streamed south from foreign lands. Mangroves covered the banks of the great river. As the pack animals straggled along behind the family, ducks floated by, and occasionally an egret appeared, hunting small fish in the shallows.

If Abram and Sarai had hoped to escape Ur and its single-minded devotion to the moon god, they were to be disappointed. Once they entered Haran, it became clear that, like Ur, this city was devoted to the worship of Nanna. The same crowds poured through the city gates to offer gifts to the hungry deity. The same prayers and blessings were murmured in the narrow passageways. Processions of priests and priestesses wound through the city and another ziggurat towered overhead. It was almost as though they had made no move at all.

In fact, some theorize that it is not a coincidence that Abram and Sarai's early years were spent in the cities of Nanna. The names of Abram's family—Sarah, Milcah, Terah, Laban—were ones associated with some sort of moon cult.[8] But it is not easy to decipher what these links to Nanna might mean. Maybe Terah specialized in statues of Nanna. Perhaps the family participated in the worship of the moon god, a shocking suggestion for those who believe that Abram devoted himself to God from the moment he was born.

All questions of faith aside, Terah's inability to resist the attractions of Haran demonstrated the difficulty of leaving the civilized world, no matter how much one might want to escape its contagions. The laden marketplace, the cheerful friends, the wealth, and the sheer comfort of settled life could help one overlook the fact that the gods seemed cruel, hungry, and whimsical, demanding ritual suicides and human sacrifice.[9] Even the dangers and inconveniences of a large urban center, such as crime and overcrowding, were not enough to dissuade men like Terah from enjoying the benefits of city living.

Accordingly, the moment God spoke to Abram, the gauntlet was thrown. If Abram obeyed God, he would have to reject his father's way of life. At age seventy-five Abram was not yet a middle-aged man by Biblical standards since he would live another hundred years. Terah was still the patriarch, the one in charge. Abram and Sarai were supposed to follow him wherever he commanded them to go. Terah's grandson Lot, who had also moved to Haran from Ur with his wife and children, was similarly obligated. To listen to God's voice would mean replacing the human father with the divine, rebelling against one in order to follow the other. In other words, obedience to God meant breaking the laws that governed the only society Abram and Sarai had ever known.

To most contemporary readers, the immensity of this commandment is unimaginable. No one was sure what lay beyond the confines of the known world. Perhaps there were vast deserts with no oases, or oceans that did not end. Few people could envision leaving Mesopotamia, even when battles broke out between warring tribes and the gods stepped up their demands for blood. The need for departure is also not immediately clear. Why did Abram have to embark on this adventure? What was so bad about the pagan cities of Ur and Haran? The modern era is not, in general, threatened by paganism. We tend to think of it as a gentle sort of pantheism, characterized by animal deities, river nymphs, and beautiful fertility goddesses, a world that induces nostalgia rather than fear and one that does not seem to represent a serious challenge to the omnipotent Lord of the Bible.

But in time it would be the pagans from Mesopotamia, the Babylonians, who would almost destroy Abram's descendants, overrunning Jerusalem and burning down the First Temple. Since these were the same pagans who believed their gods required the ritual deaths of thousands of human beings, their vast cities were places of danger for their own inhabitants, as well as for the children of Abram.

That urban centers bred corruption was not a new idea, but in Scripture, cities are also often seen as symbols of human arrogance. The Biblical scholar Reuven Hammer points out that an important theme of the Bible is this clash between Abraham's people, the Israelites, and their enemies, the urbanites. He calls the opposing groups "mountain cultures, which see the heart of the world in wilderness, revering nature and adapting to it," and "tower cultures, for whom the essence of the world is the city and the human-made environment, stripping the sense of awe from nature and attaching it to the social and technological order." Accordingly, Ur and Babylon, with their ziggurats, and Egypt, with its pyramids and palaces, are tower cultures, while "Israel from Mount Sinai to the Temple Mount, will be largely a mountain culture."[10]

Those who followed Abraham would become shepherds and traders who roamed and paused in settled places but always took to the road again. It would take centuries for them to adopt an entirely settled way of life. In contrast, those who stayed behind became the notorious heathen of the Bible, the city dwellers.

In fact, right before the story of Abram, Scripture relates a famous story about the children of Noah. Humankind had gathered together to build a tower to heaven, also known as the Tower of Babel (11:5–6). God was angered at human presumption, but after His promise to Noah, He could not destroy the entire human race again. Instead, He "scattered them over the face of the earth" and "confounded the speech of the whole earth" (11:9).

Building a city and a tall tower at first seems like odd evidence for the waywardness of humankind. Yet God had told Noah and his children not only to multiply, but to populate the entire earth. One of the most striking points of the story is that the people had congregated to create one monolithic settlement, as though they were attempting to unite against God and challenge His authority.

If this is how God regarded cities, then it is no wonder that He commanded Abram to leave Mesopotamia and that this commandment would emerge as the famous dividing line between the people of God and the ungodly.

However, this was not the only lesson God's commandment taught Abram. Travel was an essential component of faith. To the people of antiquity, allegiance to one city usually meant an allegiance to the gods of that city. Leaving Haran meant breaking free from Haran's deities. From the first moment of contact, then, God implied that His chosen man had to stay on the move and that the kind of faith He required was inextricably bound up with wandering. In this way, God could prove that He was not a local deity, confined to the precincts of one city. Abram would do best to worship Him away from large urban centers and their pagan practices.

Even as they gathered their supplies — extra goatskins, ropes, grains, wine, olives, and oil — Abram and Sarai were getting ready for a wrenching departure. They had to leave Mesopotamia with their whole hearts and not look back with regret.[11] Without the convenient definitions and protections of family and country, they would be freed from old habits and old ways.

Thus, their farewell promised to be as important symbolically as it was literally.[11] They were initiating a new kind of journey: the pilgrimage of redemption. Astonishingly, they never lamented. Instead, they threw themselves into their preparations with remarkable briskness.

CHAPTER THREE

HEBREWS

When Abram and his family and friends strapped their belongings on their donkeys and set off toward the west, they had no idea where they were heading. It is easy to forget this crucial point since most of us know that they were going toward the Promised Land, and that this land would turn out to be Palestine, or Canaan, as it is called in this early part of the story. But at this stage all God had said was to go toward the land that He would "show" Abram, as though He wanted to emphasize the departure from the old world, not the final destination. His vagueness presented His chosen man with a test: could Abram find the right country on his own?

Abram's subsequent behavior is the first evidence in the Bible that he was indeed an extraordinary man. Somehow he knew to head toward the Mediterranean, perhaps in an unconscious attempt to finish the journey his father had never completed, perhaps because of his intuitive connection to God.

Although Abram never seemed perturbed by God's lack of direction, it must have bewildered Abram's followers. No one knew what had gotten into Terah's son. It was not the custom to leave one's father and roam off into the desert, and so one might think that Abram would offer some kind of explanation. Yet Abram made no attempt to justify his unusual behavior. And he evinced no remorse over what amounted to severing his relationship with Terah.

The Bible emphasizes the split that would occur between father and son by making a confusing chronological jump. Before God even speaks to Abram, the text spells out the details of Terah's death in Haran, an event that would occur about sixty years after Abram left Mesopotamia:

> Terah took his son Abram, his grandson Lot . . . and his daughter-in-law, Sarai, and set out together from Ur . . . for the land of Canaan; but when they had come as far as Haran, they settled there. The days of Terah came to 205 years; and Terah died in Haran. (Gen. 11:32)

Earlier, the text says that Terah was seventy years old when Abram was born (11:26), which means he was 145 years old when Abram departed. If Terah lived for 60 more years after Abram left, then he had plenty of time to seek reconciliation with Abram, and Abram had plenty of time to seek a blessing from his father. Even though travel was difficult in the ancient world, a messenger could have been sent, or a token of appreciation could have been exchanged, as both of these methods of communication would be used later in the Bible.[1] But there is no record of subsequent exchanges between father and son. Abram never sent word back home, and he certainly never returned to Haran. As for Terah, he never followed Abram, and it is not clear if he missed his son or was relieved to say good-bye.

Brief though it is, therefore, this passage suggests how reluctant Terah was to break from the old world. At the same time its odd placement in the story emphasizes Terah's loneliness: fathers were not meant to die without all of their sons present. By placing God's call to Abram immediately after these verses, the Bible underlines the loss for both father and son that will occur when Abram obeys God.

It would be easy to censure Abram's treatment of his father if one wanted to undermine his saintly stature. Thus, Rashi sprang to the patriarch's defense, writing,

> Why, then, does Scripture mention the death of Terah before the departure of Abram? In order that this matter (his leaving home during his father's lifetime) might not become known to all, lest people should say that Abram did not show a son's respect to his father, for he left him in his old age and went his way.[2]

Rashi excuses Abram's departure by explaining that Abram had to leave his father behind because Terah was "wicked."[3] And yet the fact that Rashi felt the need to justify Abram's behavior indicates that Abram's actions are problematic. With this first decision to follow God and leave Mesopotamia Abram established himself as a renegade, vulnerable to attacks from all quarters.

It is possible that Abram could have spared himself some criticism if he had told everyone he was following the commandment of a strange new deity. But he remained oddly silent about God's words, a reticence all the more striking when one considers the pronouncements that later Biblical figures would make after God spoke to them. Abram's great-great-grandson Joseph would narrate his prophetic dreams to his brothers. Moses challenged the Pharaoh in the name of God. Jesus testified to God's presence on earth, quoting the words of his Father. In addition, Abram did not talk to the Lord in the presence of others like his grandson Jacob would. Instead, the first patriarch refrained from making any kind of announcement at all, even though the idea that a powerful God was endorsing this endeavor might have won his expedition more credibility.

Perhaps Abram was not quite sure how to identify who had spoken to him—a shocking thought to prominent theologians of all three religions who have declared that Abram by definition knew who God was. Still, God had not provided Abram with any sort of formal introduction. With each of the patriarchs after Abram, God would say that He was the God of Abraham. So it is strange that He did not give His chosen one a history of His relationship to humankind. He did not mention Noah or Adam and Eve. He did not mention His destruction of the Tower of Babel nor perform any miracles. No bush went up in flames. No walking sticks flared into snakes. He did not even say His own name.

Instead, God's brevity is reminiscent of the initial creation. He issued a command and Abram, like the earth and the waters before him, listened and obeyed. After His failure with Adam and then Noah, whose descendants were the builders of the infamous Tower, God had elected to try a different kind of creation, one predicated on cultivating a relationship with His chosen one. And so, in the Jewish and Islamic tradition, Abram is sometimes referred to as "the friend" of God.[4]

WHEN ABRAM AND SARAI walked through Haran's city gates, a stream of men and women followed them, carrying their possessions and leading little black donkeys with sacks heaped on their backs. Even Abram's nephew Lot had rejected Terah as the family's leader and had chosen to follow his uncle instead. These brave individuals had made the same precipitous decision as Abram — to leave their home behind — and they had made this choice even though they had not been prompted by a divine command, suggesting that Abram's charisma and persuasive force must have been extraordinary.

Nevertheless, if they had heard a rumor that their leader had been having conversations with a powerful deity, it would not have meant much to them. The last person to speak with God was Noah and that had been ten generations ago. As early Biblical figures were said to have lived for extraordinary lengths of time, from two to three hundred years, a generation was a very long time indeed.

Yet without any knowledge of God, the people were still intent on trailing Abram. It is possible they were simply participating in the general migration of the period, opportunistically following Abram because of safety in numbers, but the Bible says Abram "made souls" in Haran (12:5). This awkwardly placed verb, *asu*, or "make," has raised many questions. Some scholars have suggested that this was simply an odd way of saying that Abram and Sarai had purchased slaves. However, the writers of the Talmud argue that when one man converts another to faith in God, it is as though the proselytizer has "made" the convert. Thus, in this version of the story, right from the beginning Abram had dedicated himself to telling the people about the one true God. Later Jewish commentators concurred, although they disagreed about the number of converts who actually left Haran. The medieval scholar Maimonides theorized that there were thousands, but the Sefer Hayashar, a thirteenth-century rabbinical work, says that only seventy-two were devout enough to go with Abram.[5]

If Abram did preach about God to his would-be followers, he must have been a gifted orator, as it would have been difficult for people of the ancient world to believe in a god who was not represented by an idol. Abram's ideas were new, his behavior was strange. And yet despite the anxiety and confusion that Abram's followers must have felt about his oddities, the Bible does not record one incident of complaint, suggesting that the people might well have found his lack of dependence on the old ways inspirational. Certainly, no one accused him of neglecting the gods. Perhaps they felt liberated. If he no longer sought to appease the old masters, then they could follow suit.

At any rate, even if Abram's followers did grumble or challenge his ideas, these occasions were minor enough for the Bible to overlook. Regret was strangely absent as well. No one gazed longingly at the city they had chosen to leave. Even Lot's wife, who would become famous for a future act of looking back, marched straight ahead. Indeed, this famous pilgrimage out of Mesopotamia seems to have been one of harmonious unity, at least at first.

Such unanimity is rare in Scripture, as is equanimity and compliance. For example, in Exodus, the second book of the Bible, after Moses led the Israelites out of slavery, the Israelites lamented their fate with each step they took toward freedom. There was not enough food. There was no water. They were sick of the manna God had provided. Some even wanted to go back to Egypt, though it meant returning to slavery (Exod. 15:22–24; Num. 20:13).

Practically speaking, then, God had made a good choice when He selected Abram. People would not follow just anyone to a vague destination for confusing reasons. Few individuals would be capable of instilling confidence and faith in a people a later prophet would call "willful," "evil," and "backward" (Jer. 7:24). But Abram's followers seem to have trusted him with the same sort of intensity that the patriarch invested in his relationship to God. He was a rule breaker and careless of societal niceties, and so undoubtedly he offended those he did not inspire, but like other famous religious leaders, from Joan of Arc to Martin Luther King, Jr., the fact that his people's allegiance grew deeper with each mile suggests that he also had some mysterious quality that drew others to him.

Before they could get very far, however, the group arrived at their first significant hurdle, the Euphrates. Abram and Sarai had traveled along the river when they had journeyed north to Haran, but they had never had to consider how to cross it—a daunting prospect, since the Euphrates was not a run-of-the-mill waterway. In the Bible it is one of the four rivers that flowed through the Garden of Eden (Gen. 2:14) and is simply referred to as *Perath*, or "the river," as though it needs no other name.[6]

It is easy to understand the fame of the Euphrates. More than seventeen hundred miles long, it is one of the longest rivers in the world. In the spring, the melting snow from the Armenian mountains can cause it to flood twelve feet over its banks. Its fierce current is so intimidating that most people in the ancient world refused to cross its banks or navigate its waters until it slowed down in the south, near where it joined the Tigris. As a result, the Euphrates was generally seen as an impassable border between east and west, keeping the Mesopotamians safe from those who dwelled in the wilderness that stretched toward the Mediterranean.

A waterway that inspired such fear and reverence was clearly going to be a significant problem for the little band of travelers. And sure enough, when Abram and his party arrived at its banks, they found a torrent that was almost a quarter of a mile wide. For the first time, the group was faced with a horrifying risk. No one knew how to swim and so there was no hope of crossing the river on foot without drowning; the water was too deep and the current too powerful. They would have to pick their way along the edge until they found someone who would ferry them across—a local shepherd or one of the marsh dwellers.

There is no mention of such a ferryman in either the Bible or the Oral Torah, but one must have existed, or the group would never have reached the other side. And so we have to assume that somehow Abram located a man and a craft. From the models of boats archaeologists have found in the gravesites of Ur, we know that simple wooden canoes were common, as were log rafts bound together by reeds.[7] But one small leak or a few snapped thongs and these could fly apart, casting entire families into the deep. Even if such a catastrophe did not happen, it was hard to keep one's balance, and Abram and his people would have to squat and cling to each other while the ferryman poled them across.

As though the loss of human life was not dire enough, there was also the drowning of the herd to fear. Generally, the animals were forced into the river and swam in sheer terror to the other side, but if even one creature died, everyone suffered. Goats provided milk, yogurt, and meat. Their skin could be used to make saddles, tents, sandals, and bags. The sheep could also be eaten, but their prize attribute was wool. A man counted his wealth in terms of animals. And so the stakes of this crossing were high; the panicked goats, sheep, and donkeys, whether swimming across or braying on the raft, could all too easily be lost.

But there were no mishaps. Not one creature was lost in the passage across the dark waters. Although the river did not part to make a path, like the Red Sea and the Jordan would in later years, to the religious mind it was clear that some deity had shielded them from harm. The symbolic triumph of this crossing is marked by the name by which Abram's people came to be known. Hebrews, or Ivri, means "those who cross to the other side."[8]

This "other side" would bear little resemblance to Ur and not just geographically speaking. By choosing Abram as their leader, his people were following a divine plan they could neither understand nor predict. The hike through dry deserted land could only grow more arduous with each passing day. They wore simple tunics that did little to protect them from the heat, and rough sandals made out of wiry grasses or cured animal skin.[9] In the middle of the day the sand could grow so hot that it scalded the skin. They did not yet have sophisticated storage systems for their water. Instead, like all people throughout the ancient world, they depended on the durability of simple sheepskins, gourds, and small clay vessels, any of which could easily leak, crack, or break. The worst thing was that no one could be sure when this journey would end.

There is no Biblical account of the exact path the group followed, but it seems likely that they traveled on the ancient track used by merchants and traders from the Mediterranean and by the other emigrants who were slowly wending their way east. This meant that one of their first stops would have been Palmyra, a settlement located in an oasis just north of the Syrian desert. The city, also known as "the bride of the desert," was a welcome respite for travelers, and undoubtedly, after their hardships some in Abram's group hoped that this place of palm trees and flowing springs would turn out to be the Promised Land.

However, this would have been far too easy. Somehow Abram knew that they could not stop yet. As long as God remained silent, they had to keep plodding forward. And so after a brief rest, Abram led them away from the lovely Palmyra, probably traveling southwest until they reached Damascus, another city built on an oasis. The ancient name for the city was "dar Meshq," which some scholars suggest means "well-watered place." But another more interesting theory is that the settlement was named after "Damashq, the great grandson of Shem, son of Noah, who built the city."[10] If this is so, then Abram and his people were reversing the path of their ancestors, who had migrated from west to east. According to the logic of the Bible, this was also a symbolic trajectory. Abram and Sarai would reverse the downward spiral of the preceding generations. They were traveling toward the hope of a new life and a newly redeemed humanity.

After Abram and his followers left Damascus, they would have found frequent settlements nearer the Mediterranean. For centuries, Egyptians had traveled north through Canaan to modern-day Lebanon before heading east to trade with Mesopotamians. Northerners also traveled south to Egypt, while Greeks and other tribes arrived by sea. The Canaanites themselves were also active traders. Since everyone traveled in sizable groups or caravans, the trail would have been more crowded than we might assume. It was unthinkable to travel alone given the prevalence of banditry on the road and the difficulty of carrying enough supplies to survive.

The little black pack donkeys set the pace. These small, sturdy creatures were not like the camels of the future. They had to stop to eat and drink every few hours, and so it was impossible to travel great distances without frequent pauses. Thus, the lifestyle of a purely nomadic people, like the later Bedouins, would have been impossible for Abram and his followers to achieve.[11] Instead, like many of the people they encountered on the road, Abram's group was on its way to becoming seminomadic. After they left Mesopotamia, they traveled slowly through grazing lands, steering clear of urban centers, although they paused in cities long enough to replenish supplies.[12] In this sense, the conclusion of their journey did not matter as much as it would to us today, since once they got to the Promised Land, they would still continue to roam, pause, and roam again.

As they picked their way farther south, God did not speak. Only Abram seemed to realize that if he stopped prematurely, he might lose the blessing God had promised.[13] And so, every day the question hung in the air: Could he find their unnamed destination? So far, he seemed to be succeeding, but how could he be sure? Again, the contrast to Moses's forty-year journey with the Israelites could not be more pointed. Not once did the people ask Abram where they were going. Not once did anyone make angry remarks about the length and uncertainty of their journey. As a result, to this day we have no idea how long Abram's pilgrimage took.

Finally, just south of the port city of Tyre, they came to a wall of white mountains that seemed to block them from traveling farther south. At first it appeared that this was where their journey would have to end. But as they approached the cliffs, they saw that there was a narrow passageway between the mountains and the sea. It rose gradually, as though it had been carved by God for Abram and his people to climb. Stair by stair the party ascended what has come to be known as the Ladder of Tyre.[14]

When at last they reached the top they could see a bright green plain stretching toward the sea and the town of Acre in the south. There were lemons in the trees; the land was obviously fertile. An ancient Egyptian official who had traveled there enthused over this rich valley, writing: "Figs were in it, and grapes. It had more wine than water. Plentiful was its honey, abundant its olives. Every kind of fruit was on its trees. Barley was there, and emmer [wheat]. There was no limit to any kind of cattle."[15]

God had not yet spoken, but Abram was convinced that this bright, rolling country had to be the one the Lord intended for him and his children. He had taken his people here like a homing pigeon, even though God had not once told him where to go. The text does not tell us what Abram said to the people that day. Instead, it simply says that the little party arrived in Canaan. We are left to surmise that everyone in Abram's party must have rejoiced when they learned that their leader believed this beautiful place was their new home.

CHAPTER FOUR

SACRIFICES

Abram and his people had come upon a place that had been inhabited by the same group of people, the Canaanites, since Neolithic times.[1] These highly civilized individuals would have been shocked to hear that a wild band from the east had arrived, led by a man who believed that Canaan would one day be his.

Readers today tend to equate Canaan with modern-day Israel, but the ancient territory was much larger than the state we know. It stretched from Sidon to Gaza and was bounded in the west by the Mediterranean and to the east by the Jordan River valley. Most of our information about this land comes from excavations at the Canaanite town of Ugarit, but despite the wealth of material that has been found there, there is much that remains mysterious. For instance, even the origins of the word "Canaan" are obscure, although the various hypotheses that scholars have suggested offer compelling flashes into early Canaanite culture. One suggestion is that "Canaan" meant "purple," from a famous purple dye the Canaanites traded with the Egyptians and Mesopotamians. Another theory is that it meant "trader," as the early Canaanites were apparently very active merchants.[2] But perhaps the most interesting hypothesis is that Canaan was named after one of Noah's grandsons.

The story goes that Noah's son Ham discovered his father naked while Noah slept off the effects of a drinking binge. When he woke up and saw Ham staring at him, Noah was enraged. But instead of punishing Ham, he inveighed against Ham's son Canaan, declaring: "Cursed be Canaan, a servant of servants shall he be unto his brethren" (Gen. 9:25). Of course, one can't help wondering why Noah did not curse the son who had gawked at him rather than his innocent grandson. But to inflict a truly painful punishment on someone in the Bible, one afflicted his or her children. Descendants were more important than anything else since the next generation represented immortality.

This tale hints at early Israelite propaganda against the indigenous inhabitants of the land they wanted for themselves. Certainly, this version of the name "Canaan" reprises the Bible's theme that Abram would reverse the downward spiral of Noah's descendants. If Canaan's heirs were the men and women currently tilling the fields in Canaan, they *needed* Abram and Sarai to restore righteousness to the land. Rashi enlarged on this theme by explaining that Abram was a descendant of Shem, one of Noah's blessed sons, and that Noah had originally given Canaan to Shem. Thus, it was rightfully Abram's land.[3]

Not that the Canaanites saw things this way. They gave no sign of feeling cursed and, for that matter, showed no interest in handing over their ancestral fields to this group of shaggy goatherds. Indeed, they seem to have hardly noticed them, and as a result there were no quarrels between the two peoples until five hundred or so years later, when the Israelites returned to Canaan from Egypt under the leadership of Moses. In part, this peaceful coexistence was because Abram did not try to compete with the Canaanites for fertile land. Rather, he led his people away from the sea and through the plains of Canaan until they came to the largely uninhabited hill country in the north. There they could graze their flocks on the mountainsides and in the valleys.[4] The few Canaanites who dwelled in this region did not resent their presence, especially since Abram and his people did not plant crops or try to build any permanent homes. Instead, they gradually headed south, traveling from one grazing land to another, leaving few signs that they had been there.

At length they came to a high valley nestled between Mount Gerizim and Mount Ebal, about forty miles north of present-day Jerusalem. There, they found a small town called Shechem, which served as one of the few centers of trade in this mountainous region. Located on the only natural inland route between the northern region of Galilee and southern Judea, near the modern Palestinian town of Nablus, Shechem offered Abram and his tribe a pleasant respite after the rocky hills of the north. A grove of terebinth trees provided welcome shade from the sun, and the townspeople were eager to trade olive oil and wheat for wool and goatskins.

Abram had still not confided his mission to any of his followers or mentioned his allegiance to God, but one day, as they rested in this tranquil valley, a miracle occurred that moved him to reveal his loyalties. Again, we do not know if it was night or day, whether Abram was waiting for this event or was surprised. Instead, the Bible is terse: "The Lord appeared to Abram and said, I will assign this land to your offspring" (12:7).

In this second exchange between God and Abram, God makes it clear that Abram had indeed found the right land. However, the Bible does not explain what Abram saw when God "appeared." Instead, the brevity of the passage suggests that what is important is God's articulation of His promise and His acknowledgment that Abram had done well.

For the first time, Abram felt moved to give thanks to God, but in the Bible there were as yet no traditions in place for the expression of gratitude to this particular divine. The Mesopotamian rituals of idol worship were clearly unacceptable, so Abram was forced to come up with an idea himself. What he did might seem unsurprising to the modern reader but was in fact quite extraordinary. He did not attempt to slaughter Canaanites in the name of God or fashion the largest monument he could. Instead, he gathered stones and heaped them into a pile to create an altar, the second in the Bible. Although Abram could not have known this, Noah had also built a simple altar after the ark had safely landed. Thus, Abram was enacting an essential connection to the past and making an important announcement to his people and the Canaanites: he was a follower of a God who was not new, though He was new to them.

Abram's pile of stones may have been small, but the consequences of this action were enormous and are still felt today. Every year, Jews from all over the world gather near the site of ancient Shechem in the controversial Jewish settlements near Nablus to commemorate the moment they believe God gave the Promised Land to their people. Since this region of Israel now falls within contested territory, there have been many clashes between the settlers and the Israeli government, as well as between the local Palestinians and Jews.[5]

When Abram built his rock altar, however, all remained calm. The Canaanites showed no evidence of being threatened by this activity. These Ivri were not attempting to build giant fortresses, nor did they seem interested in staking out the fertile plains. The small group was an almost invisible presence in the land and their little pile of stones could easily be obliterated if they became a nuisance.

Although the Bible remains silent about what Abram said to his people about God, the altar publicized his devotion and allowed him to introduce his followers to his elusive deity. In addition, by piling up these stones, Abram had effectively planted the flag of his new faith in Canaan.

But it would have been understandable if Abram's followers worried. It may have been liberating to escape the rule of Nanna and Marduk, but who exactly was Abram's God? Would He take care of them? Why couldn't they see Him? Abram never mentioned God's sisters, brothers, wives, or parents, suggesting that this new deity was a loner.[6] Perhaps He was like Abram and had been unable to father sons and daughters. This idea was troubling, as it threw God's virility into question. How would such a deity have the strength to fight other peoples' gods? No one gave voice to these concerns, however, and when Abram said it was time to leave Shechem and travel farther south, his people traveled behind him, still faithful and uncomplaining.

Some scholars argue that Abram's altar building at Shechem, devout though it may seem, was actually influenced by local pagan ritual. The cluster of trees near Shechem called "the terebinth of morel" was regarded as sacred by the Canaanites, who often built altars to the gods near groves of trees. Many pagan peoples of the ancient Near East regarded trees as holy objects, as they marked the presence of an oasis or of some kind of water source.[7] However, there is no conclusive evidence that Abram was following Canaanite religious rites. Indeed, that Abram's group held themselves apart from the Canaanites suggests that they had little interest in assimilation.

When they approached Bethel, about ten miles north of Jerusalem, close to the modern Palestinian town of Beitin on the West Bank, Abram and his people paused yet again, pitching their tents outside the city and no doubt marveling at the size of its gates; Bethel was one of the most important settlements of the time. Across the hilly plains, they could also see the shadowy outlines of the enormous walled city of Ai. The power of the Canaanites was indisputable, yet Abram evinced no fear of these people. Rather, he erected another altar to God.

At Bethel, there were no terebinths, suggesting that the Bible's mention of the grove at Shechem was meant to designate a specific place, rather than to denote a pagan sacred site. However, Bethel was also a Canaanite place of worship. In fact, its name means the high place (Beth) of God (El). But although Abram's altar locations were close to Canaanite ones, there is no other hint that he was interested in worshipping the local deities. In fact, it is at Bethel that the Bible reveals that Abram somehow knew God's name, although it does not tell us what this name is. Instead, the text informs us that

"he invoked the Lord by name." Thus, the careful geography—
"[he] pitched his tent with Bethel on the west and Ai on the east,
and he built there an altar"—suggests that the Bible is not hinting
at Abram's pagan tendencies, but is instead pointing out his ability
to proclaim his faith in the face of powerful enemies (12:8).

Certainly, Abram's altar building and invocations indicate how
grateful he is to the God who has made such grandiose promises.
Still, we might wonder how Abram's nonexistent children could
ever assume possession of a land inhabited by a people who adhered
to a flourishing religion that offered a direct challenge to Abram
and his God and who were far more technologically sophisticated.
For the Canaanites were an impressive people. They were fluent
writers not only of their own language but of various Mesopotamian languages, while Abram's people were illiterate. They had
advanced beyond the clumsy system of writing known as cunei-
form, where each syllable was denoted by a different symbol, and
had invented an alphabet of consonants that the Phoenicians would
later modify and pass on to modernity.[8] The Greek, Latin, Cyrillic,
Coptic, and Brahmic family of scripts in India and Southeast Asia
all trace their origins back to the Canaanites' innovation.

The elegance of their daily life also distinguished the Canaanites from Abram and his followers. Excavations at Jericho have
revealed handsomely carved wooden furniture and elegant pottery.
Canaanite lords and ladies wore gold jewelry that was remarkable
for its refined craftsmanship. Canaanite towns were so well fortified
that later Israelites would exclaim that Canaanite cities were "great
and walled up to the sky" (Deut. 1:28; cf. Num. 13:29). Even though
these descriptions were the exaggerations of a nomadic people,
there was some truth to their claims. At the apex of Canaanite culture, a typical city could spread more than nineteen acres—an
impressive achievement if one notes that the area of the island of
Manhattan is twenty-two square miles. In addition, the natives of
the land were skilled builders. The walls of Jericho, constructed
of burnt bricks, ranged from about nine to thirty-nine feet thick,

demonstrating that the Canaanites were prepared for war and had no intention of relinquishing their land to newcomers.[9]

This impression was reinforced by the many Canaanite altars and temples that Abram, Sarai, and their followers encountered in their travels. In general, Canaanite altars were huge affairs, built on the summit of mountains or hills, although sometimes they were constructed on top of enormous mounds of stones. Like the ziggurats back in Mesopotamia, these high places, or *bamah*, as the Bible terms them, dominated the surrounding countryside and were often placed near a temple so that the overall effect was overwhelming. Whenever Abram and his band passed through the valley of one of these sites, it was impossible to ignore the sheer might of this civilization.

Even today, one can glimpse its splendor. A few of the Canaanite holy places have remained standing for thousands of years. One such site at Nahariyah, on the northern coast of modern-day Israel near the border with Lebanon, has been extensively excavated. Here, the temple consisted of a rectangular room with an entrance carved out of one of the long sides. The nearby stone altar was littered with the remains of many mysterious Canaanite ritual objects, including "lamps with seven spouts," pottery, the bones of animals, and many female figurines, suggesting that the deity who was worshipped here was probably female and probably a fertility goddess.[10]

Unfortunately, the richness of these temple excavations does not make up for the lack of written sources on Canaanite religion. We do know the Canaanites believed their god El, a warrior god usually depicted bearing a spear, was the ultimate authority on earth. El's wife was Asherah, a sea goddess, who was probably the goddess worshipped at Nahariyah.[11] She was regarded as the "creator of creatures" and the mother of the gods, producing seventy divine sons.[12] But Canaanite religious rituals continue to remain obscure, although there have been enough disturbing discoveries near the *bamah*s and inside the temples to cause many writers to argue that the Canaanites practiced human sacrifice. If so, such practices would have given Abram and Sarai another incentive to avoid these sites.[13]

As it was, the contrast between these deities and the Bible's invisible and singular God could not have been more pronounced. The Canaanites held that the power of their mother and father gods was unshakable. Like the Mesopotamians, they had statues they could produce as evidence of their gods' attributes.

Abram and his little band, on the other hand, had nothing to show for themselves. They had no definite information about God. No icons. No fancy temples. No miracles. As a group, they were neither wealthy nor powerful. The notion of a single god, rather than a pantheon, was entirely unfamiliar, and Abram's own efforts at altar building were paltry in contrast to the Canaanites' enormous structures.

Finally, Sarai's inability to get pregnant was potentially disturbing evidence against Abram's God. To individuals in the ancient world, if Abram's deity were truly powerful, He would have granted children to His loyal servant. So, despite the gruesome quality of some of the Canaanite rituals, the temptation to join in was real. A god of war and a goddess of fertility must have seemed like appealing deities — so appealing, in fact, that scholars say many of Abram's descendants adopted Canaanite beliefs and rituals. From the number of female figurines that have been excavated on sites throughout Israel, Asherah would seem to have been a prominent figure in ancient Israelite worship, or so suggests the famous archaeologist William Dever in his provocative book *Did God Have a Wife?*[14]

Yet, although it seems likely that some of Abram's descendants would ultimately follow the lead of the Canaanites, there is no Biblical record of slippage during Abram and Sarai's lifetimes. Instead, it appears that Abram and his band successfully steered clear of the Canaanite rites. This is especially striking given Abram's desire for a child. After all, Asherah's job was to increase fertility.[15]

Peace reigned between the two peoples until a different kind of catastrophe arose. As Abram and his people roamed farther south, it became clear that something was very wrong. The grasses rattled in the wind, dry and sparse. Springs vanished. The animals had nowhere to graze; the land withered before their eyes.

No one knows how long this dreadful time lasted, but soon a famine arose. The animals began to die, weakened by hunger and thirst. Abram, Sarai, and their people were adrift in a strange land, starving. It was a fairy tale gone awry. The fertile kingdom was barren. God's promises did not seem to be worth much. Maybe Abram had made a terrible mistake in following Him.

CHAPTER FIVE

BEAUTIFUL WOMAN

Famines are never just famines in the Bible. Often, they are sent by God as tests or punishments of some kind. But as the situation in Canaan grew increasingly desperate, it was unclear why this catastrophe was occurring. Neither Abram nor Sarai had done anything to anger God, at least not that they knew of. In fact, His last words to Abram were that Canaan was the right place to be. Why then would He allow the land to die before their very eyes? Had He made them leave Mesopotamia only to destroy them in the Promised Land?

Without evidence to support God's promises, Abram would have to rely on his faith and hold out against any naysayers who might claim that God was behaving capriciously and cruelly.[1] After all, now that it was God's turn to complete His half of the deal, He had let His chosen one down.

But it is possible that God was not ready, for whatever reason, to fulfill His part of the bargain. Perhaps He wanted His relationship with Abram and Sarai to deepen before they received His gifts. Without land and without children, they needed Him with an intensity that might dissipate if their wishes were granted too quickly. God, it seemed, was enjoying their dependence on Him, and one can see why. Abram was proving to be a loyal follower. Despite this disaster he did not complain about the temperamental nature of his deity, although it would have been easy enough to mutter that the Promised Land was not what it should be. Instead, he acted briskly to save his people, leading the group south, out of Canaan and toward Egypt, where food and water were still plentiful.

The barren expanse that once separated ancient Egypt and Canaan is now called the Negev desert. Although Abram and Sarai had braved the Syrian desert, this experience was nothing compared to the unsettling terrain of the Negev. The enormous sweep of sky stretching out over miles of endless craters and a wilderness shorn of grass and trees is enough to compel even modern travelers to despair. Mark Twain, who visited there in 1867, wrote that the Negev has "a desolation that not even imagination can grace with the pomp of life and action."[2]

In such an environment, it can take time to become accustomed to the overwhelming emptiness. Scale and proportion fade away, not unlike being stranded on the open ocean. But perhaps because of its bleakness, the Negev possesses a startling beauty and grandeur that has been known to inspire a kind of supernatural clarity in even the most dispirited wanderer. It was here that Ezekiel saw the dry bones of skeletons rise up and reconstitute themselves as human beings (Ezek. 37:1–14). It was here that Jesus first understood his divine mission. Modern-day pilgrims continue to view this unearthly place with veneration and as a site of potential revelation. If God speaks to anyone these days, you can imagine Him speaking here.

For Abram, Sarai, and their followers, the desert offered a route toward salvation. In Egypt, they hoped to find respite from the chaos that had befallen the Promised Land. They did not lament their desert journey, since the prospect of remaining in Canaan was far worse. However, there were many terrifying rumors about the Egyptians. The Pharaohs had made a name for themselves as warrior heroes, conquering all of the surrounding peoples, including the Canaanites. This meant the Egyptians were de facto overlords to Abram and his followers. Essentially, Abram would be delivering himself and his little band into enemy hands. Once they set foot in Egypt, they would be at the mercy of Pharaoh.

In addition, Egyptian cities had the reputation of being decadent, violent places, and the Egyptians were known to be a lascivious people. Everyone in Abram's party had heard stories about strange religious rites, drunken orgies, and other bizarre excesses in Pharaoh's palaces, practices that were even worse than the rituals of the Canaanites. What's more, the Egyptian gods were supposed to be the most powerful in the world, as they had been instrumental in helping the Egyptian army fend off invaders and grow steadily richer over the centuries. Finally, there was the sheer size of the place to consider. Abram and Sarai had managed to avoid much contact with Canaan's huge walled cities; Haran and Ur were backwaters compared to an Egyptian urban center. It would be a shock to arrive in crowded metropolitan Memphis after the quiet life Abram and Sarai were used to, like stepping off the train in Grand Central Station after having lived one's life in the mountains of Tibet.

Tradition tells us that Abram chose to follow "the Way of the Wells," a route that had been carved out years before by the Egyptians as a kind of desert highway.[3] This nomenclature is a little misleading, as there were no signposts to guide them, nor were they likely to encounter other travelers along the way who could help point them in the right direction. Unlike the passage west from Mesopotamia to the Mediterranean, few people ventured into this desert. The wells were sometimes as much as sixty miles apart, and without even the most rudimentary navigational instruments to guide the group (it would be almost two thousand years before the invention of the compass), they had to rely on Abram's ability to read celestial markers. If he made a mistake and got lost, they could easily run through their supplies.

Yet again Abram demonstrated his skills. With a sure eye, he guided them steadily toward Egypt. The best time of day to travel in the desert was the early morning. By midday it was important to find some kind of shelter, or to set up tents so that everyone could seek respite from the sun. The black donkeys could travel up to twenty-five miles a day, but the group could not have gone more than ten or fifteen miles in the early hours, and even this would have exhausted them.[4]

Accordingly, it is unclear exactly how long this three-hundred-mile trip took. Some commentators say weeks, even months or years, while others have suggested a few days. Abram and Sarai's party was composed of members of their extended family, including Abram's nephew Lot, Lot's wife and children, the herdsmen for Abram's and Lot's flocks, the herdsmen's families, as well as numerous servants, babies, and old men and women. Thus, it seems unlikely that such a large group would have been able to move very quickly. They were further slowed by the need to stop at the wells, seven in all, to replenish water supplies.[5] Despite the welcome break in their journey, each day of rest was a setback, as their food provisions, already sparse, grew leaner.

When they drew near the Egyptian border, the Negev merged into the Sinai desert, the heat intensified, and the rocky path became increasingly sandy, making each step more and more difficult. At last, one day, when they stared across the undulating white slopes, they could see the walls of a grand fortress jutting up against the horizon. This was one of the telltale markers that they had arrived, since the Egyptians had built a string of such fortifications, known as "the Wall of the Rulers," along their eastern border to ward off enemies and to discourage nomads, or "sand people," from penetrating their land.[6]

Strangely, it was at this point in their journey, when the relief of civilization was in plain sight, that Abram started to worry. As everyone else in the party rejoiced, undoubtedly anticipating savory meals of grapes, cheese, lamb, goat, bread, and flagons of water and wine, Abram became increasingly apprehensive. He knew that as "sand people" he and his family and friends could not have been less formidable. At most, his party consisted of around two or three hundred persons and this group would have appeared dusty, hairy, and appallingly uncivilized to the thousands of sophisticated inhabitants of Egypt's teeming cities. He was also well aware that the Egyptians were concerned about invading Sumerian or Canaanite armies and that it was unlikely they would bother to attack a straggling tribe of goatherds.

What, then, was causing Abram's fear? In a word: beauty.

Sarai was famous for her looks.[7] Later sources elaborate on this theme, declaring that Sarai was a prize only the finest man could win, even more desirable than Eve, who was, until Sarai, the prototype for female physical perfection. One text reveled in every detail of Sarai's body:

> How fine are the hairs of her head . . . How desirable her nose and all the radiance of her countenance. . . . How fair are her breasts and how beautiful her whiteness! How pleasing are her arms and how perfect her hands and how desirable all the appearance of her hands! How fair are her palms and how long and slender are her fingers! How comely are her feet, how perfect her thighs! . . . She is fairer than all other women. Truly her beauty is greater than theirs. Yet together with all this grace she possesses abundant wisdom, so that whatever she does is perfect.[8]

Abram knew that Sarai's beauty could occasion jealousy on the part of the officials at the gates of the city. Worse, Pharaoh might want her to join his harem. If so, then, according to the rules of the ancient world, Abram would have to be killed. Rulers did not want stray husbands interfering with their newly acquired wives.

Abram's fear was particularly pointed, because surprisingly, the Egyptians considered "sand people" both menacing and attractive.

A century or so before Abram and Sarai made the long trek to Egypt, an Egyptian artist created a mural that portrayed such Semitic travelers as strikingly handsome. The men and women are shown with dark hair and aquiline noses, and are tall compared to the Egyptians. The men are bearded and the women's long hair is tied back and neatly braided. Men and women both wear woolen tunics, although the women's tunics are more modest.[9]

The Egyptians, on the other hand, were famous for their plainness. According to their own descriptions and that of neighboring peoples, they tended to be "short, slight, long-headed." Some travelers thought of them as downright "ugly." This may have been anti-Egyptian propaganda, but to Abram, there was an obvious and therefore sinister discrepancy between his wife's "natural" beauty and the heavily painted faces of the Egyptian women.[10]

Yet Abram's anxiety about Sarai's good looks and his own self-preservation tells us more about him than about the Egyptians. Despite his later reputation as a man of unquestioning faith, his fear was not only a reflection of his own self-doubt, it was also the first indication of his anxiety about God's power and compassion. At this point in Abram's life, God had proved Himself to be inconsistent at best. Although Abram and his followers had arrived in Egypt unharmed, Abram did not know if God would intervene if his life was threatened. After all, there were no statues of Abram's God waving a spear like the Canaanite god El. Nor did Abram know if God was mighty enough to challenge Pharaoh.

Everyone knew it was foolish to deny the wishes of such a mighty ruler. If he wanted Sarai, he would simply seize her. The Egyptians considered him a god. No one was allowed to talk to him directly or touch his holy personage. In some ways, then, what lay ahead was a crucial test, not only for Abram, but for God. Unsure of the outcome, Abram quickly devised a plan, one that may have seemed logical at the time but that would have serious repercussions for both Abram and Sarai in the years to come.

As they approached the border, Abram said to his wife, "Sarai,

I know what a beautiful woman you are. If the Egyptians see you and think, 'She is his wife,' they will kill me and let you live. Please say that you are my sister, that it may go well with me because of you, and that I may remain alive thanks to you" (Gen. 12:11–13).

This is the first time Abram speaks in the Bible and, ironically, he emerges as a faithless and panicked character, rather than a staunch follower of God. His famous piety is nowhere to be seen. Although he had never before prayed to God for protection, this moment would have been just the right time to do so. But instead of asking for God's assistance and trusting to His powers, he decided that he would rather sacrifice his wife's honor to preserve his own skin. Did the great patriarch value himself over Sarai, and his own life over her safety?

Sarai met Abram's request with an astonishing silence. She did not protest, argue, or chastise her husband for his weakness, but she also did not assent. Her silence is particularly puzzling given that later in their marriage she would be perfectly able to quarrel with Abram when she felt like it. However, in this instance, it was as though she had drawn a veil across her face.

To begin with, Sarai may have been too shocked by her husband's proposal to speak. Or she may have agreed with his plan and been prepared to sacrifice herself for his sake. It is also possible she had heard Abram refer to her as his sibling on previous occasions. According to the Bible, Sarai was actually Abram's half-sister, the daughter of his father by another woman. By Mesopotamian law, close relatives such as first cousins or even half-brothers and -sisters were allowed to marry. And so, Abram was not asking Sarai to lie, just to leave some information out.[11]

Another interpretation of Abram's words may have caused Sarai to feel particularly forlorn. Perhaps Abram no longer wanted Sarai as his wife because she was barren, and so he actually did treat her as his sister, withholding sexual contact from her. According to the custom of the day, Abram would have been within his rights to take another wife, whether or not he divorced Sarai first, in order to ensure that he had heirs. It is also possible that Abram was rebellious. Sensing that his relationships with God and Sarai were somehow intertwined, he was eager to escape the hold that both had on him.[12]

A more controversial explanation put forward by scholar Savina Teubal is that Sarai was not simply Abram's wife but also an *en*, a high priestess in Mesopotamia. This would help explain the family's close relationship to the cities of Nanna, as well as their predilection for sacred groves. If Teubal is right, then it would have been Sarai's job to engage in ritual marriages with rulers in order to test the fertility of the land. However, this does not necessarily mean that she continued to serve Nanna, or any of the Mesopotamian deities, once her husband had met God.[13]

But if Teubal's hypothesis is wrong, then it is likely that Abram's request left Sarai feeling forsaken. What could a wife say to a husband who seemed more intent on saving himself than on protecting her? If Abram pretended to be her brother, she would lose her only weapon against the incursions of other men, since women without husbands were considered fair game to predatory strangers. Indeed, nothing could be more dangerous than to enter a new land as an "unclaimed" female. Without a husband who acknowledged that he "owned" her, Sarai faced danger, including rape, kidnapping, and outright murder.

And so, as the donkeys' hooves sank into the sand, and the sky glowed a hot steady blue, the band entered Egypt with a terrible plan in place. No guards waved them across a border. No trumpets blared. They were too small a group. But when at length they met their first Egyptians, Abram did exactly as he had proposed. He presented Sarai as his sister, and she remained silent.

Maybe, in part because she did not speak at this point, the rest of Sarai's life with Abram can be seen as a response to his actions at the gates of Egypt. Even Abram's staunchest allies, the ancient rabbis who were intent on depicting him as the superhero who founded Judaism, would not be able to absolve him of this act. They pointed to the Biblical phrase "going *down* to Egypt" to underline Abram's spiritual decline as he approached Pharaoh's palace.[14]

In fact, this story has so troubled Abram's admirers that some were convinced the Torah had gotten the details wrong. The Koran leaves out Abram's request altogether. In *The Book of Abraham,* a Mormon sacred text that the founder of the church, Joseph Smith, said he translated with divine assistance, God, not Abram, suggests the plan:

> And it came to pass when I was come near to enter into Egypt, the Lord said unto me: Behold, Sarai, thy wife, is a very fair woman to look upon;
>
> Therefore it shall come to pass, when the Egyptians shall see her, they will say—She is his wife; and they will kill you, but they will save her alive; therefore see that ye do on this wise:
>
> Let her say unto the Egyptians, she is thy sister, and thy soul shall live.
>
> And it came to pass that I, Abraham, told Sarai, my wife, all that the Lord had said unto me—Therefore say unto them, I pray thee, thou art my sister, that it may be well with me for thy sake, and my soul shall live because of thee.[15]

Reassuring though this depiction of Abram's actions might be, in the Biblical version, Sarai's silence wreaths Abram's actions in ambiguity. Even if she had briefly assented, uttering just the word "yes," the reader would be less troubled. As it stands, it is impossible to know if Sarai accepted her husband's request or if she despised him for it, and this leaves Abram in a disturbingly unredeemed position.[16]

There is, however, one last hypothesis about Abram's actions that paints the man in more generous colors without changing the words of the Bible, although it suggests that he was involved in a far more confrontational relationship with God than hitherto suspected. Perhaps Abram's decision to remove his protection from his wife was actually an attempt to discover God's true character. Would God rescue Sarai? Would He allow Abram to make such a sacrifice? Who was this God? Could He hold His own against Pharaoh?

After all, Abram hardly knew God. He had followed God's command and left Mesopotamia for Canaan, but he had not yet gotten any return for his obedience. Sarai's womb had remained stubbornly empty, and Canaan was still replete with farmers who did not seem to realize that their fields would soon belong to Abram. He may not have complained when the famine struck, but he certainly seemed unhappy now. God was not doing what He said He would, and so Abram would take matters into his own hands.

Seen in this light, Abram's behavior seems more understandable. He had created an opening for God to act. But if God did not intervene and Abram let the Egyptians kill him in a doomed effort to preserve his wife's virtue, Sarai would end up unprotected anyway and would be forced to join Pharaoh's harem. In addition, his death would leave his followers vulnerable to Egyptian predations. Therefore, it is possible that Abram was not being selfish, although Sarai may not have realized this. Perhaps he was deploying a strategy that would help preserve the future of his people, albeit at Sarai's expense. If so, then his actions initiate a tradition of strategic trickery among his descendants, who would often rely on deception to outsmart stronger opponents.

Still, no matter what Abram's motives were, Sarai's fate hung in the balance, underlining the many complexities of this story. Accordingly, those writers who have attempted to explain away Abram's actions miss the point of this episode.[17] Abram is not simply a model of obedience. He is not a quiet, acquiescent figure. Rather, the Bible paints a portrait of a man who struggled to reconcile the demands of God's word with his own fears and desires.

CHAPTER SIX

RAPE IN THE PALACE

Egyptian civilization was over a thousand years old when Sarai and Abram first trudged across the border with Canaan. The initial dynasty had been established around 3100 B.C.E., and the Pyramids were already considered ancient relics. The nineteenth century B.C.E. marked the end of the Middle Kingdom, and the eighteenth century ushered in the beginning of the Thirteenth Dynasty, an era so tumultuous that it is impossible to guess which Pharaoh actually sat on the throne when Abram and Sarai ventured into the empire. Two cities, Memphis and Thebes, vied to be the center of government, each putting forward its own contestant for the title of Pharaoh. But since the Pharaoh based in Memphis was probably the most powerful and wealthiest, it seems likely this was where Abram and Sarai headed, as supplies would be more plentiful there.

Even an embattled Egyptian king was a far more glorious ruler than Abram and Sarai had ever encountered before and a decaying Egypt far mightier than any civilization they had known. Memphis was just south of the Nile delta, a few days' journey from the border along the busy Egyptian thoroughfare, and as they approached, the polished limestone of the Pyramids gleamed in the sun, and the

Sphinx glowered at them, warning them away from the tombs of the dead kings. At last, Pharaoh's palace appeared on the horizon, large and garish. Rather than one imposing building, it was actually a tightly ordered system of gigantic pillared structures that included temples, theaters, and private residences. The result was daunting to anyone who might have dreamed of overpowering the ruler. Not that Abram had any such desire. He simply wanted food, drink, and rest for his family and friends and, of course, safe passage through the land.

But as Abram had expected, Sarai's exquisite beauty was noticed from the moment the Egyptians spotted her. Immediately, dazzled courtiers raced to tell Pharaoh of the bewitching foreigner who had just arrived in the city (Gen. 12:15). Intrigued, Pharaoh summoned the couple to his palace and made a stately entrance into his throne room. As was the custom, Abram and Sarai bowed so their foreheads touched the ground in deference to Pharaoh's power.

When Sarai lifted her head and the ruler saw how lovely she was, he too fell under her spell. He demanded that she come to his private quarters so that he could enjoy her beauty for himself, or so the rabbis wrote, expanding the Biblical version that simply stated, "The woman was taken into Pharaoh's palace"(12:15). Only then did Pharaoh ask if Sarai and Abram were married, the Midrash says, since at no point in the Bible does Pharaoh actually inquire about her marital status. Sarai promptly named Abram as her brother, and Pharaoh sent him gifts of gold, silver, sheep, and slaves.[1]

There is another version of this story, however, where Pharaoh did not need his attendants to tell him about Sarai's loveliness, because from the moment she arrived in Egypt, "all the land . . . shone with her beauty."[2] The extraordinary part of this tale is that Sarai was seventy-five or seventy-six years old. Neither the Bible nor the Midrash dispute this fact. Granted, Sarai was destined to live to 127, but this still meant that she was well past middle age. Her beauty did not lie in her youth, then, but in an intrinsic perfection, and something else mysterious — charisma, perhaps, or, according to the rabbis, her piety.

At any rate, everything had gone exactly as Abram had feared. Sarai had been seized by the Egyptians to become one of Pharaoh's "wives." In obedience to her husband, she did not resist her capture and had lied about her marital status. As Abram watched his wife trail into the palace to become the newest member of Pharaoh's harem, we do not know whether he felt guilty that he had preserved his life in exchange for his wife's body. Instead, we are left to wonder how Abram could have allowed her to be seized by Pharaoh without making any kind of protest.

In fact, this inaction would earn him the contempt of one famously opinionated woman: England's Queen Victoria declared on her deathbed that she did not expect to see Abraham in heaven after his betrayal of Sarah.[3] It is easy to see what she meant, especially as it is possible that Abram's fear of Pharaoh's wrath was entirely of his own invention. The ruler had made no threats, either to Abram or Sarai. Perhaps Abram could have spoken up with impunity and said, "No, you may not have her. She is my wife."

As for Sarai, all of the stories concur that she did not weep over leaving her family and friends but conducted herself with dignity. Inside the precincts of the palace, there were elegant amphitheaters, cavernous rooms with paintings of banquets, battles, and the gods making love, all in the vivid colors the Egyptians favored: red, black, gold, and green. Outside, the fountains splashed into dark pools. There were altars to strange gods and rows of tightly pruned shrubs and fruit trees. There were also more people here than in many of the towns or villages Sarai had visited. Servants scurried down hallways, tended gardens, cooked food, washed tile floors, and whispered to each other while the nobles strolled and chatted.[4] Pet monkeys, cats, and tame little dogs ran freely through the palace.

To reach her new chambers, which would have been in the most lavish section of the palace, near Pharaoh's private quarters, Sarai had to travel through courtyard after crowded courtyard. Compared to the men she knew, the Egyptians were shockingly immodest, conducting their business half-naked, with elaborate linen cloths wrapped around their waists instead of the long woolen tunics Abram and his family wore from the neck down. The Egyptians also abhorred facial hair, and men tweezed and shaved their faces until they had a smooth girlish look that Sarai had only seen on young boys. Both men and women painted their faces in odd stripes of green and black. And the women wore their hair in elaborate coils that had been hennaed red. Some even had ornate tattoos of crocodiles or cats, two of the animals they worshipped, on their arms and thighs. These strange-looking people hardly seemed human, and Sarai stood out as a foreigner in her simple smock with her long hair hanging straight down her back.[5]

Pharaoh had many wives and concubines, who enjoyed a surprising amount of independence in their section of the palace, roaming where they wanted, bossing servants around, ordering meals from the kitchens, and bathing in the formal garden pools. In Egypt, unlike in Mesopotamia or Canaan, women were treated with a respect that must have been eye-opening for Sarai. Men and women were accorded equal access to the law and shared many of the same rights. Women were free to work outside the home and could be doctors, merchants, or manufacturers.[6] For the women in Pharaoh's harem, though, work was out of the question. Most of their day was spent visiting with each other and tending to their beauty, which had won them the prized position of "wife" to one of the most powerful rulers in the world.[7]

And so, whether she liked it or not, Sarai was plunged into a world of luxury and fashion that would have been unheard-of back in Canaan or Mesopotamia. There were mangoes and coconuts to eat and wine to sip. There were elaborately ornamented chairs to sit on and a phenomenon entirely new to Sarai: beds with wooden headboards and soft mattresses placed on "stretched leather thongs that served as springs."[8] How different this was from the goatskin blankets and straw mats of nomadic life.

The women ground their own makeup out of malachite and kohl and spent hours concocting new recipes for the perfumed wax cones that they wore on top of their heads at evening parties. These were odd accessories that were designed to melt in the late-night heat so that drips of the sweet-oil aphrodisiac ran down their faces, necks, and backs.[9]

Occasionally one could see sacred processions of priests and priestesses walking the ceremonial path to the pillared temples. Despite the differences in their costumes and their deities, it would have been difficult for Sarai not to be reminded of the rites of Ur and Haran. There were cat gods, snake gods, a wolf god, and a myriad of male and female deities who played active roles in the Egyptians' lives. In addition, fortune-tellers roamed the palace grounds, selling magic creams, mysterious rituals, odd amulets, spells, and charms. It was hard to keep track of them all.[10]

Traditionally, Pharaoh's other concubines were responsible for grooming a new woman to enter his harem. After bathing the candidate in scented water, they bedecked her with jewelry — usually golden bracelets and wide beaded necklaces. They painted her face, tweezed her eyebrows, shaved the hair off her legs, oiled her skin, and dressed her in the latest Egyptian fashion, such as a pleated linen dress. Finally, they perfumed her hair and neck. By the time Sarai was brought to Pharaoh's chambers, she would have looked just foreign enough to titillate his jaded palate, but she had also been molded into a sexually appealing woman by Egyptian standards.[11]

According to many sources, one of Pharaoh's daughters was named Hagar. If this was the point at which Abram's future lover and his wife first encountered each other in the perfumed intimacy of the women's chambers, then Hagar would have had the upper hand.[12] As a princess, Hagar would seem unlikely to have noticed the new Semitic woman who had joined her father's harem, but this setting bred close relationships, since the women in Pharaoh's palaces were frequently together and their shared preoccupation with the rituals of beauty inspired friendships as well as feuds.

For Sarai, this must have been a terrible time. We do not know how long she stayed in the palace. Although some versions of the story say she was only there overnight, the Biblical version does not specify the length of her time with Pharaoh, leaving open the possibility that she was in the harem long enough to establish a bond with the women, perhaps even with the princess. She needed a confidant, and the fact that Hagar would one day join her when she left Egypt suggests that Hagar now filled that role.[13]

Although it must have been a great pleasure to have the dust and sand of the Negev sloughed off her body, to be massaged with oil, to have her long hair combed and plaited, ultimately these preparations were a prelude for Sarai's private interview with Pharaoh. If she was in fact a Mesopotamian high priestess, as Teubal has suggested, then she was used to the idea of ceremonial intercourse. Otherwise, this was a meeting for which there was no successful outcome, and which she could only dread. If she resisted his advances, she could be put to death, or Abram and her family might be harmed. If she did not, she would be ruined forever, as she would have had sex with a man who was not her husband. In her culture this act would render her a whore, no longer worthy to be a wife and liable to be executed by her own people (Deut. 22:22; Lev. 20:10).[14]

Commoners were rarely allowed in Pharaoh's divine presence. To Sarai he would have appeared both strange and mighty. Like the other Egyptian men she had seen, his face was waxy smooth, although he might have had a small patch of hair on his chin. With the long tails of green and black paint extending his eyes and joining his eyebrows, he did not look like an ordinary man but more like a statue or a painted image concocted by an artist. For ceremonial occasions, he wore a wig, and on top of this, a high triangular crown that made him look much taller than he actually was.

In the privacy of his bedchamber Pharaoh had probably removed his headdress, but this did not render him any less threatening. His arms were completely covered with golden bracelets, and around his neck was a wide beaded necklace. From his ears hung golden earrings, and even his sandals were gold. Everything that was human about him had been covered, adorned, exaggerated, or painted over until it was easy to see why people believed he was a deity.

Everywhere there was evidence of the rumored Egyptian lasciviousness. The Egyptians were, in fact, true connoisseurs of sexual pleasure. Naked girls danced in the court and "pranced, shimmied, and shook their bead collars to make them rattle."[15] Musicians played the harp and sang songs with suggestive and sensual lyrics. The ancient words of one famous song reflect their philosophy of life, one entirely foreign to Sarai:

Spend a happy day. Rejoice in the sweetest perfumes. Adorn the neck and arms of your beloved with lotus flowers and keep your loved one seated always at your side. Call no halt to music and the dance, but bid all care begone. Spare a thought for nothing but pleasure; for soon your turn will come to journey to the land of silence.[16]

Egyptian ideas about the divinity of the Pharaoh contributed to the erotic environment of the court, as the Pharaoh's sexuality was seen as a reflection of the gods' creative forces. In many of the murals found on tomb walls and in the papyri that have been discovered from this period, the Pharaoh is often surrounded by amorous young women and engaged in explicit sexual acts.[17] The Egyptians did value chastity, but it was on their own terms. For instance, anal sex was a favorite as this preserved a woman's virginity and did not lead to pregnancy.[18]

We do not know exactly what happened between Pharaoh and Sarai. Did they have sex? If they did, did she enjoy it? Did she fight him off? Did she break her promise to Abram and tell the ruler her true identity? Was she actually a high priestess? Naturally, there are many stories that attempt to explain what *really* happened. The early rabbis, in particular, believed that God would not have let Pharaoh consummate his lust. Christian commentators also vigorously argued that God had intervened, putting a stop to things before the ruler could act. Rashi gave more credit to Sarai's powers than the other commentators, writing that she spoke directly to the angel of God and told him to "Strike [Pharoah]!"[19]

However, these commentators do not mention another reading of this story. Perhaps Sarai skillfully manipulated the ruler into some kind of sexual interlude that did not include actual intercourse. This strategy would have allowed her to retain her chastity and yet not get killed for her resistance. Finally, the Bible offers the most scandalous possibility of all. The text tells us that Pharaoh "took" Sarai as his wife, using a Hebrew verb that is ambiguous enough to allow for the possibility that they did have sex. The scholar Harold Bloom insists this was the case, and that Pharaoh succeeded in making Abram's wife his concubine.[20]

Whether Sarai submitted to sex with the powerful emperor, whether she was intrigued by her time with the ruler, or whether she never had to face him at all, one thing is clear: God was ready to end the charade Abram had forced his wife to enact. He sent "mighty plagues . . . on account of Sarai" to torment Pharaoh and his family (Gen. 12:17). Although this is the standard translation of the verse, there is another more interesting interpretation. The Hebrew has an additional word that usually goes untranslated, *l'dbr*, which means "word" or "action." If one were to put this word back in, the line would read, God sent "mighty plagues . . . on account of Sarai's word/action." The importance of this overlooked word is that it gives Biblical evidence for Sarai's resistance to her husband's plot.[21] Sadly, we will never get to hear what she said or did, but at least the Bible lets us know that she was not a passive victim. In fact, some writers suggest that this episode in Sarai's life gives her more confidence as she is forced to assert herself, discovering her own worth apart from Abram. As Amy-Jill Levine writes, "Sarai's own situation of exploitation [may have] led to new self determination."[22] Perhaps she really was a priestess and Pharaoh failed his test.

The Bible does not tell us what kind of plagues God sent or if Sarai was with Pharaoh when they struck. The vagueness of this passage has allowed commentators to devise their own stories. Early Jewish thinkers were fond of describing Pharaoh's suffering as a sexually transmitted disease. One tale reports that God sent great flying insects that buzzed around Pharaoh's crotch, stinging him and causing him to suffer humiliating distress. Rashi believed that the illness was "a kind of skin disease for which marital relations are harmful." Other stories depict Pharaoh's entire family suffering from a debilitating and miserable illness no one could cure.[23]

What is most important about Pharaoh's suffering, however, is that God had struck down the most powerful man on earth. A weakened Pharaoh was a catastrophe for Egypt, as it rendered the entire country vulnerable. If Pharaoh became ill, priests and priest- esses, doctors and magicians were summoned to heal his suffering. But in this case there was nothing anyone could do to cure the ruler or his wives and children. The royal household burned with a fever that would not go away.

How Pharaoh made the connection between his suffering and his new foreign bride is unclear, and so, again, there are many ver- sions of the story. Some say God spoke to him directly, admonish- ing him for seizing Abram's wife. Others report that it was Sarai who put a stop to things, declaring that Pharaoh must not touch her if he wanted to avoid the punishment of her God.

Nevertheless, one point is clear. Pharaoh's capture of Sarai exposed him, and Egypt, to the power of the Biblical God. Although Sarai's beauty put her at great risk and caused her much anguish and fear, her charms served God well. She was a siren who drew men in so God could manipulate and control their lives. Like that other famous tool of the gods Helen of Troy, Sarai's desirability helped advance the plans of the divine.

Surprisingly, the ancient rabbis shuddered at the idea that Abram was one of the men who had been drawn to Sarai's charms. In their attempt to create a "pure" founder of their religion, they declared that the only man who could resist Sarai's beauty was her husband. In fact, they argued that Abram was so free from desire that the first time he noticed her appeal was right before their entrance to Egypt and then only because of the danger they would face once they crossed the border. Some versions of this Midrash go further, saying he was so devoid of curiosity about her appearance he did not observe her directly, but only saw her reflection in a stream.[24]

Still, this version of events seems like a stretch, revealing more about the early commentators and their efforts to cover up one of Abram's vulnerabilities—an appreciation for feminine beauty or a sexual appetite—than any new facet of Abram's character. Certainly, there is no Biblical evidence to suggest that Abram was impervious to sexual desire.

Thus, in their impulse to sweep Abram's "lust" under the rug, the rabbis missed a significant possibility, although it is not an idea they would have relished. If Abram was initially attracted to Sarai for her beauty—and why wouldn't he be?—perhaps God may have chosen Sarai *before* he chose Abram. What if Sarai's combination of beauty and barrenness was just what God wanted in the wife of His chosen man? Such a woman would be able to entice men into a relationship with her and then help them discover their need for God. Ultimately, Sarai's presence in these men's lives allowed Him to work His miracles. Neither Abram nor Pharaoh would have required divine assistance without Sarai, as the lack of children on Abram's part and the terrible plague in Pharaoh's household caused both men to look toward the heavens for help.

The cost to Sarai in all this is somewhat unclear. We will never know if she secretly enjoyed her stay in the palace, surrounded by luxuries and delectable food and drink, or if she was repulsed at the experience.[25] But when Pharaoh finally did make the connection between Sarai and the sufferings of his family and understood that he had kidnapped, maybe even violated, a married woman, he could not get rid of her fast enough.

Horrified, Pharaoh rose from his sickbed, called Sarai out of the women's chambers, and summoned her husband, asking, "What is this you have done to me! Why did you not tell me that she was your wife? Why did you say, 'She is my sister,' so that I took her as my wife? Now here is your wife; take her and begone!" (12:18–19). God had successfully made Himself known in Egypt. Pharaoh now feared Him more than his own gods.

This is where another gap in the Biblical story occurs: the reunion scene. The moment when Sarai walks across the tiled courtyard back to Abram's side is missing. At the very least, this omission is anticlimactic; at most, it prompts some disturbing questions. Sarai and Abram had not seen each other since she had disappeared into the palace to serve Pharaoh. One might expect, indeed hope for, a moment of high emotion instead of this rather stunning silence. But we never get to see whether Abram expressed relief at the safe return of his wife, thanked God, or felt chagrin. We do not know if Sarai felt any happiness at being given back to her husband, the man who had betrayed her to Pharaoh in the first place. And yet the absence of these details ends up speaking for itself: what better way to render a couple who are profoundly at odds than to shroud their relationship in silence?

Pharaoh, who was now profoundly frightened of the wrath of the foreigner's God, did not simply cast out the couple. He showered them with gifts of jewels, donkeys, camels, and cattle in hope of appeasing their deity.

Compared to Abram, the Egyptian ruler comes off as rather sympathetic. The moment he discovers Sarai is married, he stops his advances. He appears shocked at the wrongdoing that Abram has allowed him to perpetrate and appalled at Abram for delivering his wife into sexual slavery. The question he asks Abram — "What is this that you have done to me?" — is exactly the same question God asks Eve in the Garden of Eden. This is a remarkable reversal for a Biblical story, as Pharaoh is depicted as the virtuous man, the one allied more closely to righteous action than the patriarch.

Abram does not answer but remains mute as though ashamed of his behavior.

There are elements here that suggest the Biblical future as well as the past. Sarai will become a symbol for the Israelites enslaved in Egypt centuries later, while Abram becomes the "brother" who delivers Sarai into servitude, just as his great-great-grandsons will sell their brother Joseph to the Egyptians, setting in motion the Israelites' slavery in the first place. Ultimately, Moses, the great freedom fighter, will be the one to undo Abram's legacy.

To emphasize this link to Egypt, tradition says Pharaoh gave Hagar to Abram and Sarai. According to the Midrash, Pharaoh was so impressed with the power of Abram and Sarai's God that he declared, "I would rather have Hagar be a slave in Abram's household, than a princess in my palace."[26]

Whether or not this young woman was actually Pharaoh's daughter, the legends are firm that she joined Abram and Sarai at this point in the story. In this sense, her entrance into their lives is linked to the couple's tragic sojourn at the palace and Abram's betrayal of Sarai. Not only would Hagar's arrival change Abram and Sarai's lives—as well as the course of human history—she would also be a constant reminder to Abram and Sarai of a painful and divisive time in their marriage.[27]

Of course, none of the players in this drama could have known what was to come. At first, Hagar seemed like nothing more than a pleasing gift from Pharaoh. Sarai's beauty, instead of endangering her husband's life, had bought him enormous wealth. The experience had reinforced Abram's trust in God, since it was God who had saved the couple from the wrath of an angry Pharaoh. Sarai herself had not been killed and was free again, even if it is not clear how she felt about rejoining Abram as his wife. As for Hagar, she was off to see the world. Princess or not, she would now be able to discover what lay beyond the desert that stretched across the horizon.

CHAPTER SEVEN

WAR

I mmediately after Abram and Sarai's final interview with Pharaoh, the great ruler's men escorted the foreigners out of Egypt
(Gen. 12:20). With such an abrupt departure, it was impossible
to know if the situation had improved in the Promised Land during their time away. Perhaps they would find blighted crops, dead
fruit trees, and dry springs when they arrived back. However, their
uncertainty was made easier to bear by the long line of new donkeys
that fanned out behind them. Each animal was laden with sacks of
gold, jewels, and spices. Sarai and Abram were a wealthy couple
now. The sojourn in Egypt had made their fortune.

But this sudden wealth was also worrisome. The Bible's use of
the noun *kevod* to denote Abram's riches hints at Abram's ambiguous situation, as it can also mean "burden." Even more troubling,
there is another echo of the Adam and Eve story. The verb used to
describe Pharaoh's orders, "send away," is the very same one used
to describe the expulsion from the Garden of Eden, God's punishment of the first man and woman.[1]

Still, at first, nothing seemed awry. They trailed back through
the Negev without encountering any difficulties, and when they
arrived in Canaan, they could see that the crops were growing.

The springs were full of water. The famine had passed. When they reached their old campsite at Bethel, Abram prayed at the altar he had built and again called upon "the Lord by name" (13:4).

Despite the evident sincerity of Abram's gratitude to God, there was also an implicit grandiosity in this gesture. Abram's party had grown far more impressive since he was last here. The long train of donkeys indicated that a very rich man had arrived in town. Hopeful traders and curious onlookers would have been interested to witness Abram's public declaration of his allegiance. This important man did not worship El or, for that matter, Nanna or Osiris. Instead, he and his clan would now be known as those who followed a different god. Abram was spreading the word. The knowledge of God's existence was beginning to take hold in both Egypt and Canaan.

On one hand, therefore, Abram seemed to be a triumphant figure, a man who had gone down to Egypt in fear of his life and come back with the spoils of victory. But upon his return to Canaan, tensions began to flare in the camp, and he was forced to grapple with the aftermath of his behavior in Egypt.

Abram had Sarai's constant presence as a reminder of what he had done. Common sense suggests that Sarai was angry with her husband, or at least saddened by his betrayal, but Sarai had yet to speak in the Bible, and so her feelings remain cloaked. Despite their eagerness to fill in Biblical gaps, the ancient commentators never attempted to explain how the relationship between husband and wife might have been harmed by Abram's actions. Perhaps this is because they did not want to call any further attention to what Nachmanides, the formidable twelfth-century rabbi, called the patriarch's "great sin."[2] Whatever the reason, the rabbis of the ancient and medieval world refused to speculate on Sarai's ability to forgive Abram, nor did they explore the possibility that Sarai might have felt bitterness or shame. Instead, as we have seen, they focused on how she maintained her purity throughout her encounter with Pharaoh.

The silence about Sarai's response to Egypt is especially puzzling since everyone knew how crucial she was to Abram's life. One would think that volumes of commentary would have been written on her reaction to this episode. The sad fact that she could not have children swung her into focus, spotlighting a woman in the Bible in a way that had not occurred since Eve's famous conversation with the snake.[3]

Sarai's importance extends beyond her own story. Her infertility set a precedent for many of the significant women in Genesis. Rebecca, Sarai's daughter-in-law, and Rachel, Rebecca's daughter-in-law, would have difficulty getting pregnant. Later in the Bible, Hannah, another barren woman, would pray so desperately for a child that she became the model for how we are all supposed to approach God.

It is no coincidence that women who struggled with their fertility were the ones God singled out. For twenty generations before Sarai, women had conceived effortlessly, but God had been disgusted with the results. The descendants of both Adam and Noah were godless individuals, and so fertility was no longer a sufficient criterion for the selection of the new Adam and the new Eve. Now God wanted His chosen ones to depend on Him for reproduction, implying, as we have already seen, that Sarai's fertility, or lack thereof, was one of the primary reasons that God chose Abram.[1]

This idea helps explain why God's relationship with this famous couple would be far more intimate than with any that came before. Sarai's pregnancy would depend on God's goodwill, rather than her husband's virility. Thus, her infertility provided God with the opportunity to mold Abram into the man He wanted him to be. Again and again, God would use her inability to conceive as a trump card in His maneuvers with Abram. Ultimately, Sarai will serve as the catalyst that will jump-start Abram's life and convert him into Abraham, the hero. She also initiates the Biblical tradition in which God chooses the servant who seems least able to serve, from Moses the stutterer to Jeremiah the tongue-tied.

Abram might have hoped that his invocation at Bethel would help matters along, but he would soon find that God was not yet interested in working miracles. The weeks passed and Sarai remained barren. Abram could only wait while Hagar served her mistress, biding her time. Far from enjoying their new abundance, they found this period after Egypt difficult. The *kevod* of the Pharaoh seemed to be getting heavier, not lighter.

Tensions were not confined to Abram and Sarai's tent. The most direct consequence of the couple's Egyptian wealth was that there was not enough pasture for their newly acquired animals. Conflict escalated until finally Lot's shepherds quarreled with Abram's over grazing rights (13:6–7). This was the tribe's first internal conflict. Pharaoh's gifts were causing Abram's people to splinter apart, suggesting that riches gained in such a way could only bring about alienation and difficulty. In the past, the tribe had remained strong by banding together, pooling resources, and uniting against enemies. And so when this quarrel flared, it threatened the safety and well-being of the entire group. Once again, God seemed intent on testing Abram. To continue on as God's chosen leader, Abram would have to manage this crisis.

Abram swiftly made the difficult decision that he and Lot must separate before the harmony of the camp was destroyed. This was a sacrifice, as Lot was Abram's only viable heir and losing him would be like losing a son. So Abram tried to preserve a good relationship with his nephew, demonstrating both generosity and tact, skills that would come in handy in the future. "Let there be no strife between us, for we are kinsmen," he said to Lot as gently as he could (13:8).

To seal the bargain, Abram allowed Lot to choose which land would be his. If Lot wanted to occupy Canaan, he could have the Promised Land and Abram would move onto other grazing grounds. But Lot selected the rich grasslands of Sodom, even though the land was populated by locals whose way of life would probably be very different from his own.

Almost all of the early Jewish commentators declare that Lot's choice foreshadowed his future downfall.[5] In the Bible a man's virtue was often measured by where he lived. Since Sodom would become known as the city of sin, Lot would become irretrievably linked with impurity and evil. The Koran, however, resists the idea that any of the great figures of the Bible were morally flawed, and so tells us that Lot was actually a missionary who was sent by God to do good work in this evil city.[6]

However one wants to interpret Lot's choice, it was certainly understandable. Most scholars agree that Sodom was located on the rich fertile plain of the Jordan River near the southernmost tip of Canaan. It was one of five cities scattered along grazing lands that were famous for fattening sheep and goats. It seemed bucolic and pleasant, a perfect place to raise children.

Abram granted Lot's request without raising any objections, unknowingly contributing to Lot's doom. But the rabbis who studied this story absolve Abram of any guilt in the matter, arguing that Lot's indifference to Canaan spelled out his own ruin. According to the Midrash, when Lot "departed from Abram" he was implicitly declaring, "I want neither Abram nor his God."[7]

Whether Lot was a virtuous man or a sinner, he was one of Abram's last links to his father's family, and so when his entourage departed for Sodom, Abram could only mourn the loss of his nephew. Having followed God's commands, he found himself in a land that was not his own, still without offspring, and on rocky terms with his wife. If ever a man was to doubt his faith, this would be the moment. As though God suspected this might be the case, He spoke again, comforting His chosen one for losing his surrogate heir.

"I will make your offspring as plentiful as dust," said God in reassuring tones, declaring yet again that Abram's children would fill the land (13:16). Nevertheless, when Abram looked west, east, north, and south, as God commanded him to do, the land was populated by Canaanites, who were building their temples, tilling their orchards, and worshipping their gods as though they intended to stay there forever.

But God persisted, commanding Abram to walk the perimeters of his family's future holdings. Abram obeyed, and after his survey of Canaan, chose to settle in a hilly region named Hebron, where a thick grove of trees bent over a promising stream. Here Abram gave thanks for his blessings and built yet another altar, his third, to God.

At first the days passed uneventfully. Abram's herds grazed contentedly on the grassy slopes. The children grew taller. The women went about their daily round of chores, grinding grain for bread, pounding and stretching goatskins, carding wool, and weaving on small handheld looms. The men traded stories and the servants drew water from the nearby spring. Abram busied himself with exploring the hills and ensuring the well-being of his flocks. In the spring, the poppies and wild mustard burst open and the countryside seemed bright and hopeful.

For a brief spell, Abram could relax his vigilance. The neighboring farmers did not threaten them. Water was plentiful. The herd was flourishing. And yet, the tranquillity of this landscape was deceptive.

War broke out on the plain that lay below Hebron. King Amraphel, King Arioch, King Chedorlaomer, and King Tidal, the rulers of the four cities near Sodom, had set forth on a destructive march, annihilating every settlement they came across. Their violence was so devastating that traces of their destruction still remain. Twentieth-century archaeologists have unearthed a series of settlements along "the King's Highway" that were destroyed around this time (somewhere between 1900–1700 B.C.E.) and that were never rebuilt.[8]

Soon, news came that the enemy had entered Sodom and seized Lot. According to one legend, they had thrown him in a cage, displaying him as a war trophy.[9] Desperate to save his nephew and only heir, Abram revealed himself to be far more than a simple shepherd. He gathered his men and they rushed down from the hill country. Though his army was far smaller and armed with no more than knives and staffs, Abram's men quickly defeated the savage kings. Lot was released, and Abram earned a new reputation for being a great military leader. The king of Sodom, grateful for Abram's protection, marched into Abram's campsite to offer the patriarch the spoils he had acquired in the war. It was a tempting offer, but Abram asserted his virtue and independence by refusing to take any of the sinful king's property. "Not even a shoelace," he declared, because he did not want the king to be able to say, "It is I who made Abram rich" (14:23).

Abram's refusal to accept wealth from the hands of a sinner was evidence of a fastidiousness he had not exhibited in Egypt. Either Abram had changed, or he regarded the king of Sodom as more reprehensible than Pharaoh. Traditional stories speak of widespread reverence for Abram and for his success in this military venture: "Nations in Abraham's time desired to proclaim him their prince, their king, and even their god, but he indignantly declined, and took that very opportunity to point out to them that there is but one Great King, one Great God."[10]

Even if these accounts are somewhat hyperbolic, it is true that Abram was now a war hero. His eagerness to fight the kings reinforced the importance of his relationship with Lot. But it also leads one to wonder where Abram's martial fury was when Pharaoh seized Sarai. Perhaps Abram refrained because of Pharaoh's greater military force, or perhaps it was because Abram had fewer resources in Egypt. Still, it seems odd that he would fight on Lot's behalf but not on Sarai's.

Indeed, Abram's rescue of his nephew throws into relief his betrayal of his wife, revealing how complicated he was: at once a brave military commander and a deeply human, imperfect man who feared for his own life. Thus, Abram may have conquered the kings of the plain, and his actions in Egypt may have saved the lives of his followers, but his relationship with Sarai remained unsettled. As a soldier he was triumphant; as a husband it was less clear how successful he had been or was going to be.

———◆———

CHAPTER EIGHT

DINNER WITH JESUS

While Abram and his men were recovering from battle, the king of Sodom was not the only man to stride into his campsite. The Bible says that another person arrived, a strange figure whose identity has been debated for centuries: "King Melchizedek of Salem brought out bread and wine; he was a priest of God Most High" (Gen. 14:18).

A priest? Priests had not been invented yet, at least not priests of God. Abram and his family were supposed to be the only followers of God at this point in the Bible. However, the ceremonial bread and wine suggested this man did not just want to have a meal with Abram, but intended to enact some sort of ritual. In addition, the name of Melchizedek's city, Salem, seems to be a shortened version of one that had not yet been built, Jerusalem. There was something bewildering, almost magical about Melchizedek. Where had he come from and why was he there?

The standard explanation for the chronological problems of this passage is that Melchizedek was a later insertion into the text, but advocates of this theory tend to overlook the enormous emblematic weight of Melchizedek's appearance at this moment in the Abram story.[1]

Melchizedek, whose name in Hebrew means king (*melech*) of righteousness (*tzadik*), was evidently a visitor from a different world, perhaps some kind of angel. Abram took his advent in stride, even bowing his head to receive a priestly blessing, as though he knew what one was. Immediately, Melchizedek declared, "Blessed be Abram of God Most High, Creator of heaven and earth. And blessed be God Most High, Who has delivered your foes into your hand" (14:19).

Although this one moment could not wipe out the burden he had carried with him since Egypt, nor the harm that he had done Sarai, it did seem that God still regarded Abram as His chosen one. Not only had He allowed Abram to vanquish his enemy, but He had also sent His priest to proclaim His goodwill.

Before they ate, Abram demonstrated an intuitive knowledge of how to respond to a priest's blessing. He gave Melchizedek "a tenth of everything," which would be the tithe that was required of later generations. Abram had grown since Egypt. Not only had he refused the wealth of the evil kings, now he was lessening the weight of his ill-gotten Egyptian gains by bestowing riches on a man of God.

As they drank their wine, Melchizedek remained quiet. He did not describe Salem and so it is not clear if there was a tradition of Jerusalem being a holy city while Abram was alive. Nor did the stranger say in what temple he had served as a priest, or who the other followers of God were. When Melchizedek and Abram finished their meal, Melchizedek disappeared, never to be seen again. Perhaps because of the many questions he raises, Melchizedek has been viewed by Jewish and Christian scholars as a person of urgent symbolic portent.

According to Christian apologists, Melchizedek was an early example of Christ's triumph over the limitations of the Jews. By paying tithes to Melchizedek, Abram acknowledged his priestly status, leading the author of the Book of Hebrews to conclude,

> Now consider how great this man [Melchizedek] was, to
> whom even the patriarch Abraham gave a tenth of the spoils
> (Heb. 7:4).

In other words, Abram's payment demonstrated his subordination
to the priestly king. And Melchizedek's blessing demonstrated his
ascendancy over Abram, as "the lesser is blessed by the better"
(7:7).[2]

To the founders of the early church who scoured Hebrew Scripture
looking for "types"—figures, episodes, and characters that foreshadowed, or even stood for, the advent of the Messiah—Melchizedek
was an emblem of Jesus, and Abram's deference to him demonstrated
the triumph of Christ over the great patriarch of Hebrew Scripture,
an important point since many Jews wondered how Jesus, who was
not descended from the priestly tribe of Levi, could be a holy man, let
alone the Messiah.[3] By linking Jesus to the stately figure of Melchizedek, the author of Hebrews neatly solved the problem of Jesus's
credentials. Instead of belonging to the traditional Israelite priesthood, Jesus would be "High Priest forever according to the order of
Melchizedek" (6:20).[4]

Once the connection between Jesus and Melchizedek had been
established by Hebrews, later Christians developed the idea that
the priest's exchange with Abram proved the primacy of Christianity over Judaism. Indeed, there are those Christians who believe
that Melchizedek was not only a "type" or foreshadowing of the
actual Jesus, but was in fact Christ Himself.[5] Once one claims that
Melchizedek truly is Jesus, the central premise of Christianity is
strengthened to an exponential degree. Far from being preeminent,
Abraham becomes a mere historical figure, a primitive example of
what is to come in the New Testament.

Needless to say, Jewish scholars find this argument troubling
and refuse to acknowledge any connection between Christ and the
mysterious high priest. However, Jewish tradition still accords great

importance to Melchizedek. The Midrash asserts that Melchizedek was actually the 450-year-old Shem, grandson of Noah. In fact, it was his descendants, the Elamites, whom Abram had just conquered in his battle with the four kings. Accordingly, when the two met in the valley, both were anxious. Abram expected that Shem would be angry with him for killing his grandchildren, and Shem was worried that Abram would be furious at him for raising sinners.[6] When they exchanged greetings, they made peace and created a bridge not only between themselves, but between the world before the Flood and the world that came after. Shem, the direct descendant of Noah, stretched out his hand to bless the man many commentators regard as the new Noah, Abram.

Rather than noting Melchizedek's superiority to Abram, Jewish tradition takes note of an embarrassing blunder on the priest's part: his blessings are in the wrong order. Melchizedek honors Abram before God. The Talmud records that Abram was shocked and exclaimed, "Does one bless a servant before blessing his Master?" Before this incident, the rabbis say, God had contemplated making Melchizedek the father of all priests, but after Melchizedek's error, He decided the honor of the priesthood would go to Abram's descendants instead.[7]

Despite this idea of Melchizedek as flawed, the sense of mystery the visitor trailed behind him ensured that his legacy did not end here. One famous story says that on the evening of the sixth day of creation, God inscribed His sacred name on a staff and gave it to Adam. Adam passed it on to Noah, who bequeathed it to Shem. At their famous meeting, Melchizedek (or Shem) gave it to Abram, who passed it on to his descendants. Centuries later it ended up in the hands of an Egyptian priest named Jethro. Jethro planted the staff in his garden, and one day Moses came to the house, saw the staff, and claimed it as his own. At once, Jethro knew that Moses was a godly man, the hero of prophecy who would one day free the Jews from slavery, and so he gave Moses his daughter Zipporah as his bride. God, too, took note of Moses and performed His second miracle (after the burning bush) by turning the staff into a snake and back again.[8]

According to this story, Melchizedek links Abraham to both Adam and Moses, placing him in the center of the lineage of the Bible. Important though this is, however, the Melchizedek incident was only a prelude for the next episode in Abram's life. God had big plans, ones that dwarfed all that had come before.

CHAPTER NINE

SILENCES

For what more liberal and more fruitful provision could God have made in regard to the Sacred Scriptures than that the same words might be understood in several senses, all of which are sanctioned by the concurring testimony of other passages equally divine?

—Augustine[1]

In the age-old tradition of women, Sarai and Hagar stayed behind at the campsite in Hebron while Abram and the other men were at war. According to the Bible, 318 men accompanied Abram, presumably all of his retainers, although a few male servants would have been left behind (Gen. 14:14). This means that there were at least three hundred women in the camp, assuming that most of the men who went to war were married. If some households had female servants, plural wives, or young children, the number would have been even higher. Remaining also was the motley group of men who were too sickly or too old to go with Abram.

To chase down Lot's capturers, Abram and his band had to travel north to Damascus, a journey that could take many weeks. This meant he would be gone for at least several months—a long time to leave the tribe without a leader. Despite the presence of men at the campsite, the Bible does not say that Abram appointed a male deputy from among them, suggesting that he was content to leave the camp under Sarai's jurisdiction. Precisely what happened in Abram's absence is unclear, though, because for three chapters, the Bible does not mention either Sarai or Hagar, and instead focuses on Abram and his activities.

Biblical silences mean many things to many people. The naive say that silence means that nothing happened, but the Bible's earliest commentators, both Jewish and Christian, teach that it is up to the careful reader to piece together the hidden events. The ancient Jews taught that study could unlock the mysteries of Scripture in the same way that a hammer strikes sparks on a rock.[2] St. Augustine wrote, "the ambiguities of [Scripture] . . . demand no ordinary care and diligence."[3] However, because the silence in these three chapters concerns women, neither the rabbis nor the early church fathers bothered to search out what might have been happening to Sarai and Hagar. To them, the lives of women were not important enough to speculate about.

These gaps in the story are not limited to women but extend to everyday life in general. After all, the tales in the Bible recount extraordinary events, so accounts of the routine activities of both men and women are neglected in the text. Still, it is the lives of women that are largely overlooked, since many of the heroes of these extraordinary events are men. This is unfortunate, since what Sarai did while Abram was away might not be discussed by the commentators, but it is still an essential part of this story.[4]

One of the most difficult aspects of the men's departure was that the women did not know when their husbands would return. Alone in the wilderness, the little group had very little protection. If marauders attacked their campsite, it was up to the women and the few men who remained to fend off their assailants. Later in the Bible, the heroine Jael would impale the captain of enemy troops with a tent peg when he ventured into her camp (Judg. 4:19–22; 5:24–27).

This is precisely the sort of action that Sarai, as the leader's wife, had to be prepared to take.

Although it was burdensome to shoulder male responsibilities, for a childless woman like Sarai, whose status was somewhat precarious, this was an opportunity to cement her position as the "first lady" of the tribe.[5] Lot's wife was the only other woman who had approached Sarai's position of leadership and she had moved to Sodom with her husband. Alone at the top of the clan's hierarchy, Sarai could have easily faltered or doubted herself. The other women could have tried to topple her or complained about her when the patriarch returned.

Fortunately, this did not happen, or so we can surmise, as the Bible makes no mention of any crises. The habitual round of daily life ticked along. Without any record of serious quarrels or contention, we can assume that Sarai was a good arbitrator. This was an essential skill, as tensions and personal enmities could not be allowed to fester; they endangered the tribe. If aggrieved parties seceded from the clan, everyone was more vulnerable to enemies, wild animals, and starvation.

Sarai's duties were not limited to resolving disputes. She also had to be acutely aware of the weather and the condition of the grazing grounds before the animals had chewed through all the grasses. There could be no rash decision about moving. If they went too far from Hebron, the men would not find the camp when they returned from war. Generally, the little band relied on scouts, but there were probably not enough men left behind, so Sarai had to have an excellent sense of local geography when she directed the tribe's path. It was always dangerous to leave behind a water source. Would they find another spring or oasis soon enough? Would this new water source be sufficient to sustain the entire band of women, children, and animals?

The daily life of the camp was full. The women were responsible for pounding and grinding barley, hard wheat, and enmer (a wheat-like grain) before they began the sweaty business of bread-making, including mixing, kneading, and building a fire for baking. As the highest-ranking woman, Sarai was responsible for monitoring their supplies. She had to make sure they did not use their communal stores too quickly, and that the grains were well stored and protected from moisture and rats. Moldy barley would have been as catastrophic as an attack on their campsite.[6]

In addition to preparing the food, the women were the laundresses and the ones who trekked to the spring to get drinking water. They gathered roots and herbs for stews, and fuel for the fires. They tended the babies and toddlers. They pounded goatskins into felt, stretching them into the waterproof rugs that roofed their tents and protected them from wind, sand, and rain.[7]

As if this were not enough, in the men's absence, the livestock had to be tended and protected from the incursions of wild animals. Without shears, the coats of the goats and sheep had to be cut with knives or plucked. Fortunately, the sheep of the ancient world had hair more like a goat's or a yak's than the fleece of modern-day sheep, whose coats have to be sliced off with a sharp blade. Still, gathering wool was a strenuous activity and would have taken several days of hard labor. After this difficult process, the wool and goat hair had to be washed, combed, and carded.[8]

Finally, to make the wool into thread the women used a hand-held spindle, essentially a "U-shaped bent stick," and wrapped the long thick fibers around it, twisting and looping them until at last the wool began to stretch and lengthen, and a thin, strong thread began to emerge. After perhaps a month of spinning, a family might have enough thread to weave a piece of cloth suitable for one of the plain tunics worn by both men and women. Simple horizontal looms were light and easy to pack on the donkeys when they had to trek to a new site. If they had enough thread when they reached a settlement with a weaver, they could also hire him to manufacture their cloth.[9]

All the while, the children had to be taught proper behavior as well as crucial lessons about how to survive in the wilderness. Jewish tradition has always held that Sarai was as important a religious teacher as Abram. According to the Midrash, she helped educate women and girls about God, while Abram instructed the men.[10]

Given their frightening position alone in the wilderness, it is miraculous that this was such an untroubled time for the women. That there were no attacks, famines, or plagues tells us that Sarai was as talented a leader as her husband yet never neglected her duties as a woman. Indeed, she shared many of the virtuous qualities of the ideal wife depicted in Proverbs:

> *Her husband puts his confidence in her,*
> *And lacks no good thing.*
>
> *. . .*
>
> *She looks for wool and flax,*
> *And sets her hand to them with a will.*
> *She is like a merchant fleet,*
> *Bringing her food from afar.*
> *She rises while it is still night,*
> *And supplies provisions for her household.*
>
> *. . .*
>
> *She girds herself with strength,*
> *And performs her tasks with vigor.*
> *She sees that her business thrives.*
> *Her lamp never goes out at night.*
> *She sets her hand to the distaff;*
> *Her fingers work the spindle.*
>
> *. . .*
>
> *She oversees the activities of her household,*
> *And never eats the bread of idleness.* (Prov. 31:11–27)

Of course, this description is from a male perspective, yet the wife emerges as a vital character in her own right. Proverbs does not glorify either beauty or obedience. Rather, the ideal Biblical woman is supposed to be strong and vital—a manager, not a follower.

Given the extent of her responsibilities, it was fortunate that Sarai would not have to do her chores by herself. Although the Bible has yet to mention Hagar by name, Sarai will refer to her as "my servant" in the next episode of the women's story, suggesting that throughout this period Hagar was Sarai's primary maid and perhaps her only one. As a high-ranking servant, Hagar would have worked alongside Sarai. Together they would have prepared meals, attended births, cared for invalids, boiled grains, and scanned the horizon for dangerous bands of strangers. From her mistress, therefore, Hagar would have learned all the skills a woman needed to survive the harsh life of the campsite.

The isolation of the women was made more pronounced by their lack of communication with the men. Granted, it was difficult to exchange messages over such vast distances, but it also seems likely that Abram felt no need to send word because of his faith in his wife's abilities. Of course, it is also possible to read Abram's silence as evidence that he did not care about his wife and the domestic affairs he had left behind. But such behavior would have been out of character for Abram, who is consistently depicted as one of the most beloved leaders in the Bible. This man would never abandon his people. He had devoted himself to their welfare and their security for many years and he would not stop now.

However, it is likely that for Abram this act of leave-taking, like his initial departure from Haran, was liberating. Once he had turned over his worldly affairs to his wife, he was free to be a warlord. After he had achieved victory and before he returned to the campsite, he could pause and direct his energies inward.

In the meantime, Sarai had the chance to reflect on their situation: her husband was the childless leader of a band of exiles from Mesopotamia. If he did not become a parent soon, he would lose credibility as a leader, and so would she as his wife. People might believe that God was angry at them, Abram was weak, or she was cursed.

She had to take action. And who better to help her than her handmaiden, the woman who was by her side every day, pounding and spinning, grinding and baking? Such mindless tasks invite conversation, and so it seems likely the two exchanged confidences as the long, hot days passed. It is even possible that it was during this time together that the two women came up with the scheme that would change both of their lives forever.

But even if Hagar did not know for sure what Sarai had in mind, she must have understood how painful it was not to be able to have children. She might even have suspected what Sarai would ask of her. However, both women knew that nothing could happen yet. They would have to wait until Abram came back home.

CHAPTER TEN

TREMBLING BEFORE
GOD

For many men and women of faith, whether or not they are prophets, the experience of an essential loneliness seems to be a prerequisite for understanding their own nature and their relationship to God. Indeed, religious thinkers of all eras have believed that aloneness is an intrinsic part of having a divine vision. Dietrich Bonhoeffer, a Protestant German pastor who was put to death by the Nazis in 1944, wrote from his prison cell, "It is as though in solitude the soul develops senses which we hardly know in everyday life."[1]

According to Lakota tradition, to go on a "Vision Quest," one has to "vow to be isolated from one to four days or four nights." There can be no vision unless one is completely alone. The distinguished twentieth-century rabbi Joseph Soloveitchik believed that loneliness was the first evidence of man's evolving relationship to God. Only the person who is able to access such feelings is able to experience the divine, he argued.[2]

And so, when on the journey back to Hebron, Abram's men inexplicably faded away and left him alone in the wilderness, it was perhaps inevitable that this time of solitude would play an important role in his relationship to God.[3] Few Biblical prophets wanted to endure the profound separation from their friends and family that

God required of them. But the pull toward the divine was like falling in love. No one could resist it even though the pain that would result was predictable. The prophet Jeremiah complained that God was like a forceful suitor:

> *You have seduced me and I am seduced,*
> *You have raped me and I am overcome . . .*
> *I used to say, "I will not think about him,*
> *I will not speak his name anymore."*
> *Then there seemed to be a fire burning in my heart.* (Jer. 20:7–9)

The scholar Rudolph Otto summed up the divine experience as "mysterious, terrible, and fascinating." The prophet was compelled toward the call of God but the experience was frightening and entirely absorbing, even addictive. Once a mystic had encountered God, he spent the rest of his days simultaneously dreading and longing for another divine visitation.[4]

For most people, separating oneself from the world was not in itself sufficient preparation for receiving direct communication from the Lord. The writers of the Talmud argue that the recipient of the Spirit must be "strong, wise, humble, and physically imposing. He must also be rich!" The great medieval scholar Maimonides added that a prophet must be in a "happy joyous mood" to receive messages from God.[5]

This is certainly a different picture from the stereotypical image of the prophet as an outcast, dressed in rags, and despised by all, and it is based in part on Abram. The early commentators believed that one had to be physically fit and in good condition to withstand the overwhelming impact of God's presence. At this juncture in his life, having trounced the most powerful warlords in the land and having established himself as an important international negotiator, Abram was at the height of his powers—wealthy, politically savvy, and in excellent health. Perhaps this is why God chose this particular time to pay an extended visit.

It was no coincidence, then, that when Abram found himself with no companions, away from the responsibilities of the war and the campsite, suddenly "the word of God came" (Gen. 15:1). Immediately, Abram trembled in terror. "Fear not," God said rather abruptly (15:1). This brave man had not needed any solace before, though he had faced many terrifying situations: the crossing of the Euphrates, the flight from famine, the trek through the Negev, the confrontation with Pharaoh, the battle with the kings of the plain, and two previous encounters with God. One cannot help but wonder: Why would Abram be afraid now?

Rashi suggests that after the war, Abram was "in great anxiety" and was afraid that he had reached the limit of his "God-given . . . reward." Perhaps the enemy kings would seek revenge and Abram would tumble down from glory.[6] God must have thought this as well, since His next words were meant to reassure Abram that his battle victory was not the end of his triumphs and that, having spurned the Sodomite treasure, he would now receive heavenly honors instead. "Your reward shall be very great," God said, using the same word for "reward" that the king of Sodom had, as though He wanted to contrast the immensity of divine blessings with the paltry gold of the monarch (15:1).

But by now Abram may have been skeptical about God's promises. Where were the children God had said he would have? And so he continued to shake with fear. Seeing the vulnerability of His chosen one, God redoubled His efforts to soothe Abram, saying, "I am a shield to you"—in Hebrew: *maggen Avram*—words that have been so beloved to Jews that, four thousand years later, congregations throughout the world still recite them during the *Amidah*, the daily standing prayer.[7]

Abram was in the midst of the longest encounter he had ever had with the divine. According to Jewish tradition, the prophet actually left this world and entered the realm of the low-ranking angels, called the *ishim*. These were not the famous angels, like Michael and Gabriel, but they still ranked above human beings.[8] This may have been both a mentally and physically trying experience, so it seems unlikely that Abram felt much immediate comfort from God's words. Maimonides wrote, "Whenever one is receiving a prophecy, one's limbs shake, the strength of one's body weakens, and one's thoughts become disturbed, leaving one's mind free to understand what one will see."[9] To onlookers, the prophet might appear to be undergoing some kind of fit, conveying to both the recipient and his community that an extraordinary event had occurred.[10] William James writes that a "mystical state" is often marked by "passivity . . . The mystic feels as if his own will were in abeyance, and indeed sometimes as if he were grasped and held by a superior power."[11]

However, the twentieth-century scholar Abraham Heschel disagreed with this characterization of the prophet, arguing:

> The prophet is not a mouthpiece, but a person; not an instrument, but a partner, an associate of God . . . God, we are told, asks not only for "works," for action, but above all for love, awe, and fear. [12]

In other words, Abram's fear in this scene is not, according to Heschel, testimony to his passivity or his abandonment of self. Rather, it is evidence that Abram stayed intact as a person while talking to God and, even more important, that he was responding directly to God's presence, rather than becoming a selfless receptacle for God's wishes. This theory, more than the ideas of Maimonides and James, helps explain what Abram was able to do next.

Despite his terror, for the first time in his life Abram voiced his concerns to God. Even more shocking, he seemed to protest against God's will. "O Lord God," he said, "what can You give me, seeing that I shall die childless. . . . Since You have granted me no offspring my steward will be my heir" (15:2).

Abram had a right to complain. Almost ten years had passed since God had first promised him offspring, but Sarai remained infertile. Abram had no sons to fill his land, which was not his land, anyway, since Canaan remained in the hands of the Canaanites. Abram's only potential heir, Lot, was back in Sodom.

As a result, Abram's future felt empty. It was only through children that one could pass on one's legacy. The shadow of his mortality fell long and dark on all that Abram had done and would do for the sake of the Lord.

With the stakes so high, adoption was a common practice during this era and a step that some scholars believe Abram had already taken by naming his head servant as his heir.[13] But even if this was true, to Abram, it was clearly an unsatisfactory arrangement. God responded compassionately to Abram's words as though He had been waiting for Abram to express despair so that He could console him. "That one shall not be your heir; none but your very own issue shall be your heir," He declared (15:4).

This announcement was a welcome surprise. Abram had taken an enormous risk. No one had ever talked to a god like this. He had broken the conventions of both the Canaanites and Mesopotamians, who believed that one bowed down to deities, feared and flattered them. Certainly, one did not question them, complain, or demand to know their plans. But when Abram had gathered his courage and told God what worried him, instead of striking him dead, God responded by revealing more than He ever had before.

And He was not through. As though He realized that Abram needed more evidence, God "took [Abram] outside and said, 'Look toward heaven and count the stars, if you are able to count them'" (15:5). When Abram looked up, the sky was studded with constellations. Of course he could not count all the stars. Instead, he could only feel his own smallness in the face of the universe. Only then did God add, "So shall your offspring be" (15:5).

This moment of prophecy was a departure from the promises God had given before. It seemed He wanted Abram to learn something important from this vision of infinity. There is an echo here of the tradition about Abram's childhood, that he had looked at the stars and had thought at first they were gods. But now it was God who instructed Abram in the art of stargazing. Those pinpoints of light were not the divine presence itself. Rather, God was the organizing principle behind the constellations.

Glorious though this experience must have been, it may also have been confusing. By providing him with this vision, God seemed to want Abram to understand simultaneously his importance and his unimportance. The numberless descendants God promised made Abram's own existence seem like nothing, as if he were just one speck of light. On the other hand, he would be the father of an entire universe. As one eighteenth-century commentator wrote, "The descendants of Abraham seem insignificant in terms of numbers and power, but each one is an indispensable part of God's plan."[14]

This exchange also initiated a new way for human beings to establish a connection to God—by contemplating the immensity of nature. The philosopher Pierre Hadot calls this state "a cosmic consciousness" in which one "become[s] aware of the place of one's individual existence within the great current of the cosmos."[15] The early-twentieth-century German intellectual Malwida von Meysenbug was humbled by the infinitude of her religious vision: "I was alone upon the seashore," she wrote, "and I was impelled to kneel down . . . before the illimitable ocean, symbol of the Infinite. I . . . prayed as I had never prayed before, and knew now what prayer really is: to return from the solitude of individuation into the consciousness of unity with all that is."[16] Countless other writers, from Thomas Merton to Charlotte Brontë, have described this sort of existential confrontation with the universe as an essential prerequisite for a divine revelation. One could even say that Thoreau's sojourn in Walden owes its grandeur to Abram's experience of the constellations.

It should come as no surprise, therefore, that many western visionaries move from a sense of their individual isolation to experiencing their place in the vastness of the universe. Like Abram, they at once feel the enormousness of God and their own limitations. Emerson wrote, "I am God in nature; I am a weed by the wall."[17] St. Augustine described God as a circle whose center was everywhere and circumference nowhere, leaving mankind lost and overwhelmed by the mystery of God's existence. Even the mathematician Isaac Newton, a devout Christian who was devoted to discerning the rules of nature, was still acutely aware of his own limitations. He observed that the laws he found could never explain anything but the mechanics of life on earth. The universe, or the Book of God, was inaccessible to him.[18]

Rashi, who was particularly struck by this episode in Abram's life, wrote that God did not simply take Abram "outside" his tent but instead swept him off the earth and revealed the entire universe from the "outside" or from God's all-encompassing point of view. For one miraculous instant, then, Abram got to share God's perspective. Understandably, this moment of vision resulted in greater closeness between God and His chosen one. As the Bible says, "because [Abram] put his trust in the Lord, God reckoned it to [Abram's] merit" (15:6).[19]

Ironically, this moment of mutual trust between God and Abram has sparked centuries of controversy between Christians and Jews. In his letter to the Romans, whom he was trying to convert to the new faith of Jesus, Paul used God's "reckon[ing]" as evidence that Abram was granted God's grace without following any commandments, since God had yet to communicate Jewish law to Moses at Sinai. Abram, Paul argued, was an example of how all one needed to enter into the New Covenant with Christ was faith. He wrote, "We have come to believe in Christ Jesus, so that we might be justified by faith in Christ, and not by doing the works of the law, because no one will be justified by the works of the law" (Gal. 2:16).

Later Christians used Paul's words in their polemics against Judaism, arguing that Abraham and God forged their relationship on the basis of love and love alone. There was no need to accept the covenant of the Torah to be one of the righteous. All that mattered was the acceptance of Christ. Thus, faith triumphed over law and Christian over Jew. But as the modern theologian Kenneth Vaux argues, Paul is simply seeking to revive piety, not eradicate Jewish law.[20]

Religious politics notwithstanding, it is puzzling that what seems to have spurred God to take action was Abram's complaint. Complaints are not generally seen as meritorious—parents punish children for this behavior—whereas God rewarded Abram, bestowing His vision of Abram's place in the universe only after the patriarch had questioned God's pronouncements.

And yet, although God's timing may seem counterintuitive to the modern reader, by waiting until after Abram spoke directly to Him, God ensured that Abram had the courage required to bear the weight of the prophecy. When God told Abram that his descendants would be as infinite as the stars, He had to be sure that His prophet could truly comprehend infinitude without being paralyzed and that he could retain his sense of self without indulging in grandiosity.

This frank exchange between man and God was such a valuable exercise that it seems odd that God never enacted this ritual with either Adam or Noah. Some may argue that this was because Abram was the greatest of the three men and was, therefore, the only one capable of speaking directly to God. He was not silent like Noah. He was not dishonest like Adam.

But it also seems possible that God had learned something from His experience with these two earlier partners in creation. He had not allowed them to be invested enough in the future. He had not shown them enough of His plan for the world. Now He chose to give Abram an inkling of what He Himself saw. This does not necessarily mean that God Himself had changed. It could simply mean that human beings had evolved, and God, like any good teacher, needed to adapt His strategies to meet the needs of His students.

———◆———

CHAPTER ELEVEN

COVENANT OF
THE PARTS

Despite their newfound rapprochement, all was not settled between God and Abram: there was still the matter of the land. God brought up the subject in the formal manner of a king.

"I am the Lord who brought you out from Ur to assign this land to you as a possession," He said (15:7). Since He had already had a prolonged exchange with Abram, not to mention several previous encounters, it seems odd that God would choose to announce His identity here.

However, Abram would have recognized the language God used as the same language used in treaties between masters and their vassals. A legal announcement of identity was an essential part of any real estate transaction. Indeed, it is highly possible that Abram had already made such contracts in both Canaan and Egypt. Thus, he knew that God was not drawing back from him by using overly polite language; instead, He was declaring that He was now ready to enter into a covenant with His chosen one.[1]

Previously, God's promises about the land had been vague. He had used the future tense — "I will give" — in His first statement, indicating that the gift of land would happen at some unspecified time in the future. Although He did firm things up in His second promise by using the present tense, He still did not enter into a formal agreement with Abram. It was not until His third promise that He outlined the extent of Abram's ownership, declaring that Abram would possess the length and breadth of the land, "the north, south, east, and west."

Contrary to expectations, this time Abram did not act the part of the obedient vassal. Nor did he express gratitude for God's sudden willingness to forge a contract with him. Instead, he questioned God, again asking for evidence that the Lord would truly abide by His covenant. "O Lord God," Abram said, "how shall I know that I am to possess [the land]?" (Gen. 15:8).

The Bible had just declared that Abram had put his faith in God. So it seems unlikely that he was being rebellious. Instead, Abram's second question sounds like another admission that he could no longer abide by the vagueness of God's earlier pronouncements, not because of God's limitations, but because of his own. In other words, Abram was neither challenging nor testing God. He was uncovering his vulnerability.

Rashi, who was disturbed by the thought that Abram might be distrustful of God, suggested that what Abram meant to say was "Tell me by what merit they (my descendants) will remain in the land?" Abram felt so undeserving of God's gift, Rashi said, that he needed a sign to help him believe his own good fortune.[7]

Abram's self-revelation makes this dialogue revolutionary. As we have seen, the idea of an honest exchange with a Mesopotamian or Canaanite god was unthinkable. Marduk, El, and Anak did not want to hear skepticism or self-reflection from their worshippers. They wanted flattery and slavish devotion. And so, Abram's expectations of God were as unusual as God's requirements for Abram. Abram confided his personal doubts in the hope that God would provide him with answers, and God seemed to delight in this intimacy. Moreover, Abram's ability to engage God in this kind of question-and-answer session demonstrates how much he had grown since leaving Haran, when he had silently obeyed God's word in the manner of a Mesopotamian. In turn, God's expansiveness suggests how much He wanted His chosen man to become an assertive companion rather than an obsequious follower. Now Abram had a voice, a respectful voice, but a voice all the same. Perhaps it was not even important what Abram asked God. What was important was that he asked at all.

Evidence of God's approval came immediately. Just as his previous question had ushered in the vision of the stars, Abram's new query prompted the next stage of the prophecy. God ordered Abram to bring Him a heifer, a goat, a ram, a young bird, and a turtledove in order to perform the ancient Covenant of the Parts (15:9). Abram, who a minute before had appeared to be alone in the wilderness, promptly found these animals, suggesting that God had already gathered them for the upcoming ceremony.

The modern reader can be excused for wondering why these were the creatures God wanted Abram to present to Him, but in Abram's world, each of them had a ritualistic meaning, and so God was communicating in a way that Abram, at least, would have understood. Although it is impossible to recover the precise symbolism of God's language, Rashi, who steeped himself in the interpretation of ancient sacrifices, suggested that the heifer was meant to beg God for guidance, and the goat was the correct sacrifice for an individual who had sinned, as was the ram. The turtledove was special, though, because in the Song of Solomon the dove is a symbol of Israel. In this way, the animals embodied a kind of code, so that if Abram had spoken, his words might have sounded something like this: "Dear Lord, please help me to understand your pronouncements [the heifer]. Please forgive my sins and accept my atonement [the goat and the ram]. Also, please give me hope that my children will inherit the land of Canaan [the birds]."[3]

As the sun sank lower in the sky, the ram brandished its horns, the heifer lowed in terror, the goat tried to flee over the sands, and the birds flapped and cawed, but Abram had no pity. He took out his sharpest knife and killed each creature before it could escape.

Then, his hands warm with blood, he hacked each of the animals in half, except for the birds, which he left limp on the ground. If they truly did stand for the nation his children would found, he did not want to split them in two.[4]

To carve the dead bodies of the ram, the heifer, and the goat was a difficult and sweaty chore, especially when it involved breaking their breastbones. But he did not give up, even as the afternoon darkened to twilight. He knew that if he wanted to discover exactly what God had in mind, he had to perform this laborious task. Perhaps he had seen someone else enact such a ceremony, as it was a Mesopotamian tradition to ratify a treaty in this way.[5] Certainly, he carried out the ritual without hesitation, as though he were following some kind of recipe.

Once he had finished splitting the animals, Abram pulled and pushed each half until they lay exactly across from each other. When he was done, he could stroll down a kind of corridor between the carcasses. The lungs arched like birdcages, the spill of intestines uncoiled outside the arc of bone. The slope and heft of the animals' anatomy was testimony to God's inventiveness. Even Abram, who was used to seeing the insides of dead creatures, as he regularly slaughtered them for food, must have found this array somewhat stupendous, like a tour through God's creation.

The strange, sweet smell of blood was thick in the air and, before long, kestrels and sparrow hawks began swooping down from the sky, eager to feed on the fruits of Abram's labor, but Abram "drove them away" (15:11) and stood guard until the sun set.[6] When it was dark, a "deep sleep fell upon [him]" (15:12), and a great "dread" filled his soul. As Abram lay in a stupor next to the dead animals, God spoke out of the darkness:

Know well that your offspring shall be strangers in a land not theirs, and they shall be enslaved and oppressed four hundred years; but I will execute judgment on the nation they shall serve, and in the end they shall go free with great wealth. As for you, you shall go to your fathers in peace; you shall be buried at a ripe old age (15:12–15).

To those who argue that the Bible is a compilation of different sources, this passage is an example of a later addition to the story. But this pragmatic interpretation, useful though it is, can undercut the awe the reader is supposed to feel about God's foreknowledge. By predicting the Israelites' slavery in Egypt, God reveals that He knows the future. And, of course, He does—He knows all the stories in His book.

This is also the first time God's predictions about Abram's descendants are not wholly optimistic. Although He promised Abram a gentle end to his own life, His prophecy about Abram's descendants is truly horrific. Trapped in sleep, Abram could not respond or protest against this vision. Perhaps this was why God had decided to relay this news to him in a dream. A sleeping Abram could not express his devastation or argue on behalf of his people.

Still, it is difficult to know what to make of God's pronouncement against Abram's offspring. Some suggest that it was divine punishment for Abram's betrayal of Sarai in Egypt.[7] This would explain why Abram cannot protest the fate of his descendants, since his own behavior had been so execrable. God's own explanation was that Canaan was not yet ready for occupation, because "the iniquity of the Amorites [Canaanites] is not yet complete" (15:16). In other words, the Canaanites had to reach the peak of their sinfulness before Abram's descendants could inherit the land. But this delay in their inheritance does not explain why Abram's children would have to be enslaved while they waited for the Canaanites to self-destruct. The prospect of slavery dangled in the air, an inexplicable prophecy of pain.

This connection between blessing and suffering is disturbing to consider from a theological standpoint. What kind of God requires His people to suffer? Many Christians answer this question with the principle of original sin: we are still paying for Adam and Eve's initial act of disobedience in the Garden of Eden. The Koran leaves Abram's nightmare vision out of its account of his life. But Jews are left with a conundrum and, true to form, have argued about the meaning of God's words for centuries without coming to any particular conclusion.

God's troubling pronouncement sheds new light on the idea that the Israelites are "God's chosen people," as this covenant was clearly not based on any "divine favoritism."[8] God promised the land to Abram's children not because He loved them better, but because the Canaanites were wicked.

This was a new idea: ownership of Canaan was not based on who was there first, military prowess, or wealth. Instead, inheritance was based on a people's moral standing as determined by God. In case any future Israelite became smug about his rights to the land, the Book of Deuteronomy warned, "Say not to yourselves, 'the Lord has enabled me to occupy the land because of my virtues . . .' It is not because of your virtues and your rectitude that you will be able to occupy their country, but because of the wickedness of those nations" (Deut. 9:4–6).[9] In other words, God did not want His people to think they were intrinsically superior to other nations. Instead, He reinforced the principle that immoral behavior would result in divine repossession of land. If the Israelites became as sinful as their neighbors, they too would forfeit their claims to Canaan.

God reinforced this point in later books of the Bible, declaring, "So let not the land spew you out for defiling it, as it spewed out the nation that came before it" (Lev. 18:28). Of course, as every reader of the Bible knows, the exile of Abram's descendants from the Promised Land was exactly what would happen: first, at the hands of the Babylonians, and then again in 70 C.E., when the Romans destroyed the Second Temple and drove the Israelites from the land.

For now, however, Abram still slept beside the carcasses he had prepared. The dark sky became ever darker and, before Abram could move, it grew entirely black and an unearthly fire suddenly appeared. It floated toward the animals like a torch held by an invisible hand. God had arrived. As the dreaming Abram watched, stunned, He "passed" between the carcasses, right near Abram's resting place, walking the corridor between the split animals. The supernatural quality of the vision is extraordinary to imagine: the bloody halves, the spiral of black intestines, and the clouds of smoke and flame rising up to the heavens.

Abram may have sensed that if he did not adhere to his part of the agreement, he would be torn apart, his body open to the sky. After all, the underlying meaning of this ancient Near Eastern ritual was that if the vassal disobeyed the overlord, he would meet the fate of the slaughtered animals. And yet, since this tableau also represented a mundane traditional practice—sealing a real estate contract between men—the other surprising aspect of the scene was its human quality. God had descended in order to demonstrate His reciprocal relationship with Abram. If Abram had reached up to heaven with his questions, God had in turn, come down to earth.

But the darker meaning of God's mystical appearance was still hard to avoid. The Bible uses the verb *avar* for God's walk between the carcasses. The same word appears later, in Exodus, when God passes through Egypt the night He kills all the firstborn sons of the Egyptians. The parallel may have been invisible to Abram, but it is apparent to any reader. God's benevolence was clearly dangerous. He was capable of performing miracles on behalf of those who served Him with love and obedience. Yet He was a deity who could divide a man against himself, split legacies in two, and slaughter the sons of those who did not heed His word.

Once He had passed between the animals, God paused to speak, again using the language of a formal legal contract and pronouncing the covenant's terms with the greatest clarity He had yet used: "To your offspring I assign this land, from the river of Egypt to the great river, the river Euphrates" (Gen. 15:18). Then He vanished, having made no promises about how long Abram's descendants would get to keep the land, nor about their ultimate well-being.

When at last he woke up, Abram remained mute. He did not express gratitude or joy. God may have quieted his anxieties about the land, but the servitude of his children in Egypt shadowed the future.

There was also another problem to consider, one of a more personal nature. If Abram was to fulfill God's mission that his children inherit the land, he would have to repair the breach with his wife. He would also have to believe that God could render the impossible possible, and that his infertile wife would give birth. Otherwise, his chance for immortality was gone, and he and Sarai would fall into extinction, swimming in wealth, but doomed like the Canaanites.

CHAPTER TWELVE

SARAI'S PROPOSITION

I t is always difficult to heal a wounded marriage, and Sarai and Abram's troubled relationship was no exception. But just how troubled it was is unclear. Up to this point, the only recorded exchange between the two was Abram's request that Sarai claim she was his sister in Egypt. There is no Abram monologue, no Sarai reverie, and no conversation between the two that tells us what they thought of each other, either before or after the incident with Pharaoh. Instead, the reader is forced to experience their relationship secondhand, never knowing whether Sarai raged, Abram apologized, or Sarai ever forgave him.

Once again, the Bible's reticence can have as much of an impact on the reader as what it does say. In this case, the lack of recorded dialogue between Abram and Sarai leaves the couple in a state of permanent suspension. If the Bible had documented an exchange between them after Egypt, this episode might have lessened in importance. If Abram had had the opportunity to explain his actions or if Sarai had expressed her resentment, the reader could feel some kind of resolution, even if Sarai and Abram could not entirely come to peace.

The optimistic reader might hope that some kind of behind-the-scenes rapprochement did occur, but this seems unlikely, as the

Bible tends to emphasize tales of forgiveness. For example, three generations later, the story of the couple's great-grandsons Joseph and his brothers underlines the principle that relationships can heal after terrible episodes of betrayal. Joseph's jealous older brothers had sold him into slavery in Egypt (just as Abram had sold Sarai), a seemingly unforgivable offense. But unlike Sarai, Joseph confronted his brothers with their deed, making it clear that he had suffered at their hands. When they (unlike Abram) begged for forgiveness, Joseph embraced them, and the brothers were reunited (Gen. 45:4–15). Here lay the foundation for the future of Israel, as these brothers would become the fathers of the twelve tribes that would constitute the Israelite people.

Joseph's willingness to expose his grievances opened the door to healing. This suggests that if the Bible had wanted the reader to see Sarai draw closer to Abram, it would have described some kind of exchange between them. Instead, the Biblical silence only serves to make Abram's action loom large, like the proverbial elephant in the room. He is eternally at fault and Sarai is eternally wounded. They remain in a limbo of complicated and unexpressed emotions, a miserable condition and a reflection of the withdrawal that happens in any strained relationship when silence replaces conversation.

Yet, to some extent, the Bible's refusal to tell the reader more about this marriage is because deeds, not feelings, are the building blocks of this story. What Abram and Sarai *did*, particularly to each other, is what matters. And what they did next was calamitous, or wondrous—depending, of course, on your point of view.

WHEN ABRAM RETURNED from his journeys, a war hero and a prophet, a tribal leader and a wealthy man, he found a woman who had become accustomed to running not only his household, but also the affairs of his entire people. Having had to make crucial decisions on behalf of the tribe, she was no longer the demure beauty Abram had married years ago.

The vision Abram had endured also set him apart. He did not radiate a strange unearthly light as Moses did after his encounter with God (Exod. 34:29), but he was like a person who had climbed a great mountain and then descended back to ordinary life. To someone who knew him well as Sarai did, it must have seemed that he had left her and all those he loved far behind.

Such a reunion could only be heartrending. The once devoted couple were now strangers. Until Egypt, Abram and Sarai had faced the unknown together. They had fled Mesopotamia, endured the pioneering life in Canaan, and had even persevered through the pain of childlessness side by side. But now a chasm separated them. Though Abram knew the challenges Sarai had had to meet while he was gone, he could not imagine what it was like to be a woman assuming responsibilities that were never meant to be hers. And Abram's experiences were incomprehensible to Sarai. She had never been to war. Prophetic visions from the divine were beyond anyone's wildest imaginings. She had been immersed in practical problems, while Abram had been lost in contemplation of the universe.

It is fitting, then, that Sarai initiated their first conversation. She was the one who had been living in the campsite, facing the reality of their childlessness. "Look, the Lord has kept me from bearing," Sarai said bluntly. "Consort with my maid; perhaps I shall have a son through her" (Gen. 16:2).

This was a strange way to welcome one's husband home from war. Where was the joyful greeting? Where was the relief at his safe return? Instead, Sarai announced her plan so imperiously that it sounded as though she were ordering Abram to obey her. She did not employ any "womanly" stratagems to cajole or convince him. She did not even bring him to her tent for another try at conception.[1]

According to one ancient tradition, Sarai was perfectly within her rights to act so boldly. If she could not have babies, she was legally entitled to bring in a "second wife" to have them on her behalf.[2] The children would be considered Sarai's, with the "second wife" continuing to serve as a handmaiden, or nanny. The urgency behind Sarai's demand stemmed from a disturbing law that if a woman did not bear children, her husband could cast her aside and take another wife. Thus, as the scholar Nahum Sarna writes, Sarai may have been acting to protect her rights as Abram's first wife, forestalling any efforts on Abram's part to displace her.[3]

The first wife's status would be enhanced according to how many children the second wife bore, or that was supposed to be the case. Sometimes the second wives, or concubines—it is unclear what their actual title was—sought to better their social position after they bore a child. However, the documents are stern about the punishments that should befall a second wife who forgot her place. Children and the transfer of property from generation to generation were the most important elements of marriage in the ancient world, not romance or fidelity. Although Scripture does include a few stories where a husband's love for his wife is seen as a virtue, the fact that these examples are set apart indicates that romantic love between spouses was not a given.[4]

The Bible underscores the seriousness of Sarai's proposal, as the first word Sarai uses, "look," or *hanneheh*, is actually the same word the prophets would use centuries later when they were trying to get the people to heed their warnings. *Hanneheh* told listeners to pay close attention.[5] Perhaps Sarai was inspired by God or at least *seemed* inspired by God. Indeed, Jewish commentators would later refer to Sarai as *Iscah*, or Seer, as she was supposed to have been an even greater prophet than her husband. Accordingly, it is possible that Sarai was following God's instructions when she offered Hagar to Abram, but the Bible remains stubbornly reticent about the origins of her idea, introducing an ambiguity to everything that would occur as a result of her proposal.

Those who would like to view Sarai and Abram in the best possible light argue that Sarai's actions were generous. Even if the appropriation of another woman's child might be regarded as selfish, she knew her husband required an heir in order to carry on his line. To the ancient and medieval readers of this story, Sarai's role as Abram's wife permitted her to take these actions. She had accepted that she could not bear a child herself and wanted Abram to have the opportunity to be a father. If Abram had told her about God's promises of children, perhaps she also felt that she was fulfilling God's prophecy for her husband. This is what Josephus, a Jewish historian of the first century, believed. He wrote that Sarai "brought" Hagar to Abram's bed in accordance with "God's bidding." To Josephus, Sarai's actions were intrinsically selfless.[6] Similarly, many Islamic stories praised Sarai for her noble self-sacrifice.[7]

It is significant that this is the first time in the Bible that Sarai's words are recorded. Up to now Sarai's silence had suggested that she was a conventionally submissive wife, although in the case of Egypt, we have seen that her silence might have been more complicated. Still, at least on the surface, she had mutely followed Abram and had not initiated any plans of her own. Now, Sarai had clearly decided that it was time to take charge. And although she did not mention Egypt directly, the subject was implicit in every word she spoke.

First, there was the matter of Hagar's identity. Before Sarai makes her proposal, the Bible sets the stage by declaring, "[Sarai] had an Egyptian maidservant whose name was Hagar" (16:1). The naming of Hagar's origins is not an accident. No one else in the story merits such a reference (except once, when Abram is referred to as "the Hebrew" [14:13]). Whether Hagar was a princess or not, the maid's native land linked this new episode directly to Abram and Sarai's troubled past.

How conscious Sarai was of this connection to her own experience is unclear. It is possible that Sarai was testing her husband to see if Abram had enough faith in their marriage and, therefore, in God's ability to work miracles, to veto her idea. But if this was her intention, it was doomed to failure. Sarai's invitation, following on the heels of Abram's last encounter with the Lord, seemed in perfect accordance with God's plan to make His chosen one's children as plentiful as the stars. Even if Abram did not think that her words sprang directly from God's covenant, her proposal dovetailed so perfectly with his own desires that it would have been almost impossible for him to say no.

There are also other possible explanations for Sarai's suggestion. Perhaps after her sojourn in the Pharaoh's harem and her time alone as the tribe's leader, she no longer wanted to be intimate with Abram, and this was her way of escaping that responsibility. Or maybe the memory of her own slavery in Egypt was so disturbing that she asserted her power by abusing another. She certainly seemed determined to place Hagar in exactly the same position she had endured in Egypt. As the Bible scholar Tikva Frymer-Kensky writes, "Sarai's own experience as a slave does not make her more empathetic to the slave in her own home. On the contrary it makes her want to assert her dominance and authority so she won't lose it again."[8]

Regardless of her deeper motivations, on a pragmatic level, Sarai's presentation of Hagar to Abram must have seemed the best way to preserve her status as Abram's wife. Her infertility was a crisis that needed to be solved. But unlike the other barren women in the Bible, Sarai never discussed her desperation for a child or her shame at being unable to produce one. Not once did she display her misery for her husband to witness.

Her granddaughter-in-law Rachel, on the other hand, raged at her husband, Jacob, "Give me children or I shall die." And Jacob showed his desperation when he shouted, "Can I take the place of God?" (30:1–2). Still, he continued to love Rachel best, and her children were his favorites. When Hannah, the mother of the prophet Samuel, wept over not being able to conceive, her husband begged to know what her sorrow was about so that he could comfort her (Sam. 1:8). But the stalemate between Abram and Sarai remained intact. No rage. No sorrow. No tears. Sarai issued her orders and subsided. If he said yes, he would at last have a child—this much was certain. Hagar was young and fertile. If he said no, he would be expressing a loyalty to Sarai that she did not seem to require from him anymore. And he would have no heir.

However, Abram did not say anything. He let silence drift between them while he "listened to Sarai's voice" (Gen. 16:2), tacitly acquiescing but allowing her to take responsibility for what would come next.

CHAPTER THIRTEEN

DO WITH HER
AS YOU WILL

No one knows what Sarai was thinking when she brought the young Egyptian woman to Abram's tent. The Bible reverts to its customary reticence about the details of women's lives, so there is no scene that describes Sarai bidding farewell to the couple and walking back to her quarters alone. As for Abram, at no point did he express any opinion about Sarai's plan, although he did not hesitate when Hagar tiptoed into his chambers. Instead, he took her straight into his bed.

Abram would have had difficulty turning his back on Hagar, not because of the Egyptian maid's beauty—Hagar was never famous for her looks—but because of her youth and evident fertility. Perhaps he believed he was doing nothing wrong and that conceiving a child with Sarai's maid was part of God's plan for giving him an heir. Still, some argue that, by taking this next step, Abram was displaying a dangerous impatience. Rather than waiting for God to heal Sarai's infertility, he decided to father a child through his own initiative.[1]

Of course God had yet to mention who the mother of Abram's children would be. Also, at no point does God say that He will view Abram's independent actions to fulfill the promise as an act of faithlessness. Instead, in other Biblical passages, God makes it clear that He prizes action, not passivity. Thus, there could be no way that Abram would know that he was departing from God's plan. And perhaps he was not. Perhaps his union with Hagar was part of God's scheme right from the beginning.[2]

Islamic thinkers have tended to skirt this issue since, according to Islamic law, Abram was perfectly within his rights to have marital relations with Hagar. It was his duty to father children. If his first wife was barren, then he had to move on to another woman, whether he wanted to or not.

Furthermore, while in the West, a culture that disavows polygamy, the story of Abram and Hagar is viewed as essentially problematic, in Islamic countries, where the practice of polygamy is often embraced, the story of Abram's marriage to Sarai is frequently one of harmony and peace, even when Hagar is introduced. This reveals how closely linked our interpretation of the original stories is to our modern cultural practices and values.

There are some exceptions to the West's skepticism about Abram's new familial arrangement. For instance, Joseph Smith, the founder of the Mormon Church, believed that polygamy played a crucial role in a righteous life. While in the midst of prophetic ecstasy, Smith glorified Abraham's "marriage" to Hagar:

> God commanded Abraham, and Sarah gave Hagar to Abraham to wife. And why did she do it? Because this was the law; and from Hagar sprang many people.... Was Abraham, therefore, under condemnation? Verily I say unto you, Nay; for I, the Lord, commanded it.[3]

According to Smith's logic, if an individual resisted plural marriage, he would lose his chance at salvation. He glossed over the tragedies that would erupt in the lives of the three Biblical figures as a result of Abram's union with Hagar, proclaiming the right of every man to marry as many women as he desired. Despite the outrage of some of his closest friends and his wife Emma's efforts to dissuade him, Smith persisted in his beliefs. The issue would divide the fledgling Mormon Church and destroy Smith's marriage. According to his biographers, Smith "married" at least thirty women, many of them under the age of eighteen. Eventually, Smith would be shot to death for promoting plural marriage.[4]

Although the contemporary Mormon Church has outlawed the practice, splinter groups like the Fundamentalist Church of Jesus Christ of Latter-Day Saints (FLDS) still base their support of plural marriages on the words of Smith, decreeing that a man must have at least three wives in order to get to heaven.[5] To these ten thousand or so believers, Sarai's offer of Hagar to her husband is evidence of her heroic devotion to God. Every first wife should be a Sarah, willing to share her husband with many partners. Every man should be an Abraham, willing to shoulder the responsibility of many wives.

LIKE ABRAM, Hagar had maintained a firm silence when Sarai made her proposal. She had not even spoken when Sarai brought her to Abram's tent. Her wordlessness could simply reflect the Biblical silence that surrounds the lives of women. Or it could suggest she had accepted her lot as Abram's new bedmate with equanimity. Certainly, up to this point, Hagar seems to have been a compliant servant.

Traditionally, Islamic and Jewish commentators say that Hagar greeted this opportunity with gladness, because she knew that she was lucky to have such a holy one as her husband. Of course, these commentators were men who lived during eras when the course of a woman's life was determined by her father, husband, or brother. To them, Hagar's fate could only improve if she was intimately linked to a wealthy and powerful man. Indeed, it is possible that Sarai believed she was honoring Hagar and rewarding her for her loyalty when she selected her as her husband's second wife. Thus, the early rabbis record Sarai as saying to Hagar, "How fortunate you will be to cleave to this holy body [of Abram]."[6]

And yet, if Sarai's silence back in Egypt may have indicated protest, then Hagar's mute acquiescence must also be viewed somewhat
suspiciously. As a slave, what other choice did she have? Her wordlessness was potentially smoldering, particularly since she would
have plenty to say later on in the story once she was convinced of
her freedom.

Nevertheless, the ancient Jewish and Muslim writers tend to
depict Hagar as grateful and obedient. They all say she was a pious
woman who had converted to the worship of God. As one writer
put it, "Hagar walked in the same path of righteousness as her mistress, and thus was a suitable companion for Abraham."[7] Linked by
their patriarchal ideals, if not their theology, these commentators
did not spend much time thinking about Hagar, but when they did
they agreed on yet another point: Hagar was a virgin. It was vital to
these thinkers that Abram's second wife be worthy of his love, and
thus it was crucial that Hagar had not had intercourse. Since the
Egyptians were notorious for their creative sexual practices, even if
Hagar had indulged in such activities at Pharaoh's palace, it seems
possible that she was still technically a virgin.[8]

And so, at first, Sarai could believe that she had chosen an
exemplary mother for Abram's child and that she could be proud
of helping to fulfill God's prophecy by devising this plan. However,
the situation soon soured.

Before long, Hagar discovered that she was pregnant. The
Bible does not tell us whether it was a month after her first night
with Abram or a year. In fact, how long their relationship lasted
and how often they made love has been the subject of intensive
debate among Jewish scholars. Rashi wanted to downplay the idea
of the great patriarch's sexual appetite and argued that the couple
only had sex twice. His logic was that Hagar got pregnant the first
time she slept with Abram but then miscarried. Thus, they had to
make love one more time. Afterward, there was no need for further
intimacy.[9]

But this argument has more to do with what Rashi wanted to see in the text than with what is there, as there is no evidence to suggest that Hagar got pregnant immediately. Instead, it is just as likely that it took her months to conceive, forcing the couple to sleep together on a regular basis. It is even possible that they continued to make love after she got pregnant and after she bore a child—a truly troubling idea to those who want to believe that Abram only slept with Hagar out of necessity.

To the secular reader, this might seem like a bewildering problem: Why does it matter if the great patriarch had a long-lasting sexual relationship with Hagar? But to many, the idea that Abram conducted an affair with Hagar for any reason besides having a child implies that he was weak or lascivious. In addition, to those Jews and Christians who seek to elevate Sarai over Hagar, it is disturbing to consider Abram forging a bond with his second wife. According to this way of thinking, Biblical polygamy was acceptable as long as the husband stayed emotionally faithful to his first wife. For instance, Abram's grandson Jacob was married to the sisters Rachel and Leah and slept with their serving maids to increase the number of his offspring, but his loyalty and love for his favorite wife, Rachel, remained unshakable.

Regardless of how long it took Hagar to conceive, the Bible is clear that once she realized she was going to have a baby, she felt contempt for Sarai. As the Bible puts it, "Her mistress was lowered in her esteem" (Gen. 16:4). These words are the first Biblical indication of Hagar's feelings. She had done what her mistress had not been able to do. She was fertile; Sarai was barren. Soon, she would have Abram's child, while Sarai remained childless.

The commentators differ on what happened next. As we have seen, the Islamic tradition is often silent about this sequence of events, but according to Jewish and Christian accounts, Hagar began to be cruel to Sarai. Rashi was specific about this cruelty, writing that when neighbors came to visit, Hagar would pull them aside and whisper that Sarai was not really as virtuous as she appeared. She would say things such as "My lady Sarah . . . is not inwardly what she appears to be outwardly. She makes the impression of a righteous, pious woman, but she is not, for if she were, how could her childlessness be explained after so many years of marriage, while I became pregnant at once."[10]

Sarai, who had not been jealous before, was now enraged. Instead of relishing the promise of a new baby, Sarai shouted at Abram, "The wrong done me is your fault! I myself put my maid in your bosom; now that she sees that she is pregnant, I am lowered in her esteem" (16:5).[11]

Surprisingly, Sarai did not blame Hagar or herself. She was not angry that Abram had slept with Hagar or that Hagar was pregnant. Rather, she was angry at the blow to her dignity. The union between her maid and her husband had been her idea, but now that Hagar wanted to undermine Sarai's status in the household, Sarai placed the responsibility for this outrage on her husband's shoulders. Her words can be seen as an attempt to shift culpability, but they also point to an important aspect of Near Eastern law.

To elevate a concubine or second wife over one's first wife was taboo; the first wife was supposed to reign supreme in the household. Accordingly, the master of a home was not supposed to tolerate arrogant behavior in a second wife, unless he felt his first wife was truly unworthy. Seen in this light, Abram's tacit support of Hagar suggested that either he was so smitten with his young lover that he was unable to set any limits with her or that he had drifted so far from Sarai that he no longer cared. In either case, he was not behaving with the husbandly fidelity that was highly prized in the Bible. Angry at what must have seemed a second betrayal by her husband, Sarai invoked God, declaring, "The Lord decide between you and me" (16:5).

There have been centuries of shock waves over Sarai's speech. With few exceptions, the early and medieval Jewish commentators condemn Sarai's words, arguing that she is suggesting that God might support her over her husband. To these thinkers, it was as though she had tattled on Abram to their heavenly Father. The writers of the Midrash agreed. For this arrogance, they argued, Sarai's life was later cut short. Ultimately, she would die forty-eight years before her appointed time.[12]

Instead of condemning Abram for his insensitivity to his wife, these foundational texts use Sarai's story as an example of how one should not focus on judging others but should instead concentrate on one's own flaws. The idea that Abram was weak and had failed his wife, just as he had in Egypt, did not seem to trouble the writers of either the Talmud or the Midrash, and their interpretation has persisted for almost two thousand years.[13] Sarai should have focused on herself, not her husband. And she certainly should not have summoned God as a judge. To these rabbis, Abram is the victim of Sarai's plot rather than an accomplice in an impatient scheme to beget children.

In Islamic legends, since this entire section of the story is often omitted, there are few records of any quarrels between the two women or between Sarai and Abram. Even the climactic argument that will occur seventeen or so years later is frequently not mentioned. Instead, Sarai is usually the unwaveringly gracious first wife of Abram, and Hagar the beloved and fertile second wife. What matters is the conception of Hagar's baby, not the power struggle behind his birth. Similarly, Islamic thinkers were less concerned with explaining the age-old strife between the descendants of Ishmael and Isaac. They focused instead on telling the story of Mohammed's forebears Hagar and Ishmael, as this mother and son would become famous as the discoverers of Mecca and the founders of the Muslim legacy.

However in the Bible's version of the story, it seems both of the marriage partners were at fault: Sarai for complaining to God about Abram, and Abram for his lack of faith and his weakness in the face of temptation. Together, they formed the perfectly unhappy, aggrieved couple.

Hagar, too, seems wrong for treating her mistress with disdain. Although the modern reader might be troubled by Abram and

Sarai's assumption that Hagar's womb was essentially their property, it was considered a great honor to be chosen as the tribal leader's second wife. According to the mores of the era, Hagar should
have been grateful, not dismissive of her mistress. Abram and
Sarai's behavior was the standard fare of the time. The legal code
gave masters the right to control the fertility of those they "owned,"
and Hagar's new role as second wife was seen as an elevation in her
social status. If a slave wife attempted to step out of her servitude,
she could be sold or "demoted" back to her status as a simple slave.[14]
Accordingly, Sarai and Abram never refer to Hagar by name. They
did not think of her as a person, at least not yet. At this point in the
story, she is simply their possession.

Even if up until now Hagar had been silently rebelling against
her situation, her pregnancy may have been the first time since her
servitude began that she had something of her own to be proud of.
Although at first glance her jeers seem the pent-up expressions of
her rage at being a slave, perhaps her attitude can also be seen as
the typical reaction of a young woman for the first time feeling her
power and value in the world.

If Hagar's behavior seems justifiable, the manner in which Abram
and Sarai proceeded to discuss her fate casts them further in the
wrong. In answer to Sarai's accusations, Abram retreated, declaring, "Your maid is in your hands. Deal with her as you think right"
(16:6). Abram uses the same troubling language as other Biblical
characters who have wanted to distance themselves from a difficult
situation. As Tikva Frymer-Kensky writes, "The phrase sounds
evil and immoral" when the speaker knows that harm will probably
come to the individual he is throwing into enemy hands.[15]

This sort of callousness makes it easy to view Abram as heartless. How could he leave the woman he had slept with in the hands
of his irate wife? Surely he knew what would happen. Was he being
spineless in the face of his wife's attack? Or was he at last showing
his loyalty to Sarai?

One can argue this was the only action Abram could take. Hagar was a servant and Sarai was his wife. Since Hagar had been her handmaid, it was Sarai who had authority over Hagar. To disrupt this system was potentially dangerous. Chaos would result if men intruded in the areas of domestic life traditionally assigned to women or if masters and mistresses permitted slaves to reach beyond their proper place.

It is also possible to see Abram's surrender to Sarai as evidence of his own lingering love for her. If Abram no longer cared about his first wife, he could have ignored her words and replaced her with Hagar. But clearly Sarai still mattered enough for him to listen to what she said. Torn between the two women, Abram had to choose which one to disappoint. He and Sarai had a history together. They were family. They had spent most of their lives in each other's company. She was a woman of stature, a leader; her name even meant "princess." Hagar was a slave. His relationship with her had just begun. The choice was clear. He aligned himself with Sarai.

As a result, "Sarai treated [Hagar] harshly," and Abram did not stop her (16:6). Rashi fills in the blanks of this story, suggesting that Sarai humiliated Hagar by making her walk behind her mistress on the way to "the bathhouse" to make it clear that Hagar was a slave. He also says that Sarai gave Hagar "the evil eye ... so that she miscarried."[16] The Midrash declares that Sarai kicked Hagar out of Abram's bed and slapped her with a slipper.[17] Writer David Klingoffer suggests that Sarai's "afflictions" of Hagar have the same tenor as the "afflictions" Jews are supposed to impose on themselves during Yom Kippur, the Day of Atonement. But according to Jewish law, no one should impose these on another person. The individual must repent on his or her own. According to this way of thinking, Sarai was again demonstrating her tendency to judge others rather than leaving this responsibility to God.[18]

The Bible does seem to indicate that Sarai is in the wrong here as the Hebrew phrase for Sarai's abuse of Hagar, *watte anneha*, is the same phrase the Bible will use to describe the Egyptian oppression of Israel many centuries later.[19]

But it also makes it clear that there did not have to be these tensions. In the other famous case of surrogate motherhood in Genesis, Jacob's wife Rachel named the children of her maids and raised them as her own. At no time did she mistreat the women who bore "her" children, nor was she jealous of their fertility. Instead, she celebrated each birth, declaring, after her first adopted son was born: "God has vindicated me, indeed, He has heeded my plea and given me a son" (30:6). Rachel's sister Leah followed suit and also rejoiced in her maid's children. It is clear that the behavior of these women was the norm, while Sarai was breaking the rules, just as Hagar had when she had attempted to assert her priority.

There is an important implication here: By mistreating Hagar, Sarai gave up her rights to the maid's unborn baby. And so, before Hagar even bore her child, the ideal of polygamy had broken down. How odd, then, that it is this story, not the later one of Leah, Rachel, and Jacob, that became the model for men like Joseph Smith. Sarai was far from an ideal first wife, and Abram was a flawed husband. Even Maimonides, who revered Abram, felt that the patriarch had behaved just as badly as Sarai. He wrote, "The matriarch sinned by such maltreatment, and Abraham too by permitting it."[20]

Even though Abram didn't stand up for her, Hagar had too much self-respect to allow herself to be mistreated for long. When Sarai's cruelty became too much to endure, she would take fate into her own firm hands.

CHAPTER FOURTEEN

HAGAR AND THE WILDERNESS

One night, while everyone else slept, Hagar tiptoed out of her tent, past the terebinth trees that marked their campsite, and into the open land. She would not have to go far to disappear from sight. The night would soon fold her into its darkness.[1] Still, those first few steps were difficult, as they were steps toward an almost certain death. No one could survive alone in the wilderness.

Yet she did not hesitate. Dignity mattered more than life. She was breaking every law, departing from all conventions, yet no one stopped her, no one heard her, no one followed her, and after a few minutes of determined walking, she had left them all behind. She was alone now. But where was she? And where was she heading?

Prophets are hard to recognize. The rantings of a strange man might be inspired by God, or his odd words might simply mean he is crazy. Not that most people worry about this problem anymore. For most modern readers, the necessity of recognizing prophets has largely evaporated, since with the exception of the Mormons and certain other Protestant groups, the prophet is generally considered extinct. Although all three of the great monotheistic religions hold that there can still be revelatory experiences between God and the individual, according to Christians true prophecy ended with Jesus and according to Muslims with Mohammed.[2] Jews are a little more vague, but most scholars write that the prophetic era ended some time after the destruction of the First Temple, in 586 B.C.E., and before the Great Assembly to canonize the books of the Jewish Bible, around 410 B.C.E. Thus, the modern dilemma tends to be distinguishing between mental illness and eccentricity, or hallucination and inspiration.

In the time of the Bible, however, everyone knew there were moments when God spoke to people. The problem was not *whether* He spoke, but when and to whom. Had these people really heard God's voice, or were they deluded? Were they the victims of a demon, or had they truly experienced divine prophecy? A bizarre act—for example, cutting one's hair off with a sword, as God asked Ezekiel to do—could be evidence of profound prophetic gifts, since God seemed to delight in asking His chosen ones to provoke their onlookers with shocking antics.

A person who fled into the desert by herself would have been particularly difficult to regard as inspired by God. If wild animals did not kill the lone wanderer, then thirst or bandits would. Safety lay in numbers, and only one bent on suicide would willingly abandon the tents of her people. Of course, if someone had been touched by God and led by Him into the wilderness so that He could commune with her in privacy, this person was not crazy. Instead, she was simply obeying the will of the Lord.

But it crossed no one's mind that Hagar might be following a divine command, as she seemed an unlikely candidate for the Lord to choose: Why would God take note of a woman, let alone a servant? Once they discovered she was gone, most people, including Abram and Sarai, assumed they would never see her again. Indeed, if God had not intervened, Hagar's story could easily have ended here as a footnote: the crazy woman who fled her mistress and died alone in the wasteland between Canaan and Egypt.

But Hagar had been marked by God for an extraordinary mission, although she had no idea that God had any particular interest in her. She had not heard a voice instructing her to leave. She had received no indications about what she should do or which trail she should follow. In hindsight, it is clear that her flight was divinely inspired, but when Hagar left, she could only believe that she was following her own instincts by taking the path back toward Egypt. Her plan was to go southward into the wilderness, toward the dreaded Negev desert, with few supplies and no companions — an indication of how desperate she was to escape Sarai's abuse.

Once she was in the desert, however, any sense of purpose she might have had soon vanished. Rust-colored rocks jutted upward; the sky was scorching and unending; the main road forked around the mountains, snaking up and down until it was unclear where she was and where she was heading. It was impossible to retrace her steps, just as it was impossible to discover which trail Abram had followed when he had led their band through this wilderness. There were endless yellow and pink ridges lined with black and green mineral deposits of magnesium and copper; here and there, ravines opened up underfoot. Occasionally, herds of wild asses cantered by, their sharp hooves clicking against the hard rock; lizards scuttled under boulders; fan-tailed ravens swept overhead, waiting for any sign that Hagar was weakening. And she was, both mentally and physically. One needed a strong body to survive the arid conditions, but one also needed an alert mind to cope with the unavoidable dehydration, confusion, and despair of wandering alone in a vast desert.

It was easy to doubt oneself in the Negev. And it was even worse to endure the heat, silence, and loneliness while pregnant. For Hagar, however, the situation was not entirely bleak. The moment she walked into the unknown was also the moment her real story began. Like her master and mistress, she had to cast off her bonds to the old world in order to set the course for her own life.

But at what a cost. Unlike Abram and Sarai, who had set off on their journey together and with their tribe of followers, Hagar had no comrades to protect her and no one to rally her spirits when her energy flagged. Instead, she was by herself for the first time in her life. In both Pharaoh's palace and Abram's campsite, there had been no such thing as privacy. The women of the harem slept and ate and played in the same quarters. In Canaan the tents were bunched so closely together that everyone knew what everyone else was doing. If a couple quarreled or a child coughed, everyone heard.

Despite the many annoyances of this kind of communal living, for a vulnerable young woman such as Hagar, there was also comfort in tight quarters. The group provided protection against invaders and allowed its members to share tasks and resources. There was also an overriding sense of certainty in the campsite. One rarely had to face the existential questions that trouble the modern individual: What am I going to do with my life? What should I do today? Who am I? Where am I heading? Not that life in the ancient world should be romanticized. People lived in tightly knit groups because they had to; there was no other way to survive. Although this kind of cheek-by-jowl lifestyle could be smothering at times, privacy came at too steep a price for anyone to seek it out. Independence was not worth losing one's life.

And yet, Abram's experience had proven that isolation was one of the key elements to a divine visitation. Perhaps this is because of the pointed contrast to ordinary life that such times offered. It would have been difficult to hear a divine summons over the din of the campsite. In addition, being lost was often a natural prelude to mystical experiences, perhaps because it produced a sensation of such disturbing uncertainty that it was almost impossible not to confront one's limitations. Therefore, when Hagar trekked through the Negev, she joined the long line of God's elite who lost themselves in the desert—in this desert, in fact—in order to receive the Lord's word.[3]

Although we do not know how many days Hagar wandered, we do know that she walked far enough to approach the desert of Shur, a continuation of the Negev that lay along the northern Sinai Peninsula, on the northeastern border of Egypt. This region of the

Negev was an in-between place, since it was the land that had to be traversed if one was moving from Africa to Asia or simply making one's way between the Promised Land and the land of the Pharaohs. In this border country there were no fabulously ringed mountains, no green copper on the jagged rocks, and no herds of wild asses. Instead, it was monotonous, an unending roll of yellow sand, gravel, and rock so terrible that one can understand why a person would cry out to God.

Few places on this planet are as forbidding, at least to human beings. God, on the other hand, seemed to feel perfectly at home here. Somewhere in this wilderness was Mount Sinai, the famous mountain where God would have His most intimate encounter with mankind, showing Himself to Moses. Also nearby was the cave where generations later the prophet Elijah would have his important encounter with God:

> And lo, the Lord passed by. There was a great and mighty wind . . . but the Lord was not in the wind. After the wind — an earthquake; but the Lord was not in the earthquake. After the earthquake — fire; but the Lord was not in the fire. And after the fire — a soft murmuring sound. When Elijah heard it, he wrapped his mantle about his face and went out and stood at the entrance of the cave. Then a voice addressed him: "Why are you here, Elijah?" (1 Kings 19:11–12).

Clearly, there was a powerful link to God in this desert. It was a place where anything could happen. What was hidden would become clear. What was impossible could become possible. But Hagar had no expectation of revelation. She was a fugitive. Tradition says her name was linked to the Arabic word *hajara*, which means "to flee."[4] She had wanted to escape, not to experience a vision. And if she was looking for anything, it was water.

However, since it was almost impossible to find a well in this part of the Negev, Hagar's chances for survival were slim. She was only a woman, albeit an unusual one, as she embodied a long list of contradictions. She was a slave who had freed herself. She traveled alone — something no one ever did, let alone a female. She was a wife without a husband; she was a pregnant woman without a father for her baby (or, if she was no longer pregnant, she was a woman who had miscarried with no man to protect her). Any one of these paradoxes would have distinguished Hagar from other women in the Bible, but it was when something extraordinary happened that Hagar's true nature became clear.

No one knows what first caught her eye. Perhaps little patches of green abruptly appeared, disrupting the monotony of the desert, or maybe there was suddenly a pile of stones where there had been nothing a minute before. Or maybe telltale reeds nodded in the distance, beckoning her toward hope. All we know is that Hagar was astonished to find a steady trickle of water flowing out of the earth. Although the Bible uses the words for "spring" and "well" interchangeably, later events make it clear that this water source was probably a well, which means that someone had surrounded the spring with rocks to protect and mark the opening.

At this point Hagar should have suspected something unusual had occurred. No one had ever found water so easily in this wilderness. Elijah discovered neither a well nor a spring when, battered by sandstorms, he stumbled through this desert. And the Israelites who would trek into the waste of Shur only three days after the shock of the Red Sea crossing would almost die of thirst before God intervened (Exod. 15:22–25).[5] Even today, it is unclear exactly where Hagar's well was located. Some scholars have pointed to a spring called Camel's Jawbone near Kadesh. But this spring no longer exists. Modern Bedouins make pilgrimages to a spring in Muweilih, twelve miles to the northwest of Kadesh, believing this is actually the well of Hagar.[6]

Although no one knows for certain where the well was, the fact that Hagar found it marked her as truly exceptional. In fact, the root of the Hebrew word for prophet, *navi* (*nun-bet-alef*), is related to another root (*nun-bet*), which means "emptiness" or "receptiveness," suggesting, as Rashi writes, that to receive a divine revelation, you had to be like a well and make yourself hollow or "open" in order to hear the word of God. In the Bible, water was often linked to the divine and, therefore, to prophecy. Thus, Moses made the bitter waters at Marah drinkable for the Israelites, and many of the later prophets found water for themselves or for their people to drink.[7]

For women in the Bible, springs and wells were also symbolic sites. Abraham's daughter-in-law Rebecca would be discovered at a well. Moses met his bride, Zipporah, at a well. Thus, water and the promises it offered desert dwellers was an especially apt metaphor for human fertility and for femaleness itself.

But ultimately water was water. For Hagar, the miracle of discovery was enough. She knew this well would save her life, and she drank her fill. Only when she was done did something even more extraordinary happen. Suddenly a voice spoke, a voice she had never heard before. An angel of the Lord called her by name.

CHAPTER FIFTEEN

THE WELL

Given the misery of her initial circumstances and her ultimate triumphs, it is no wonder that Hagar has come to be seen as a sort of guardian angel of African American women. She is the quintessential escaped slave striking out on her own. Understandably, modern interpreters, who associate slavery with race, often depict her as a black woman who is oppressed by her white mistress.[1] But even if Hagar had been a black woman, race relations as we know them did not exist in the ancient world. Sarai herself was not European, or "white," and which woman had darker skin is unclear and has no bearing on the story. Still, this tradition of interpretation does demonstrate that Hagar's saga is largely about power and freedom. As the feminist scholar Phyllis Trible argues, Hagar is "a symbol of the oppressed. . . . She is the faithful maid exploited, the black woman used by the male and abused by the female of the ruling class, the surrogate mother, the resident alien without legal recourse . . . the homeless woman, the indigent relying upon handouts from the power structures, the welfare mother . . ."[2]

But Hagar was not simply a victim. She had gotten into her predicament by leaving behind the group and in doing so had begun to forge her own life. Thus, it should come as no surprise that when she drank from the miraculous well, her desolation was suddenly broken. The angel, the very first one to appear in the Bible, asked two probing questions: "Hagar, slave of Sarai, where have you come from, and where are you going?" (Gen. 16:8).

Angels in the Hebrew Bible are understood to be extensions of God rather than independent entities, and so the point of this story is that God had interrupted His customary silence to speak to this Egyptian servant. Although Hagar did not feel dread, as Abram had in his last trancelike encounter with the divine, she could only answer the first of God's two queries, saying, "I am running away from my mistress, Sarai" (16:8). The second question she ignored because how could she know where she was going? She had escaped from an unbearable situation and had not planned what might come next. She was not even sure that she would get to Egypt. For all she knew, she would die in the desert.

Although Hagar may have appeared arrogant to Sarai, her silence about the future revealed her humility. As King Solomon, the traditional author of the Book of Proverbs, would write many centuries later, "Do not boast of tomorrow, / For you do not know what the day will bring" (Prov. 27:1–2). And as the preacher declared in Ecclesiastes, "Indeed, man cannot guess the events that occur under the sun. For man tries strenuously, but fails to guess them" (Eccles. 8:17; 9:1). In other words, the future is God's territory. Only a prophet can have a glimpse of what will come, and Hagar did not think of herself in such exalted terms. Admittedly, she had attempted to climb the tribe's social ladder when she became Abram's second wife, but social aspirations were an entirely different matter from claiming to have a special relationship with God.

Although the angel's queries seemed practical, their implications were immense. To begin with, Hagar had never been asked to consider such questions before. A serving maid was even less in control of her destiny than an ordinary member of the tribe. If regular people were not used to self-reflection of this kind, imagine Hagar's shock at being asked to examine her intentions.

But God wanted Hagar to consider her life in larger terms and His words were meant to raise the questions that have haunted the faithful ever since: What are your origins, and what is your destiny? The sixteenth-century Catholic St. Ignatius recorded these conundrums as the centerpiece of his devotions: "Where did you come from? . . . Or whence did this come to pass?"[3] It was time for Hagar to see herself as an individual with an important destiny. She was no longer one of the lowliest members of the tribe, entirely at the mercy of others' orders. Her choices and actions were her own, as she, like Abram and Sarai, was one of God's chosen.

Perhaps it is their confrontation with mortality that has led these questions to resonate over the centuries. These are the words that Paul Gauguin scrawled across one of his most famous paintings, which is still known as *Where Do We Come From? . . . Where Are We Going?* The title of one of Joyce Carol Oates's most famous stories is "Where Are You Going, Where Have You Been?" A famous Zen koan is based on these questions.[4] But for Hagar, and indeed for most people of faith, these queries function as a kind of test where one is asked to consider one's divinely appointed responsibilities and assess how well one has fulfilled them. In addition, these questions direct the devout to contemplate the role God plays in the world. According to this way of thinking, Hagar's existence did not consist of random events and coincidences. Instead, there was a divinely infused order to her life that she now had to try to search out.

Thus, when Hagar did not answer God's second question by saying, "I am going to Egypt to escape from Abram and Sarai," or "I have no idea where I am or where I am going," she left the door open for larger, more metaphysical answers. However, the next words she heard were bitter indeed. The angel gave a bewildering command that has troubled generations of readers: "Go back to your mistress, and submit to her harsh treatment" (Gen. 16:9).

In the face of such an order, it would have been understandable if Hagar had protested, run away from the well, or at least insisted on staying on the path to Egypt. But she remained mute, leaving it unclear if she was assenting or inwardly rebelling. Undeterred, the angel continued, making an astonishing promise to someone who was only a fugitive slave, "I will greatly increase your offspring, and they shall be too many to count" (16:10). If Hagar complied with the first part of God's command and returned to her life of suffering at the hands of Sarai, she would enjoy the very same blessing God had just promised Abram. Even the word "countless" was the same.

Even more surprising, the angel referred to Hagar's children as "your offspring," confirming that Sarai had indeed lost her claim to Hagar's babies. The angel's phrase also indicates that Abram would have to acknowledge Hagar's offspring as her own and not his first wife's. This is strange since one would think that in the age of the patriarchs any child of Hagar's would be considered Abram and Sarai's property. However, God has made a striking differentiation: Hagar would be the bearer of His promise in her own right, a remarkable role for a woman to play in the ancient world.[5]

Instead of expressing astonishment or gratitude, however, Hagar did not speak, and her silence has provoked controversy. The Bible scholar Devora Steinmetz has argued that Hagar's silence during this divine interview represented her direct rejection of God's terms. To Steinmetz, Hagar's inability to respond to the angel's second question demonstrated her refusal to enter into a covenantal relationship with God. Because she did not want to endure pain, an intrinsic element of God's pact, she refused to utter any word that might indicate her acceptance of the future that God laid out for her.[6]

But Steinmetz does not make this claim about Abram, who was also silent when God told him his descendants would have to endure four hundred years of captivity. In fact, no one has concluded that Abram's muteness in this exchange constituted a rejection of God's covenant. Granted, the angel speaks to Hagar repeatedly, and she initially remains quiet, but Steinmetz's interpretation of her silence seems odd, as Hagar will go on to obey God's words, and God will fulfill His promise to her. Seen in this light, her silence is better read as piety and as evidence that Hagar does not question God's will.

Still, it is true that Hagar's speechlessness in this passage is provocative. There are many words she might have uttered and did not.
For instance, she could have asked the question that still puzzles
many who read this story: "Why do I have to go back and suffer more
years of hardship?" Rashi believed the answer to this question was
simple: after having miscarried, she had to return to get pregnant
again. But this interpretation does not solve the bigger mysteries.

The Bible is asking the reader to wrestle, once again, with the
problem of suffering. Like Abram's children, Hagar would have to
endure slavery before she could be free. In her commentary on this
story, Tikva Frymer-Kensky writes, "Why does God insist that suffering come before reward?"[7] More specifically, why must Hagar
return to her mistress, especially since it seems entirely unacceptable that God would act against the rights of a fugitive slave? The
Bible itself declares, "You shall not turn over to his master a slave
who seeks refuge."[8] Even in the context of the Biblical world, then,
God's response to Hagar seems unjust and downright unsympathetic.
To make this commandment even harder to understand, years later,
when the Israelites had escaped slavery in Egypt and were wandering the desert under Moses's leadership, God would not allow them
to return to slavery, even though many of them longed to hike back
to their masters to avoid the terrors of their expedition.

God's apparent cruelty might be explained as a case of a woman's
suffering being less important than a man's destiny. By this logic,
Hagar had to return for the sake of Abram, to help him grow and
to put him to God's test again. If she was pregnant and bore her
baby in the wilderness, Abram would never know the child he had
lost. But if she went back to the campsite, Abram would become
attached to the baby and learn the joys and anguish of fatherhood.

The fact that Abram did not seem overly concerned about
Hagar's initial flight supports this idea. He did not chase after her
or express any grief and anxiety. He had allowed Sarai to mistreat
her. Perhaps Abram needed to learn how to care for the women in
his life more tenderly. Maybe God was unhappy with how he had

abdicated responsibility for the conflict between Sarai and Hagar and had decided to give him another chance.

Yet there are other ways to view God's commandment that do not prioritize Abram's development over Hagar's well-being. For example, God may have wanted Hagar's baby to bear Abram's stamp. It was important that the nations acknowledge her child was indeed Abram's. It was also crucial for this child to know his father, so he could learn the customs and rules of an extraordinary leader. Finally, God may have wanted Hagar to have Abram's protection while she raised her son.[9]

These theories notwithstanding, what is most important is that the angel's visitation had transformed Hagar from slave to mystic and from oppressed woman to tribal leader. It was as though the wilderness itself was speaking, pushing her to think of herself in new terms, as a free person with an important role to play, rather than as a serving maid subject to the will of others. A more timid person would never have tried to escape Sarai's oppressive hand. By fleeing to the Negev and allowing the unknown into her life, Hagar had demonstrated that she was willing and able to experience the mystery of the divine and the loneliness of the prophet. Certainly, God thought so.

The angel declared,

[You] shall bear a son;
You shall call him Ishmael,
For the Lord has paid heed to your suffering.
He shall be a wild ass of a man;
His hand against everyone,
And everyone's hand against him;
He shall dwell alongside all of his kinsmen. (16:12)

The modern reader will be excused for thinking that God is saying some unpleasant things about Ishmael. But to be called a "wild ass of a man" was not an insult; in Biblical times the desert asses were a symbol that would have made the slave mother's heart rise in joy. There was no better emblem of freedom than the wild creatures she had seen roaming in the rocky Negev. And what could be more tantalizing for a slave woman to hear than that her son would be free? In fact, this would be Ishmael's dominant characteristic, just as his mother's was currently her slavery. Even more significant, he would be a fighter, asserting his independence against anyone who attempted to oppress him. Thus, his "hand" would always be ready for battle.

Naturally, many Jewish and Islamic scholars have seized on this final verse to prove their contrasting political points. Rashi expresses Jewish hostility toward Muslims by writing, "All will hate [Ishmael] and attack him." But the Koran declares that Ishmael "was a man of his word, an apostle, and a prophet." Certainly, neither the Koran nor the hadith describe Ishmael as a particularly aggressive person or as a fierce warrior. Rather, he is painted as a loyal, trustworthy man of God.[10]

But though the portrait of Ishmael varies, one point is indisputable. God was sympathetic to this slave woman's pain, and He had just confided more directly in her than He had in His chosen father of nations. He had even told her the name of her child, information He had yet to disclose to Abram, though Abram was the man upon whose shoulders the great western religions were to be built.

Not surprisingly, the announcement of Ishmael's birth could only bolster Hagar's confidence in God and in her own destiny. Never again would she try to escape her fate. And yet, despite the powerful ramifications of this moment in Hagar's life, this scene has often been misinterpreted as a symbol of Hagar's distanced relationship with God, since an "angel" is doing God's talking for Him. However, this argument misses the point of the text and underestimates Hagar's role in Abram's story. Even worse, it diminishes the Biblical import of Hagar's descendants, the Arabs.

However, as we have already seen, angels are not lower than

God on some divine totem pole. They are an inextricable part of the divine will. As the eighteenth-century kabbalist Moshe Luzzato writes, "God had thus willed and organized things so that his decrees should be translated into action through angels . . . "[11] Later on, for example, angels will speak to Abram, conveying to him some of the most important information of his life.

CHAPTER SIXTEEN

A SECOND CONCUBINE

If Hagar's sojourn in the desert served as a catalyst for her meta-
morphosis from slave woman to one of God's chosen, there is
another intensely disturbing Bible passage that serves as a shadow
story to Hagar's experience. Indeed, without knowing this darker
version, it is difficult to understand the uniqueness of Hagar's destiny and how important she was to God.

The parallels between Hagar's life and this bleak tale from
Judges 19–21 are too pointed to be a coincidence.[1] Most scholars
believe that Judges was composed after Genesis and as a result
echoes some of the central episodes in Abram's life. On a symbolic
level, the early rabbis argued that the central incidents in the patriarchs' lives would be repeated throughout the rest of the Bible,
while Christians believe that Hebrew Scripture foretells Christ's
redemption of the world and points to the need for this redemption. Certainly, this tale would seem to fit the bill from both perspectives: it recapitulates details from Abram's life and it shows us a
snapshot of an entirely unredeemed world.

Both tales feature a fugitive concubine and both pivot around
the questions that Hagar must confront in the desert. Yet this
second story, set hundreds of years later, is important because it

demonstrates what could have happened to Hagar as a woman on her own. In addition, it highlights Hagar's relationship with God, as the Judges concubine does not have the benefit of God's shield. Finally, it shows the disasters that might occur if one answered the angel's questions lightly, without understanding their wide-ranging implications.

The Book of Judges is set in the chaotic period of Biblical history after the Exodus and the settlement of Canaan, but before Israel had kings. In this tale, a nameless young concubine flees from her husband back to her father's house. Immediately, the link to Hagar's story should become clear. Not only were both women concubines or second wives, but both attempted to leave behind the men in their lives and return to their childhood homes, although Hagar did not succeed. In the Judges story, the woman's husband also held a leadership position in society, although of course he did not have Abram's stature. Still, he was a member of the highly respected Israelite tribe of Levi.

All Israelites traced their family lines back to the twelve sons of Jacob. The Levites, the descendants of Jacob's third son, Levi, were the only tribe to remain loyal to Moses and God during the Exodus. As a result, they became the priests, responsible for the ritual life of the community, performing the sacrifices, and guarding and maintaining the Temple once it was built in Jerusalem.

The Levites traveled from place to place, serving as ritual experts, and were dependent on the goodwill of the other eleven tribes to survive. This was important for two reasons: Levites were meant to adhere to higher moral standards than other people and were often on the road, as Abram and his flock had been, rendering them vulnerable to the hostility of marauders, thieves, and enemies.

When his concubine ran away, the Levite, unlike Abram, pursued the woman—though he did not do so immediately. At first this seems like a more loving gesture than Abram's inaction when Hagar took flight, but there were some disturbing elements to the

Levite's pursuit. When he arrived at her father's house, there is no evidence the Levite ever spoke to the fugitive, although his intention had been to "woo her" (Judg. 19:3). Instead, he negotiated her return with her father and never consulted with the concubine about her wishes or asked why she had fled in the first place. He laid claim to her as though she were a piece of property that had gone missing.

The young woman's father urged the Levite to stay a few days and enjoy himself, drinking and feasting. At last, late one afternoon, the concubine's husband decided it was time to depart, never a wise decision in a countryside where the night was thick with bandits.

At first nothing seemed amiss. When the sun set, the couple stopped in Gibeah, an Israelite town populated by members of the tribe of Benjamin. It was the duty of the Benjaminites to offer the couple hospitality, but none of the inhabitants invited them to stay overnight, and so the couple remained stranded in the town square until at last a stranger approached them.

In an emphatic echo of the Hagar story, he asked the same two questions the angel had asked Hagar: "Where have you come from and where are you going?" In this story, though, the questions were not directed toward the woman but toward her husband. The Levite responded to the stranger's questions with a confidence Hagar had lacked: "We are traveling from Bethlehem in Judah to the other end of the hill country" (19:17–18). Apparently, the Levite did not suspect that these questions had a symbolic meaning that transcended the literal or that they might be intended to make him think about the larger issues of his past and his destiny. Instead, he stayed entirely in the concrete world, missing an important chance for introspection.

The stranger was happy with these answers and asked the Levite and his concubine to stay with him for the night. Believing they had found a safe place to sleep, the couple followed him home. But later that evening, "the men of the town, a depraved lot," banged on the door and demanded that the Levite be given to them so that they could "be intimate with him" (19:22). Though English translations often attempt to mute the Benjaminites' clamor, the Biblical Hebrew suggests that the men wanted to rape and abuse the Levite.

This obscene demand was taboo for many reasons: the Levite was a member of an Israelite tribe, and thus the Benjaminites should have greeted him as a brother. But even if he were not an Israelite, the Benjaminites were breaking the ancient world's fundamental rule of hospitality. They should have greeted a guest in their town with generosity and kindness.

The couple's host, desperate to appease the rowdy mob, did something so shocking that the Benjaminites' violent predilections almost fade in comparison. He offered them his virgin daughter and the Levite's concubine in place of the Levite. "Have your pleasure of them," the stranger pleaded. "Do what you like with them, but don't do that outrageous thing to this man" (19:24). It is true that Abram's nephew Lot will say almost the same thing to an angry crowd of Sodomites who are attempting to attack his guests, but there is another echo here that is less obvious. The host uses the language Abram used after Sarai complained to him about Hagar's disrespectful behavior: Abram had said, "Do to her what is good in your eyes," and so, clearly, the reader is meant to connect all three of these stories — Sodom, Hagar, and the Levite's concubine — although the reason is not yet apparent.[2]

The host's words may dismay the modern reader, but, according to the rules of the ancient world, the lives of women were worth less than those of men. As we have seen, Abram felt free to offer Sarai to the Pharaoh to preserve his own life, thus the stranger was doing his duty by trying to protect his guest. The Levite, however, had another choice: he could have offered himself in place of the young women. But, eager to save his own skin, the Levite does not protest. In fact, he is the one who carries out the terrible act the host proposed. The Bible puts it tersely: "[the Levite] seized his concubine and pushed her out to [the Benjaminites]" (19:25). There is no mention of the host's daughter, suggesting that the host, at least, thought better of his offer.

Left alone to face the Benjaminites, the concubine had little hope of survival. The men "raped [the Levite's concubine] and abused her all night long until morning." The text says they only released her "when dawn broke" (19:25), making it clear she had endured an entire night of unthinkable torture.

The Bible does not tell us what the Levite did while the shouts of the crowd floated through the windows of the stranger's house. It would have been impossible to avoid hearing the screams of his concubine as the men carried her off. The only thing we know is what he did not do. At no point did he go out into the streets to protect the young woman. Indeed, he waited until the sun came up and the Benjaminites had retreated to their homes before he opened the door and found the young woman lying on the doorstep "with her hands upon the threshold" in a desperate last plea for help. She was beaten and bloodied, but whether she was alive or dead is unclear (19:27–28). All we know is that when the Levite told her to get up, there was no answer.

The Levite loaded her body onto his donkey and finished his journey, returning to his home in Ephraim. But once he arrived at his destination, he did not bind the woman's wounds, nor bury her, if she was in fact dead. Instead, he picked up a knife and chopped her into twelve pieces. One presumes that she was not still alive and that he did not murder her himself, but the text is not particularly reassuring, leaving it possible that he killed her. After all, for him, her value had been ruined, not only because she was disfigured and wounded, but because other men had had sex with her. At any rate, he did not pause or pray for guidance. Instead, he sent twelve portions of her flesh "throughout the territory of Israel" as evidence of the Benjaminites' crime (19:29).

The reaction among the Israelites was profound: "Everyone who saw it cried out, 'Never has such a thing happened or been seen from the day the Israelites came out of the land of Egypt to this day'" (19:30). The tribes, with the exception of the Benjaminites, gathered to express their outrage. When the culprits refused to appear and make amends for their crime, the other eleven immediately declared war. They massed 400,000 men against 26,000 Benjaminites, but it still took them three days to win (20:2; 20:17).

The concubine's terrible fate had occasioned war. Like Hagar, her story would spark a chain reaction that would affect thousands, but, unlike Hagar, who under God's aegis would go on to found a people, this concubine's death almost destroyed the Israelites.

When at last the battle was over, only six hundred Benjaminite men were left, and now a new problem faced the Israelites. According to the tradition of warfare in the ancient world, the Benjaminite women and children had also been slaughtered. However, the purpose of the war had been to punish the Benjaminites, not annihilate them. After all, the Benjaminites were descendants of Abraham too. God had promised Canaan to all twelve tribes, so it was important that the Benjaminites survive. The situation was made more extreme because the tribes had sworn not to allow their daughters to marry a Benjaminite. Unless their fellow tribes came up with a solution, the Benjaminites faced extinction.

In response, the Israelites concocted a twofold plan based on yet more destruction. First they urged the Benjaminites to massacre the men and capture the women of Jabesh-Gilead. Although the Benjaminites followed their brothers' instructions, this still did not yield enough women. So, the tribes pushed the Benjaminites to capture and rape the girls of Shiloh, who were gathering nearby for a festival. Again, the Benjaminites did as their brothers suggested, and yet more women were seized — this time in the name of regenerating the twelfth tribe of the Israelites.

Ironically, the Levite's pursuit of his "wife" had resulted not only in her downfall, but also in the suffering of countless other women. However, despite the obvious differences between the two stories, it is still puzzling to consider why the Judges story turns out like this when Hagar's tale would end with the creation of a new people. After all, both women were runaway concubines.

The most straightforward explanation is that the two tales take place in two different books of the Bible. Genesis is dedicated to showing the active role of God in the creation of the world, while Judges seeks to show the violence and the lawlessness of the Israelites when they fall away from God.

In addition, the husbands and their relationship to God have little in common. Although at first glance his behavior seems heartless, Abram, who was in despair about the continuity of his line, let his fertile concubine flee. The Levite, on the other hand, fetched his concubine, and his pursuit brought about her downfall. It can be argued, therefore, that Abram's apparent neglect of his second wife allowed room for God's intervention and Hagar's freedom, whereas the Levite trampled on the free will of his concubine.[3]

The cycle of violence against women in Judges is by no means unique to the Bible. For instance, the Roman story of the Rape of the Sabine Women offers a striking parallel to the concubine's sad story.[4] To find wives for themselves, the founding fathers of Rome stole women from the kingdom of Sabinium. For both the Israelites and the Romans, then, the capture of women from neighboring peoples was an essential aspect of their origins.

The astonishing thing, then, is that rape is not the centerpiece of the story of Abram and Hagar. Although, in essence, Hagar was forced to sleep with Abram, she was proud of her pregnancy and seems to have regarded her alliance with Abram as advantageous rather than abusive. As for Abram, he was in just as desperate a situation as the Benjaminites and the Romans when it came to the continuity of his line. Hagar was a fertile foreign woman just like the women of Shiloh and Sabinium. She was even in a subordinate position as a serving maid. Yet Abram did not hold her captive when she wanted to escape. He did not attempt to overpower her, nor did he try to steal her back or seize her baby. Instead, he let her go, although she was probably carrying his child.

That Hagar's story is not a story of violence is extraordinary. She escaped the fate of the concubine and the Sabine women in part because of Abram's piety but largely because God "heeded [her] suffering." In contrast to the Judges tale, God plays an active role in her story, watching, intervening, protecting, guiding, and talking to both Abram and Hagar about their lives and destinies. Consequently, Hagar's story offers an alternative creation myth to that of the Romans and the Israelites: one that is based on freedom, not slavery, and one where there is no need for brutality and rape.

Perhaps this is why Hagar could not speak when the angel asked her about her destiny. How could she have foreseen such a miraculous future? It was inconceivable that a slave woman would become the free mother of a free people. Indeed, the torture and murder of the Levite's concubine was the most likely fate for an unprotected single woman. Thus, any attempt on Hagar's part to predict what would happen to her would have fallen short. Even if she had dreamed of escaping slavery, she could never have imagined the independence that lay ahead for herself and her descendants.

CHAPTER SEVENTEEN

NAMING GOD

B ut who was this God whose voice rang forth at the well, who sometimes offered help and at other times was silent? Who was He who created the heavens, strode through the Garden of Eden, bestowed visions, and told Hagar the name of her baby? Where did He come from? Why did He have to be so elusive?

Hagar did not complain about God's vagaries. Instead, she acknowledged the moment of her selection in the desert by doing something extraordinary. When God finished His predictions, Hagar spoke for the first time in the Bible, as though she had been saving her voice for the Lord: "You are El-roi," she said (Gen. 16:13). In the future, other people in Scripture would refer to God by the names He would teach them to use—Adonai or Yahweh—but no one had ever invented their own, and no one else ever would. Thus, Hagar reveals an originality, a willingness to break from convention, and an eagerness to connect to this bewildering deity that sets her apart from every other Biblical figure, male or female. Clearly, rules did not matter to this servant woman.

However, the phrase she uttered is almost as mysterious as her previous silence. To begin with, "roi" can be translated as "seeing," and "El" denotes a deity of some kind. Thus, Hebrew scholar

Reuven Hammer writes that El-roi could mean "God of seeing, that is, the all-seeing God. Also, God of my seeing, that is, whom I have seen; and God who sees me."[1]

In other words, no one is quite sure what Hagar was really saying, except that she was searching for a way to make sense of God's identity, something earlier men had not done. Adam had disobeyed God and never attempted to address Him directly. Noah had performed God's bidding but had never called God by name. Abram was different, of course, but unlike Hagar, he never had to create his own language for the divine, and this leaves his innermost thoughts about God's identity somewhat obscure. When Hagar pronounces the name El-roi, however, she lays bare her ideas about God as well as her struggle to know Him and express herself to Him. In this one moment, Hagar emerges as a more resourceful partner than many of the human beings God would speak to in the long history of His conversation with the world.

The Bible attempts to clarify her mysterious phrase, saying, "She meant, 'Have I not gone on seeing after He saw me!'" (16:13). But most readers have been even more confused by this second sentence, and sadly, commentators have not spent much time trying to decipher her words. Either they did not deem Hagar important enough to analyze her phrase because she was "just a woman," or, if they were Jewish, they discounted her because she is the traditional mother of Islam. Most Muslim scholars have not corrected this oversight, since Hagar's encounter with God does not appear in the Koran.

Such scholarly neglect is unfortunate, since not only was Hagar's conversation with God unique, as we have seen, but she was also the first to define God as a being who could "see" people.[2] To modern readers, who are used to the idea of a deity who is aware of and cares about each individual, this seems an obvious attribute. But in ancient times, that God could "see" Hagar—take note of her—was a revolutionary idea, as it demonstrated that He was unlike the other deities of the ancient world, who routinely ignored their followers unless they were coaxed and fed expensive delicacies by specially trained priests. Hagar's God, on the other hand, was a democratic God, a divine who was actually concerned about a poor woman.

Of course, Hagar was going to bear the child of God's chosen man. Still, in His appearance at the well, God demonstrated a remarkable willingness to enlarge a slave woman's view of the world. In fact, it is this closeness to God that Hagar's descendants would claim for themselves over both the Israelites and the followers of that strange messianic rabbi Yeshua, or Jesus.

However, all three religions were fundamentally shaped by Hagar's observation that God is El-roi—the One Who Sees Me—since the God of Judaism, Christianity, and Islam is conceived of as a deity who is capable of forming relationships with human beings, in contrast to other deities "with [their] mouths that cannot speak and eyes that cannot see" (Psalms 115:6). In fact, Ishmael's name actually means "He hears," or to translate it another way, "God hears the voice of those who cry to Him."[3]

Just as important, Hagar's sojourn with God had not killed her. Where she came from, people did not talk to the high gods. The reason priests and priestesses mediated these exchanges was that the divine overlords would destroy ordinary petitioners. Thus, in addition to seeing Hagar, God had allowed her to pierce through what one medieval mystic called the "cloud of unknowing" and actually perceive Him.[4] Then, He had allowed her to separate from Him unscathed. After such an exchange, Hagar could not refuse God's commands. He had said that Hagar must go back, so return she would. But their time together had left a definitive mark on her. She was now no longer just a servant or a second wife; she was a woman who had met the divine.

Even the desert was transformed by this dramatic event. The Bible announced that the well where Hagar and God had spoken was "now" known as Beer-la'hai-roi, or "the Well of the Living One Who Sees Me" (Gen. 16:14). In the same way that Hagar had been elevated by her divine interaction, so the well was no longer simply a spring in the desert but was forever linked to God. This name change suggested that Hagar's experience could extend beyond the confines of her own memory—it was marked for posterity by the well.

The new world Hagar helped launch, in which human beings had a closer relationship with the divine, placed a new emphasis on human morality. If she taught her children that God could see and hear them, perhaps they would behave with more circumspection than previous generations. If a human being committed a sin, God took note. On the other hand, if a person needed help, as Hagar had, God would come to her rescue.

To place Hagar's experience in the historical record, the Bible assures the reader that one can find the actual well "between Kadesh and Bered" (16:14). These details seek to locate Hagar's revelation in geography so that the reader will be convinced this event "really" happened. But the danger is that the reader might also attempt to lock God's location into this particular spot—a misreading, as the Biblical God was depicted as being everywhere at all times. He was in the raging whirlwind and the black ocean, the sin-ridden city and the desert oasis. God's intangible nature made Him portable, a characteristic that further distinguished Him from the pagan deities of other peoples, who were generally conceived of as "living" in particular places such as wells, mountains, and springs.

So, although the Bible is clear that this was God's well, it was not His home. Similarly, God may have been the God of the Israelites, but He was also the God of Egyptians, Canaanites, and all humankind—another lesson of His appearance to Hagar. Contradictory as it may seem, though God sometimes destroyed the enemies of Abram's children, He was their God just as much as He was the Israelites' God. He could not be held to one location, one people, or one individual; even Abram had to share Him with the rest of humanity, including his second wife.

THERE IS NO RECORD of Hagar's journey back through the wilderness. It seems unthinkable that she had the strength for another trek through the Negev, but somehow she found her way back to her master and mistress. Hagar's safe return indicated how closely God was watching over her. Given her limitations—a single, possibly pregnant young woman—God must have helped her make it back to Hebron. Otherwise, she might well have collapsed somewhere in the desert, been devoured by wild animals, assaulted by roaming tribes, or lost forever in the Negev's monotonous hills. Thus, although the Bible does not mention any extraordinary event occurring on her way home, the fact that she survived the journey was itself a miracle and represented yet another divine intervention in her life.

In tacit acknowledgment of the impossibility of Hagar's return and, for that matter, of her entire experience in the desert, the Bible seems intent on fixing this story in real time and space, a striking difference from the vagueness surrounding Abram's prophetic encounters. Thus, the specifications of Ishmael's name, the location of the well, and later, the timing of his "actual" birth, are intended to demonstrate not only that Hagar received a divine call, but also that everything she heard would one day come true. After all, it would be easy enough for cynics to say that she had made the whole story up to avoid being punished for running away. How could a simple serving woman have heard the voice of God?

Still, the similarities between her experience and that of Abram are remarkable. Like Abram, Hagar had to separate herself from the trammels of family and home life before she could have a prophetic vision. And like his, her journey into the wilderness helped shape her into the founder of a people.

Generally speaking, though, Hagar is not regarded as a prophet by most scholars in either the Jewish or Christian traditions. In part, this is because she was a woman. But there is an irony here, as she fits the most important criterion given for a prophet by Abraham Heschel, whose book *The Prophets* is widely regarded as one of the authoritative works on the subject. At the well, she discovers what he terms "theotropism," God's personal concern for humanity.

As Heschel writes, "Prophecy is the voice that God has lent to the silent agony . . . of the world."[5]

Muslim writers do not usually address this story, as most say that Hagar never ran away from the campsite in the first place. Only later, after the birth of Ishmael, did she wander alone in the desert. And it was then, with her baby in her arms, that she had an important encounter with God. However, again, in Islam, she remains simply the woman to whom God spoke and is rarely regarded as a prophet in her own right.[6]

Despite these shortsighted interpretations, Hagar's relationship with God is one Abram and, for that matter, any of God's chosen might well envy. With her, God was direct, clear, and highly detailed, and most of what He foretold happened without delay. He even gave a specific reason for His actions: He had seen her suffering and was now comforting her. With Abram, God had offered no such guidance. His chosen man would never know why God selected him, nor could he predict when God would finally enact His promises.

Indeed, it would not be until much later that angels would announce to Abram the imminent birth of another child—information Abram could have used much earlier on. Hagar, not Abram, receives the first divine annunciation of a son's birth. Conventional hierarchies are overturned. The slave woman gets to hear the news her master has been waiting for all of his adult life.

CHAPTER EIGHTEEN

ISHMAEL

Having a baby was as dangerous an undertaking as going to war. It was impossible to know if one would emerge from the experience alive. Although there are no precise records of how many women died in childbirth during the Biblical era, a woman's chances of surviving this ordeal were far from certain.[1] Too many things could go awry. A baby could be turned the wrong way in the womb, and unless there were skilled midwives or experienced older women available to help shift the child, the mother might well die from the dangerous task of trying to push out an infant feetfirst. The umbilical cord could get wrapped around the neck of the unborn child. A mother's contractions could mysteriously stop. Fevers could result from an infection. Internal bleeding could continue days after the baby was born.

So, when her labor began, Hagar faced a terrifying ordeal. Although she could hope that God would protect her as He had promised, the trial that lay ahead was daunting. Birth was a public event in the world of women, and with so many people involved in the deliveries of the tribe, the disasters that occurred were common knowledge. Hagar had undoubtedly witnessed at least one death during childbirth and had seen or heard how other women suffered in labor. On the positive side, she had also learned what practices to employ to have a safer, easier delivery. But there were no guarantees and, of course, no way to escape suffering. Most women leaned on their friends, sisters, and mothers to help them through their travail.

With no family to support her, Hagar would have to rely on the woman to whom she was most problematically connected, Sarai. In some ways Hagar was fortunate in this, since, as one of the elders, Sarai would have expertise as an herbalist and a childbirth attendant. Still, to have one's enemy play a prominent role during such a vulnerable time would have troubled any woman, let alone Hagar, who had already been abused by Sarai. In such a tiny community, however, neither woman had any choice. Sarai had to help and Hagar had to receive her help. Indeed, it is a credit to both that they accepted their roles with apparent grace, since Hagar did not complain, and Sarai did not try to sabotage the birth.

There was a lot riding on this event. If Hagar successfully gave birth to Ishmael, as God had said she would, she would push Abram and Sarai into a new stage of their lives as surely as she pushed her baby into the world. Abram's legacy would be guaranteed. Sarai, on the other hand, who thus far had no baby, no direct communication with God, and a strained relationship with both Abram and Hagar, would be the odd woman out. Nothing would demonstrate her inadequacy more than the birth of a child to her husband's upstart concubine.

As for Hagar, there would be no looking back. There was no better way to cement her position at Abram's side than by bearing a healthy son—a fact that must have helped her greet her labor with anticipation and excitement. But no amount of anticipation could mask the pain when the contractions began. Fortunately, Sarai and the other women knew exactly what to do. Over the centuries many rituals had been created to help ease labor. Sage, which grew plentifully in the dry land of Canaan, could be sipped as a tea or rubbed on a woman's belly to help soothe cramps. Nard was an herb that also grew in the desert and had strong sedative powers if a woman required respite.[2] Rubbing Hagar's back and feet, holding her hand, and encouraging her to breathe, scream, and pray could also help her endure her agony.

Labor was an intimate experience, and so the servant and the mistress, the abused and the abuser, were forced to enter a new stage of their relationship. Hagar needed Sarai, and it was Sarai's duty to grit her teeth and stand by her handmaid while Hagar sweated through the pain that Sarai longed to endure. In addition, a strange inversion occurred, since Sarai's job was essentially to serve Hagar during the labor: the mistress became the handmaid and the handmaid the mistress. At last, thanks to the efforts of both women, Abram's firstborn crowned and then spilled into the waiting arms of Sarai and the other attendants, healthy and whole, just as God had said.

Despite Hagar's delivery of a healthy baby, her future was still uncertain. Although it seemed likely that her status would rise now that she was the mother of Abram's child, it was hard to predict what would happen next. She did not know if Sarai would renew her persecution, or if Abram would now protect her. Perhaps it would be impossible for her to remain at the camp. The lesson of the desert — that God was aware of her suffering — did not necessarily mean that He would save her from any harm her master and mistress might inflict. All that Hagar could count on was that God would witness her distress.

She might have worried less if she had known that her earlier exchange with the angels marked her as one of the most blessed women in the Bible. The divine communication she received bore an uncanny resemblance to later famous annunciations. Angels spoke to Hannah, the mother of the prophet Samuel, and to Samson's unnamed mother. Perhaps the strangest parallel of all, though, is between Hagar and Mary, mother of Jesus. Even Mary's two significant differences from Hagar — that she was a virgin and that the father of her child was God — did not release her from having to undergo the same labor pains as Hagar, suggesting that it was the father's role, not the mother's, that underwent a decisive transition in the Christ story.[3] Indeed, it seemed as though there was something so important about labor that it needed to be experienced by the mother of the Christian God as well as by Hagar and all the other Biblical mothers.

This is an odd thought, since it is the general scholarly consensus that the women of both the Hebrew and Christian Bibles were second-class citizens. But if women were so unimportant to God, then it would have made sense for Him to create His son entirely out of His own Being, as Zeus had with Athena. Instead, God consistently relied on women as partners in His creation. Although the pain women experience giving birth can be traced all the way back to God's punishment of Eve, this story also demonstrates that the Bible regards labor as a divinely sponsored occurrence. Birth, then, that supremely "natural" event, can also be read as a symbol of God's participatory role in human life, whether it takes place in the Hebrew Bible or in Christian Scripture.

But though Scripture begins by emphasizing that God is responsible for human fertility, until the story of Abram, Sarai, and Hagar, He had not foretold or been personally involved in any human birth. Ishmael was the first baby God had deemed worthy of individualized attention. He had even predicted the boy's name, a rare phenomenon in the Bible and one associated with some of the most important births in Scripture. This might seem counterintuitive to the modern reader, unaccustomed to seeing Ishmael as one of the most significant figures in the Hebrew Bible. But Ishmael was a man chosen by God to create a new people. Like the later men whose names were also foretold—Jesus, Isaac, and Samson—Ishmael was destined for greatness.

Born under the shelter of God's blessing, Ishmael was the wonder of the campsite, and Abram could assume that the prophecy about his offspring had been set in motion. As for the two women in his life, a truce of sorts seemed to emerge. While Hagar nursed the little boy in the shade of her tent, Sarai was forced to reconcile herself to the bitterness of her fate. As the days passed and Hagar walked freely around the campsite, her baby in her arms, Sarai did not provoke any conflicts. Indeed, she seems to have stopped tormenting Hagar entirely. Perhaps Hagar could rest easy. Calm prevailed and Ishmael flourished; again, just as God had foretold.

MOTHERS WERE RESPONSIBLE for the early education of their children, and so Hagar taught her toddler his first lessons while he lived in her tent, until he was weaned at around age three.[4] Although traditional Jewish and Islamic teachings hold that Hagar was a devout follower of God, as befit a partner of Abram, her childhood had been spent in Egypt, and so it seems natural that many of the stories she told her little boy would be about the land of her birth. Pharaoh, the palace, the dancing and singing, the strange statues people worshipped as gods, the Pyramids, the huge city, and the swampy, changeable Nile—all of these would have fueled Ishmael's imagination about the larger world. He would have understood right from the beginning that Pharaoh's people were his mother's people, not a foreign race to be feared. From his earliest years he would also have been aware that he and his mother were different from everyone else in Abram's camp. Indeed, he was different from his mother as well, since, to use a modern term, Ishmael was biracial, both Semitic and Egyptian.

But even if some of the members of the tribe regarded Hagar and her son with suspicion, Ishmael was the son of the leader. From Abram, the boy would have gleaned the essentials of survival in the wilderness, including hunting, tending the flocks, and trading with other tribes. He could also observe his father's determination not to be ruled by any overlord, a legacy Ishmael would take to heart. In addition, Ishmael would have been granted privileges that not everyone received. From the moment of his birth, the little boy enjoyed more food, thicker blankets, and finer clothing because of his father's wealth. No one could treat him as a servant. Ishmael, the son of a slave woman, was raised by his father to prize freedom.

And yet, although it is clear that Abram loved his son and wanted to include him in all aspects of the camp's daily life, ultimately Ishmael could never be fully integrated into the community. Hagar may have taken a few steps up the social ladder when she gave birth, but she had started life in the camp as a servant woman, and so it would have been difficult for Abram's followers to completely accept Ishmael as one of their own.

Despite the challenges he faced, Ishmael remained remarkably untroubled. Both his mother and father loved him dearly and protected him from harm. Indeed, Abram valued him so overwhelmingly that in just a few years he would argue with God on Ishmael's behalf, jeopardizing his relationship with the Lord for the sake of his firstborn's rights of inheritance.

As time passed, the boy grew, defying his enemies by developing into a strong teenager, while his father watched with pride and pleasure. According to Jewish and Muslim traditions, Ishmael soon became famous for his skills as an archer. As Abram's son, he was one of the leaders of the boys his age and shared with them the responsibility of herding the goats and sleeping under the stars with the animals when they roamed far from the family's tents.[5]

With each new achievement of her son, Hagar gained stature in her community. Her joy in Ishmael could not be diminished, even by those who despised her. For Abram, this period was probably the happiest of his life. Every day his son grew stronger, braver, and more independent. Abram would not have to leave his wealth to his head servant, as he had once feared. He had an heir.

Sarai's feelings, on the other hand, were more opaque. She remained quiet during this period. She may have been seething, anguished over her own childlessness, or she may have been reconciled to Hagar and her husband's son. It is impossible to know for certain, but given the uninterrupted tranquillity of this period, it is probable that any truce Sarai and Hagar had established during Hagar's labor held steady.

Of course, it is also possible that Abram may have put his foot down and declared that Sarai could no longer tangle with his second wife or her son. But such assertive behavior would have been out of character for a man who had deferred to Sarai's authority during the original struggle between the two women.

At any rate, it seems unlikely that Hagar now reigned supreme as the mother of Abram's child. Given Sarai's stature as a leader, it is hard to imagine that she would have endured a demotion without protest or that the people themselves would have allowed Hagar to treat her as a subordinate. What seems most plausible is that Sarai had decided to accept Ishmael, or at least appear to accept him.

Thus, Ishmael's birth brought peace to the campsite — a precarious peace, of course, but peace all the same. The boy grew up at the center of things, secure in the protection of his family and his tribe. And Sarai, who was capable of instigating an argument at a moment's notice, desisted from stirring the pot.

CHAPTER NINETEEN

EL SHADDAI

One day, about thirteen years after Ishmael was born, the serenity of the campsite was shattered, never to return. Without any warning, God arrived, and He did not seem happy. He had been remarkably quiet since His encounter with Hagar in the desert, but now He was impatient to be heard, appearing under the cloak of an ominous-sounding new name, "El Shaddai," or the Lord Almighty. No one knows for sure what this title means, but most scholars agree that *Shaddai* has stern overtones, with some suggesting that the phrase means "God of the mountain." As Jack Miles writes, "Of all the titles applied to God in Hebrew, it is the one most intended to convey raw power."[1] Certainly, this was a different face than the one God had showed in His visitation with Hagar.

Before Abram could wonder why God was there and why He was speaking in such authoritarian tones, Gods issued a commandment. "Walk in my ways," He declared (Gen. 17:1). God's abruptness suggested He was angry, as though Abram had *not* been walking in His ways. Perhaps He suspected Abram no longer felt he needed God now that he had Ishmael. If this is true, God's sudden shift indicates He had decided to clarify things, as well as exercise stricter control over His chosen man, despite His earlier hands-off approach.

God's next words support this idea, as, for the first time, He placed an ethical stipulation on Abram's behavior, telling Abram that he must "be blameless" (17:1). Since God had never before made any sort of statement to Abram about how he should conduct himself, it seems He now felt a need to remind Abram of his moral obligations. Still, it is hard to be definitive here, as this commandment was also reminiscent of Akkadian treaties where the overlord would remind his subject that his behavior must be flawless for the contract to remain valid.[2] Perhaps God was simply observing an ancient tradition inherent to formal agreements and was casting no aspersions on Abram's past behavior.

Unclear though God's reasoning is, it is only after this pronouncement that He reiterated His promise that Abram's descendants would be "numerous" (17:2), further indicating that the fate of Abram's children would be directly linked to his good behavior. Initially, all Abram had had to do was obey God in order to reap his rewards, but El Shaddai had just upped the ante.

Abram had not said anything when God arrived, nor did he speak after God issued His promise. Like Hagar during her interview at the well, he was silent. However, he departed from his earlier behavior by "[throwing] himself on his face," an appropriate response to this new attitude of God (17:3).[3]

True to form, God did not explain His intentions. Instead, while Abram groveled, God suddenly changed the subject, declaring that He would give Abram a new name. From now on, God proclaimed, Abram would be known as "the father of a multitude of nations," or Abraham (17:4–5). According to ancient rabbinical texts, the addition of the letter *hei* to Abram's name "represent[ed] the name of God" because *hei* is used three times in the Lord's name. (More accurately, the *hei* appears in the approximation of God's name that Jews have used for thousands of years, since His actual name is believed to be too sacred to speak or to read.) Accordingly, Abram's name change was meant as a "reward" for "pious behavior."[4] If so, this announcement represents a sudden reversal on God's part.

God implied that Abram had been guilty of straying from His path a moment before, so it seems strange that now He would want to reward him.

But perhaps God was not being as contradictory as at first He seemed. Implicit in God's declaration was the principle that to be the father of multitudes, Abram had to become a new person. In other words, who Abram had been before was no longer sufficient. So God's idea of a name change seems less like a tribute to Abram and more like another divine attempt at creation, although it is unclear why God would want to erase the past and keep a tight rein on Abram's future behavior. Had Abram proven himself to be unsatisfactory in some way?

Scholars of all religious persuasions resist the idea of a failed or, even worse, a rebellious Abram. Many argue that Abram had been so virtuous in the years since Egypt that God wanted to honor him by helping him become an even holier man who could adhere to a stricter version of the covenant. As Nahum Sarna writes, "Now the patriarch is told that he will not only have an heir and be the progenitor of a nation but that he will even become the 'father of a multitude of nations.'"[5]

Although many of these same commentators criticize Abram's behavior in Egypt, they blame this episode on factors besides the man's cowardice: the corrupting influence of the land of the Pharaohs or the mores of the ancient world that valued a man's life more highly than a woman's. Few address the more central question of Abram's fidelity, or lack thereof, to Sarai. And even fewer comment on the possibility that Abram had lost faith in God's promise of offspring and had acted on his own to get the son he wanted, Ishmael. But this kind of whitewashing misses the real issue, at least from God's perspective. God's chosen man seemed intent on keeping himself apart from God. He did not budge when El Shaddai spoke, keeping his face buried as though he did not want God to know what he was feeling. For His part, God persisted in His aggressive attitude. He could have relieved the tension by saying,

"Do not fear," or "Do not hide from Me," but He chose to leave these words unsaid, just as Abraham never said, "Forgive me, Lord, if I have disappointed You."

Unperturbed by his vassal's abject demonstration or perhaps finally moved by his show of subservience, God chose this moment to broach a new, frightening topic. "Every male among you shall be circumcised," God announced. "Thus shall My covenant be marked in your flesh as an everlasting pact" (17:10; 17:13). Building on the principles laid out in their last covenantal exchange (15:1–21)—that Abraham must swear fealty to God in order to receive His blessings—God now demanded a strange, almost incomprehensible price to seal their agreement: Abraham's foreskin, that of every man in Abraham's household, and that of each of his male descendants.

The irony of this command is extraordinary. At this point, Abraham did not have the multitudinous offspring that God had said would appear. Only Ishmael existed, the boy who was born because Abraham and Sarai took matters into their own hands. Given these circumstances, why would Abraham do anything to please God, let alone cut off a piece of skin from one of the most vulnerable areas of his body? Embedded in God's order was a threat, as though He was anxious about Abraham's devotion, and maybe He was right. Abraham had made no altars to the Lord after Ishmael's birth, nor had he called out to God in gratitude as he did after his sojourn in Egypt. Instead, for thirteen long years he had ignored God.

But there was no pretending God was not present now, and so even if Abraham had been feeling complacent, he appeared terrified by El Shaddai's arrival. To make matters more alarming, the covenant of circumcision was clearly meant to be like the Covenant of the Parts—ritualized enactments of what could happen if there was a disagreement between God and Abraham. Both represented a kind of violent invasion, of the animal carcasses on one hand and of Abraham's body on the other. Indeed, the metaphor of being split is connected to God's commandment to Abraham to walk in His ways. If Abraham had indeed been divided in his loyalties, if he had strayed from God's path, then he had been living a divided life. To walk with God meant to walk with a whole heart, leaving other paths behind. If Abraham had been following the dictates of his own desire for a child, and not God's, then it was no wonder God would demand his foreskin. God was insisting that He be included in Abraham's decisions concerning his fertility.

God's new covenant, therefore, appears focused on eradicating any division between Himself and Abraham, and inside Abraham's own heart, suggesting that Abraham's attempts at self-reliance could only produce a feeling of being torn between his own inclinations and God's will. It was difficult to follow an often invisible, absent-seeming Lord. This is why another covenant had to be struck, complete with visible evidence of God's presence.

But for Abraham the act God demanded could not have been welcome. Perhaps this is why he continued to say nothing. As far as God's chosen man was concerned, it would have been far less alarming if God had set a restriction against cutting his hair, or a dietary law, or even a limit on how often he had intimate relations with his wife. Unfortunately for Abraham, these would all be later strictures God would impose to help His people remember Him and their own identity. To change Abram into Abraham, God required something more drastic than a simple change of lifestyle. If God wanted a more faithful, more obedient servant, He knew that He had to target Abraham's source of potency, anxiety, and pride.

Some modern readers miss the weight of God's words, however, arguing that circumcision simply reflected the hygienic concerns of the ancient Israelites and that medical issues were probably the anthropological origins for the practice. It is true that other Near Eastern peoples practiced circumcision during this era—more than one mummy has been found to be circumcised.[6] But entirely pragmatic explanations fall short of comprehending the complexities of the power struggle between God and His chosen man.

Certainly, circumcision would demonstrate Abraham's obedience to God, an important point if God was truly worried about

Abraham's fidelity. But it is easy to wonder, as the church father Paul did many centuries later, why there had to be an actual incision of the flesh. Paul saw the act of circumcision as "nothing," writing that God's initial promises were made to Abram before he was circumcised. What was important, Paul argued, was the inner man. He wrote, "Circumcision is that of the heart, in the spirit, and not in the letter."[7]

In fact, this is one of the most profound innovations Paul made when he converted people to his brand of Judaism, which has come down to us as Christianity, and it is one reason he was such a successful missionary. If the heart and the spirit could be circumcised, or dedicated to God, then the Gentiles could keep their foreskins. Paul took it one step further, arguing that Jesus welcomed the circumcised and the uncircumcised, and so no one needed to endure any physical indignities to follow God. This declaration made it far easier for a man to join the church than to become a traditional Jew.

Abraham's experience suggests that God, or at least the God of the Hebrew Bible, had a different point of view. Before He and Abraham could move forward, He needed a tangible demonstration of commitment. If a declaration of a pure heart or of true love and devotion had been enough for Him, He would have asked for that instead. Still, it is puzzling that God waited until now to make this demand. If circumcision was so important to Him, why had He not required it years before? Indeed, it was only after Abraham fathered Ishmael that God thought to appropriate control of the male sex organ. This strange timing suggests that God believed Abraham had been too hasty in pursuing his desire for a child.

On the other hand, God had never condemned the birth of this baby. As we have already seen, He foretold Ishmael's future to Hagar with a certain amount of relish. Yet His intervention at this moment in the story makes it seem likely that God did not want such an independent act of reproduction to happen again, at least not now. Once Abraham was circumcised, his sexuality would become a symbol of his fealty to God, and this would be a new, more powerful symbol of devotion, as circumcision required more of Abraham than the traditional sacrifice of animals. This time Abraham had to surrender a part of himself.

Of course, it is possible to view circumcision as a demonstration of divine power, with the story becoming oedipal in nature—father and son trapped in an eternal wrestling match for dominance. Accordingly, God's commandment can be interpreted as a warning to Abraham not to rebel against his father.[8]

However, it is not necessary to view this story solely in Freudian terms. If God was interested in creating, or "fathering," a new man, His demand for Abraham's foreskin could also be a symbol of their stronger relationship. When Abram gave a piece of his flesh to God and was, figuratively speaking, reborn as Abraham, he would be demonstrating an irrevocable allegiance. It was this loyalty and closeness to God that would make Abraham new.

Many Jewish theologians support this principle and add that circumcision is meant to be a spiritual instrument that places reproduction squarely in the hands of God. According to this interpretation, during the most intimate human act, God's presence is unavoidable. By giving up part of the organ that controls human fertility, Abram would make the statement that his penis was no longer entirely his own to do with as he wanted, and neither were his children. As Klinghoffer writes, "Traditionally . . . *brit milah* [the covenant of circumcision] is performed in public, in daylight. The reason is that what a man does with his penis is not just his business. It is everyone's business. At the very beginning of life, a Jewish male's sex organ is exposed before his community and cut, signifying that the community has an interest in his sexual future."[9]

This helps explain why God says that the act of circumcision is to be "an everlasting pact" among Himself, Abraham, and Abraham's offspring. God's mark on each man would be invisible to others except in an intimate setting. But it would also be inescapable. Women who had relations with uncircumcised men, or men who were not Israelites, were condemned. And each man would understand that with his circumcision came blessings and responsibilities. There could be no release from one's relationship to the divine.

To support this argument, Maimonides suggested that a man's sexual pleasure was also lessened after circumcision, and thus it was easier for a circumcised man to control his lust and think of God. This seems a quiet admission, for once, that even Abraham had difficulty controlling his sexual drive. Seen in this light, circumcision can be viewed as a God-given tool in man's struggle to master his instincts.[10]

But the question of obedience remained. If Abraham did comply with God's wishes, circumcising himself and the men and boys in his household, would the covenant hold? Would God change His ways and make good on His promises? If God did give him another son, Abraham's life would become far more complicated. What would happen to his beloved Ishmael if he had more children?

Abraham and God's relationship did not seem particularly promising. Abraham remained prostrate in the dirt, listening to God's words in mute resignation. A new life as a new man seemed a long way off.

———◆———

CHAPTER TWENTY

SARAH AND GOD

God had not forgotten about Sarai. She may have made her peace with being the woman in the background and she may have decided that she was not meant to be the mother of her husband's child, but God would soon reveal that He had kept His eye trained on her for years.

Thus, while Abraham continued to lie facedown, God suddenly brought up Sarai, informing the patriarch that his first wife also needed a new name, Sarah. This new name was not a tremendous departure from Sarai, as both essentially mean "princess." The only difference between them is that Sarai can be translated as "*my* princess," suggesting that Sarai was owned either by her husband or by her tribe, whereas Sarah has no such implication.[1] It seems God no longer wanted Sarai to be known simply in relation to her husband or her people. Her new name would allow her to be "recognized generally" as a woman of independent stature.[2]

Like the transition from Abram to Abraham, Sarai's name change would result from the simple addition of the letter *hei*. This was a clever sleight of hand on God's part. Although adding the same letter to both Abram's and Sarai's names might seem trivial, it was actually a provocative way of connecting the two to each other and to God. Because *hei* does not actually make a sound like an *a* or an *s* and is instead a forced exhale, not unlike our own *h,* the newly minted Abraham and Sarah would each have to add an extra breath every time they spoke their partner's new name. Breath has long been associated with prayer and meditation, as well as with God's name. In fact, many scholars have suggested that the root of God's mysterious name Yahweh is "to breathe."[3] Some traditions have even said that human inspiration is literally caused by God's breath. This idea persists in English, as one of the original meanings of the word "inspiration" is "to breathe in."

After many years of being married, therefore, husband and wife would be forced to remember the Lord each time they called each other. At the same time, they would be jarred out of old habits. It might seem small, a fresh appellation for one's spouse, but it is always difficult to break the customs of a life spent together, especially because such customs generally help people manage the difficult feelings and memories that accumulate over time. Thus, with the names God bestowed on His couple came another implicit mandate: to consider each other from a fresh standpoint.

However, the prospect of gaining perspective on his marriage must have seemed easier said than done to Abraham, who remained silent while God came to the most extraordinary part of His declaration. "I will bless [Sarah]," He declared. "Indeed I will give you a son by her. I will bless her so that she shall give rise to nations; rulers of people shall issue from her" (Gen. 17:16).

This was the most specific pronouncement God had made to Abraham about his legacy. Abraham could not know that these words would resound throughout history, since this was the prophecy that would ultimately give rise to the Jewish people: Sarah's son would father Jacob, and Jacob's twelve sons would found the twelve tribes that would constitute the Israelites. But there was an irony here, as God made this announcement only *after* Hagar had given birth to Ishmael. Indeed, the fact that Abraham already had a child made this declaration oddly disturbing, as though Sarah's baby was meant to compete with Hagar's. Everything would have been far easier if only God had revealed this information before Abraham slept with Hagar, but perhaps God had not wanted to do anything that would have impeded the birth of Ishmael.

As for Abraham, he finally interrupted God's speech "and laughed." After so many years of waiting, his reaction was not all that surprising. As Maimonides wrote, "This was certainly something to laugh about: it was totally astonishing."[4] After his hilarity subsided, Abraham muttered, "Can a child be born to a man a hundred years old, or can Sarah bear a child at ninety?" (17:17).

Talking to himself in front of God and laughing at God's words were actually rather shocking things to do. According to the rules of the time, it was considered disrespectful to smile or laugh around those who wielded more power. A person of lower status had to be unfailingly deferential and thankful for the overlord's gifts. What Abraham should have done, therefore, was declare gratitude. But instead he exclaimed, "O that Ishmael might live by your favor!"(17:18). These are the first and only words Abraham spoke to God during this encounter and they demonstrate Abraham's loyalty to his firstborn son. He had not protested over the name changes or even the circumcision. Rather, it was Ishmael who mattered to him.

Oddly, God did not respond to this outburst and continued to give more details about Sarah's incipient pregnancy, none of which Abraham gave any appearance of caring about. This is not surprising. God's chosen man had endured more than fifty years of empty-seeming pledges — he had arrived in the Promised Land and found it inhabited; famine struck; Sarai had not had a child — and so it would have been strange if he had jumped at this new pronouncement. Besides, he loved his real son, not the child of God's vague proclamations.

Abraham's question about Ishmael and his skepticism about God's plan suggest the patriarch's willingness to challenge God — an idea that contradicts the conventional reading of this tale. For instance, Rashi writes that when Abraham laughed, he "had faith and rejoiced."[5] But aside from laughing, Abraham showed no other signs of happiness. He did not stand up to greet God's announcement with joy or start piling up stones to make an altar. If he had nodded quietly or uttered a prayer of gratitude, it would be easier to argue that he unequivocally accepted God's pronouncements. This would also be true if he had laughed but not inquired about Ishmael. But to laugh in God's face and then ask about his firstborn son implies that Abraham questioned God's credibility, as well as the overall good judgment of His plan. And why wouldn't he? How could he welcome this news when he already had a son whose fate would be endangered by the arrival of a new boy?

Besides, it was ludicrous to imagine an old man and an old woman having a baby. Sarah was ninety and he was one hundred. Even though they would both live for many more years, they were beyond the age of conception. Certainly, Sarai was postmenopausal (18:11). Thus, God would have to restore Sarai's fertility and enhance Abraham's masculinity as well as help them achieve some sort of rapprochement. In fact this reconnection may well have been what He had in mind when He told Abraham to change their names. Maybe a new identity for both partners would help matters along.

Still, for Abraham, the prospect of taking Sarah to bed as though she were a bride and he an eager, virile groom could only seem absurd. It was difficult to picture convincing Sarah to make love again. Even if he told her about God's new promise, why would she believe him? They were going to need more than new names to renew their romance. First, they would have to desire each other. Second, they would have to believe they were young enough to create a baby. Third, they would have to act on this belief. Either way, this kind of intimacy would be a miracle after the years of bitterness they had endured.

Ultimately, then, whether Abraham was laughing at his own inability to create a child or Sarah's or God's, God was clearly struck by Abraham's response, since, in an interesting twist, He would see to it that this laughter would be passed down to the next generation. "You will name your son, Isaac, or Laughter," He declared (17:19).

Although God may have meant these words as an olive branch, illustrating that He understood Abraham's fears and forgave him, it is also possible that His own sense of humor suddenly emerged. Even God might find it funny that an old man and woman would have a baby. A more sinister interpretation, however, is that God may have seen nothing humorous in any of these events and intended Isaac's name to serve as a chastening reminder to Abraham of his skepticism. As usual, His intentions were opaque.

AFTER DESCRIBING SARAH'S future child, God finally relieved Abraham's suspense. Ishmael would also be "blessed," He said, and would grow up to be the "father of twelve chieftains" (17:20). He would not only survive the advent of Isaac, but would go on to flourish as the leader of his own nation. God was emphatic that Ishmael would have a share in His legacy and in that of his father, Abraham. Like Isaac, Ishmael would spread the seed of God, but he would not have to abide by the covenant Sarah's son would have to keep. Truly, he would be a free man, as he would be liberated from the obligations that would rest on his brother's shoulders.[6]

Yet despite God's intentions that each son would receive His blessing, history has not respected His wishes. Rashi represents the traditional Jewish hostility to Ishmael's descendants, the Muslims, writing, "All will hate [Ishmael] and attack him."[7] Ishmael would have no place in the future of God's chosen family, the newly created Abraham and Sarah, because Ishmael was conceived *before* Abram was circumcised.[8] Of course, as we have seen, this is an entirely erroneous reading of God's words. At no point does God say that Ishmael should surrender his claims to his father's legacy. Instead, He repeatedly refers to Ishmael as Abraham's rightful son and makes it clear that Ishmael will found a great nation in his own right.

If, despite God's efforts to be inclusive and evenhanded, His words have been interpreted in a divisive, even prejudicial way, it is in large part because of the many mistakes Abraham made with the women in his life. His inability to mediate between them brought about their initial conflict, which would soon erupt into a far more serious struggle. Even if he should have resisted sleeping with Hagar—a stance that generally serves an anti-Ishmael agenda—after this crucial act Abraham did not protect Hagar from Sarai's abuse, nor Sarai from Hagar's cruel teasing. Many years earlier, he had not sheltered Sarai from Pharaoh.[9] Far from being the pious and loving father of monotheism, therefore, Abraham treated both Hagar and Sarai with a disturbing selfishness and insensitivity that would in turn provoke centuries of animosity among his descendants. Even worse, his difficulties with the women would result in the displacement of a beloved little boy who had spent the first thirteen years of his life as the apple of his father's eye.

WHEN ABRAHAM HEARD God's blessings for Ishmael, he must have known that the old jealousies between his wives would be renewed if Sarah had a baby. Once he stood up and started things in motion, Abraham would be embarking on an entirely new relationship with his first wife, a bond that would now necessarily exclude Hagar. This was potentially exciting, as there was the promise of another child, but there was the threat of tremendous loss as well. Given the characters of the two women, their truce would inevitably come to an end. Thus, it is no wonder Abraham did not move, but stayed flat on the sand while God spoke. He knew there was trouble ahead.

God must have known this, too. Indeed, it is easy to wonder why God, who was presumably an expert on human nature, would want to introduce a second baby into this family. Sarah, Hagar, and their children would undoubtedly compete for Abraham's favor. Even

Abraham, who by definition should have wanted as many sons as possible, had made it clear that he did not particularly want Sarah to have a child and ruin the peace of his home; instead, he wanted Ishmael to thrive. At this point, then, it seems puzzling that God did not let Sarah stay barren. She appeared to have accepted her fate, and if she had not and was still suffering, her pain would spare countless generations the tragic legacy of division.

However, God remained dedicated to Sarah, although it is not at all clear why. Those Jews who have attempted to discern God's motives have all too often resorted to blame and hate, arguing that Ishmael was inadequate and could not carry the weight of Isaac's mission or that Hagar was unworthy to be the mother of a chosen son.[10] Christians also depict Ishmael as the son who does not deserve God's blessing. According to Paul, Abraham's eldest son is a symbol of the Jews who have forfeited their right to Abraham's patrimony because they have closed their hearts to the truth of Christ's word.[11] Isaac, on the other hand, as the rightful inheritor of God's covenant, represents Jesus. His descendants will be Christians, not those who adhere to the Law of the Torah. Naturally, Islamic thinkers disagree with this anti-Ishmael stance. They trace their lineage through Abraham's eldest son, unshaken in the belief that Hagar was selected by God to bear the child of the promise.

It has been difficult for the human imagination to conceive of both of Abraham's sons as blessed or to believe that both mothers were elected by God. And so although God's timing is somewhat controversial, it is human limitation, rather than God's will, that has created the family quarrel between Muslims and Jews, and Muslims and Christians. Each side tends to perceive the "other" son as unnecessary and, worse, as a hindrance to their own candidate's claim of primacy.

One of the reasons this divide seems unbridgeable is that it is based on emotional positions that have little to do with the original

Biblical text. All three religions stumble over the idea of the two boys' sharing Abraham's legacy, in part because of the problematic belief that only one child could inherit Abraham's crown and also because of a troubling, overriding desire for a single inheritance rather than a multilayered tradition.

However, religious leaders who hold such opinions need to reconsider their positions. Abraham did not have a crown, a throne, or a kingdom. Isaac would inherit the Promised Land, but Ishmael would become a great nation. The world was large enough that the boys never had to fight over territory. Ishmael and his descendants would migrate toward Egypt and, even after centuries had passed, never contested the ownership of Canaan. Isaac and his descendants roamed farther north and rarely had contact with Ishmael's children.

This legacy, then, was broader than land or scepter. Abraham bequeathed to his sons a blessing and a covenant—intangible but limitless commodities, since both stemmed from Abraham's intimate relationship with God. As a result, anyone and everyone could benefit from Abraham's inheritance; he could be the father of the world precisely because he had no empire to pass along. Any follower of Ishmael would receive God's protection; any follower of Isaac would benefit from God's covenant. All they had to do was commit to a relationship with Abraham's God and not allow the pagan gods who crowded their neighbors' lives and lands to seduce them with their charms.

AFTER GOD HAD REASSURED Abraham about Ishmael's future, He announced that Isaac would be born in a year. In the silence that ensued, Abraham had the opportunity to reflect on the challenges that lay ahead. Soon he would have to call Sarah by her new name and then, somehow, consummate their union. Would she consent to embrace him? How would Hagar accept this turn of events? As usual, God had not given him any directions. He had made sweeping proclamations and then left before Abraham could ask Him how to proceed.

It should come as no surprise, then, that Abraham made up his mind to concentrate on the task of circumcision first. Daunting as it might be, it was a male ritual and had nothing to do with love affairs, at least not directly.

———◆———

CHAPTER TWENTY-ONE

GOD THE FATHER

Although he did not appear particularly eager to launch himself back into a relationship with Sarah, Abraham should have been grateful that God had preserved a hands-off policy regarding his estranged wife and had decided to leave it up to Abraham to make Sarah pregnant, a generous act for a deity of the ancient world.

Indeed, God's preservation of a sexual boundary between humans and the divine was actually an important precedent in the world of the gods. A Sumerian deity would not have hesitated to mate with a human female. Egyptian divines, or at least the Pharaohs, who were considered gods, famously lusted after women. And of course the Greeks were famous for their immortals' sexual adventures with mortal men and women: Zeus fathered Helen of Troy; Aphrodite was the mother of Aeneas. There were a plethora of hybrid Greeks who were half mortal, half divine.

Even in the Bible, there was a strange race of people, the Nephilim, who were the product of divine-human unions (Gen. 6:4). God disapproved of these demigods and destroyed them in the Flood, making it clear that He did not countenance the mating of divine and mortal.[1] Of course, the advent of Jesus would render the human father irrelevant once again, but for now, God was content to let Abraham father his own child with only a little help from Himself. The Flood had been His attempt to redelineate the boundaries between human and divine and He was not going to ruin things now.

Thus, God's insistence that Abraham father Sarah's child can be seen as reassuring. He would not be the sort of god who tangled with human women. This is an implicit announcement of where He stood in the sexual politics of the era's divines. He would intervene in fertility issues only by bestowing His blessing and nothing more. However, faced with the difficulties that lay ahead, Abraham may have wished that God would climb into bed with Sarah and make the miracle happen Himself.

His Canaanite neighbors would have sympathized with Abraham's sentiments. Neither the Canaanites nor the Egyptians would have been impressed with God's respect for the dignity of Sarah and Abraham, nor His reliance on Abraham to impregnate his own wife. If an important woman like Sarah could not get pregnant, her God was clearly impotent.

This was an understandable prejudice in the ancient world. For example, the father of the Canaanite gods, El, was so notable for his virility that Canaanite poetry described his penis in graphic, very human terms:

> El, his rod sinks.
> El, his love-staff droops,
> He raises, he shoots skyward.
>
> . . .
>
> The women are El's wives,
> He bends, their lips he [kis]ses.
>
> . . .
>
> As he kisses, they conceive,
> As he embraces they become pregnant.[2]

Of course, poems like this do not mean that the gods' involvement in sex entirely precluded the human male's role. Rather, the gods' blessing might well have been seen as the necessary component in human conception. The most interesting point, however, is that the God of the Bible is never referred to in such explicitly sexual terms. In fact, unlike El, God did not seem to possess a penis, or at least it was hidden from human view. And while El was often depicted with a "long flowing beard," any physical characteristics that might identify Abraham's God as definitively male are absent in the Bible, although the pronoun that refers to God is always masculine.[3] This lack of a body, particularly the genitalia, was meant to be one of the distinguishing characteristics of the Biblical God. Later, God's second commandment to Moses would prohibit the creation of graven images, emphasizing God's identity as a transcendent, spiritual being, or so the modern world has liked to believe.

But this does not fit the role He played in the lives of Abraham and Sarah or, for that matter, in the lives of many of the Biblical figures who lived after the first patriarch and matriarch. At no point in the Hebrew Bible does God seem particularly intangible, although He always retained His air of mystery. Indeed, although the idea that God did not have an actual body is supposed to be one of the cardinal elements of the religion Abraham passed on to his children, the principle of a god without physical form was such an alien idea to the ancient world that many scholars argue that Abraham and his family assumed God had a body of some sort and that the notion of a fully spiritual being was of much later origin. As Harvard professor James Kugel writes, "The Bible's prohibition of image making did not derive from any notion that God had no physical form — the God of Old, numerous texts imply, did indeed have some kind of physical being."[4] The reason for the second commandment, Kugel argues, is that God's physical form was unsteady and unpredictable and therefore could not be housed in the permanent stone of an icon. He explains, "God may be conceived to have a body, but it is not a consistent presence."[5]

That the ancient world conceived of God in physical terms is suggested by one of the earliest verses in the Bible, "God made man in His own image" (1:26–7). Although this verse is often interpreted figuratively—God gave humankind some of His spiritual attributes, such as the soul—the implication is there: God had to have some kind of form on which to base His creation. If humankind looked like God, then God looked like humans. Certainly, since He kept appearing to people, He had to have a physical form or at least the ability to assume a human shape. After all, Abraham, Hagar, and in later years Jacob, Manoah, Joshua, and many others "saw" God. In fact, in many cases, they thought God was a fellow human before He revealed His identity.[6]

Even the prophets who lived many years after Abraham and Moses had visions of God in human form, but the reports they brought back from this experience were vague and did not focus on His appearance. When Isaiah and Daniel saw God, for instance, His body was draped in robes (Isa. 6:1–2; Dan. 7:9–10). Only Ezekiel gazed upon the naked midsection of God, where he saw "a gleam of amber—what looked like fire encased in a frame" (Ezek. 1:26).[7] Although Ezekiel used metaphorical language to record his vision, Jewish students were traditionally warned against reading his words, as they were apparently too shocking for the unschooled mind. It is unclear if this was because Ezekiel saw God's genitals. What we do know is that for many centuries Ezekiel was regarded as a kind of X-rated prophet, since most people believed that only the truly faithful would be able to translate the potentially erotic elements of his vision into an inspirational meditation on God's nature.[8]

Provocative as Ezekiel's prophecies might have been to the ancient world, his account now seems rather tame and quite confusing. Indeed, if this is the most explicit view the reader receives of God, it pales compared to other Near Eastern traditions. El was not the only ancient god whose male attributes were lovingly depicted by his followers. Sumerian and Egyptian artists carved naked images of their gods so that anyone could pick up a statue, study the god's anatomy, and examine his masculine attributes.

In addition, there were many stories and poems about the gods that emphasized their sexuality. One famous Sumerian tale with which Abraham and Sarah were probably familiar attributed the creation of the river Tigris to the masturbation of the god Enki, who ejaculated into the empty banks of the river until he flooded its walls with his semen. Then he used his penis as a shovel to create the famous channels that farmers used to irrigate their fields.[9]

The Biblical God never did such things. But Abraham and Sarah would not have considered His restraint a sign of the lack of a physical body. Instead, it is likely they thought God simply *refrained* from using His sexuality, a far more complicated idea than the principle of incorporeality.

One explanation for God's refusal to use His sexual powers is that this was one of the ways Abraham and Sarah knew their God was different from other divines. On a more emotional level, God's refusal to act as a human lover and His discretion surrounding His masculinity helped create His image as God the Father. This idea is reinforced by the Bible's emphatic lesson that it was dangerous to gaze upon the father's loins, whether the father was divine or mortal.

As we have seen in the story of Noah's son Ham, who "uncovered" his father's nakedness, this act was so taboo that Ham's descendants were cursed for eternity. Ham's brothers, on the other hand, reaped their father's blessings, as they covered Noah and did not look at his naked body (Gen. 9:21–27). Accordingly, even imagining God's nakedness could be considered a lethal act of disrespect.[10]

Of course, other religions of the ancient world conceived of their gods as mothers and fathers. But God's insistence on keeping His naked body shielded from the eyes of His followers created a different relationship between humanity and the divine, one that was at once more remote and more intimate. This was a God who would not sleep with His followers but instead would behave like a true parent, looking after their safety and advising them about their mistakes.

Still, the Noah story invites the question: Why should looking at a father's nakedness be worthy of a curse? And why would beholding God's masculinity be so threatening to Abraham and his descendants?[11]

At first glance, the notion of a sexually potent male divinity was too threatening to consider. Of course, this was precisely what other ancient peoples had had to endure for centuries, but they had other deities they could turn to for help—Hera could rescue Zeus's victims. Baal could temper El's excesses. But God was not part of a pantheon. As a single deity, He was the all-powerful, and so there was no recourse for human beings. If God chose to behave like other divines and father children, then human husbands would have no way of guarding against His incursions. For that matter, nor would women, as at any moment they might face divine sexual aggression. In a flash, God could potentially render human virility superfluous and human femininity vulnerable.

Certainly, God's proclamation that Sarah would become pregnant after years of barrenness trained a spotlight on Abraham's helplessness and God's dominance. Even in His role as Father, God was more of a "man" than Abraham. Sarah's inability to conceive—whether because of her infertility or his old age—had been a condition that Abraham could neither heal nor end. God, not Abraham, was in charge of fertility. He may have decided not to play the role of lover, but until He chose to intervene, Sarah would not get pregnant.

Although Abraham might well have been relieved at the thought of God taking over his marital duties, for Sarah, the idea of surrendering to the lust of a divine being was probably not inviting. William Butler Yeats attempted to capture what such an experience would have been like in his poem "Leda and the Swan," where he imagined the experience of a mortal woman seized by Zeus in disguise.

A sudden blow: the great wings beating still
Above the staggering girl, her thighs caressed
By the dark webs, her nape caught in his bill,

He holds her helpless breast upon his breast.
How can those terrified vague fingers push
The feathered glory from her loosening thighs?[12]

However, the act of conception with her husband did not seem to appeal to Sarah either. When Abraham returned to the campsite after his vision, he found his wife going about her business with no suspicion of what lay ahead. She did not race to greet him, but neither did he rush to tell her what God said. Instead he summoned the men to prepare for the moment when God's involvement in their lives became irrefutable.

Despite the multiple dimensions to God's commandment, at this juncture, when Abraham stood with his knife sharpened, there was no escaping the fact that circumcision was a kind of injury. The Bible itself depicts its shadow side. For instance, after an uncircumcised, non-Israelite man raped Abraham and Sarah's great-granddaughter Dinah, her brothers would use the ritual as a tool of revenge. They demanded that all the men in the tribe of the rapist be circumcised as a pledge of brotherhood to the Israelites. The tribe complied in good faith, but while they were recovering, Dinah's brothers attacked and killed them all. Circumcision had rendered the foreign men so weak they could not defend themselves. They had been successfully unmanned.[13]

Those who unquestioningly revere Abraham's piety argue that Abraham recognized the injurious implications of God's commandment and relished the prospect of subordinating himself to God. Some scholars even say that circumcision allows a man to consider himself female in relation to the male God. As the historian Howard Eilberg-Schwartz writes, "What makes an Israelite man into God's beautiful female lover is his circumcision."[14]

According to this way of thinking, the symbolic feminization that occurred during circumcision removed any possibility of viewing the love between God and the patriarch as homosexual. Depicting the passion between divine and human as a male-male affair was troubling to many of the devout, both in the ancient and modern world. So troubling, in fact, that it was preferable to depict Abraham as female rather than as engaged in a homosexual affair with the divine. Thus the Midrash compared the uncircumcised Abraham to a gorgeous woman with one flaw:

> Thus the king said to her, "You have no defect except that the nail of your little finger is slightly too long; pare it and the defect will be gone." So said God to Abraham, "You have no blemish except this foreskin. Remove it and the defect will be gone."[15]

Whether or not Abraham would think of himself as a woman once he was circumcised, a fascinating principle of devotion has flourished in many Jewish and Christian circles: the idea that a man should "unman" himself in testimony to his love for God. This might be a problematic thought for some, but it is a devout and absorbing one for others. Lest one think that this idea was confined to the ancient world of the Israelites or early followers of Jesus, a modern Christian poet declares,

> *Annul me in my manhood, Lord, and make*
> *Me woman-sexed and weak,*
> *If by that total transformation*
> *I might know Thee more.*
> *What is the worth of my own sex*
> *That the bold possessive instinct*
> *Should but shoulder Thee aside?*
> *What uselessness is housed in my loins,*
> *To drive, drive, the rampant pride of life,*
> *When what is needful is a hushed acquiescence?*
> *"The soul is feminine to God."*[16]

Though he may have inspired this ideal of "feminine" obeisance to God by hastening to fulfill God's commandment, Abraham did not actually seem to share the poet's joy at self-subordination. In fact, the difficulties that still lay between God and Abraham would center on issues of potency. His required surrender to the divine would provoke Abraham to resist God in other, less obvious ways.

At this point, however, only one sign of his rebelliousness surfaced. Abraham delayed drawing closer to Sarah. Instead of explaining his actions to her, he focused on organizing the men for the ordeal ahead. Sarah, meanwhile, was left on the outside, puzzled and excluded from the proceedings.

CHAPTER TWENTY-TWO

CIRCUMCISION

Abraham did not hesitate. He took a stone knife and pared off his foreskin and that of thirteen-year-old Ishmael. Although no trumpets blared and no angels came down from heaven, he had succeeded in enacting his own transformation. It would have been reasonable for him to pause and nurse his wound, but he turned to all of the "homeborn slaves and those that had been bought from outsiders" and circumcised them as well (Gen. 17:26–27).

The men of the camp—outsider and insider, leader and servant, man and boy—were now united. There was no mistaking what tribe they belonged to. Although other peoples practiced circumcision, they were few and far between, and this would become increasingly true over time, so that circumcision would eventually become a mark that set Jews apart. Indeed, in later times, those who were not circumcised were called *arel*, meaning "having foreskin," and were considered impure by the Israelites.[1]

Abraham's haste to fulfill God's commandment was in keeping with his past behavior. When God told him to leave Ur, he left immediately. When God said to sacrifice the animals for the Covenant of the Parts, he promptly obeyed. He was the opposite of later prophets, such as the very human Jonah, who tried to hide from

God and ended up inside a whale rather than carry out His orders. Abraham, for all his rebellious spirit, never procrastinated when it came to God's pronouncements. In fact, the contrast between his speed and God's tortoiselike methods was somewhat startling. The faster Abraham rushed to carry things out, the more ponderous God seemed to become.

This time Abraham had outdone himself, since there was a qualitative difference to the circumcision commandment. Moving from the land of his fathers into the unknown had not been easy, but adhering to this new painful demand took a different kind of bravery. Of course, Abraham was not an ordinary person, but still, the urgency with which he approached this new task suggests that he was being more than obedient. Perhaps there was something he wanted to achieve for himself.

Despite God's reassurances, Abraham could not help but worry about Ishmael's fate. It was crucial the boy be regarded as legitimate, since once Sarah had a baby, Ishmael stood the risk of being disinherited. If the lack of foreskin was going to be God's symbol of His chosen family, then it is no wonder Abraham rushed to circumcise himself and his firstborn. What better way to create an irrevocable link between father and son as well as to the divine? Abraham could not know that circumcision would also help him cure the division he felt between his living son and his soon-to-be-conceived son, and thus end much of his contention with God. But this reconciliation would, in fact, occur. Once they were circumcised, both Ishmael and Isaac would be indisputably his. The brothers and their descendants would be linked to one another, since they shared the common mark of God. As sons of Abraham, both boys would be bound by the covenant of circumcision.[2]

However, the distinction between their ages at circumcision — eight days for Isaac and thirteen years for Ishmael — pointed to an important innovation on the part of God. The other accounts of circumcision in the ancient Near East depict the practice as an adolescent ritual. Thus, when God commanded that infants should be circumcised on the eighth day, He was initiating a new custom. Isaac would be different from his brother, his father, and their pagan neighbors.[3]

The generations that came after Abraham, inspired by the alacrity with which he approached circumcision, came to regard this ritual as a spiritual as well as a physical duty. For instance, Moses ordered the faithful to "circumcise the foreskin of your heart" (Deut. 10:16), and the prophet Jeremiah complained that his listeners' ears were "uncircumcised" because their spirits were so clogged with impurities they could not hear his words (Jer. 6:10). Long before Paul's idea of the circumcised heart (Rom. 2:28–29), then, Abraham's descendants believed that one needed to approach circumcision as a soul-cleansing event. If the cut figured as a kind of brand, a mark of one's belonging to God, it could also be seen as evidence of spiritual purification.

Yet Abraham had no idea this would be the legacy he would pass on to future generations. Indeed, he would not realize the implications of his own circumcision until after the blood started to flow. God appeared, as though He had been anticipating this moment for centuries. Indeed, the Hebrew verb that announces God, *Va Yera,* means literally "He was seen," suggesting that He allowed Abraham to view Him, though there is no record that Abraham saw God's actual shape. Instead, what is important about this verb is that it underlines the sudden intimacy that had arisen between God and His chosen man. Before this, the closest glimpse Abraham had gotten of the divine was the eerie light that appeared during the Covenant of the Parts.

The suddenness of God's entrance cannot be overestimated. As we have seen in their last exchange, when Abraham—or, actually, Abram—had interrogated God about Ishmael's future and refused to rejoice wholeheartedly in the news of Isaac's imminent arrival, God and man had seemed more adversaries than friends. Now it seemed that the swiftness with which Abraham had performed the circumcision, as well as the circumcision itself, had wrought a miracle. Rather than His typical game of cat and mouse—thirteen years of silence and then a sudden thunderous arrival—God stepped right into Abraham's presence. Even more surprising, He did not issue any orders or impart any divine information. Apparently, He just wanted to be close to His chosen man.

The Bible uses only one sentence to describe this event: "The Lord appeared to him by the terebinths of Mamre; he was sitting at the entrance of the tent as the day grew hot" (Gen. 18:1). The early rabbis were so struck by this passage that they composed countless stories and treatises on the meaning of each word. Rashi cites one scholar who says God appeared "to enquire after the state of [Abraham's] health." This tradition has persisted, so that today the Jewish principle of *bikkur holim,* the virtue of visiting the sick, is traced back to this Biblical verse. Even the fact that Abraham remained sitting was considered significant. Rashi writes, "[Abraham] wished to rise, but the Holy One, blessed be He, said to him, Sit and I will stand."[4]

This tradition of interpretation emphasizes Abraham's weakened physical condition, a state that could easily have prompted a vision of the Lord, especially since the heat of the day would have intensified any symptoms from blood loss, pain, and exhaustion. Moreover, God was being inordinately respectful of Abraham's vulnerable state. The two did not speak about any important business, and this must have been a relief. At least temporarily, the struggle between God and His favorite had been laid to rest. Abraham did not beg God to tell him when He was going to fulfill His promises. And for the first time in God's history with humankind, He did not command or punish anyone. For a moment, He, too, could rest.

It is not immediately obvious why circumcision changed the relationship between Abraham and God so profoundly. Neither party's agenda had changed. God still wanted Sarah to have her baby. Abraham was still devoted to Ishmael and suspicious of the new infant's arrival. Yet Abraham had acknowledged God's overwhelming importance in his life and symbolically expressed his willingness to share his role as father and husband with his own divine father. Thus God's sense of satisfaction and even gratitude spilled over into these quiet moments.

As a result, the gentler meaning to the ritual unfolded. It seems God really did want greater intimacy with both Abraham and Sarah. Once Abraham surrendered, God could give Himself in return, reinforcing the idea that He would refrain from divine trespasses and that Abraham's circumcision would act as a seal against divine intrusions.

THEIR INTERLUDE did not last long, however. Abraham suddenly saw "three men standing near him"(18:2). Like God, they materialized out of nowhere. There had been no advance notice of their approach, no telltale cloud of dust, and no warning from Abraham's scouts. It was also an odd time of day for visitors to show up, as most people did not travel in the desert during the heat of the day. In fact, Rashi says that God had made it particularly hot because He did not want His chosen man bothered by visitors during his convalescence.[5]

But Abraham was such an eager host that according to the Talmud, "he was grieved that no travelers came."[6] Welcoming newcomers and offering them respite from the rigors of travel were among the most important virtues of the ancient and medieval world and ones the commentators were sure their founding father embraced. One famous Jewish tradition says that Abraham and Sarah's tent was open on all four sides in order to help the couple spot potential visitors.[7]

When the strange trio approached Abraham, it was immediately clear there was something mysterious about the men, but well-bred and generous as he was, Abraham did not ask any questions.[8] It was his job to welcome them, so he raced to fulfill his obligations even though this meant wrenching himself away from his tranquil enjoyment of God. In fact, his haste to help the three strangers became an emblem of how one should treat his or her guests. The eighteenth-century Hasidic rabbi Aaron of Karlin wrote, "When we turn our attention from God to tend to the needs of people, we do God's will. Conversely, God is not pleased when we place such a great focus on God that we ignore needy human beings." The Talmud states, "Hospitality to wayfarers is greater than welcoming the Divine Presence."[9]

"My lords," Abraham exclaimed, "if it please you, do not go on past your servant" (18:3). He called for water so they could bathe their feet and rest in the shade of the terebinth trees. Then he offered them a "morsel of bread," bowing to them with all the graciousness he could muster (18:4–5).

Abraham's zeal is reminiscent of the speed with which he had just circumcised himself. Some say that once Abraham had experienced the healing waters of God's sympathy after his circumcision, he was better able to express concern for others. Other commentators suggest Abraham knew he was doing God's will by welcoming strangers to his household.[10]

Whatever Abraham's motivations, his behavior made it clear that he would not exact a price from travelers, nor would he order his men to attack the three men or hold them prisoner. He would take the risk of welcoming them. Selfless though his actions were, there was also a pragmatic aspect to his decision. Despite the value placed on hospitality, many tribal leaders routinely killed wayfarers, stealing their goods and protecting themselves from attack. Abraham had experienced the costs of war and did not choose violence. His strategy was to convert these new arrivals into friends before they could menace the tribe.

As the men settled themselves in the shade, Abraham hurried to his tent to look for Sarah. "Quick," he said "make cakes," and while she busied herself finding the choicest flour and mixing the oil and the honey, he "ran to the herd," chose the most tender calf to be slaughtered for a meal, and gave the calf to a lad to carve up in preparation for roasting (18:6–8).

Interestingly, Rashi writes, "This was Ishmael whom [Abraham] bade to do this in order to train him to the performance of religious duties (in this case the duty of hospitality)."[11] This story became so popular in Islamic circles that there is actually a large saucepot on display in the Topkapi museum in Istanbul that is reputed to be the vessel Ishmael and his father used to cook this famous meal.[12]

Although Ishmael is always presented reverently in the Koran — he is one of the great prophets, famous for his patience and piety — according to some Islamic tales, the boy sometimes made mistakes.[13] For instance, one tale records Ishmael's failure to help his father erect the Kaaba, the famous centerpiece of the Great Mosque. Abraham sent Ishmael to find the right boulder for the cornerstone, but Ishmael protested, saying, "Father, I feel tired and lazy." Abraham replied, "Go! No matter what you feel." But Ishmael took so long on his errand that at last the angel Gabriel intervened and brought the perfect rock, "the Black Stone." When Ishmael returned, he asked, "Father! Who has brought [the stone]?" And Abraham responded, "It was brought by one who is more active than you and never gets tired."[14]

Jewish legends add that, in this instance, "the lad" made a crucial error — he let the calf get away. When Abraham saw the animal gallop from the campsite, he charged after it. However, the calf was much faster than Abraham, who was likely slowed down by his recent circumcision and by the fact that he was one hundred years old. After scampering up and down the hilly landscape for many miles, its skinny tail receding farther and farther into the distance, the calf disappeared into a cave in one of the Hebron valleys.[15]

Although this story begins comically, it quickly assumes a more serious tone, as what appeared to be Ishmael's blunder becomes a godsend in disguise. Abraham dove after the little creature and suddenly found himself in a chamber perfumed with "the sweet fragrance of Paradise."[16] This was the Cave of Machpelah, a place Abraham would make famous a few years later. Candlelight flickered, and when he stumbled through the narrow door of the chamber, he discovered two bodies, a man and a woman lying on separate couches. Lanterns burned without going out and the entrancing smell seemed to emanate from the bodies themselves. Abraham had stumbled into a magical chamber, the hiding place of Adam and Eve.[17]

It seems no accident that Ishmael helped his father find this place, even if his assistance was inadvertent. Adam and Eve cannot be claimed by any one religion: they are the parents of Jew, Muslim, and Christian. That Abraham's eldest son, the ancestor of Mohammed, led his father to their cave is an implicit reminder of these faiths' common origins.

This encounter suggests that Abraham had to go back to his origins before he could move forward with his destiny. God had talked to His chosen man about the future and the children he would bear, but He had never mentioned his parentage or his link to the beginning of time. In the same way that Odysseus had to visit the land of the dead before he could reach home, it makes sense that Abraham had to understand his connection to the source of all humanity before he could assume the mantle of patriarch. After all, he was supposed to be the new Adam.

However, Abraham did not have much time to ponder the past. The calf lowed, the shadows lengthened, and Abraham scooped up the little animal and rushed home to feed his visitors. But as he ran through the hills of Hebron, the calf protesting and trying to kick itself free, he resolved that someday he would find a way to purchase this cave for himself. It had been difficult to leave this beautiful place.

Back at the campsite, Abraham slaughtered the calf. As the meat roasted over a low fire, its aroma filled the air. Meanwhile, he prepared a yogurtlike dish of milk curd and poured fresh milk to drink. Truly, this would be a meal fit for a king. Only a very rich man could offer such a banquet, but Abraham was not interested in proving his wealth or his power. Instead, once the calf was done, he himself "waited on" the strangers while they ate and lounged in the shade of the trees. This was an extraordinary effort for a tribal leader, not to mention an old man who had just endured a self-circumcision and a noontime jog through the dry foothills of Hebron.[18]

After their meal, the strangers turned to him and, instead of expressing their gratitude for his generosity, asked him, "Where is your wife, Sarah?" This was an unusual question. Men did not generally ask about other men's wives. Besides, how did they know her name? This could easily have been perceived as a threatening gesture, and Abraham would have been well within his rights if he had chosen not to answer. But instead of trying to protect himself or Sarah, he pointed them to Sarah's tent.

Perhaps as a reward for his trust or perhaps out of impatience that Abraham had not yet told Sarah himself, the moment they knew where she was, the strangers made it clear they were messengers from God. "Your wife Sarah shall have a son!" one of them declared (18:10).

This time Abraham did not laugh. In fact, he did not say anything at all. He had already heard about the miracle baby, and he had just circumcised his firstborn. Ishmael was safely part of the family now, and Abraham could worry less about his fate. But Sarah, who had crept to the entrance of her tent to hear her husband's conversation with the strangers, "laughed" just like her husband had (18:12).

However, Sarah's astonishment took a different turn than her husband's. "Now that I am withered," she muttered to herself, "am I to have enjoyment—with my husband so old?" (18:12). The English translation of Sarah's Hebrew makes her words sound far more polite than they really were. The Hebrew word *ednah*, which is usually translated as "enjoyment," actually has a pointedly sexual connotation, as it means "abundant moisture."[19] So, while Abraham had wondered how they could have a child when he was one hundred years old and she was ninety, Sarah focused on the act of intercourse. How could her elderly husband be potent? How could she have sexual pleasure again?

Before she could say anything else, God spoke abruptly. "Why did Sarah laugh?" He demanded. Abraham had no answers for God, as he had not actually heard Sarah's voice. So God continued, saying something very tactful but also somewhat shocking. He lied about what Sarah had said, misquoting her as saying, "Shall I in truth bear a child, old as I am?"—these words were in accord with Abraham's own sense of wonder and also protected his dignity by not revealing Sarah's doubts about his potency (18:13). In His defense, the rabbis argued, "Sometimes truth has to be compromised to maintain love and harmony between husband and wife."[20]

God went on to ask, "Is anything too wonderful for the Lord?" suggesting that not only could He lie with impunity but also that any questioning of Abraham's virility was a challenge of God's powers (18:14).

Sarah, however, knew that God had just covered up the truth and that His uncharacteristic bluster could well be an attempt to conceal His own falsehood. Although she was the only one who was aware of this, she did not correct Him. Instead, she denied her previous action: "I did not laugh," she declared. The conventional interpretation of Sarah's disclaimer is that she was so terrified she wanted to take back her words so that God would not be angry with her. But it also seems possible that she was asserting her own will in the face of the divine Lord. If God was going to utter a lie, then she would, too, even though she was "frightened." After all, she understood she could not undermine His authority directly by telling Abraham what she had really said, but she could still let God know she had noticed His misrepresentation of her words. God, however, did not acknowledge any misdeed on His part and instead took issue with her, saying, "You did laugh" (18:13–15).

In many ways, God and Sarah sound like an old married couple bickering over who said what. But this was the first and only time God spoke directly to Sarah. Compared to the long conversation He had had with Hagar at the well, this exchange seems brief and a little prickly. In addition, it is odd that He chose to ask Abraham about Sarah's laughter instead of speaking to her from the start.

Perhaps He was following a rule of the ancient world that said married women should not be addressed directly or that one should talk to their husbands first. Or perhaps He felt she did not require as much attention as Hagar, since she was the powerful wife of a tribal leader, not a helpless servant woman.

As for Abraham, he had not been aware that either Sarah or God was listening to his conversation with the angels or that his wife and deity were engaged in a negotiation at his expense. Despite the brevity of the exchange, there was an intimacy about God and Sarah's quarrel that suggested a connection to each other that excluded him. God had just found out something Abraham did not know—Sarah had wondered how her husband could have sex with her—and Sarah had just witnessed God lying about her words.

Moreover, it seems strange that God would be offended by Sarah's laughter. It had not mattered to Him when Abraham had laughed at His announcement of Isaac's birth. Of course, in those days, a woman's questioning masculine potency was far less acceptable than a man's doubts about his wife's fertility, so perhaps God's rewording of her statement was less to protect Abraham than to assert that He was the one who oversaw these affairs.

But the shared secret between God and Sarah could also suggest that God had not been bothered by Sarah's words and that His response was a kind of smoke screen that hid another meaning. He needed Sarah to love and trust Him just as much as she needed Him to open her womb. Thus, the words they uttered were like the slippery vows exchanged by adulterous lovers, since they were meant to insulate Abraham from their intimacy. After all, God did not want to do anything to endanger the already precarious relationship between husband and wife. The couple had entered a new phase of their lives, and it was not at all clear how they should conduct their relationship. God knew it was important that Sarah not alienate Abraham at this point in their marriage. He wanted them to become parents, and Abraham was edgy enough about the prospect of a second child. They would never get into bed with each other if they quarreled.

Finally, there is another possible meaning here. Though God appeared to condemn Sarah for lying by declaring, "You did laugh," it is also possible that He simply wanted her to acknowledge her own happiness. At last Sarah had something to laugh about. After thirteen years of playing second fiddle to Hagar and many more years as a barren woman, it was time for Sarah to take delight in her future rather than question her good fortune. Of course she should laugh.

The angels, meanwhile, had grown restless. They had other errands to accomplish, so Abraham helped them depart, "walking with them to see them off" (18:16). Naturally, neither he nor Sarah had any clue where they were going next, but God and Sarah's strangely coded exchange about sex and male potency would actually foreshadow the terrible events that lay in the future. As for the angels, they gazed down at the valley of Siddim without saying a word (18:16). Seen from the slopes of Mamre, the cities of Sodom and Gomorrah sprawled, tiny in the distance.

CHAPTER TWENTY-THREE

THE DEBATE

The valley of Siddim was a mysterious place. Unlike Hebron, Bethel, or Shechem, other locations visited by the patriarchs, no one is sure where the valley really was. The best guess of scholars is that it was located somewhere near the Dead Sea.[1] The Bible tells us that this valley was where the kings of the plain banded together to fight Abraham. We also know that it was lush and fertile, a tempting place to live, as this is where Lot decided to move when he split off from his uncle.

While Abraham watched the angels travel down the path to Sodom and Gomorrah, the two famous cities located in the valley, God took the opportunity to do something He had never done before and would never do again. In an eerie mirroring of Abraham and Sarah's brief soliloquies, He spoke to Himself, although, like Abraham and Sarah, He used a stage whisper to make it clear that He wanted someone to hear His quandary. "Shall I hide from Abraham what I am about to do?" He worried (Gen. 18:17).

Since the only audience for God's question was Himself, it seems that God could be divided against Himself and could therefore suffer the same anxiety as His human counterparts. Although it was not yet evident what God wanted to conceal, one cannot imagine

El or Osiris hesitating or second-guessing their decisions. But here was Abraham's God, uncertain and engaging in an internal debate.

The theological implications of such divine behavior are enormous. To begin with, in this case at least, God had not already preordained His own actions, nor was He certain of the responses of human beings. This glimpse into His psyche tells us that Abraham and Sarah's God was not the distant God of later centuries, such as the Watchmaker of the eighteenth century, who had already measured out all events, but was instead a figure who experienced inner conflict, not unlike a character from a twentieth-century existentialist novel.

Indeed, God's apparent uncertainty subverts definitions of the divine as timeless, living at once in past, present, and future. Perhaps He also lived through time like His human subjects and reacted to events as they did. If so, in this extraordinary moment of divine angst lay the origins of human freedom. Although most of the time He seemed to know exactly what would happen, there were times, like now, when it seems that He had not predetermined anyone's fate, any more than He was certain of His own actions.

At length, after brooding over the matter some more, God arrived at the conclusion that He would have to divulge His plan to Abraham. He had chosen this man to be the father of future generations and needed him to know His hidden intentions. He declared, "For I have singled him out, that he may instruct his children . . . to keep the way of the Lord by doing what is just and right" (18:19). Abraham had to know God's rationale so he could emulate His righteousness in his own role as a leader and father.

Having reached this conclusion, God suddenly cried, "The outrage of Sodom and Gomorrah is so great, and their sin so grave!" (18:20). Like any human being, God had reached His limit; He could no longer restrain His frustration with these cities. And now it became clear what His secret was. Just as He had once determined to destroy the wickedness of Noah's generation, He had made up His mind to eradicate the evil of the valley. This time, however, He was going to reveal His scheme to a human being, not to save the man's life, as with Noah, but to explain the logic of His ways.

Before this, God had never felt any impulse to explain His actions to a human being. He had imparted information to Adam, Noah, and Abraham but had never thought to include them in His thinking. In fact, it was His inscrutability that would prompt John Milton to try "to justify the ways of God to men" in his epic poem *Paradise Lost*. Now He treated Abraham as He would treat the later prophets, "disclosing His plans to him," and thereby opening a new chapter in His relationship to His creation.[2]

As for Sodom and Gomorrah, up to this point in the Bible, there had been no evidence of their waywardness. Yet God declared that the sheer enormity of their iniquity had passed all boundaries. "I will go down to see whether they have acted altogether according to the outcry that has reached Me," He said (18:21). The cry that reached him, says one of the Midrash, had come from a young woman who was hospitable to a stranger. The Sodomites were so outraged at her humane act that they "smeared her with honey" and left her to the mercy of bees that "stung her to death." Another story says that after one of Lot's daughters had taken pity on a beggar and fed him, the Sodomites burned her to death for her "crime," and God heard her anguish.[3]

However, God allowed for the possibility of false reports, saying, "If [there is no evidence of sin], I will take note" (18:21). He was a fair judge, one who would rely on facts rather than rumor and one whom sinners should fear but whom good men and women could trust.

But Abraham was still worried. Would God get carried away by His own anger? With remarkable bravery, he confronted his deity. "Will you sweep away the innocent along with the guilty?" he exclaimed. "Will you . . . not forgive [the cities] for the sake of the innocent fifty who are in it?" And he did not stop there. In his longest speech so far to God or, for that matter, to anyone, he went on, "Far be it from You to bring death upon the innocent as well as the guilty so that innocent and guilty fare alike. . . . Shall not the Judge of all the earth deal justly?" (18:24–25).

This final point was a far more challenging question than Abraham's query before he circumcised himself. (How can I, an old man, have children with my elderly wife?) And this time it was directed straight at God rather than as a muttered aside. In addition, the last time Abraham and God had had an exchange, Abraham had crouched on the ground and kept his head down. Now he stood upright and faced God directly.[4] Truly, Abram was no more.

By allowing Abraham to know His intentions, God had thought to teach His chosen man how to live in a morally upright manner, but He may not have expected to receive a lesson from Abraham. However, like a grown child whose maturity surprises his father, Abraham had some insights to offer God, ones that God seemed to value. Instead of being shocked at what could be seen as Abraham's effrontery, God responded as though He was impressed with Abraham's point, saying, "If I find within Sodom fifty innocent ones, I will forgive the whole place for their sake" (18:24).

This was breathtaking. God had just reiterated that He was not sure what He would find in the valley, and was amending His plans in response to a human being's advice. He was also continuing to model the right way for a judge to proceed. As a tribal patriarch, Abraham had often had to play this role and would have to do so again in the future. Thus, God wanted His chosen man to observe the decision-making process of an ethical leader. This included not only observing and weighing the evidence before issuing a sentence, but also listening to the counsel of wise advisers, just as God had with Abraham.

However, Abraham was not done cross-examining God. While this might seem like unforgivable insolence, God had invited this behavior by allowing Abraham to hear His logic, giving Abraham the opportunity to assert his own ideas about justice. Indeed, it is possible to view this whole episode as one of God's tests. Was Abraham truly a just man? Could he stand up for the rights of strangers?

The answer was yes. Abraham went step by step, lowering the number of innocents that would buy a reprieve to forty-five, to forty, thirty, twenty, and then finally stopped the negotiation at ten. Unfortunately, Abraham never explained why he ended here. Perhaps he decided that he had pushed his luck far enough, or maybe he believed that any number under ten could not merit saving an entire city. Whatever his reasons, ten has come down to modernity as a crucial number for the shaping of a community, especially a community of virtue, since ten is the traditional number for a *minyan*, or "the quorum for public worship," in Judaism.[5]

The revolutionary aspect of Abraham's debate with God is that he called God's capacity for both justice and mercy into doubt. This was not how you talked to gods in the ancient world. But instead of killing him on the spot, God listened to him and promised to be compassionate. This may have been because Abraham was deferential in his remarks, saying, "I who am but dust and ashes" (18:27). At any rate, both Abraham and God had accomplished their goals. God had provided Abraham with the chance to express his convictions. Unlike Noah, who remained mute when God informed him of the incipient Flood, Abraham showed that he was able to think of others. And he went even further, demanding that God obey the same ethical guidelines He had decreed for humans. As the Conservative Jewish prayer book puts it, "If God is to be obeyed when commanding moral behavior, God must exemplify that moral behavior."[6]

Incredibly, God seemed pleased. As for Abraham, whether or not he had heard God's inner debate, he had discovered that with God there was room for both negotiation and debate, because God Himself was not always sure what He was going to do. For His part, God confirmed that He believed it was His responsibility to listen and respond to the petitions of human beings.

THE ANGELS, MEANWHILE, continued down the hills of Hebron, presumably toward the Dead Sea — at 1,378 feet below sea level, the lowest point on earth. Today this region is a desert with strange white pillars of sand and limestone, and dark hollows of gravel and dust. But as we have already seen, in those days it was famous for being green and abundant.[7] The Jordan River trickled through the valley, providing water for crops, and many prosperous towns sprang up along its banks.

However, the beauty of the land masked a terrible geological reality. Buried under its rich abundance lay pits of oily tar so highly flammable that all it would take was one well-placed lightning bolt to set the entire valley on fire. Indeed, many believe that this is the natural explanation for the ultimate destruction of the famous cities.[8] Others suggest that the story is a myth to explain the barrenness of the region. There is archaeological evidence, however, that something catastrophic happened approximately four thousand years ago. The theory is that methane trapped under the earth ignited when an earthquake struck; the rock in the area liquefied in the heat and buried the cities.[9]

Some scholars suggest that the remains of Sodom and Gomorrah are in modern-day Jordan, along the eastern shore of the Dead Sea, and others theorize that they are under the sea's salty waters. Since it is impossible to know for certain, archaeologists have relied on the excavations of the Jordanian sites Bab-edh-Dhra, Safi, Feifa, and Numeira to provide insight into what the Biblical cities might have been like.[10]

Each of these ancient settlements was constructed near a wadi (ravine) of the Dead Sea and ringed by a huge stone wall with a tower on one end. There was only one wooden gate to let people in and out. All of this is fairly typical of Bronze Age sites, but there is one strange element that makes these sites distinctive. Outside the walls stretch acres of graves, each cemetery housing up to 500,000 corpses. This phenomenon may simply suggest that the area was once extremely heavily populated. But these cities do seem to share a preoccupation with their dead. The evidence suggests that many of the townspeople were stonecutters who made their living designing tombstones and other ceremonial markers. Naturally, there were other professions as well, including merchants, potters, storekeepers, farmers, and shepherds, like Abraham's nephew Lot. Still, the overwhelming focus of the cities seems to have been on commemoration, a tremendous irony given what might have happened here.

Of course, there is no obvious connection between the construction of enormous graveyards and sins. Thus those Biblical archaeologists who are intent on proving that these sites are indeed Sodom and Gomorrah point to the discovery of many luxury goods—including fine linens, jewelry, and beaded pottery—as evidence of these people's wealth, one of the most important characteristics of the Sodomites. Also, in Numeira, ancient grapes were found preserved under thousands of years of sediment at the site of an old vineyard, providing more evidence that the site is either Sodom or Gomorrah, as later in the Bible both cities are mentioned as famous wine producers.[11]

Still, the mystery of where these cities might have been should not obscure the drama of what happened next. When at last the angels entered the gates of Sodom, the first man they saw was Abraham's nephew. Lot, as befitted Abraham's close relation, immediately displayed exquisite courtesy by bowing and offering the angels the same sort of warm hospitality his uncle had shown earlier in the day. He invited them to his house, bathed their feet in water, "prepared a feast," and "baked unleavened bread" (19:3).

But while the strangers had enjoyed Abraham's meal in the quiet of his campsite, they had an entirely different experience in store at Lot's house. As they settled down to their dinner, a crowd could be heard gathering outside the house. When it grew dark, a terrible din arose. The Sodomites catcalled and shouted, screaming, "Where are the men who came to you tonight? Bring them out to us, that we may be intimate with them" (19:5). As we have seen before, English translations are generally more circumspect than the Hebrew. In this case the word the Sodomites used means "to rape."[12] In fact, this is the same verb used to describe the violence of the strangers against the Levite's concubine in Judges 19:19.

The angels continued to sit at the table, and although they could have stopped the clamor, they did not say a word. God had told them to ascertain the corruption of each individual before passing judgment on the entire city, and they needed to know if Lot was virtuous like his uncle or a sinner like the rest of the Sodomites.

Lot did not realize the elegant strangers were angels or that he was being assessed, but he did know it was his job to protect them. He jumped up from the table, went straight outside, and carefully locked the door behind him. However, when he saw all the townspeople gathered on his steps, he knew he was in a terrible predicament. His house could not withstand the onslaught of this angry crowd. If he had hoped to have a reasonable discussion with these men, he now understood this was an impossible prospect. So he made a desperate proposition: "I have two daughters who have not known a man. Let me bring them out to you, and you may do to them as you please; but do not do anything to these men, since they have come under the shelter of my roof" (19:8).

Lot's offer echoes what Abram asked Sarai to do in Egypt, though on a much more horrible and violent scale. As we have already noted, many centuries later, the Levite's host would follow suit, offering two helpless young women to the angry crowd. On the one hand, these offers demonstrate a criminal carelessness about the lives of women. But in Lot's case, another point becomes clear: the overwhelming value placed on hospitality. Evidently, Lot felt it was so important to protect his visitors that he had to surrender his daughters. Like the Greek myths and European fairy tales of a later date, these Biblical tales underline the virtue of being kind to strangers, no matter how unprepossessing they are. The hag might be a princess in disguise; the hermit, a king; the shepherd, a god.

However, later commentators concur that the virtue of hospitality does not excuse Lot's action. For instance, Maimonides wrote that a man should die "rather than permit his wife or daughters to be dishonored."[13]

Fortunately for Lot's daughters, the Sodomites refused his offer, as they were motivated by something more than lasciviousness. Pointing at Lot, they shouted, "[He] came here as an alien, and already he acts the ruler! Now we will deal worse with you than with them" (19:9). Their words show that, even after all these years, the Sodomites regarded Lot as an outsider—and worse, an outsider intent on bossing them around. The foreshadowing of the fate of the Jewish people in the diaspora is inescapable here. From Hellenistic Greece to twentieth-century Germany, the Jew has been considered the definitive foreigner and persecuted accordingly.

Certainly, the Sodomites lived by different rules than Lot and his family. Although they have come down to us as primarily sexual sinners, with the name Sodomite becoming synonymous with orgiastic indulgence and homosexuality (at least to those who condemn homosexuality), their central problem was not sexual perversion, but rather their obsession with power and autonomy. They did not want to be told what to do by anyone, not by Lot, not by God. Accordingly, they demanded sex in order to intimidate and assert their authority.

Enraged, the men shoved Lot, pressing him against the walls of his house, while others hammered on the door, trying to break in. But just before the door gave, the angels lifted Lot to safety and blinded the crowd with a terrible light. Having stilled the violence, at least temporarily, and revealed that they were supernatural entities, the angels told Lot that God had not found one worthy soul inside the city and, therefore, intended to destroy Sodom. However, He would save Lot and his household if they fled from the valley.

Lot had two other daughters who were married, so once the angels had dispersed the crowd, he raced to warn his sons-in-law. But the young men only laughed, and their mockery caused Lot to hesitate (19:14). Surely, the angels did not really mean everybody would be destroyed. There was no evidence of a storm coming. The night was peaceful and clear. Lot delayed. He did not want to leave behind everything he had built.

At first, the angels did not press him, but when morning came and Lot was still not ready to leave, they dragged him, his wife, and his two unmarried daughters out of the city, leaving behind the married daughters and their husbands, since they had refused to believe doom was coming.[14] Once the city was a safe distance away, the angels allowed their charges to rest while they gave them instructions about what to do next. "Flee for your life!" they exclaimed. "Do not look behind you, nor stop anywhere in the plain; flee to the hills, lest you be swept away" (19:17).

Oddly, instead of obeying the angels, Lot argued with them. He did not want to go up to the hills, he said, because he was afraid he was not strong enough to make it as far as Hebron before he was killed. "Look," he begged the angels, pointing to a small settlement that lay, gray and unimposing, against the horizon, "that town there is near enough to flee to; it is such a little place! Let me flee there . . . and let my life be saved" (19:20). It is telling that Lot chooses to speak in the singular here. Of course, he could simply be implying that he and his family were one entity, since a man's wife and children were considered part of his person. But his phrasing does suggest a selfishness that does not bode well for his future.

Unfortunately, Lot also reveals his foolishness here. To argue with one's divine rescuers about where to flee was not only ungrateful, but also jeopardized the entire endeavor. Surely, the angels knew best. Perhaps because Lot was Abraham's nephew, God did not get angry, and allowed Lot and his family to head toward the town, which came to be named Zoar, or "Little Place," after Lot's description. Though he had gotten his way, Lot still dragged his feet until suddenly the angels evaporated and God spoke. "Hurry, flee there, for I cannot do anything until you arrive there" (19:22).

Many readers have found this episode of Lot's recalcitrance puzzling, and Jewish tradition has attempted to explain his behavior by suggesting that Lot was afraid of something far more complicated than distance. He wanted to appear righteous, commentators say, and therefore did not want to live near his uncle Abraham because then his lack of true virtue would be exposed. When he had dwelled in Sodom, he had enjoyed appearing pious next to his dreadful neighbors.[15] But his virtue was only skin-deep. The angels had saved him because he was Abraham's nephew, but in reality he was a misguided man who moved to Sodom because he did not understand that Canaan was the Promised Land. However, Islamic commentators disagree, arguing that Lot was sinless from the day of his birth until he died.[16]

Whether or not Lot was a paragon of virtue, he had demonstrated one important difference between himself and his uncle. Abraham had leaped to do God's bidding at all times, even when he did not want to. In addition, Abraham's debate with God had been about the well-being of others, including his nephew. Lot, on the other hand, was slow to fulfill God's orders. Although he had shown bravery in defending the strangers from his neighbors, he was reluctant when it came to leaving Sodom.

But God did not punish him, at least not yet, and stood by His word to release Abraham's nephew from the destruction of the plains. He waited until the man and his family entered the gates of Zoar before He "rained . . . sulphurous fire" (19:24) down upon Sodom and Gomorrah, igniting the underground bitumen and tar pits. The wind blew the terrible rotten-egg smell of sulfur across the valley while flames tore through the houses and the grasslands. Nothing was spared. No plants, no animals, not one person.

Even though Zoar was safely removed from the annihilation, there was no escaping the fog that drifted across the horizon. Lot and his daughters staggered through the streets of the town, but Lot's wife lingered. She had had to separate from two of her children and, it seems likely, a flock of grandchildren as well as her neighbors and friends. Every person she had once known in these cities was incontrovertibly dead, struck down in a few seconds. It was too much to bear. She turned her back on her husband and her two unmarried daughters and peered through the valley, trying to see through the dense smoke. But of course this sad moment was also the moment of her destruction. Suddenly, she stood rooted in one place, transformed into the legendary pillar of salt.

The fate of Lot's wife helps illustrate the suffering involved in such a flight. Salt, after all, is the essential ingredient of tears, and it is also a "preservative."[17] Lot's wife, unnamed though she is, represents those survivors of tragedy who are annihilated emotionally and spiritually, if not physically. Like many who endure such experiences, she desperately attempted to cling to what was gone. Thus, her destiny can be read as a reflection of her true orientation. She could no longer dedicate herself to life, as she could not leave behind the past.

Other commentators, however, have a harsher interpretation. Rashi writes that God told the family not to look back because it was "not fitting that [they] should witness [the Sodomites'] doom whilst . . . escaping." In addition, it would be wrong for them to think about their possessions when God had saved their lives.[18] Just as centuries later the Israelites were not meant to gloat over the destruction of the Egyptians, so Lot's family was not meant to rejoice over their safety at the expense of all those who had died. Besides, witnessing the sheer force of God's destructive power was akin to seeing God face-to-face. To have such a direct encounter with the divine was too much for any human being.

Today, near the Dead Sea, there is a strange cylindrical formation of salt. Tourists group themselves at the bottom to have their picture taken with "Lot's wife," little knowing they are commemorating the tragedy of survival, which in itself is sometimes too difficult to bear.

CHAPTER TWENTY-FOUR

GERAR AND A CAVE

The day after the destruction of the cities, Abraham went to the peak where he had stood with God and looked out over the plains. All he could see was black air "rising like the smoke of a kiln" (Gen. 19:28). Never again would this land be a garden. The orchids, the sorrel, and the wild mustard were all gone. Instead, it would become famous as one of the most barren regions in the world, devoid of vegetation and all but the sturdiest of insects and creatures. Even the sea that was the centerpiece of the region had almost been destroyed. Today, its saline content is so high that just one mouthful can poison a swimmer.

Zoar, the town where Lot had sought refuge, was so close to the valley that the smoke hung over the rooftops, blotting out the daylight. An awful stench filled the air, and the residents of Zoar and the three refugees from Sodom shivered in fear. To Lot, Zoar no longer seemed like a wise choice for a new home. As for the Zoarites, they had reason to be suspicious of this strange little band.

Lot and his daughters had arrived with ash-streaked faces and parched throats just as the flames began to rise from the cities a few miles away. It was strange that they had appeared at the exact moment the destruction had begun. Perhaps they had set the fires themselves or been involved in bringing about the obliteration. No Zoarite suspected that the presence of the old man and his two young daughters had saved their town from the same fate as Sodom and Gomorrah.

However, these miserable, bedraggled strangers were in fact their saviors. The Zoarites owed Lot and his daughters gratitude and a particularly warm welcome. But as the refugees wept, grieving the loss of their mother and wife, and of their home, the Zoarites revealed their iniquitous nature by making no offer of hospitality. Instead, they huddled in their sandy houses, avoiding the old man and his daughters. According to the Midrash, they had no knowledge of God and prayed to their own gods for escape from the catastrophe that had struck their neighbors.[1]

Fortunately for both sides, the townspeople did not need to endure Lot's company for long. Abraham's nephew found himself gripped with terror at the thought of staying in Zoar. Indeed, the moment he arrived he was ready to leave, displaying a restlessness that is common to those who have suffered calamity. Nowhere was safe. No new town could replace what was lost.

To make the situation even more ominous, Lot had just witnessed the savagery with which the Sodomites treated outsiders. Now, he and his girls were strangers in a strange town inhabited by the neighbors, cousins, and friends of the people who had just been destroyed. The angels who had protected Lot and his daughters in Sodom were gone. Even if the Zoarites did not harm them, they would always regard Lot's family as interlopers, just as the Sodomites had.

It did not seem wise to wait until the Zoarites recovered from witnessing the annihilation of their neighbors. After resting a few hours, Lot set forth for the very hills he had originally resisted, dragging his reluctant girls along with him. Having been given a second chance at life, he was dedicated to saving his daughters from more violence.

As they climbed the steep path toward Hebron, the smell of

burning lessened and the air became lighter. Slowly, sun broke through the smog. Crows cawed. The lizards, unused to human visitors, scuttled out of the way. Here, there were no cities. No murderers or rapists. No mobs demanding satisfaction. It was the perfect setting for an old man who had lost everything. The world was a dangerous place. Better to stay clear of it.

And so, when at last Lot glimpsed the dark mouth of a cave in the jagged rocks along the trail, he stopped his daughters. This would be their new home. He would not continue up the mountainside and set up camp with his uncle, as his daughters might have hoped. As we have seen, some commentators have said that this is because he did not want to live too near his virtuous uncle. Certainly, to arrive destitute—having lost his herds, his servants, everything—would have been a difficult acknowledgment of failure. At any rate, even in Abraham's small settlement, there were too many people, too much potential evil.

As his girls helped him set up camp, they could not protest except behind Lot's back. Their father was in charge of their destinies; to argue with him was out of the question. But though they had found safety, it was at the expense of life itself. Their father's condition was not so different from their mother's. Just as she had refused to walk with them into the future, so he refused to reenter the world. He would preserve himself and his children but would ignore his primary responsibility as a father of daughters, which was to help them find husbands.

Here in the wilderness there were no angry crowds or sulfurous rain, but neither were there servants, friends, markets, or neighbors to gossip with. Most important, there were no men. Although Lot had spent the early years of his life as a nomad like his uncle, he had raised his family in a wealthy city. Sin is a terrible thing, but a sinful city can also be terribly appealing to its inhabitants, especially adolescents. After all, there is shopping and flirting. Eating and drinking. Parties, girlfriends, boys. In the mountains, there was nothing to do all day except prepare food and carry heavy buckets of water from the nearby stream for washing and cooking and drinking.

MEANWHILE, back in Hebron, after the smoke rose up from the cities, Abraham was suddenly just as discontented and restless as his nephew. He had lived in Hebron since Lot had left for the cities of the plain, but now he did not know where Lot was. He could only assume his nephew was dead along with thousands of others. Black ash floated up from the valley, covering all of their belongings. It was impossible to go on living as though nothing had occurred. Perhaps he felt betrayed by God. Or maybe it was difficult for him to accept that God had not found ten good people in either Sodom or Gomorrah. Had the Lord gone back on His word? Had He allowed His anger to get the better of Him?

Rashi has no truck with such explanations. Instead he puts forward two other theories. Travelers stopped coming to the region after the destruction of the cities of the plain, he argues. For Abraham, who was at least partially dependent on trade for a livelihood, such isolation could only bring about a sharp economic downturn.

On a practical level, then, Abraham had to leave the area to drum up some business. But Rashi speculates that there was another, more interesting reason: somehow Abraham did know Lot had survived, but instead of being happy about this, he wanted "to get away from Lot who had gained an evil reputation."[2]

Of course, it is impossible to know for sure why Abraham decided to pick up and leave Hebron. All the Bible says is that soon the entire household was on the road to Egypt. Once again, they struggled through the heat and dust of the Negev, but instead of pushing through to Pharaoh's palace as they had years before, they rested in Kadesh, an oasis on the southern border between Egypt and Canaan. Although it was pleasant there, Abraham was still restless and led them back north until they reached the great Canaanite city Gerar. They set up camp in the rich grazing lands just outside the city walls. Instead of retreating to the wilderness like Lot, Abraham and his family were now perched outside the largest settlement in this part of the world. Abraham had chosen to escape the psychological aftermath of the burning cities by plunging himself and his family into contact with yet another new civilization.

The name Gerar, based on the Hebrew root *ger,* means "outsider" or "stranger."[3] But in this case it was hard to tell who was strange and who was familiar, who the interloper and who the host. Abraham and his party had arrived uninvited and parked themselves outside the gates of the city, a provocative act, no matter how small their band. To Abraham's people, however, the Canaanites who lived inside Gerar were equally threatening. They were strangers who were not bound to Abraham's tribe by blood or treaties. If they decided the travelers were dangerous, they were capable of inflicting real damage. War, rape, pillage—anything was possible.

While they waited to see how the Canaanites would respond to their presence, the new arrivals could still enjoy the beauty of this new land. Located in the western Negev, Gerar was about halfway between Beersheba and Gaza.[4] Despite the lack of rainfall, the region was fertile, thanks to an underground aquifer. All one had to do was dig down fifteen or twenty feet to tap into an almost limitless source of water, fresh from the hills of Judea. The land itself was flat and inviting, as though it had been created for planting. Sunflowers, citrus, cotton, onions, lettuce, and cabbage were just some of the crops that flourished here and still do. In the spring, the plain was truly spectacular. The sunflowers glowed. The lemon trees blossomed. The greens sparked against the dark earth. Abraham and his family had arrived in a veritable breadbasket.

The fertility of the land notwithstanding, it was here that Abraham would have to repeat one of the crucial tests he had endured as Abram. While the servants set up the tents and the children played under the citrus trees, Abraham let it be known to all interested outsiders that the beautiful woman by his side was his sister and not his wife. This act has an odd déjà vu quality, as the only distinction between this incident and Abraham's encounter with Pharaoh years earlier is that this time he did not ask Sarah's permission or offer any explanation for his behavior. Instead, he simply advertised their relationship as that of siblings.[5]

There are different theories about why important stories such as this one are repeated in the Bible. Those scholars who believe that Scripture was written by God look for the emblematic or theological meanings of these moments. For instance, it is possible that Abraham had to repeat an earlier test because he was symbolically reborn after circumcision, and thus he had to reexperience the important events of his life.[6]

But for those who see the Bible as a product of one, or even multiple, editors, the reason for these repetitions is complex and rooted in the politics of the Bible's creation. These scholars suggest that different versions of the same story had to be included in Scripture in order to keep various groups happy. For instance, if the northern kingdom told a story one way and the southern kingdom another, then both versions had to be included. This was also true of powerful groups within early Israelite society. The priestly class had to be mollified, so many of the long passages on law were written by a member or members of the priestly class, or so argue proponents of what is now called the Documentary Hypothesis.[7]

However, although this version of who might have written the Bible offers compelling hypotheses about the historicity of the text, ultimately it does not attempt to explain the cumulative effect on the reader of encountering repeated tales, nor does it offer an interpretation of the psychological and emotional implications for characters who undergo the same events twice.

Thus, strange though it may seem, the secular literary scholar and the religious interpreter have more in common than one might think. Just as the orthodox scholar believes each word of the text has encoded meaning for the reader, so does the literary scholar, albeit for different reasons.[8] Regardless of whether the story of Abraham's test was repeated to please some constituency, the interpretative problem remains: why does he present his wife as his sister for a second time?

Predictably, no sooner had Abraham announced that Sarah was his sister than Abimelech, the king of Gerar, sent his men out to the fields to collect her for his vast stable of wives. Once again, Abraham had sold his wife's honor to save his own skin even though there had been no open threat to him. This act is particularly shocking as it looks like a huge step backward in his relationship with both God and his wife.

There are many different explanations for his behavior. Perhaps he was trying to forestall the conception of a new baby to save Ishmael from a brother's competition. Maybe he was not sure he could make Sarah pregnant and hoped Abimelech would do it instead. Or perhaps he preferred Hagar and wanted to be married to her in place of Sarah. After all, Hagar was still a vital member of the tribe, and mother of his heir. He could see her busying herself around the campsite even as he spread the news to the Canaanites that Sarah was his sister.

At any rate, Abraham's denial of Sarah indicates that the truce between Abraham and the divine had ended. Surrendering his wife was an insurrectionary action on Abraham's part, since God had just told him that Sarah would bear his child. Despite his bargaining with God beforehand, Abraham may have been enraged after witnessing the carnage of the cities on the plain and felt compelled to stage some kind of protest. Could he have doubted God's word? Had there really been no righteous men left to redeem the cities? Or it is possible he was heartbroken, believing that Lot and his family had been killed. As Jack Miles writes, "Abraham's misbehavior in Gerar stands as defiance not just of the Lord's claims on Abraham's body, but also of God's demonstrative destruction of Sodom."[9]

Suddenly the reprehensible Lot seems more virtuous than his famous uncle. Once they had escaped from Sodom, Lot had dedicated himself to keeping his daughters from having any contact with men — a misguided and even jealous action, but one meant to keep them from harm — while Abraham was intent on pushing his wife into a liaison with a foreign ruler. Sarah was again his bargaining chip.

Of course, by now, Sarah was used to lying. Not only was this the second time her husband had attempted to cover up their marriage, but she had overheard God misrepresent her words. Yet she did not protest. On one hand, she was well aware that she was being used for her husband's gain and that it was her responsibility to promote his scheme. On the other hand, she might have had her own plot brewing since she knew her husband well enough to know he would attempt to pull this stunt.

Abimelech's home at Gerar was not as elaborate a structure as Pharaoh's elegant palace in Egypt, but it was enormous compared to the tents of the desert dwellers. There were countless sleeping chambers and reception rooms. Statues of strange gods stood in the corners. The walls were painted and hung with weavings. The ladies of the court smelled almost as sweet and strange as the Egyptian ladies. They wore exotic perfumes of sandalwood and myrrh and coated their hair in expensive oils. Their jewelry was thick and gold.[10] Sarah might well have felt out of place, although now as a wealthy woman in her own right, it is possible she wore jewels, too.

As in Egypt, Sarah would have been taken to the women's baths in order to prepare for her encounter with the king. Once again, handmaidens would have washed and combed her hair. This time, however, she was far more prepared for what she would meet next. Not only had she been through this routine before, she was an older and more confident person than she had been in Pharaoh's palace.

Of course, the moment Sarah set foot in his palace, Abimelech was doomed. Even before the king could lay hands on her, God appeared to him in a dream and threatened disaster. "You are to die because of the woman that you have taken, for she is a married woman" (20:3). Although the Bible is clear that Abimelech had not yet "approach[ed]" Sarah (20:4), God still chastised him, making sure he understood who she was. This was the same role God had played back in Egypt, and it seems likely that Abraham and Sarah had already known He would protect her at all costs. If so, then perhaps Abraham was not as culpable as he seemed. Maybe he had suspected that this was how things would turn out and was not trying to get rid of Sarah but was instead using her to manipulate the ruler of the land.

In great fright, Abimelech asked God the same question Abraham had when he learned of God's plan to obliterate Sodom and Gomorrah. "O Lord, will You slay people even though innocent?" It did not seem fair he would be punished, he complained, since Abraham had told him Sarah was his sister. He also added an interesting detail, claiming that Sarah had corroborated Abraham's story (20:4). This suggests that Sarah actively supported her husband's plot, raising the possibility that the married couple had come up with it together.

If this was true, then Abraham and Sarah were far more united than they had seemed when they arrived outside the gates of the city. In addition, the idea that this was a joint scheme cleared Abraham's name; he could no longer be accused of committing the same crime as in Egypt. Nor was he like Lot, since, far from being helpless like Lot's daughters in Sodom, Sarah appeared to be a willing actor in the drama. She had lent her voice to support the plan.

Accordingly, a great reversal in fortunes occurred, the kind that always seemed to happen when Abraham and Sarah were involved. Instead of being attacked, robbed, or humiliated when confronted with a powerful foreign ruler, they emerged triumphant. As in Egypt, the king was laid low, begging for mercy before the desert dwellers and their God. What could be better proof of the omnipotence of the Lord? For that matter, what could better prove the strategic thinking of Abraham and Sarah?

Before Abimelech could say anything more, God responded to him as He recently had to Abraham, by declaring that He had no intention of punishing anyone who had not sinned. "I knew that you did this with a blameless heart," God assured the hapless king. But although in many ways the shaking Abimelech was actually the wronged party in this exchange, God ordered him to "restore the man's wife—since he is a prophet" (20:7), and He "closed the wombs" of the women in the palace until Sarah was allowed to go back to Abraham.

A prophet. This was a sobering thought for the king. No wonder Abraham appeared so confident. If he had the ear of such a powerful deity, he had to be treated with caution. Though Abimelech was angry, he knew the limits of Canaanite gods. None of them had ever spoken directly to him. The next morning the king summoned Abraham and demanded reasons for his deceptive behavior: "What wrong have I done that you should bring so great a guilt upon me and my kingdom? You have done to me things that ought not to be done. What then . . . was your purpose in doing this thing?" (20:9).

Abraham responded in a thoroughly self-righteous manner, displaying his contempt for the strange customs and beliefs of Abimelech and his people. "I thought . . . surely there is no fear of God in this place," Abraham said, "and they will kill me because of my wife. And besides, she is in truth my sister, my father's daughter though not my mother's; and she became my wife" (20:11–12). Abraham had not bothered to give this explanation back in Egypt. But now he wanted to make it clear he was not at fault. In fact, it sounds like he was trying to shift the blame for his actions to Abimelech.

Seen in this light, it seems possible that the entire plot was simply another way of creating publicity for God. When confronted with God's omnipotence, the Canaanites' gods must have seemed weak to Abimelech and the people of Gerar. As for Abimelech, he was now indebted to the deity he had unintentionally wronged.

Abraham could be seen as a successful spokesman for God at this point in the story, but his behavior remains unappealing, especially as he relied on the same tired excuse as in Egypt: that he was afraid the king would murder him in order to possess his beautiful wife. At no point did he acknowledge to God or to Sarah, if not to Abimelech, that he was the one who stood to benefit most from the whole series of events.

Abimelech did not pursue the matter but, chastened by God's words, gave Abraham sheep, oxen, slaves, and a thousand shekels of silver. He also told him to settle anywhere on the rich land surrounding the city, a privilege usually reserved for princes or relatives of the king. At once, Abraham was no longer a stranger in a strange land. Now that he and Sarah had forged an alliance with the most powerful man in the region, their situation was as secure as if Sarah had indeed married Abimelech. As for Abimelech, he had learned of God's existence. Abraham and Sarah had succeeded in spreading the word about their deity.

Satisfied, Abraham could now enact the true role of the prophet and "prayed to God" on Abimelech's behalf. Immediately, God healed the women in the palace and everyone in Gerar could breathe a sigh of relief. They had escaped the curse this peculiar couple had brought upon them. As for Abraham, he was an even wealthier man than he had been before Gerar. Everything had occurred just as it had in Egypt.

Yet there was something odd about this repetition. It was too perfect. Abraham appeared too disingenuous, Sarah, too yielding. Even more strangely, Abraham and Sarah's son, Isaac, would later reenact exactly the same drama, pretending that his wife, Rebecca, was his sister in order to fool the very same ruler—or perhaps his son—Abimelech (26:7).

After reading these three stories, it is easy to feel bewildered. The men in this family appear to be selfish and weak as well as tricksters. They do not seem to be messengers of God. The women do not seem blameless, either. One cannot help but wonder how much power the wives had to shape their destinies. Were they really helpless pawns in these exchanges? Or is it possible that they were the force behind the great men, masterminds of the deception?

After all, it is difficult to think of Sarah as a victim. Ishmael's birth is testimony to the fact that she was perfectly capable of initiating her own schemes. At this stage of her life, she was strong enough to resist participating in a plan that did not meet with her approval. Each time she had encountered a situation she did not like, she had used all of her skills to change it. She had already proven her influence over Abraham several times and God had backed her up on each occasion. Therefore, although it is possible that she went along with Abraham's idea but did not originate it, it is also possible that the whole plan was of her making, reinforcing Teubal's theory that she was actually an *en*.

The evidence for Sarah's strange religious role is more convincing now that a second episode has occurred. Teubal bases her theory that Sarah was really a priestess of international fame and enacted "marriages" with foreign rulers on several key points: the fact that the rulers rewarded her husband after she spent the night with them; that she was childless until divine intervention; that she came from Ur, one of the centers of Mesopotamian religion; and that her marriage with Abraham could potentially be seen as chaste, suggesting they were indeed brother and sister spouses.[11]

A high priestess, or *en*, performing a fertility ceremony with kings or princes was an essential characteristic of the Mesopotamian royal house, particularly in the regions where Abraham and Sarah once lived. These female religious leaders would take part in what was called the *heiros gamos*, or sacred intercourse, for two reasons: to test and renew the ruler's virility and to assess the health of the land and the future of the crops. Sarah's encounters with Pharaoh and Abimelech mirror much of what is known about these religious encounters.[12]

Mesopotamian fertility ceremonies were intricate and took many hours to complete, so if Sarah was indeed an *en*, she would have been thoroughly trained in these rituals. As for the king, if he made any mistakes in his completion of the important details — washing his hands at the wrong moment, saying the wrong words during the exchange of love poems or songs, or performing poorly in the ritualized act of intercourse — he would bring destruction and infertility upon his land. Interestingly, the plague suffered by Abimelech's household was perfectly in keeping with a failed sacred marriage ceremony. God closed "the wombs" of the women in Abimelech's palace "because of Sarah" (20:18). Thus, according to Teubal, Sarah was playing precisely the role a Mesopotamian priestess was supposed to. She arrived, tested the king, found him wanting, and so God punished him.[13]

While the idea that Sarah was a priestess may sound fascinating, she did not have to have enacted a ritual fertility ceremony in order to be distinguished by God. God's readiness to act on her behalf shows that she was a sacred individual in her own right, a person who, like her husband, could mediate between the divine and fellow mortals. In fact, it would soon begin to seem that God wanted to work miracles more for her sake than for her husband's.

CHAPTER TWENTY-FIVE

INCEST

As far as Lot and his girls knew, the lineage of Abraham's father, Terah, was heading toward an abrupt end. The destruction of Sodom and Gomorrah had killed Lot's married daughters. Sarah was barren. They were the only other women in the family who could continue the line, but, entombed in their wilderness cave, their chances of experiencing motherhood seemed slim. They saw no one but each other and their father. Each spring, the mating calls of the thrushes and rock doves rang against the sky. The nests of the alpine swifts crowded together in the nooks and crevices of their cave. All of nature pushed toward procreation while they were slowly withering away.

But the young women did not give up. If God was not going to send them husbands, they would have to take matters into their own hands. It was in this spirit that the older daughter made a shocking suggestion to her younger sister. "There is not a man on earth to consort with us . . . Come let us lie with [our father] that we may maintain life through our father" (Gen. 19:31–32).

Sleep with one's father? The older daughter's suggestion was meant to be appalling, since incest was as much a taboo in her society as it is today. Even if Mesopotamian children were not generally considered siblings unless they shared the womb of the same mother, the idea of a child sleeping with either parent was a horrific suggestion. Only the royal family of the infamous Egyptians practiced incest, with Pharaohs routinely marrying their sisters in order to doubly secure the throne and the bloodlines of the royal family.[1] But no descendant of Terah would have wanted to be compared to an Egyptian.

The elder daughter's words should have scandalized her sister, but the younger girl evinced no dismay. Instead, she agreed instantly, and together they devised a plan. They would get their father drunk, and when he could no longer discern their identities, they would slip into his sleeping quarters and seduce him.

In due course, both daughters successfully completed their mission and became pregnant. But when at length they bore their sons, the names they bestowed on the babies drove home the incestuous nature of their actions. The elder daughter named her child Moab, which was based on the Hebrew *me-avi*, or "from my father." The younger daughter called her son Ben-ammi, which meant "son of my [paternal] kinsman."[2]

Despite their repugnant conceptions, these children were not entirely beneath the notice of history, as each boy would go on to found famous peoples: Moab gave rise to the Moabites, and the younger daughter's son produced the Ammonites. Modern critics suggest that this story was an example of the Israelites' mockery of their enemies' origins.[3] But this explanation seems too pat, as the Moabites would ultimately produce one of the most distinguished women in the Bible: Ruth, ancestress of King David. And David himself would send his parents to the king of Moab for protection during a time of danger. Far from punishing them, then, God rewarded the girls, particularly the eldest daughter.

One explanation for God's favor is that the girls were trapped and so the ordinary rules of human decency no longer held true. Their father had seen to their utter isolation, enforcing their chastity with a vigor that seems overblown, as though he were suddenly (and inappropriately) aghast at the thought of sharing his daughters with other men. Although he did not make any predatory advances toward the girls himself, there was an unhealthy quality to his behavior that rendered his possessiveness suspect. It could be argued, therefore, that the girls' response to the situation their father had created was brave. They persisted in continuing the family tree in the face of Lot's self-destruction.

The modern reader may nevertheless wish that they had either escaped from their father and found husbands for themselves or surrendered to being childless. But both of these options might have been disastrous. In the first case, it is probable that they would have been murdered or raped, like the Levite's concubine. In the second, their story would have ended in the cave. Israel would have lost her great king. And, for all the daughters knew, the line of Terah would have ended.

Thus, it is lucky for their descendants that sheer creative fortitude drove the sisters forward. In fact, their legacy endures today. The Moabites built a famous city named Qir that has never died, although it is now known as Kerek. Located on a mountaintop just south of Amman in modern-day Jordan, it is famous for its view of the Dead Sea and the Jordan Valley. Indeed, there are few settlements on the western side of the Jordan River that allow one to inspect Israel quite so intimately, suggesting that no matter how many battles were fought between the Israelites and Moabites, their close relationship could never be denied. Cousins and neighbors for thousands of years, they have lived eye to eye and ear to ear. From Kerek, you can see Israeli cars driving on Israeli highways. From the Israeli resorts on the Dead Sea, you can see the red rooftops of Jordan stretching below the mountain.

Given this ancient legacy, it is tempting to speculate that God destroyed Sodom and Gomorrah to create two more peoples. But surely, this was not God's intention: to obliterate the cities of the plain so that Lot's daughters would sleep with their father. Instead, it seems possible that God saved Lot for the sake of Abraham, and

yet Lot had been so corrupted by his sojourn in Sodom and so traumatized by the city's destruction that his daughters had to resort to
desperate measures to continue their line.

To those who try to glean a lesson from it, Lot's fate remains
disturbing. Certainly, it was so to Mohammed and subsequent
Islamic thinkers who viewed the Bible's version of events as erroneous. As we have seen, according to Islamic theology, the prophets
were flawless, so the Koran emphasizes only Lot's virtues, reporting that Abraham sent him to Sodom and Gomorrah to teach faith
in the true God. In the Muslim version of the tale, Lot offered his
daughters as brides to the angry crowd to save the Sodomites from
their homosexual desires, not to save the angels or his own skin.[4]

When he failed to convince the Sodomites of their sinful nature—
because of the evil of the people and not because of any mistakes
on his part—the angels rescued him and his daughters, and this is
where the story ends. There is no hint of a disturbing relationship
with his girls. Rather, Lot is repeatedly praised for his "judgment
and knowledge" (Koran 21:74). To Muslim thinkers, therefore, the
Torah's story of Lot's failings is one of the most important examples
of error in the Jewish and Christian Scriptures.

It is ironic that the relatively minor character of Lot became
an essential point of debate in the battle for identity among Jews,
Christians, and Muslims. Muslims' belief in Lot's inherent virtue
contradicts those who claim that the Koran is simply derived from
the Hebrew Scripture rather than being God's words as recorded
by Mohammed. Accordingly, the quarrel over Lot's true character
has become a battle over the legitimacy of Islam versus Judaism and
Christianity, suggesting that, in some ways, the argument between
the herdsmen of the uncle and nephew never ended.[5]

The story of Lot and his daughters takes place immediately
before Abraham and Sarah's encounter with Abimelech, suggesting
an uncomfortable parallel between the two episodes. If Sarah was
not her husband's pawn in Gerar and acted, at least in part, on her
own initiative, the possibility arises that she was not so different

from Lot's daughters. She did not commit incest, but perhaps she arranged things so that she could have a child by Abimelech, as her miracle baby would be born shortly after their encounter.

That Sarah may have engaged in such a plot may seem like a large leap and, to some, an offensive one. And yet ancient commentators were well aware of the possibility that people would be suspicious about the identity of Isaac's father. In their anxiety over potential challenges to the child's paternity, the rabbis recorded many stories to prove Isaac's legitimacy. In one such tale, Sarah begged God to make Isaac look like Abraham so that no one would doubt his parentage.[6] Rashi bypassed all of these concerns by saying that Sarah was actually already pregnant before her encounter with Abimelech.[7]

Of course, if Sarah was indeed an *en*, then being impregnated by Abimelech would not have troubled anyone. According to the matriarchal Mesopotamian tradition, the king had no claims on the child; what mattered was that Sarah was the mother. Indeed, in a matriarchy, children are often raised by the mother and her relatives, so, in this case, Sarah's husband, who was also her brother, would be the father. Sarah had fulfilled her duties to Abimelech by predicting his future and that of his land. In return she had gained what she had come for — a baby son.[8]

However, the text insists that Abimelech did not touch Sarah. Thus, one could argue that the two stories are placed near each other so that the daughters' scandalous response to childlessness would throw Sarah's nobility into relief. According to this interpretation, Sarah did not stoop to tricks or immorality to become pregnant. Instead, she was so sure that she was the recipient of God's blessing, she had no reason to trick the king into fathering her child. Abraham would father Isaac, with God playing a supporting role.

But even with this overwhelmingly positive interpretation of Sarah's actions, one question remains: If Sarah was truly going to give birth to Isaac within the year, as God had said, then why would such a string of disasters occur in the months before he arrived?

Blasted cities, incest, abduction by a foreign king—these were not auspicious events and they did not bode well for the future of Isaac. According to the heroic tradition of the ancient world, the advent of great leaders was supposed to be marked by wondrous signs— miraculous harvests, comets, and the advance notice of notables in the community—not the catastrophes and scandals that marked the twelve months before Isaac's birth.

Was God trying to warn His favorite couple of some disaster that lay in their future? Or was He trying to frighten them into closer obedience to His word?

CHAPTER TWENTY-SIX

LAUGHTER

When Sarah did at last become pregnant, with true discretion, the Bible does not tell us how this event came about. But if Abraham was the biological parent of the child, as seems most likely, then a miracle had indeed occurred. To begin with, the elderly couple had established enough of a rapprochement to climb into bed together and make love. Both of them had gone through significant changes since their youth. Abraham had slept with Hagar; Sarah had become embroiled with Abimelech. Abraham had circumcised himself; Sarah and God had reached an agreement. The rules had changed. Despite the hurts they had dealt each other, this new woman and this new man, whose very names marked their transformation, could at last hope that their relationship would bear fruit.

Whether this consummation was a one-time event or was a prelude to a long and loving relationship is unclear. All we can assume is they made love once. Although, as we have already noted, the baby's conception was worrisomely close to Sarah's sojourn in Abimelech's palace, Abraham did not make any accusations, nor did anyone else in her community. Indeed, the whispers about Sarah's virtue did not begin until many centuries later. Instead, the camp-site seemed almost entirely joyful. Even Hagar was silent.

Despite Sarah's age, her pregnancy went smoothly. For Sarah, after so many years of being a slender, a self-contained woman, it was undoubtedly strange to grow large and clumsy. For the tribe, to watch Sarah's stomach grow was like watching a rock change into water or a bush burst into flames. The baby in her womb was a tribute to God's ability to work magic. If this woman could have a child, then God could do anything.

Finally, the day came when Sarah felt the fluttery cramps that meant her time was near. At length, her contractions began in earnest and she underwent the misery and terror of labor just as Hagar had thirteen years earlier. When she finally pressed the infant into the world, it would have been fitting if the earth had shivered or if an eclipse had darkened the sky. Isaac's birth was as crucial a moment in the history of humankind's relationship to God as Noah's rainbow or the creation of Adam. The Midrash underlines the momentousness of the event:

> The whole world rejoiced, for God remembered all barren women at the same time with Sarah. They all bore children. And all the blind were made to see, all the lame were made whole, the dumb were made to speak, and the mad restored to reason. And a still greater miracle happened: on the day of Isaac's birth the sun shone with such splendor as had not been seen since the fall of man, and as he will shine again only in the future world.[1]

God had fulfilled His promise and had declared Himself willing to intervene in individuals' lives; that is, if such an intervention suited His purposes.

Sarah, though, was not thinking about the future or what would happen to the rest of humanity. Rather, she could not believe her good fortune, and as she held the baby in her arms, she exclaimed, "God has brought me laughter; everyone who hears will laugh with me" (Gen. 21:6).

In this decisive moment, Sarah, unlike Abraham, made sure to acknowledge God's gift. He had proven Himself to her, and Sarah was so moved that she continued to overflow with words, uttering her longest recorded speech:

Who would have said to Abraham
That Sarah would suckle children!
Yet I have borne a son in his old age. (21:7)

In her joy, Sarah used a strange plural—children, instead of child—as though Isaac were not one infant but many. Her statement would become true in a metaphorical sense, as Isaac's descendants would multiply into countless generations. Ultimately, however, Sarah's wordplay gave some interpreters the idea that her breasts had so much milk that she could nurse many babies. The Jewish commentators say that at the celebratory feast for Isaac's birth, Sarah suckled all the infants there and "they who drew from her breast had much to thank her for," as they would go on to become "pious proselytes." Indeed, the early rabbis were so struck by this thought that they deemed her the spiritual mother of converts to Judaism. Long after her death, therefore, Sarah has been held responsible for nurturing all those who join the Jewish faith.[2]

But Sarah's words were weightier than they first appeared. In God and Sarah's lexicon, laughter and lying were linked. Before the birth of her son, when Sarah had denied laughing, she had also denied the possibility that God's promise would come true and that "Laughter" would indeed be born. No wonder God had seemed irritated at Mamre; Sarah had had the nerve to doubt His word. By telling Abraham that the child would be named "Laughter," God made sure that Sarah would never forget Him or their initial conversation about her pregnancy. As for Sarah, when she acknowledged that God had indeed given her "laughter," she proclaimed to the world that God had wrought a miracle. He had singled her out, and she would return the favor now that she held Isaac in her arms. He was not a liar. And neither was she. At least, not anymore.

Abraham did not follow Sarah's example. At no point did he praise God for the birth of the little boy, although he did adhere to the new commandment of circumcision, ensuring Isaac's place in God's covenant. But even after this ceremony, Abraham did not make an altar to express his thankfulness, nor did he slaughter any animals. Perhaps he thought circumcision was a sufficient expression of gratitude. He might have been tired of God's control over his destiny and may not have wanted to concede the importance of His role in the arrival of his new baby. Or maybe now that he had a second son, he felt he had no need for God. Certainly, this was not new behavior on Abraham's part. He had not given thanks for the birth of Ishmael either.

But to later generations, Abraham's seeming lack of gratitude loomed as a terrible breach of etiquette. Tradition has it that this omission would give rise to the terrifying final test Abraham would have to face — the sacrifice of his beloved son. But not yet. Whether or not Abraham had made a grave mistake, there was no hint of any disaster to come. God did not rage. Hagar was quiet. Sarah was overjoyed. So, when Abraham held the new baby in his arms, he was at liberty to enjoy his role as Isaac's father.

No one knows how long this calm lasted. During the initial years of Isaac's life, Sarah cradled him in her tent, just as Hagar had Ishmael, and when at last she weaned him, it was probably with reluctance, as this meant it was time for the boy to leave her lap and her protection. Daughters could stay with their mothers until they married, but sons were expected to venture out into the wider world of the campsite, playing with the other children and spending more time with their fathers. Even those mothers who had many sons and had not just given birth to a miraculous baby faced this time with some trepidation.

But if this was a bittersweet moment for mothers, it was an exuberant time for fathers. Their sons had survived the most dangerous years of life and were ready to be instructed in the customs of the tribe. Now Abraham could begin to teach Isaac the skills he would need to survive and to lead. Of course, Abraham had had the chance to do this once before with Ishmael, but it was exhilarating to have the opportunity again, especially with a son who had been born to Sarah. The impossible had come true.

Overflowing with pride and happiness, Abraham held a feast in three-year-old Isaac's honor to mark the boy's departure from infancy and his entrance into the communal world of the camp—something he had not done for Ishmael. Perhaps this was because the boy was the son of his second wife or because Hagar had not insisted upon it. Or perhaps this was how Abraham had decided to acknowledge Isaac as his primary heir. The reasons are not clear. All we know is that this was the last happy event of Isaac's childhood.

Calves were slaughtered. Wine was poured. The women baked honey cakes on the hot stones of the fires. There was anticipation in the campsite as Abraham's followers and friends prepared to welcome the little boy. No offerings were made to the Lord, however. The servants ran back and forth to fill the serving bowls. The women rested after having spent hours preparing the meal. The roasted lambs were eaten down to the bones.

Yet even as the guests chewed their meat and drank their wine, the old tension was heating up between Sarah and Hagar. With Isaac ranging beyond the immediate orbit of his mother, he had begun to have frequent encounters with his much older half-brother. Sarah, suspicious and vigilant, watched over Isaac's safety like a hawk. If Ishmael made any misstep, she would be there to protect her boy. As for Hagar, she knew that her future and that of her son depended on how successfully they carved out a relationship with Sarah and Isaac. At no point would she have tried to provoke a confrontation.

For a little while longer, everything remained tranquil. It was not until after the feast that something awful happened. No one is sure exactly when this event transpired. Years, weeks, or days could have passed since the festivities, and this uncertainty would become an important point of debate between Islam and the other monotheistic religions. But in the Bible, the lack of clarity about timing was less important than what happened and who raised the alarm.

One day, Sarah saw Ishmael "playing" or "laughing" with Isaac in a dangerous fashion, or so she implied. The Hebrew word used to describe Ishmael's behavior, *m'tzahek,* has many meanings. Some Jewish commentators suggest that Sarah witnessed Ishmael tormenting Isaac. Others argue that *m'tzahek* can have sexual connotations and that Ishmael was abusing his little brother.[3] Still others suggest that he was mocking him and "laughing" at him. One scholar has even suggested that Ishmael was actually "playing at being Isaac," declaring that he was the firstborn and, therefore, the recipient of God's covenant. But one thing is clear: *m'tzahek* is closely related to Isaac's name, Yitzhak, as it is actually the present tense of the verb "laughing, playing."[4]

The shadow side of laughter had been an essential element of Isaac's identity right from the beginning. Sarah knew that laughing could be subversive and alienating as well as joyful, since she herself had laughed at God. Thus, the Bible's use of the verb *m'tzahek* was clearly meant to remind both Abraham and God, as well as the reader, of God's promise: that Sarah's son, not Hagar's, would be the heir to His covenant about the land. Abraham might still argue that Ishmael's circumcision and the fact that he was his father's firstborn kept him in the running as the primary recipient of his legacy, but he could never deny "Laughter" his God-given rights.

The troubling part of this story, though, is that the Bible never confirms that anything terrible really happened; all it reports is that after Sarah watched this mysterious "playing," she stormed over to Abraham and ordered him to "cast out that slave-woman and her son." The only explanation she offered for this cruel demand was that she did not want Ishmael to "share in the inheritance" of Isaac (21:10).

Sarah had come full circle. She was the one who had helped bring about Ishmael's conception; now she would bring about his banishment. It seems that once Sarah had a son of her own, she did not want to share her husband or his legacy with anyone else. Most modern readers miss the complexity of Sarah's compromised situation, so her rigid stance when it comes to Hagar and Ishmael has been a difficult pill to swallow. Because she appears to behave unkindly and out of jealousy, for many she has become an example of how not to be, and Hagar has become a symbol of those who are victimized, from African American slaves to exiles.

However, there are other interpretations that cast Sarah in a gentler light. For instance, the same scholars who view Sarah as an *en* or some sort of Mesopotamian priestess tend to see this incident as a legal issue. Sarah, as the priestess or head matriarch in the clan, had to send Ishmael away because Hagar's son threatened her matriarchal line.[5] In other words, Sarah's insistence on Isaac's inheritance was not a personal issue.

Of course, this can be said for God's covenant, too. Even if Sarah was not a Mesopotamian priestess, she still had to protect God's legacy, and He had declared that it was Isaac who would bear the weight of His promise. Clearly, Abraham was divided by his love for his sons, whereas Sarah was not. Accordingly, she had to speak on her son's behalf, not just because she loved Isaac, but because this was what God wanted her to do. She had become His agent.[6]

In an attempt to heal this traditional conflict between Hagar and Sarah, Rabbi Phyllis Berman suggests that Hagar's "expulsion" was actually the result of a scheme concocted by Sarah and Hagar. According to Berman's Midrash, Sarah had a dream that God told Abraham to sacrifice his firstborn son, so Sarah and Hagar "talked and planned and plotted" until they came up with a plan: Sarah would tell Abraham "this preposterous story about Ishmael teasing Isaac." He would send Hagar and Ishmael away, and Ishmael would be safe. When Hagar leaves, Sarah is heartbroken. Berman writes that after the expulsion, "Sarah was never the same. Although she believed that her deception had saved Ishmael's life, it had taken from her most of her own life energy."[7] What is interesting about Berman's interpretation, according to Rabbi Arthur Waskow, is that it lifts this moment in the story "beyond both the Jewish/Christian and the Muslim versions." The idea of Sarah and Hagar being allies emphasizes the principle of "a warm relationship, rather than conflict or distance, between the mothers of both communities and traditions."[8]

Whatever Sarah's intentions, whether she was being selfish, fulfilling the demands of a prophecy, or protecting Ishmael, she did not hesitate to push her position even though she knew that doing so would place her husband in a terrible spot. She fought fiercely, fueled by the memory of thirty painful years without a child. To a woman on such a mission, it did not matter if Abraham was upset.

Her husband did in fact experience pain. Deeply saddened by his angry wife's words, he did not know what to do. For the first and only time, the Bible tells us that Abraham was "distressed" (21:11). In fact, the ancient commentators claim that this was the most difficult moment of Abraham's life.[9] Ishmael was his firstborn and, according to Islam, his favorite son, so instead of racing to obey Sarah, he became paralyzed with indecision. Should he listen to his first wife or to his own desire? Either way, he would make someone unhappy; one of the women in his life would suffer, and so would one of his sons. But which woman and which child?

As he paced back and forth, unsure of what his next move should be, God intervened, signaling the importance of this decision by speaking directly to Abraham for the first time since His announcement of Isaac's birth. "Do not be distressed over the boy or your slave; whatever Sarah tells you, do as she says, for it is through Isaac that offspring shall be continued for you," God said (21:12). These were stern words for Abraham to hear, but God comforted him as well, reminding Abraham that Ishmael would also be blessed. "As for the son of the slave-woman, I will make a nation of him, too, for he is your seed" (21:13).[10]

According to this passage, then, it was not only Sarah who wanted Ishmael gone, but God as well. He could have told Abraham to ignore Sarah or to keep Hagar and her son by his side, but instead, God made it clear they had to be sent away. Once again, God and Sarah seem aligned. In fact, when God declared that it was Isaac who would "inherit" His covenant, he used the same Hebrew word to denote inheritance that Sarah had used, anointing Sarah's child as His primary heir, though He reiterated His blessing of Ishmael. Left to his own devices, Abraham might well have chosen his eldest son. As it was, Abraham had to do what God and Sarah told him to do, ignoring the promptings of his own heart.

But Abraham knew when to rebel and when not to, so the very next morning he sent for Hagar and Ishmael. The land rippled away from the tents, fading into yellow hills along the horizon. The sky was vast and cloudless. There were no trees and few shrubs, a forbidding prospect for travelers who knew they would have to endure long hours under the dangerous sun.

Hagar and Ishmael arrived at Abraham's tent, but the Bible does not record how Abraham broke the news of their exile. Perhaps this is because he did not say anything at all. Abraham's second wife was not stupid. After Sarah's speech to their shared husband, Hagar's fate was clear. Mother and son preserved a stoical silence as they stood in the doorway of the patriarch's tent. Hagar had endured exile before and knew that desert wanderings could transform a person's life. But even if she was able to place her faith in God at this difficult moment, leaving behind the safety of the campsite and the father of her child still represented an enormous challenge. She was eighteen years older than she was during her first sojourn in the desert. Could she keep her son alive? Could she bear the suffering? Was she strong enough?

Abraham said good-bye to her as best he could. First, he took some bread and filled a skin with water. He did not want to send this woman into the desert until he had made sure she was well equipped. Although the Bible does not say that he was heartbroken, it does slow down the action in this section of the story, describing how he "placed" the supplies "over her shoulder," a tender act and one that would have been especially meaningful to a woman who was used to serving others (21:14).

Then something odd happened. The Bible says that Abraham laid Ishmael "over her shoulder," though it would have been impossible for a woman to carry her sixteen- or seventeen-year-old son (21:14).[11] Most scholars see this passage as evidence of how two different versions of the story got spliced together, with awkward results, as suddenly Ishmael was represented as an infant instead of a teenager. The argument goes that baby Ishmael was from a different, earlier version of the story and that the older Ishmael came from a far later source.[12]

However, this confusing depiction of Ishmael's age can also be read as an emblem of the trust between Abraham and Hagar. If Ishmael was indeed old enough to walk under his own steam, then Abraham's action of laying the boy "upon her shoulder" can be seen symbolically. Abraham did not truly intend Hagar to carry a teenage boy; rather, this was the Bible's way of saying that Hagar, not her son, would lead the expedition. Seen in this light, Abraham's actions indicate a transferal of power from father to mother. Now that he was leaving Abraham behind, teenage Ishmael would have to listen to Hagar.[13]

To most Islamic thinkers, however, the strange back-and-forths — was Ishmael an infant, or a grown man? — serve as another example of the "corruption" of the Jewish and Christian Bible. The Koran simply states that Ishmael was an infant. In fact, in some Muslim versions of the story, Isaac was not yet born when Abraham sent Hagar and her son away — not because of Sarah's jealousy, but to spread the true faith in Allah. Although Muslim commentators do mention that Sarah was angry with Hagar, this has never been the central emphasis of the story. As we have already seen, a number of Islamic tales emphasize Sarah's selflessness. In these versions, Hagar's banishment is depicted as a blessing that would prove to be the beginning of her new life, the one God had wanted for her all along.

———◆———

CHAPTER TWENTY-SEVEN

EXILE

M other and child trailed off into the unknown, small indom-
itable figures heading south under the blue-white sky.
Hebron, where they had lived so long with Abraham's tribe, lay to
the north of their current Gerar campsite. Clearly, Hagar was intent
on heading away from the home she had shared with Abraham and
Sarah. She was shaping her own destiny now.

At first she did not panic. She "wandered" toward Egypt as she
had during her last period of exile, but this time no angels came to
her.[1] Soon she and Ishmael became lost in the wild lands near Beersheba. Before long, they had drunk their water and in despair "she
left the child under one of the bushes" (Gen. 21:15).

Hagar's action is yet more evidence to Islamic thinkers that Ishmael was indeed a baby, and certainly, leaving him beneath a bush
would have been an odd thing for Hagar to do if Ishmael was seventeen. Yet perhaps he had lost consciousness, or this might be a
Biblical metaphor for the fact that the teenager had somehow broken down, whereas Hagar was made of tougher stuff, at least physically. At any rate, the important thing was that Hagar left Ishmael
for a moment and "sat down at a distance, a bowshot away; for she

thought, 'Let me not look on as the child dies.'" Then "she burst into tears" (21:16).

If Ishmael was old enough to register his mother's behavior, then perhaps another reason Hagar left him behind was to prevent him from seeing her cry. Her sadness was deep and relentless. In contrast to Sarah and Abraham, who had laughed at the thought of Isaac's birth, Hagar wept at the prospect of her son's demise. The woman who had rejoiced at her ability to gaze upon God and live no longer wanted to see. Her child was dying. Her special gift, vision, could only cause her pain.

Interestingly, Hagar is the first person in the Bible to cry. Her tears are the natural expression of her despair, but they can also be seen as an attempt to communicate her vulnerability to God. At the well, God had told her that He saw her *because of* her anguish, reinforcing the personal nature of their relationship. Lost and grief-stricken, Hagar reached out emotionally to the deity she had named, He Who Sees Me, initiating an important way of communicating with the divine. She needed His help, and her open display of sorrow was an invitation for Him to enter and heal her desolation.[2]

God, in the form of an angel, responded instantly, saying, "What troubles you, Hagar? Fear not, for God has heeded the cry of the boy where he is. Come lift up the boy and hold him by the hand, for I will make a great nation of him" (21:17–18).

Ishmael had not made any audible cry, yet God had "heard" his misery. This was not a coincidence, as God had given Ishmael a name that meant "the one who is heard." He comforted Hagar by reminding her that Ishmael was destined for greatness. It was not time for the boy to die.[3]

God's merciful words demonstrate yet again that He cared about the fate of this woman. She was bound by His blessing, if not His covenant with Abraham. After His revelatory speech, He made a miracle happen. "God opened her eyes and she saw a well of water" (21:19). Significantly, it was not enough for God to create the water. He needed Hagar to *see* it. Just as God had insisted that Sarah laugh,

He now required Hagar to use her eyes. In both cases, He made the women do exactly what they felt unable to do: forcing Sarah to move from bitterness to joy and Hagar to move from blindness to vision. Neither woman wanted to embrace the future, yet their futures were far brighter than they could possibly know.

When she saw the spring, Hagar did not hesitate. Relieved, "she went and filled the skin with water, and let the boy drink" (21:19). It was impossible to forget what had happened the last time God had shown her water, and now she knew that what He had promised back then would come true. For Hagar, the wilderness was never truly a wilderness. God always made sure she found an oasis.

Now that she was safe, she could confront the possibilities that lay ahead. Although God had seemed cruel when He had told Abraham to obey Sarah's demand, it was evident He had wanted Hagar to leave the campsite for good reason. Despite the dangers Hagar and Ishmael faced, she was now free and so was her son. Indeed, this hope for freedom could well have been the reason behind Hagar's lack of visible sorrow when she bade farewell to Abraham. She knew she was heading into the unknown but that she was doing so as a liberated woman. After her years of servitude, Hagar had earned this reward, and perhaps she preferred the terrors of freedom to the security of slavery.

However, the Prophet Mohammed believed that Hagar did not have to ask herself any of these existential questions. According to Islamic teaching, instead of sending Hagar and Ishmael off on their own, Abraham actually took Hagar by the hand and led her to what would one day become Mecca, settling her near the ruins of the original Kaaba, the cube-shaped mosque that Adam had built and that Abraham would later return to rebuild with Ishmael.[4] As the story goes, Abraham felt that those who lived on the Arabian Peninsula needed to know the true God. Thus, long before the birth of Isaac, he brought Hagar and his beloved son there to serve as missionaries and role models. Although the patriarch felt pain at this separation, he knew it was the right thing to do.[5]

In some of the hadith, Hagar needed to be convinced to stay alone in the desert. Two small mountains guarded the barren plain where she stood holding her child. As she regarded the blankness of the landscape, she could have no idea that she was about to fulfill her famous destiny. So when Abraham turned to leave her and his infant son, she ran after him and asked why he was abandoning her in such a barren land. When he did not answer, she guessed that he was acting in accordance with a divine commandment. "Has Allah ordered you to do so?" she asked.

"Yes," Abraham said.

"Then He will not neglect us," she said.[6]

Abraham had completed his mission, but he was heartbroken to say good-bye to his beloved wife and baby. When he had traveled far enough that Hagar was out of sight, Abraham stopped and prayed to Allah, saying, "O Our Lord! I have made some of my offspring dwell in a valley without cultivation . . . in order . . . that they may offer prayer perfectly. So fill the hearts of men with love toward them, and O Allah provide them with fruits so that they may give thanks" (Koran 14:37).[7]

At first, it seemed that God did not listen to His prophet's prayer. Before long, Hagar ran out of water and was no longer able to nurse Ishmael. As in the Bible, she could not bear witnessing the child's agony and put him down under a bush. But in the hadith, instead of sitting down and weeping, she ran toward the nearest mountain, As-Safa. Despite her thirst, she climbed to the top to see if there was anyone who could rescue her and her son. There was no one, so she stumbled back down and ran across the valley to the facing mountain, Al-Marwa. Once more, she climbed to the top, but when she gazed across the entire valley, she could see nobody to help her.[8]

Weak from dehydration but still driven to survive, she struggled back down Al-Marwa, across the valley, and back up As-Safa. She repeated this arduous circuit seven times until at last a voice spoke to her as she stood on top of Al-Marwa. A woman of faith, Hagar was silent "and listened attentively." Then she spoke: "O whoever you may be! You have made me hear your voice; have you got something to help me?" Then she looked down in the valley and saw an angel strike the earth with his heel; fresh water bubbled out of the hole he had made, creating the spring that is known to Muslims as Zamzam, the famous holy water of Mecca, Allah's holy city.[9]

Hagar's desperate attempt to save herself and her child has been immortalized in Islamic tradition through one of the most important elements of the hajj, or pilgrimage to Mecca, a requirement for all faithful Muslims. Each pilgrim, male or female, must travel Hagar's path between the mountains seven times to commemorate her search for Allah and to internalize her courage and faith. Then they must drink the waters of the Zamzam from the coolers that are set up throughout the Masjid al-Haram, or Sacred Mosque, that surrounds the Kaaba.[10]

Although the discovery of the Zamzam is the most famous part of her story, Hagar's travails did not end with the angel's intervention. Despite her fatigue, Hagar raced to the spring and dug a basin to collect the flowing water. This was an ingenious act, according to Mohammed, who declared, "May Allah bestow mercy on Ishmael's mother! Had she let the Zamzam flow without trying to control it, the Zamzam would have been a stream flowing on the surface of the earth." In fact, tradition has it that the name Zamzam comes from Hagar's command, "Stop, stop!" ("*Zome, zome!*").[11]

Mohammed was right to be struck by Hagar's resourcefulness. What Hagar and her descendants needed was a well, or collecting basin, as surface water would only dry up in the heat of the Arabian sun. An experienced desert dweller, Hagar dug a small trough so that the water would pool in one place and be useful to all who came there. After she drank the water, Hagar was able to suckle her child, and before long Ishmael revived. She found them food to eat, and together, mother and son lived in peace next to the Zamzam.[12]

How long Hagar and Ishmael were alone is not clear in the hadith, but at length, some nomads caught sight of a bird circling overhead and realized there must be water nearby. They followed the bird's flight to the Zamzam and, when they saw Hagar sitting by the side of the spring, asked if she would allow them to stay with her. She responded that she would be happy to have their company but that they would have no rights to the water. These she would deed to Ishmael.[13]

Astonishingly, the nomads agreed, but no one knows why. Hagar was only a woman, and the nomads greatly outnumbered her and Ishmael. They could easily have overpowered her or ignored her demands, yet somehow Hagar had the authority to make them obey her terms. God was clearly supporting her enterprise, and Hagar had the kind of temerity and strength of character that people did not question. Like Abraham, she was a natural leader.

At the close of their negotiations, Ishmael and Hagar joined the tribe of the nomads. Ishmael learned Arabic and Hagar became one of the tribe's matriarchs. When Ishmael was old enough, she selected a wife for him—a task usually reserved for men.[14]

Though the fact that Hagar arranged Ishmael's marriage occurs in both the Bible and the hadith, it seems that later Jewish and Muslim commentators did not like the idea of a woman with this degree of power and influence. Sages from both religions attempted to "correct" this problem by relating a story about Abraham's role in Ishmael's marriage that discounted Hagar's competence. For once, the traditions were united, albeit by their distrust in the capabilities of females:

One day, after many years had passed, Abraham decided to go visit his son Ishmael. When he arrived at Ishmael's house (which was either near the Zamzam or somewhere in the wilderness near Egypt, depending on the storyteller's origins), his son was not there. However, Ishmael's wife was home, busily sweeping and doing other domestic chores. When Abraham asked where her husband was, she said he was away and complained bitterly about her lot as his wife. Abraham was displeased and said to her, "Tell your husband that the threshold of his house is not sturdy and that he must get another one."[15]

When Ishmael returned home, his wife told him what had taken place and Ishmael instantly knew who the strange visitor had been. "That was my father," he declared, "and he wants me to divorce you."

His wife was shocked. "How do you know this?" she asked.

"Because he speaks in parables. You are the threshold. You are ruining my house. I must put you to the side and get another wife." Accordingly, Ishmael obeyed his father, cast out his old wife, and took a new wife.[16]

Once again, Abraham visited Ishmael, and once again, Ishmael was not home. But when Abraham talked with his new wife, she glowed and said how lucky she was to be married to Ishmael. "Tell your husband," Abraham said, "that the threshold of his house is sound and that he is a lucky man."

When Ishmael returned home, his wife told him all that had passed, and Ishmael was grateful. "You are the threshold," he told his wife, "and my father has approved of you."[17]

Yet, despite their doubts about her skills as a matchmaker, according to the hadith, Hagar was the founder of a city and a people. She had fought off the nomads' claims to the Zamzam and the holy site of Mecca. Thanks to her, Ishmael and all Arabs would inherit a vital legacy. Despite western preconceptions about Islam, from its beginnings Muslims have revered Ishmael's mother as a heroine, illustrating that the respect of women is inherent to the faith.

In Judaism, however, Hagar remains an emblem of suffering rather than triumph. The rabbis seized upon the Biblical account of Hagar's misery in the desert as one of the most important passages in the entire Torah, so significant that it is among those recited each year on the first day of Rosh Hashanah, the Jewish New Year. There are many theories about why this episode, which does not involve an Israelite, should play such a prominent role in the ritual life of Jews. One of the most common is that Hagar's relationship with God and with Abraham is a model for all devout people. Another idea is the boy and his mother became examples of God's benevolence. Abraham's deity was the God who hears everyone's suffering.

Christians have inherited the portrait of Hagar the victim from Judaism. According to Phyllis Trible, "[Hagar] experiences exodus without liberation, revelation without salvation, wilderness without covenant, wanderings without land, promise without fulfillment, and unmerited exile without return." Trible concludes by declaring that Hagar is "a theological challenge" rather than a pioneer, an understandable assessment since the triumphant end to Hagar's tale does not occur within the scope of the Hebrew or Christian Scripture.[18]

But the Bible does hint at Hagar's later success by listing the names of Ishmael's twelve sons, each of whom would found a tribe, in direct parallel to the twelve tribes of the Israelites (Gen. 25:12–17). Like Jacob, Abraham's grandson, Hagar's child would give rise to a new nation, demonstrating that Hagar fulfilled the mission God had given her at the well. She had created a new people.

Still, in the Jewish and Christian lexicon, Hagar is largely worthy of note because she foreshadows the enslavement that would face Abraham's children in about four hundred years. God had released her from servitude and allowed her to claim her freedom, so it was only natural for Jews and Christians to view her journey as a symbol of what the Israelites would undergo when they fled Egypt.

The fact that she was Egyptian—a culture the Bible portrays as sinful—made her story all the more complicated to ponder. Early Jewish commentators were struck by the fact that she never returned to her homeland. She would live near Egypt, but not in it, and the rabbis saw this as proof that, although she was not entirely righteous, she was more pure than the immoral denizens of the land of the Pharaohs.[19]

In Islam, Hagar is the essential link between Mohammed and Abraham, so she represents the extraordinary qualities of Muslims everywhere. She is above all a founding mother and a brave leader.

As we have seen, after the angel dug the spring that saved Hagar, she built a well, whereas in Judaism and Christianity, God opened Hagar's eyes to a well that was already there.

Moreover, the Biblical version of Hagar leaves out any account of Hagar's ability to negotiate real estate deals. The well God reveals to her in the Bible never becomes hers, whereas the Zamzam is hers right from the start. This is one reason why the Islamic tradition needed to place Hagar at the Zamzam. Ishmael could never inherit any of his father's wells, but he could claim the rights to the well his mother had dug, especially as it was God who had given the spring to her.[20]

Scholars have often pointed to the many commonalities between Jewish and Muslim religious traditions, explaining that Mohammed and the later Islamic commentators borrowed freely from early Jewish sources. But this crucial difference in water rights creates an essential distinction between the two traditions. In the Bible, Hagar does not earn rights to the well that saves her. In the hadith, she does.

THE STORIES ABOUT HAGAR and the Zamzam echo an important Biblical incident that occurred in Abraham's life immediately after he sent Hagar into exile. After banishing his wife and child, Abraham did not have any time to grieve or even contemplate what he had just done. Instead, he immediately became embroiled in a nasty debate about, of all things, water rights. Reports had come to Abraham that Abimelech's men were stealing water from a well in Beersheba, perhaps the very well God had shown Hagar. Now Abimelech's tribesmen were preventing Abraham's herdsmen from using it.

Abraham was furious and met with Abimelech, accusing the king of taking the well from his people. Miraculously, Abimelech did not put up any fight but acquiesced so quickly it was clear that he was still afraid of Abraham and Sarah's God. However, Abraham was not content with the fact that he had just cowed one of the most powerful kings of the era. He announced that the well should belong to his descendants in perpetuity since he had dug it with his own hands. Again, the frightened king agreed and Abraham walked away from these negotiations the victor.

What is important here is the debate over ownership. Abraham had made a significant incursion into the king's land by claiming a water source. It was truly remarkable that Abimelech bowed to this claim and made every possible concession in order to please this man. The Bible's intent seems to be to show that Abraham had come far: from being a nomadic stranger in the land, to being a leader respected and feared by the king. The disputed well was in a spot that would come to be known as the "well of oath," or Beersheba, named after the agreement between Abimelech and Abraham.[21] To mark his triumph, Abraham planted a grove of trees (21:33).

However, if this well was the same one that had saved Hagar—and the placement of the story suggests this, since it occurs immediately after Hagar's discovery—then the Bible is drawing an implicit parallel between husband and estranged wife. One is saved by the water in a well. The other saves the well. She plants her son under a tree. He plants trees. What does this mean? Why are the two stories placed side by side? How are Abraham and Hagar connected to each other after he sends her away from the campsite?

As we have seen, this interpretative gap is filled in by Muslims. Recognizing that Hagar's fight to preserve her son's rights to the Zamzam closely mirrors Abraham's negotiations over the well at Beersheba, Muslims paint a picture of a strong, forthright woman.

Indeed, the Muslim portrayal of Hagar is of a woman who is in many ways Abraham's equal. Nowhere could he have found a more suitable wife. But Hagar had left him far behind, and neither he nor his descendants by Sarah could know her capabilities. Sarah's children would always believe that Hagar was a helpless victim, blessed by God only because of her relationship to Abraham rather than through any merit of her own.

But this doesn't have to remain the case today. Even without reading the Islamic tales, one can observe Hagar's bravery, stoicism, and leadership shining through the words of Genesis.[22]

She began life as a slave and ended it as a free woman who gave rise to a proud nation. Hagar's partnership with God took her far, but so did her initiative. After all, the first time she set out for the desert she went of her own accord. No angel told her to flee. No voice from heaven said that she would be rewarded. By choosing this path, she opened the gates of freedom for herself and her children.

CHAPTER TWENTY-EIGHT

MOUNT MORIAH

At least there was one little boy left to greet him when Abraham got home from his negotiations with Abimelech—Isaac, the child whose name reminded everyone of his miraculous birth. As Abraham struggled to make his peace with missing Hagar and Ishmael, it was undoubtedly a comfort to have the company of his younger child. He could teach the boy how to tend the sheep and the goats as well as how to use a knife to slaughter and skin them. Together, they could walk in the fields and check the pasturage. When merchants passed through, Isaac could watch his father barter and learn how to bargain from a master. Abraham could take hope from the fact that his boy was growing strong and tall and was learning his people's customs. When the time came, he would have a worthy successor.

The family moved back to Hebron, away from the scene of Hagar's expulsion and Abimelech's incursions, back to the campsite where the angels had announced Isaac's birth. The journey north put some distance between them and the difficult events of Gerar. If they could forget what had happened there, they had a better chance at happiness. With Hagar and Ishmael in exile, there would be no more competition between the women and no more teasing and fighting between the boys. Of course, there was always Abraham's broken heart and his worries about his second wife and his older son, but perhaps the pain would have lessened over time and Isaac could have grown up snug and secure in the love of both of his parents, if only God had let them live in peace.

But this was not to be. Once more, God broke the tranquillity of the campsite, summoning Abraham by name.

"*Hinneni,*" Abraham answered instantly. *Hinneni* has been variously translated as "Here I am" or "I am ready." But "ready" is something of an understatement, since this English word fails to capture the urgency of Abraham's Hebrew. Essentially, *hinneni* means "Yes, I am ready *right now.*"

Oddly, Abraham seemed to know that God had something pressing to say. Perhaps there was something in His tone, or maybe Abraham suspected that it would be too simple for him to quietly enjoy what was left of his family. But no matter how well he prepared himself, Abraham could never have anticipated God's next statement:

Take your son, your favored one, Isaac, whom you love, and go
to the land of Moriah, and offer him there as a burnt offering
on one of the heights that I will point out to you (Gen. 22:2).

Burn his son on top of a mountain? Sacrifice the miracle child? As Elie Wiesel points out, the word God uses is "*ola,* which means an offering that has been totally consumed, a holocaust."[1] Nothing would ever be the same after God uttered these words. Not in Abraham's life, nor in Isaac's or Sarah's, nor in any of their descendants', including us. God had bugled a chilling note, a warning call to Abraham. It was an illusion for parents to believe they owned their children, God declared. All human life came from Him and was ultimately His to reclaim. He was in charge of who lived or died, and nothing could stand in His way.

Truly, this was a terrible moment of reckoning, and as usual, Abraham was alone when he heard these words. Either everyone else in the campsite had scattered, or God had come to Abraham when he was by himself. This was standard procedure for God, but still, Isaac might have benefited from hearing His commandment even if it terrified him. Otherwise, it would be all too easy for him to see his father's subsequent actions as a personal betrayal. On the other hand, if he had been there, he might have wondered why his father did not protest.

For Abraham was speechless and apparently frozen as well. He did not throw himself onto the ground. He did not mutter to himself. He did none of the things he had done during other difficult interviews with God. Instead, he did not respond at all, leaving us to wonder what he felt.

God, however, was unperturbed. He did not wait around for Abraham to speak, but vanished the moment He had delivered His statement, leaving Abraham to brood over His words, which were oddly familiar.

Indeed, God employed many similar techniques and much of the same language as in His first communication with Abraham. When He had told Abraham to leave Ur, He piled up phrases in order to emphasize the sacrifice Abraham would have to make if he chose to obey. Not only did Abraham have to leave his "native land," but he also had to depart from his "father's house." Similarly, it was not enough for God to say that Abraham would have to surrender his son; He added that Isaac was Abraham's favorite. In addition, since this final commandment was His tour de force, He chose to drive home the preciousness of their relationship by introducing a new verb into the Bible, *ahava*, or "to love." Thus, when God declared that Isaac was the boy Abraham loved, Isaac became the first person to be "loved" in the Bible.[2]

Before this moment, the only evidence that Abraham loved Isaac was the feast he had held for the boy when he was weaned, and this was not particularly conclusive, as the feast could easily have been to fulfill a patriarchal duty. Otherwise, Abraham had revealed his feelings as a father only when he expressed his concern for his firstborn, telling God that he was worried about Ishmael and his legacy. Furthermore, the most emotion he had ever displayed about either of his sons was when he had been "distressed" about having to exile Ishmael a short while ago.

At no time did Abraham pray on Isaac's behalf or ask God if Isaac had received God's blessing. Of course, he did not have to ask God about Isaac's fate, as God had been clear about the boy's special privileges since the moment He had announced his birth. But as a result, there had been no opportunity for Abraham to reveal the extent of his love for his new little son — that is, not until now.

His reticence makes it possible that Abraham's love for Ishmael was so strong that God needed to spell out that it was Isaac, not Ishmael, who was the "beloved one," or that he *should* be. God and Abraham's potential disagreement about the identity of the favorite son has given rise to centuries of conflict, as Abraham's legacy was at stake. Indeed, the question of who was the favorite son has never been satisfactorily answered. Jews and Christians say Isaac. Modern Muslims say Ishmael.

Even in Islam, however, there was originally disagreement over this question. Because the Koran, unlike the Bible, does not provide a name for the boy, for the first two centuries after Mohammed's death, Muslims were divided on the issue. It was only gradually that the majority decided God must have meant Hagar's child. Today, the claim that Isaac was the son of the sacrifice is seen by some Muslims as yet more evidence of the inherent flaws in Jewish and Christian interpretation of Scripture.[3]

Nevertheless, in the Bible, what mattered to Abraham at this point in his life was that he had only one son left. If obeying the orders to leave Mesopotamia and his father behind or to cast out Hagar and Ishmael had been difficult, fulfilling this commandment was much harder. God had asked Abraham to sever ties with yet another child — his second son — and in a much more violent and final way than the exile of Ishmael.[4] To obey this new commandment would mean watching his son die.

Despite the many differences between His first commandment to Abraham and this new dread order, God clearly felt the two were linked. Indeed, they book-ended His relationship with Abraham, as they were His first and last commandments.[5] Both times, He used the famous phrase "go forth," or *lekh lekha* ("Go forth from your native land" and "Go forth to the land of Moriah"). And, just as He had failed to give the precise location for Canaan, He did not reveal the exact location where the sacrifice of Isaac should take place. Instead, Abraham would have to wait until he got near the right spot and then guess.

But these strange parallels do not explain why God insisted on magnifying the nature of the sacrifice. His puzzling step-by-step recitation of loss — your son, your favored one, the one you love — caught the attention of the early commentators. One story goes like this:

After God told Abraham to sacrifice his favorite son, Abraham said to God, "I have two sons. Which son?"

God said, "Your favored one."

"Each is the favored one of his own mother," Abraham said.

God replied, "The one whom you love."

"Is there a limit to the affections?" Abraham asked.

At last, God answered, "Isaac."[6]

According to this tale, it was God who identified the favorite, not Abraham. Each phrase allowed Abraham to guess a little bit more accurately the nature of God's intentions, but he never named the boy, suggesting that he was parrying with God, resisting His pressure to identify Isaac. But this story is open to interpretation, and how one reads it depends on which side one takes in the inheritance battle that ensued in the years after Abraham's death. It could be argued that Abraham was trying to protect Isaac. On the other hand, perhaps he was unprepared to name Isaac as the favorite because of his loyalty to his eldest son.

Abraham was right to worry. In the Bible, the election of one child over another often portended loss of some kind. Indeed, the problematic status of the favorite can be traced all the way back to Cain and Abel, another story about two brothers. When God chose Abel as His favorite, Cain murdered his brother out of jealousy. Abel's unlucky glorification brought about the young man's doom.[7]

If this is what happened to the first "favorite," it was not a good omen for other Biblical favorites, especially since there is an even more disturbing aspect of being the chosen child that Abraham would have realized instantly but which most modern readers would miss entirely. When God addressed Abraham, the word He used for "favorite child" was *yahid*, a word used only twelve times in the Bible, each time in association with child sacrifice.[8] Thus, when he heard these fateful syllables, a chill would have gone down Abraham's spine. To choose a *yahid* meant that a beloved child would soon face immolation for the sake of the divine.

God's use of this troubling word has led Harvard scholar Jon Levenson to suggest that child sacrifice was far more prevalent in the world of Abraham and his descendants than previously believed and that this practice was not just the province of the Canaanites, but was actually part of Abraham's ideology and that of his children.

To support this rather shocking argument, Levenson points out that, in the list of six hundred or so laws that God issued after the Ten Commandments, God declared, "You shall give Me the first born among your sons" (Exod. 22:28). In other words, all firstborn children were meant to be sacrificed to God. Of course, in terms of the inner chronology of the Bible this declaration came long after Abraham had died, and besides, as Levenson demonstrates, not all Biblical laws were meant to be fulfilled at all times. Still, he argues that the laws represent a theological and cultural ideal that we should not dismiss from this story and from Abraham's imagination.[9]

Indeed, Levenson points to one Biblical tale in which Jephtha, the captain of the Israelite army, vowed that if God would let him vanquish his enemies, he would offer "the first thing" he saw when he got home as a sacrifice to God. Tragically, after he had won his battle, the first creature he encountered was not a calf or a lamb, but his daughter, a *yehida* (the feminine of *yahid*). Although in this case the word could mean "only daughter" rather than favorite child, still the unhappy father had to slaughter his child to fulfill his oath (Judg. 11:29–40). Although, as Levenson says, the connection to Isaac is uncertain, it is "highly suggestive," especially since God made no protest over Jephtha's actions.[10]

In addition, Levenson argues that God used the word *yahid* when He commanded the Israelites to paint their doorways with the blood of the Paschal Lamb so that the Angel of Death would pass over their homes and not kill their firstborn, or their *yahid*, since the eldest son was generally assumed to be the favorite child. Of course, in this version of child sacrifice, a lamb replaced the eldest son of the Israelite's household, but only because God had partic-ularly commanded this replacement. If He had not, the Israelites would have also lost their sons, suggesting that such an event—the sacrifice of a child—was all too possible in the Biblical world.

Whether or not child sacrifice was part of Abraham's repertoire of experience, it is true that Abraham and his family lived in a land where the sacrifice of small children was a form of worship, even if an infrequent one. As late as the fifth century B.C.E., more than a thousand years after Abraham lived, the Phoenicians, descendants of the Caananites, were still actively sacrificing little boys and girls to appease the gods. In 1971, archaeologists discovered an image of what some of these rituals looked like. The remains of a stone tower in a Phoenician colony in southern Spain depicted a grisly banquet scene where a god with two human heads stacked on top of each other held a bowl filled with "a small person" whose "head turned to look at the upper head of the monster."[11]

Thus, God's words—impossible though they seem to the mod-ern ear—posed a real threat to Abraham. He had to proceed, knowing full well that God was capable of requiring Isaac's death and—this was the worst part—that it was His right to do so. He had given Abraham the boy, and now He could take him away if He chose to.

The idea that God could ever accept a human sacrifice is a blasphemous thought for many. Most Christians, Jews, and Muslims do not like to think that their God would ever command the death of human beings for His own pleasure. As the contemporary Jewish theologian Shalom Spiegel writes, God's intention through this whole episode was to advertise the new idea that He wanted His people to "abolish human sacrifice [and] substitute animals instead."[12]

Much of the debate that has swirled around God's commandment to sacrifice Isaac stems from the fact that the Bible introduces this episode with the sentence "God put Abraham to the test" (Gen. 22:1). In one Jewish prayer book, the notes on this story say that the use of the word "test" is "to remove any possible misunderstanding on the reader's part that God requires human sacrifice."[13] Søren Kierkegaard, the nineteenth-century Christian philosopher whose masterpiece *Fear and Trembling* was based on this story, believed that Abraham's real trial was to retain his faith that God, the all-loving, would never follow through on such a commandment.[14]

But if Abraham believed that God was incapable of making such a demand, then he did not undergo much of a test. What seems more likely is that Abraham assumed God was going to take his *yahid*. Thus, Abraham's challenge was to place his love for God before his love for his son. In defense of the idea that Abraham believed he was going to have to sacrifice his child, the medieval philosopher Joseph Albo wrote, "The reward for potential good deeds is less than the reward for actual good deeds." Therefore, he argued, God "wanted Abraham to discover the great depth of his faith" by requiring him to do what would be most difficult for him.[15] If Abraham did not believe he was going to lose his son, his "good deed" in this story was merely hypothetical.

But it is disturbing to consider the idea that Abraham willingly embraced God's test. This was the man who had initiated the famous debate with God on the hills of Hebron about Sodom and Gomorrah, but not once did he protest the commandment to kill his own son. All he said was that one eager word, *hinneni*. What kind of hero was this? What kind of man would willingly give up his child? And, even more problematic, what kind of God would make such a demand? No wonder Kierkegaard and others wanted to whitewash God's intentions.

Of course, as some scholars argue, the two cases are very different. The death of an innocent person in Sodom and Gomorrah is a scandalous idea and "requires protest." But in the context of a ritual sacrifice for God, there should be no resistance. In fact, the gift should be given freely and with joy. Still, even if this argument releases Abraham from any blame, it reinforces God's culpability.[16]

Abraham had no time for contemplation of God's motives or, for that matter, his own. He knew he had to act quickly, since God had ended His commandment with *lekh lekha*, emphasizing that Abraham had to leave immediately. In practical terms, however, Abraham had no accurate idea where he should go. All he knew was that he should head away from the camp and that God would point out which mountain he should ascend.

So, without complaint, early in the morning, Abraham made his preparations for the journey. He "saddled his ass" and "split the wood for the burnt offering" (22:3). When he was ready, he selected two of his servants to accompany him and, with Isaac in tow, began the hike toward Moriah.

Over the centuries there has been debate over where Moriah actually was. The only other reference to Moriah in the Bible is when God "appeared" to King David in "Moriah" to show him that his son Solomon should build the First Temple of the Jews in Jerusalem.[17] Therefore, for thousands of years people have believed this was the location of the fateful mountain. On a symbolic level, the Temple Mount makes sense as the place designated for Isaac's sacrifice.[18] However, modern scholars say it is impossible to know where Moriah really was.

It is unclear how old Isaac was at this point in the story; guesses have ranged from age six to thirty-seven Abraham could have been traveling with an adolescent, a grown man, or even a small child. All that is certain is that Isaac was old enough to talk and to walk without being carried.[19] Yet, no matter how old he was, the sense of doom that hung over his father's head must have been evident to Isaac, as well as to the servants. Abraham did not speak during the long trip, and neither did anyone else. No one asked where they were going or why.

If Moriah was indeed located in what would become modern-day Jerusalem, it would have taken about one full day of walking from Hebron. But the Bible says that it took the travelers three days to reach Moriah (22:4). This inconsistency in the Jerusalem argument has been explained in different ways. Some commentators say that the number three has mystical meaning, and others argue that three days is the Biblical formula for a long journey.[20]

One ancient rabbinical legend says Satan wanted to block Abraham from reaching Mount Moriah. Transforming himself into a deep river, Satan placed himself directly in Abraham's path. The patriarch could not be stopped, however. He plunged into the river until the waves came right up to his neck. Just before he was about to drown, he raised his voice and told Satan to release him from the currents, saying, "Begone, for we go to Moriah by the command of God." Immediately, Satan vanished and the land became dry once again.[21]

This story illustrates the rabbis' conception of Abraham's suffering and how often he must have been tempted to give up and disobey God. Rashi says Abraham proved his faith in God by wandering, lost and uncertain, until God showed him which mountain was the right one.[22] In the Biblical text, however, God remained silent. Just as he had once recognized Canaan as the Promised Land, Abraham somehow understood when they had reached their destination. He led the way to the foot of one of the hills and told the servants to wait for him and Isaac at the bottom, adding cryptically, "The boy and I will go up there; we will worship and we will return to you" (22:5).

This remark has occasioned much controversy over the centuries. Many have wondered what Abraham meant by saying *"we will return."* Some have argued he had an inkling that Isaac would survive, while others have suggested that he lied so that the servants would not get suspicious about his plans and try to stop him. Rashi believed that Abraham had had a vision of what would happen on top of the mountain. After all, Abraham was a prophet; thus he knew God's plans.[23] However, Rashi's idea is problematic, since, as we have discussed, it is difficult to describe Abraham as brave or faithful if he already knew his son would be spared.

Another conundrum is whether Isaac understood what was happening. If he did not, it is quite possible that Abraham lied to the servants so Isaac would not guess the true nature of God's commandment. There was still the long hike up the mountain to endure. Even if Abraham told his son the truth and Isaac accepted the idea, the boy would only have longer to dread his own suffering. Besides, there were Abraham's own misgivings to quiet. If he acknowledged what he was going to do, he might not have the courage to proceed.

While the servants watched, Abraham strapped the wood for the fire onto Isaac's back. Suddenly the connections between Abraham's last loss and this impending one became glaringly obvious. Just a short while ago, he had strung a water skin onto Hagar's back, knowing full well that he had not given her enough to survive if she did not find a well. The parallels were inescapable: once the water skin was emptied, once the wood was burned, he would have lost both of his boys.[24]

But again Abraham did not hesitate. Instead, he took the instruments for the sacrifice out of his donkey's saddlebags, the firestone and the long sharp knife he might well have used for the Covenant of the Parts and to fulfill God's commandment of circumcision. Then he and Isaac started up the mountain path, Isaac undoubtedly struggling under his burden of logs. As one of the ancients wrote, it was as though Isaac "carri[ed] his cross on his own shoulder."[25]

Before long, the servants were out of sight, and the southern desert stretched below them, yellow and vast. If Abraham and Isaac gazed downward, they could see where they had come from and could trace their journey through the thick, pitted landscape of the wilderness. But soon, the lower world was lost to view, and father and son could only see the path stretching before them. Occasionally, a thrush called, or a breeze rattled the branches of the scrubby pines that clung to the sides of the hill. Otherwise, everything was silent until finally Isaac spoke. "Father!" he said, letting the word stand by itself so that Abraham could hear the full force of the two syllables, *Avi*.

"Abraham answered, 'Yes, my son, here I am,'" falling back on the word that he had first spoken to God, *hinneni* (22:7). Since *hinneni* had been Abraham's attempt to articulate his eagerness to serve God, perhaps this was his effort to show Isaac how "ready" he was to talk with him. If so, his strategy worked; Isaac responded immediately, asking the very question that his father could not answer directly.

"Here are the firestone and the wood; but where is the sheep for the burnt offering?" (22:7).

The poignancy of this exchange is almost unbearable. There was little that Abraham could say. He was caught between God and his son. But it is puzzling that Isaac had waited so long to ask about the nature of the sacrifice that lay ahead. Surely he had noticed that there had been no animal trailing along behind them for the last three days. Why had he said nothing until now?

If Isaac was a young boy, say six or seven, then the timing of his question makes sense. One would not expect a small child to notice the lack of the sacrificial offering until this point in the story. But if he was the young man that tradition has seen him as, then the question seems to have many more meanings than the literal one, since only a very dim-witted individual would have missed the absence of a sheep or a goat before now. Thus, maybe he waited to ask this question to investigate his father's motives. Or perhaps he guessed the role he was supposed to play in the sacrifice and was pushing his father to acknowledge what was about to happen.

This last idea, that he had implicitly accepted his fate, gave rise to a tradition that God was testing Isaac just as much as he was testing Abraham. In the Middle Ages, when European Jews faced martyrdom at the hands of the Crusaders and other enemies, Isaac became a famously inspirational figure. Many stories featured him trudging forward with his father, "the one to bind, the other to be bound; the one to slaughter, the other to be slaughtered."[26] After fleeing from a murderous onslaught, one twelfth-century Jewish rabbi prayed to God for safety, crying,

> O Righteous One, do us this grace!
> Recall to our credit the many Akedahs,
> The saints, men and women, slain for Thy sake.

According to these portraits of Isaac as a martyr, father and son were united in their dedication to God and in their knowledge of what was going to ensue. The principle that Isaac embraced his own death as the intended sacrifice would also influence the writers of the Gospels, which describe Jesus as fully aware of his own fate as the sacrificial Lamb of his Father.[27]

Whatever the motivation for Isaac's question, Abraham's response was cryptic. He did not tell the whole truth. Nor did he console Isaac in case he was afraid. Instead, all he said was "God will see to the sheep for His burnt offering, my son" (22:8).

This remark, too, has given rise to pages of speculation. Many readers have seen it as evidence of Abraham's faith that God would in fact provide the sacrificial offering and that he would not have to kill his son. Kierkegaard wrote, "He believed that God would not require Isaac of him," or that, if he did indeed have to kill him, "God would give him a new Isaac, could recall to life him who had been sacrificed."[28] Kierkegaard based much of his thinking on the writings of the early church fathers, including the unknown author of the Letter to the Hebrews, who declared that Abraham had faith in God's omnipotence throughout this ordeal.[29]

However, even if Abraham believed he would have to sacrifice his son on the mountain, it seems clear that he did not want Isaac to spend his last minutes fearing this event. Perhaps he intended his white lie to be comforting, although Isaac gave no indication of feeling consoled. The silence that surrounded Abraham's words became ominous as father and son continued to walk up the mountainside. However, the Bible emphasized that Abraham and Isaac still felt close to each other, saying Isaac was still "as one" with his father. The ties that bound them were as yet unbroken (22:8).

CHAPTER TWENTY-NINE

THE BELOVED SON

When they reached the top of the mountain, Abraham recognized the place God intended for the sacrifice and gathered stones for a makeshift altar. There must have been something very distinctive about this particular spot, as Jewish legend says that Abraham was not the first man to this site. Adam had made the first sacrifice to God here. His sons, Cain and Abel, had followed suit. This was also where Noah had built an altar after the Flood.[1]

Abraham went right to work, removing the wood from Isaac's back and stacking it into a pyre on top of the stones. He labored in utter silence, and his son did not break the quiet. What was Isaac thinking? Did he guess what was to come, or was he still in the dark about what lay ahead? It is difficult to imagine what he felt or what his response was when the climactic and horrifying moment came. Abraham reached for him, took out the rope, and bound him. The Hebrew word *akedah*, or binding, is the title by which this story has come to be known in the Jewish tradition because it is this action more than any other that reveals Abraham's intentions. The father, it seems, was really going to sacrifice the son.

The strange thing is that God had not commanded "the binding" as part of the ritual. Abraham came up with this idea himself although his reasons are mysterious. We know he was not following the procedure for animal sacrifices. These offerings were usually killed before being placed on the altar, so binding them was not necessary. Instead, it seems likely Abraham was following the tradition for a far more troubling kind of sacrifice: the binding of "the beloved child whom the devout father is obliged to sacrifice and immolate." If this is the case, then, as Jon Levenson argues, "the *aqedah* is the only account we have of the procedure for a human sacrifice."[2]

But one ancient Jewish tale has a different interpretation. In this Midrash a heroically resigned Isaac speaks to his father.

> Father, make haste . . . and bind my hands and feet securely, for I am a young man, but thirty-seven years of age, and thou art an old man. When I behold the slaughtering knife in your hand, I may begin to tremble at the sight and push against you. Also, I may do myself an injury and make myself unfit to be sacrificed.[3]

This version helps explain why Isaac needed to be tied, even if he was compliant. At the same time, it underlines the idea that Isaac was an active participant in the sacrifice.

But if Isaac was still a young child, there are two other explanations for the binding: Abraham was worried his son would struggle and ruin the sacrifice, or Abraham was stalling, since binding Isaac allowed him to stretch out his final seconds with his son. If Abraham was reluctant to kill Isaac, however, this is the only hint we get. He continued steadily on his mission, picking the boy up — which reinforces the idea that Isaac was not yet an adult — and placing him "on the altar on top of the wood" (Gen. 22:9).

Isaac did not protest. And this is one of the most surprising aspects of the story. It is possible, of course, that he was so young that he did not realize what was happening. But perhaps he was as heroic as medieval Jews believed and simply submitted to his father's will. Even when Abraham "picked up the knife to slay his son," Isaac did not cry out. He remained utterly and inexorably silent. Perhaps he was preparing himself to be the perfect sacrifice, accepting that he was about to die. On the other hand, he could have been hating Abraham or praying to God. All that is clear is that it was eerily still on top of the mountain.

Thankfully, at this very moment God intervened.

"Abraham, Abraham," called an angel.

"*Hinneni*," said Abraham, relying on the word that had gotten him through most of this ordeal.

The angel continued, "Do not raise your hand against the boy, or do anything to him. For now I know that you fear God, since you have not withheld your son, your favored one, from Me" (22:11–12).

Oddly, Abraham did not express relief, nor did he offer thanks or embrace his son. He seems to have been in shock at how close he came to killing Isaac. Indeed, in contrast to Kierkegaard's reading of the story, if this reprieve was not a surprise to Abraham, the entire charade seems without purpose. Still, no one is sure what God hoped to achieve by "testing" the patriarch in this way. If Abraham was supposed to exhibit his ability to obey his deity without questioning His will, he had succeeded. But to what end? Why would God ask such a thing of His chosen one?

What is indisputable is that God had finally played His cards. To begin with, He did not want a corpse. Certainly, He did not need Isaac to be burned on the pyre his father had built. Instead, He revealed some interesting and complicated truths about Himself. First, He needed to find out something He did not know, demonstrating yet again that His foreknowledge of events is not always complete. As the New Interpreters' Bible states, "The only one said to learn anything from the test is God: 'Now I know' (16:12)." Thus, God underwent His own suspenseful ordeal: Would Abraham obey Him? Was He a worthy partner in their joint enterprise?[4] Second,

God needed to test Abraham's loyalties, exhibiting a strange insecurity as though He were a jealous lover doubting His beloved.

Although Abraham seems to have passed the test, staying "true"
to God, he had not actually killed his son. Isaac was still alive.
Abraham was still his father. Jack Miles sees this as evidence that
Abraham had managed to defy God's command. He points out that
when Abraham says to Isaac, "God will see to the sheep for His
burnt offering," the verb form can either be future or jussive ("God
will see to" or "Let God see to"), so that it is possible that Abraham
is actually commanding God to provide the offering. Thus, Miles
writes, "Abraham resists even as he goes through the motions of
compliance."[5]

But while Abraham had not actually killed Isaac, he had shown
himself capable of slitting the boy's throat. At the moment he raised
the knife, he ceased to be the man who gave life to Isaac and became
the one who intended to take it away. It was God who got to play the
role of savior. As a result, Isaac became a loyal adherent of his
father's deity. In fact, Jewish legend claims that Isaac was so pious
he spent three years in Paradise before resuming his life here on
earth.[6] To God's way of thinking, Isaac's transfer of allegiance was
as it should be. If Abraham had ever believed that he was in charge
of either the birth or death of his children, he had been fiercely dis-
abused of this notion.

Now that Abraham had proven that his "fear of God" was greater
than his allegiance to his son, he had also implicitly declared that
his role as a worshipper of God superseded his role as a father.
Although this was a bitter loss, God's test rescued Abraham from
what some would term the sin of idolatry, that is, too much love for
his son. Or, to put it another way, God's insistence that Abraham
offer Isaac to Him reminded Abraham that God was more important than his child. After all, it would have been understandable if
Isaac's miraculous birth had blinded Abraham to every other reality, including God's existence. Mount Moriah showed Abraham

that he had been a mere intermediary in Isaac's birth; God had the power to grant life, so Isaac's real father was God. For that matter, God was also Abraham's father. The first fruits and, indeed, all fruits were God's.

God did demonstrate some empathy for Abraham's divided loyalties by repeating the phrases "your son, your favored one" when He saved Isaac from his father's knife. God's refrain made the poignancy of Abraham's surrender of his son all the more acute as He emphasized that He understood how much Abraham loved his boy even as he prepared the sacrifice.

Before Abraham could respond, there was a rustle in the bushes, and a ram appeared (22:13). There is a tradition that this creature was not an ordinary ram but was one that God had created during the first week of the world and had saved for exactly this purpose, the rescue of Isaac.[7] Certainly, it was miraculous that it appeared when it did. This is why Jews blow the shofar, or ram's horn, in celebration of the New Year. The sound is meant to remind Jewish congregations that even when things appear at their bleakest, God will provide. Furthermore, the blowing of the horn is meant to provoke compassion in God for human suffering, suggesting that there is a darker side to this tradition as well. God's empathy for human beings must be summoned. It is not intrinsically there for us to depend on.

Meanwhile, the young man who lay on the pyre of wood his father had constructed did not move, speak, or sigh with relief. He lay as though already dead. Oddly, Abraham said nothing to his son. Not one word of consolation or love. In fact, the two who had been "as one" would never speak again. This silence between father and son has kept what happened next shrouded from the reader. We never get to hear if Abraham helped his son down from the pyre and whispered how sorry he was. We don't hear Isaac weep or shout at his father in rage or give thanks for being spared. All we know with any certainty is that Abraham slaughtered the ram, throwing it on the pyre "in place of his son" (22:13).

This was an independent action on Abraham's part, as God had not commanded him to make an offering of the animal. Indeed, God was now as quiet as father and son. He made no statement that human sacrifice was against the rules, nor did He declare that animals should be burned instead of human beings.[8] Rather, He left the decision to kill the ram up to Abraham, while His words about how Abraham had proved that he "feared" God continued to echo in the air on top of the mountain.

As the flames licked at the logs beneath the dead animal and the ram began to roast, the mouthwatering smell of burning meat filled the air. But even this sacrifice did not create a climactic scene of release and rescue or of joint worship by father and son. At least symbolically, Isaac would remain forever bound by his father while Abraham would remain forever the man who had raised a knife to his own child. The great Hasidic teacher Menahem Mendel of Kotz wrote, "Although it was hard for Abraham to bind Isaac on the altar, it was just as hard to release him. For Abraham realized that Isaac, for the rest of his life, would remember that his father had almost killed him."[9]

However, God's chosen man recognized that he had sustained another vision from the Lord, one that had permanently estranged him from his miracle child but that linked him to his God forever, even if it was now a bond tinged with bitterness. And so he directed his eyes heavenward and gave Mount Moriah the name *Adonai-yireh*, which has been translated variously as "on the mount of the Lord there is vision" and "on the mount the Lord appears."[10]

In a certain way, then, both Abraham and God had gotten what they wanted. Abraham had proved that he was more faithful than God Himself, since it could be said that God had gone back on His word by demanding Isaac, whereas Abraham had consistently been loyal to God, obeying His most difficult commandments. As for God, He had gained more knowledge about His chosen man Abraham. The patriarch would obey His word even when it meant performing incomprehensibly painful duties. In addition, God had secured His relationship to Isaac, as Isaac would never be able to see Abraham as his trusted father again. As a result, God's lineage was secure. Isaac's children would be God's children.

Still, one cannot help but wonder about Isaac's point of view. Although the Midrash says that on the mountain he transferred his primary loyalty to God, it is also possible that this beloved son felt betrayed by both of his fathers. The mystery that surrounds him is deepened by the fact that he did not speak again until after his father died. When he does finally talk, we do not hear his actual words. Instead, he simply "pleads" with God for children, in an uncanny echo of his father (25:21).

There is a notable resemblance between the events on Mount Moriah and the wanderings of Hagar and Ishmael. Both Hagar and Abraham used the word "vision" to describe their encounter with God after their sons are spared. More disturbing is the fact that both boys almost died at the hands of their father. Ishmael's close call came about through Abraham's command. Isaac's encounter with the knife needs no further explanation. In both cases, God saved the boys, reaffirming His blessing.

In current Muslim thinking, though, these parallels are not given much weight. As we have seen, to modern Muslims, the child who was nearly sacrificed on top of the mountain was not the son of Sarah. They base their ideas on some central problems in the Biblical text. First, God commanded Abraham to sacrifice his only son, but, in the Biblical version of the story, God uttered His commandment when Abraham already had *two* sons. Jewish and Christian thinkers have explained this contradiction in one of three ways: (1) Abraham had only one son by God's anointed woman Sarah; (2) Ishmael had been exiled at this point and so was no longer, for all intents and purposes, Abraham's son; or (3) Ishmael was included in God's blessing but not in His covenant about the Promised Land.

Muslims counter these arguments by saying the chronology of the Bible is wrong and that Mohammed and Islamic theology corrected its mistakes. Clearly, God ordered Abraham to sacrifice his son *before* the birth of Isaac, back when Abraham had only one child. This leads Muslims to point to the second apparent contradiction in the Bible: the problematic question of Ishmael's age at the time of his expulsion. In the Bible, as we have seen, his age at exile appears to swing back and forth. Abraham could not have "laid" a teenager on Hagar's shoulder. Hagar could not have laid an adolescent under a bush. And an adolescent would not cry like a baby. This seems to indicate that Ishmael could not have been sent into the desert when he was seventeen years old. Accordingly, Islamic thinkers say that Abraham must have exiled Hagar when Ishmael was an infant.

However, a problem arises with the Muslim version, since Ishmael was circumcised at age thirteen, and it is unclear how this would have happened if he were already in exile. Islamic thinkers solve this conundrum by explaining that Abraham was a loving father who regularly visited his little boy in Mecca and that during one of those visits he performed the operation. In fact, Islamic tradition holds that Abraham visited Ishmael every seven years and that it was on his first visit that the sacrificial event occurred, a test that involved Ishmael, not the as-yet-unborn Isaac.

As Muslims tell it, when they were catching up on all that had occurred during their time apart, Abraham said to Ishmael, "O my son! I have seen in a dream that I am offering you as a sacrifice to God, so what do you think?"

Ishmael responded with alacrity: "Do what you are commanded," he said. "You shall find me very patient." So Abraham laid his son prostrate, put his forehead on the ground, and directed a sharp knife toward his neck. At this very moment, God called him: "O Abraham! You have fulfilled the dream! Thus do We reward the good doers!" A ram was sent down from heaven to be slaughtered instead of Ishmael, which Abraham did, and they both had a big celebration that day.[11]

In this version of the story, not only are the sons switched, but a few other ideas change as well, although the central point of Abraham's obedience stays in place. For instance, Ishmael's earnest participation in the potential sacrifice is explicit. He becomes a second Abraham, modeling devotion to God and adherence to His commandment. Thus, God's reprieve is a joyful occasion that father and son can share. In fact, Muslims have a holiday each year called Eid al-Adha, the Feast of Sacrifice, to commemorate how Abraham and Ishmael "submitted to the will of God."

While Islam celebrates the obedience of Abraham and his eldest son, Christianity joins Judaism in discounting Ishmael's role in the story of the sacrifice. To most Christians, Ishmael is to be pitied for his exile, whereas Isaac's ordeal foreshadows the fate of Jesus of Nazareth. In the same way that Isaac's status as the beloved one necessitates his encounter with his father's knife, so Jesus's identity as God's "beloved" marks him for the crucifixion. Thus, in many Christian congregations, the story of Mount Moriah is read on Good Friday as a prelude to the Gospels' rendition of the death of Jesus.[12]

To Paul, this interpretation of the sacrificial story offered an opportunity to prove that Christians were the real descendants of Abraham. He wrote, "For not all descendants of Israel are truly Israel, nor, because they are Abraham's offspring, are they all his true children. . . . It is not those who are born in the course of nature who are children of God; it is the children born through God's promise who are reckoned as Abraham's descendants" (Rom. 9:6–9). In other words, if Abraham passed his legacy of faith directly to Jesus, then the real recipients of God's covenant were not the literal descendants of Abraham and Sarah (and certainly not the descendants of Abraham and Hagar), but those who had accepted Jesus as the Messiah. The chain of inheritance went like this: Abraham, Jesus, and the community of the faithful. This, Paul said, was because the Jews had based their "efforts" to achieve righteousness on "deeds" not "faith."[13]

To Paul, those who did not believe in Christ were exiled like Ishmael, marooned in the desert, cut off from the true worship of God.[14] Unfortunately, Paul's ideas paved the way for many of the stereotypes that still fuel the flames of modern-day anti-Semitism. Although Paul believed that the Jews would be "grafted" back onto the tree of true faith, his insistence on the primacy of faith over deeds led to future misconceptions. One of the most damaging is that Jews are "slaves" to the law, blindly following the rules of Torah and missing the path of the spirit.[15]

Of course, this is a misrepresentation of Judaism, and of Paul's words, as Jews have a venerable history of spiritual practice, from the teachings of Talmud to Kabbalah. But those who formulated these ideas were fighting to gain legitimacy for a fledgling religion. To the early church leaders, both religions could not be Abraham's rightful heirs, so Paul's theology could only pit the two faiths against each other.

Even now, the quarrel over which son was sacrificed on Mount Moriah continues, implying an argument about which religion is truly legitimate. Of course, there are those who do not participate in this debate, but they are few and far between. If this contention over the identity of the beloved son could cease, perhaps the legacies themselves—the traditions the three sons stand for—could rise gently to the surface. Then at last we might view these three great religions in all their complexity rather than as opponents in a war where winner takes all.

CHAPTER THIRTY

THE DEATH OF SARAH

The moment after his reprieve from the flames would seem to be the moment for Isaac to inherit his father's mantle and become the patriarch of the next generation. But the Bible does not depict him as an eager prince; in fact, it does not bother to describe him at all. The boy who had almost been slaughtered was nowhere to be seen. This did not worry God, who declared to Abraham:

> Because you have ... not withheld your son, your favored one, I will bestow My blessing upon you and make your descendants as numerous as the sands on the seashore (Gen. 22:16–18).

The lack of Scriptural information about Isaac at this point in the story has given rise to much speculation and even some suspicion. One Midrash says that the angels carried him off in their arms and flew with him to Paradise, where he sojourned for three blissful years.[1] But some ancient Jewish thinkers believed that Isaac was not standing next to his father listening to God's final words because he had actually perished in the flames. When God had said, "You have not withheld your son," He meant it literally. Abraham had placed Isaac on the pyre and watched the fire consume his body.[2]

This shadowy tradition about Isaac's death persists despite the fact that he would soon reappear, alive and well. For example, one Talmudic story says that during the time of David, God sent a plague to Jerusalem to punish the king for his sins. But when God looked down at the suffering city, He caught sight of a pile of ashes heaped on top of Mount Moriah. He realized that this black mound was all that was left of Isaac, and the memory of Abraham's sacrifice persuaded Him to be compassionate and spare the people.[3]

Another Talmudic tale recounts a dilemma about where to build the Second Temple after the First Temple was destroyed. As the people were pacing around Mount Moriah, arguing about the site, they discovered Abraham's altar and "the ashes of Isaac." This, they knew, should be the precise location for the new building. Rashi said that God had compassion for humanity because of "the ashes of Isaac." And a twelfth-century rabbi wrote, "When Abraham bound his son Isaac on the altar, and slew him and burned him, [the lad] was reduced to ashes, and his ashes were cast on Mt. Moriah."[4]

Although the idea that Isaac did not survive his trip up the mountain contradicts the Bible's version of events, these accounts of Isaac's death demonstrate the power of the Akedah. At the last moment, God had stayed Abraham's hand, but He had asked Abraham to turn away from his son in his imagination and his heart. Perhaps it is this assertion more than anything else that gave rise to the Talmud's tales of Isaac's ashes. After all, Abraham and Isaac's relationship was severed so effectively, it was as if Isaac were dead to his father. Once the possibility of the father killing his son had been raised, it was hard to put it back into safekeeping. A dangerous idea had surfaced and the ancient commentators could not help but examine its implications.

Though most readers do not accept the interpretation that Isaac died, many still wonder why God would issue such a commandment. Abraham had already proclaimed his loyalty to the Lord many times: he had circumcised himself, left his father behind, and sworn off all other gods. As for God's pronouncement about the covenant, there was nothing new about this; the patriarch had already received God's word that he would have numberless descendants. Thus, there did not seem to be a need for this final test. God's behavior seems arbitrary and cruel, and this has troubled generations of believers and nonbelievers alike.

In an attempt to grapple with God's inexplicable "test," the ancient legends claim that even the ostensibly loyal Abraham was bewildered. In one story, Abraham actually interrogated God about the injustice He had inflicted. The scene took place on top of the mountain while the ram was still burning. As the smoke wound its way up to heaven, Abraham's anger overflowed and he declared to God, "I will not leave this altar until I have said what I have to say."

After God politely agreed to listen, Abraham said, "Did You not promise me that Isaac would be the child of Your covenant, and that he would go on to father multitudes?" God agreed that this was so.

Abraham continued, saying, "I might have reproached You, and said, 'O Lord of the world, yesterday You told me that Isaac would be the father of multitudes and now You say, "Take thy son, thine only son, Isaac, and offer him for a burnt offering."' But I . . . said nothing."

God did not interrupt, so Abraham went on. If he could convince God of his righteousness, the consequences would be enormous. "When the children of Isaac sin . . . and fall upon evil times," he said, "You should be mindful of the offering of their father, Isaac, and forgive their trespasses and deliver them from their suffering."[5]

God was not affronted at Abraham's boldness, just as He had not been disturbed by Abraham's arguments on behalf of the potentially innocent citizens of Sodom and Gomorrah. Instead, as in the earlier episode, He credited Abraham for his concern about the generations to come and replied in a compassionate and careful manner, saying, "Your children will sin in the future, and I will sit in judgment upon them on the New Year's Day. If they desire that I should grant them pardon, they shall blow the ram's horn on that day, and I will remember the ram that was substituted for Isaac as a sacrifice, and will forgive them for their sins."[6]

Given the prevalence of this idea—that the ram was a kind of mnemonic device for God—almost as many tales exist about the ram's remains as about Isaac's ashes. Some say that King David used its sinews to make the strings for the harp on which he composed and sang the Psalms. Others declare that the prophet Elijah fashioned the ram's skin into his belt. As for the ram's horns, they were truly extraordinary. One was blown at the end of God's delivery of the Ten Commandments to Moses on Mount Sinai, and the other one would be blown at the end of days.[7]

In many ways this legend helped to redeem God as well as future sinners. If God had indeed listened to Abraham and said that He would reciprocate for the great gift Abraham had given Him, then He revealed Himself to be far more compassionate than in the original Mount Moriah story.

Of course, this tale was created to soften the edges of the Bible's version, although it is notable that the rabbis do not picture Abraham petitioning God *before* the Akedah. That would have made him appear far too disobedient. As it stands in the stark Scriptural telling, the central question remains unanswered: What could have prompted God to "test" Abraham in such a terrible way? As we have seen, some commentators argue that God needed to learn about Abraham's faith. But why was He uncertain about Abraham's loyalties? Had Abraham done something wrong? Had he not been virtuous enough? Perhaps God had ferreted out his moments of rebellion. Maybe it was not sufficient that he had left his homeland, his father and brothers; endured decades of childlessness; been forced to flee to Egypt during a famine; and been compelled to part with Ishmael and Hagar, all at God's behest. Once again, it is hard not to wonder what kind of God would require so much from His chosen man.

In an attempt to explain this puzzle, some stories point to Satan as the origin of Abraham's suffering, as though the idea of God coming up with these ordeals on His own was impossible. In the most common version, Satan taunts God, saying, "At the feast he had for Isaac, Abraham did not offer you any thanks. No calf was slaughtered for you. No sheep, nothing at all. You know how human beings are. Once you give them what they want, they forget all about you."[8]

God had no answer to this. He believed that Abraham was loyal to Him, but did not want anyone to have questions about his piety. Thus, just as He would test Job many centuries later when Satan challenged Him again, He devised the most difficult trial He could imagine so that Abraham would have the opportunity to prove his virtue to the world.[9]

Still, perhaps God secretly agreed with Satan, in which case His command was meant not just as a test, but as a stern wake-up call to Abraham. As we have already discussed, there is little evidence that Abraham was delighted by the arrival of Isaac, since, when God announced his birth, Abraham had remained focused on Ishmael. Maybe Abraham himself had anxieties about whether he had been grateful enough for the birth of his second son. As modern commentators have noticed, in many of these ancient tales, Satan seems to represent the inner doubts of the characters.[10]

Yet there is another Midrash that makes the opposite claim, saying that God tested Abraham because he loved Isaac too much. As Elie Wiesel writes, "This hypothesis has the merit of 'justifying' the order that Abraham received from God and which otherwise would seem incomprehensible." Yet, as Wiesel notes, the questions still remain. Why does God "inflict a worse—and supreme—punishment on the son?"[11]

If any of these stories about Abraham's mistakes were true, then Abraham's trek up Mount Moriah would surely make up for the neglect of duties to God or discrepancies in his love for his two sons. However, in the wake of such a trial, his feelings about God could only undergo an irrevocable change. If God had wanted to draw closer to His chosen man, He had failed. Never again would Abraham and God speak. He had offered God his last sacrifice, and although God would shower blessings down upon him, he would not respond. Indeed, Abraham acted as though he never wanted to hear God's voice again.

Sadly for Abraham, his own son appeared to be having the same reaction to him. The Bible says that the great patriarch returned to his servants alone (22:19). Where was Isaac? Of course, this could be a simple gap in the text, but just as the lack of mention of Isaac after the ram's sacrifice has given rise to many Midrash, so has the sentence describing Abraham's return. After all, Scripture was particularly pointed about the fact that the father and son climbed the mountain together. Wiesel asks, "Are we to understand that . . . the experience they just shared had separated them — albeit only after the event? That Isaac, unlike Abraham, was no longer the same person, that the real Isaac remained there, on the altar?"[12]

Aside from the story about Isaac in Paradise, many hypotheses have emerged about where Isaac had *really* gone. One of the most popular is that he vanished to study Scripture at the Bible school of Noah's son Shem.[13] Of course, this does not make chronological or historical sense, since there was as yet no recorded Bible to study, and Shem could not still be alive. Yet the point of the story is that even though Isaac may have felt estranged from Abraham, his faith in God had not diminished. Instead, he wanted to draw closer to the deity who had saved him.

The Bible offers no such consolation for Abraham. Rather, it emphasizes his alienation from his entire family by stating that he did not go home to Sarah, who was still in Hebron. He traveled instead to Beersheba, the same land where Hagar and Ishmael found their well and where Abraham had successfully negotiated with Abimelech. Perhaps the patriarch was mourning his second wife and grieving the absence of his first son.

Beersheba lay southwest of Sarah's campsite and was far enough away that husband and wife could not easily visit back and forth (though it was close enough that they could travel the distance, if necessary). The only way to get to Beersheba from Moriah (if it was indeed Jerusalem) was to cut straight through Hebron, so either Abraham saw Sarah briefly as he traveled through, or he made his way around the settlement, adding days to his travel, simply to avoid seeing his wife. Either way, his choice of Beersheba did not speak well for his marriage, though it is unclear if he was avoiding Sarah, or if Sarah did not want to see him.[14]

Certainly, Sarah may have been the one to cast him out. After all, she had waited ninety years to give birth to Isaac. She loved her son passionately. If she had gotten even a whiff of what Abraham had intended to do, she might well have condemned his actions. In a recent Midrash written by Arthur Strimling, when Sarah gets wind of Abraham's plans, she, and not an angel, is actually the one who stops him from killing their son.[15]

The Jewish sages put a more positive spin on Beersheba, suggesting that Abraham wanted to protect Sarah from what had almost happened to her son. Why force her to confront the fact that she almost lost Isaac? Better to distance himself from her so that she would not learn the truth.[16] However, given the parameters of their relationship, what seems most likely is that Abraham felt guilty about what had just transpired and wanted to avoid a confrontation with his spitfire wife. Even at a distance of thousands of years, it is perfectly easy to imagine her anger. How could she not have felt betrayed by her husband? Consequently, separation became an excellent strategy for keeping the peace.

Interestingly, just as Abraham tried to distance himself from one part of his past, another caught up with him. A messenger from the brother he had left behind in Mesopotamia tracked him down in Beersheba. This was truly a remarkable event, given the enormous distances that separated people, the difficulty of actually locating them, and how long it took to travel on foot. Yet the Bible does not say how the messenger found the patriarch, or how he came by the news he bore. What was important was contact with the family Abraham had left behind. This moment is made all the more poignant by the fact that Abraham had effectively isolated himself from everyone he had ever loved. He was on his own now. No sons. No wives. No brothers. No nephew. Even his relationship with God had become tenuous.

While Abraham listened eagerly, the messenger revealed that Nahor, Abraham's brother, had had a total of twelve children by his wife and his concubine. This was important information, and Abraham stored it away for later use. If Isaac ever did reappear, he would need a wife, and maybe one of Nahor's daughters or granddaughters would be the right woman. Then Isaac would not have to marry a Canaanite. The number twelve was also strangely predictive as, in just two generations, Abraham's grandson Jacob would produce twelve sons, the founders of the twelve tribes of the Israelites, and Jacob's wife would be descended from Nahor. In addition, Ishmael would soon have twelve sons of his own.

But Abraham could not know any of this. He had to face the contrast between himself and his brother, which could hardly have been more striking. Nahor had an enormous family, ensuring that the line of Terah, the father of both men, would not die. In contrast, all Abraham seemed to have left were his servants. Before he had time to brood on his lonely situation, however, another messenger hurried into the camp with terrible tidings. Sarah had died. Although the Bible does not tell us how much time elapsed between the Akedah and Sarah's death, many of the ancient rabbis connect the two, saying that the reason the text tells us about her death right after Mount Moriah is that she died from sorrow when she heard about the events on the mountain.[17]

However, other commentators have different explanations for this tragedy. Some said that while Abraham was preparing to sacrifice Isaac, Satan paid a nasty visit to Sarah. He had figured out that Abraham was going to succeed at his test, so to hurt the God he hated, he would do his best to destroy Sarah. Accordingly, he "appeared to her in the figure of an old man, very humble and meek," and whispered in her ear, just as the snake had to Eve, "Dost thou not know all that Abraham has done unto thine only son this day? He took Isaac and built an altar, slaughtered him, and brought him up as a sacrifice. Isaac cried and wept before his father, but he looked not at him, neither did he have compassion upon him."[18]

Sarah did not think to question the veracity of the evil talebearer and wept bitterly, crying, "O my son Isaac my son, O that I had this day died instead of thee! It grieves me for thee!" When she had finished her lament, Sarah fell into the embrace of one of her women friends and "became as still as stone."[19]

Satan was even more cruel in another tale. Disguising himself as Isaac, he arrived at Sarah's tent in apparent distress. In concern, Sarah said, "My son, what has Abraham done to you?" Seizing the opportunity to drive a wedge between the married couple, Satan reported what Abraham had done to Isaac, including the binding and building the flames of the sacrificial fire. Although he did say that Abraham had spared Isaac's life, he left out the fact that God had required these actions, so Sarah leaped to the assumption that Abraham had chosen to inflict suffering on their child of his own accord. So shocking was this information that she died immediately.[20]

Because commentators tend to regard Satan as an emblem of the "internal conflicts" of each character in the story, some interpreters suggest that Satan reveals an essential character flaw in Sarah: she assumed Satan's report was accurate when she should have doubted him. Worst of all, in the second version, she distrusts Abraham. Indeed, according to the ancient legends, it was this lack of faith in her husband that warranted her death.[21] Despite all appearances to the contrary, Sarah should have believed the best about her husband and, for that matter, about God.

Finally, other ancient sources hearken back to Sarah's outcry to God when she was angry with Abraham for not protecting her from Hagar's effrontery. She had declared, "May God judge between you and me." As the Talmud says, "He who calls down judgment on his neighbor is himself punished first."[22] Thus God shortened her years on earth.

Many readers, however, resist these stories of blame. As Wiesel argues, Sarah's death represents the impact of the terrible events like the Akedah on innocent family members and suggests that Abraham "became unwittingly an accomplice to his wife's death."[23] Even the Midrash stories, far-fetched as they may seem, point to the basic fault line in this marriage. No matter why Sarah died, the abruptness of her death precluded any kind of resolution between husband and wife and rendered Abraham even more alone.

When he heard the news, Abraham traveled to Hebron as quickly as possible and went straight to Sarah's tent to sit beside her body and mourn. This moment in Abraham's life fascinated the early rabbis. Although he may well have been enacting the ancient traditions of his tribe, this is the first recorded instance of a devout follower of God observing any kind of ritual having to do with death. Thus, many Jewish and Christian practices come from this passage. For example, the fact that he did not leave Sarah's body alone but stayed with her has made sitting with the dead an important rule in many mourning rituals. Also, he did not talk, and as a result, silence has become a solemn mourning tradition in some religious circles.

In contrast, the Midrash says that the behavior of the other members of the campsite was far from exemplary. One story depicts everybody weeping so inconsolably over Sarah's death that Abraham had to comfort them rather than receive any comfort himself.[24] Perhaps as a result of this tale, this sort of behavior is absolutely taboo in the Jewish tradition of mourning. No one is supposed to address the mourner unless he or she asks a question or invites one to speak.

So what did Abraham do while he sat beside his dead wife? The rabbis decided that he composed the famous Biblical poem that praises the ideal wife: "Who can find a woman of valor? Her price is far above rubies. Her husband's heart relies on her."[25] Of course, scholars have long since argued that this verse was written many years after Abraham lived. But even if we did not turn to the historical record, given the state of things between Abraham and Sarah when she died, it seems surprising that anyone would think Abraham wrote this poem. His heart did not necessarily rely on her. He had had no difficulty receiving payment for her charms from two different rulers. Yet the idea that Abraham penned this love poem remains part of the Jewish tradition, reflecting an age-old hope among readers for reconciliation between husband and wife, as though the Biblical silence that surrounds Sarah's death leaves the story too painful and too incomplete.

The Bible does not tell us how long Abraham sat there, but the Midrash says that before he began the burial procedures for his wife, Satan made one more return visit. "Abraham," Satan said, preying on Abraham's conscience, "it is your fault that Sarah died."[26] If Satan represents some aspect of Abraham's own psyche, it must follow that Abraham was tempted to believe he was guilty of this crime. But why?

David Klinghoffer suggests that Satan's appearance here represents the problem of self-glorification. Abraham had to resist the idea that he was responsible for other people's destinies. Klinghoffer writes, "It is a temptation we have all felt—to think that everyone else's fate depends on us. Self-aggrandizing and infantile at the same time, it pictures us at the center of not only our own world but that of every other person we know."[27] Sarah's death rested on God's shoulders, not her husband's. The rabbis who told this story believed that an essential aspect of the sacrifice of the beloved son was the necessity for Abraham to surrender to God's will. Muslim thinkers concur. Even self-blame on Abraham's part could too easily undermine this crucial point of faith. It was the divine who had power over life and death, not Abraham.

True to form, Abraham did not succumb to Satan's blandishments. Instead, he set about discharging his last practical duty as Sarah's husband: finding a place to bury her body.

CHAPTER THIRTY-ONE

BURIAL AND MISSION

Abraham had a particular place in mind to lay Sarah to rest. The Bible says that he went to the leader of the men who lived in Hebron, the Hittites. Tradition has it that the meeting took place at the gates of the Hittite city near the hill of Tel Roumeidah, where archaeologists have excavated the remains of a four-thousand-year-old town wall.[1]

Abraham began the meeting with the diplomatic skills he had honed over the decades, formally asking the Hittites for the right to purchase "a burial site" (Gen. 23:5). By "site" he did not mean one small plot of land to house his wife's body. Instead, he wanted an entire acreage, large enough for generations of his descendants to claim as their own. This was a remarkable testimony to his belief in God's covenant, since at this point there was still little evidence that these generations would come to fruition. Isaac was unmarried. Ishmael was not supposed to be the son to inherit the Promised Land. Who else besides himself and Sarah would be buried in this ground? Who else would cultivate this field?

Since Abraham and his people were only "resident aliens" (23:4), the Canaanites would have been perfectly within their rights to refuse his request, especially as they were famous for resisting foreigners' claims to their land. God, however, must have been working behind the scenes to make sure Abraham succeeded, as the Hittites proved surprisingly eager to please, saying, "My lord: you are the elect of God among us" (23:6).

Apparently, Abraham's blessings were so visible that even the Hittites had noticed. Angels had visited this man. Foreign kings had sought his assistance. He had been chosen by his God to be the leader of a people; no one in his right mind would want to displease a divine emissary. Thus, the Hittites made an offer that expressed their admiration for Abraham as well as their fear of his deity: "Bury your dead in the choicest of our burial places; none of us will withhold his burial place from you for burying our dead" (23:6).

The Hittites' gesture was a significant tribute to Abraham, as such an offer meant they were willing to share the afterlife with him and his family. According to their tradition, people who were buried near one another would travel together on the final expedition to the Kingdom of Death. If Abraham bought this land, therefore, there would be no distinction between his descendants and the Canaanites.

But Abraham did not want Sarah to lie with the Canaanites in their grave compounds. He wanted to preserve his people's identity for future generations. It was a difficult proposition, however, to say no without offending the Hittites. So Abraham "bowed low to the people of the land," demonstrating his deference and his gratitude, and asked to buy "the cave of Machpelah." This was a skillful twist on Abraham's part, as he managed to make it sound as though he were eager to be "in [the] midst" of the Hittites (23:9), even as he suggested that his wife and family be buried separately from them.

The owner of the Machpelah cave, Ephron, stepped forward immediately and, observing the intricate rules of Canaanite negotiation, promised to give Abraham the land for nothing. But Abraham knew better than to accept such an offer. If he took Ephron at his word, the man could reverse the deal, reclaiming the land as his own. Or he could later exact some kind of tribute from Abraham as a tenant on his land. This was not acceptable to Abraham, who was determined to own this land for himself and for his future children. So, again, he "bowed low to the people" and said to Ephron, "Let me pay the price of the land; accept it from me that I may bury my dead there" (23:13).

Ephron pretended to demur, saying, "A piece of land worth four hundred shekels of silver—what is that between you and me?" Again Abraham saw through this ploy and, in front of the elders, paid Ephron exactly what the Hittite had said the land was worth, four hundred shekels.

Abraham was now the proud owner of a rocky, infertile field and an undistinguished cave. There was so little that was appealing about this particular patch of land that the Canaanites must have wondered why Abraham had pushed so hard to attain it. Even today, his choice is puzzling. Perhaps this was all he could afford. Or maybe he suspected that the Hittites would agree to sell it to him, since it was not worth much. Hebron is located in one of the most mountainous regions of modern-day Israel. Although the altitude, up to a thousand feet in some places, makes it a good climate for grapes and plums, the site where Sarah and Abraham are reputed to be buried is unprepossessing. This is disguised by the fact that all three monotheistic religions have erected enormous monuments in Abraham's honor. But if you took down the imposing mosque, the wall built by Herod, and the chapel erected by medieval Christians, the rough and barren feeling of the land would resurface.

Yet Abraham must have known that this purchase would be a proclamation to the future of his family's rights to this terrain, as well as, on a more human scale, his complicated love for his wife. According to Jewish tradition, it was this purchase of the Cave of Machpelah that gave rise to the ritual of a groom "purchasing" his wife with a gold band at the wedding ceremony. Even today, when a man places a wedding ring on the finger of his bride, Orthodox Jews believe that he reenacts "the exchange of money for Ephron's field" that took place almost four thousand years ago.[2]

Furthermore, in Hebrew, the name "Hebron" means "to join together," reflecting the city's origins as the home and burial site of this famous couple.[3] So, despite their final estrangement, Abraham declared his loyalty to Sarah in the way his world would best understand, a real estate purchase that would announce the stature of their family.

However, Teubal argues that Sarah, as a Mesopotamian priestess, was actually the one who selected the site. According to this theory, Sarah regarded Mamre as a sacred grove, and since she was in charge, Abraham was simply performing his duty by burying his powerful wife in a ritually approved location. Although few scholars adhere to this theory of matriarchal power, there is some evidence to back it up. For instance, it is in Mamre that God promised Sarah a baby and where she bore the child of that promise, Isaac. In addition, it would be in Mamre, in Sarah's tent, that her grandchild would be conceived.[4]

On the other hand, according to the Midrash, there was a supernatural reason to buy this particular land, as the Cave of Machpelah was not just any cave. It was the mysterious cavern that Abraham had discovered when he had chased the calf for the angels' banquet all those years ago, before Isaac's birth. This was the cave that contained the bodies of Adam and Eve. One story says that when Abraham entered the cave with the body of Sarah in his arms, Adam and Eve wanted to leave, because they were "ashamed" of the sins they had committed, especially when faced with the virtues of the patriarch and his wife. Abraham attempted to "soothe" them by promising to intercede with God on their behalf, but only Adam listened to him; Eve still "resist[ed]" so vigorously that Abraham had to lift her up and carry her "back to her place."[5] As though it were not enough that he had to bury his wife, he also had to rebury the mother of all humanity.

After he had laid Sarah (and Eve) to rest, it was time for Abraham to return to his duties as a leader and a father. But the early commentators believed that the events on Mount Moriah and Sarah's death had taken their toll on the 137-year-old Abraham, giving rise to a kind of "just so" story. Up to this point, the legends say, Abraham had been so youthful and vigorous that he had often been mistaken for Isaac. But after Sarah died, he prayed to God that the symptoms of age would mark his face and slow his step. God granted this petition and Abraham's request set into motion the human aging process. This was the first time a human being experienced the physical symptoms of growing older, and ever since, "the appearance of men changes in old age."[6]

Certainly, Abraham seems to have understood that he was no longer the vital man he had been. Soon, he would be too weak to be the leader anymore, and Isaac would have to assume his father's post as the next patriarch of the tribe. But it was not immediately clear that Abraham would be able to get his son to shoulder his duties. The Bible does not say how old the boy was or how much time had passed after Moriah. At this point, Isaac could have been a young child, a teenager, or even a middle-aged man.

The Bible does imply, however, that even if by now Isaac had accepted the circumstances of his sacrifice, he was still intent on avoiding his father.[7] Father and son are never described as being in the same place after the Akedah. The text does not mention Isaac's presence at his mother's deathbed, nor does it say that he helped his father with the burial rites. The legends attempt to repair this bitter aspect of the story, and the most famous tales declare that Isaac suddenly appeared and wept over Sarah's body, crying, "O my mother, my mother, how hast thou left me, and whither hast thou gone?"[8]

Even in the ancient stories, though, Isaac does not speak to his father. But Abraham did not have the luxury of waiting until his son felt like communicating. He needed to prepare Isaac to assume his new role. If Isaac was to carry on God's covenant, he had to have children, so Abraham's first order of business was to find him a wife. However, as Isaac seemed resistant to his father's overtures, Abraham required a trustworthy adviser to help guide his son.

The man he turned to was his intelligent and worthy senior servant. Although the Bible never names him, tradition says this man's name was Eliezer.[9] This was the same servant to whom Abraham had thought he would leave all of his worldly goods before the birth of his sons, a testimony to the high esteem Abraham had for the man. Eliezer had been with him longer than any of his other servants, presumably since they had arrived in Canaan.

Therefore, Abraham summoned Eliezer and made the man swear fealty to him, asking him to "put your hand under my thigh" (24:2). This odd request was a euphemism for a rather intimate gesture. Abraham wanted the man to swear by "the sign of the covenant," that is, to touch the mark of circumcision. The circumcised penis was a visible sign of the relationship between the two men and of Abraham's loyalty to God.[10] After circumcision, the whole camp, servants and masters, could be considered members of the same family. Although such a request might sound suggestive to modern ears, Abraham did not intend any kind of sexual innuendo. Instead, he wanted to impress upon his servant the seriousness of the occasion as well as to emphasize the importance of producing future generations who would abide by God's covenant.

Abraham demonstrated his esteem for Eliezer by carefully describing the errand and giving him the chance to refuse it. The job, after all, was deceptively simple. Abraham needed him to return to Mesopotamia "and get a wife for my son Isaac." There were many pitfalls to such an expedition and Eliezer could not help but be alarmed. "What if the woman does not consent to follow me to this land, shall I then take your son back to the land from which you came?" he asked (24:5).

This was a perfectly reasonable question, but it was one that Abraham dismissed immediately. He did not want Isaac to return to Mesopotamia under any circumstances. "On no account," he declared, "must you take my son back there!" (24:6). Abraham's vehemence might at first seem misplaced, but it was only through Isaac's continued presence in the Promised Land that the family's legacy could continue. Abraham's vision during the Covenant of the Parts had shown him that his children and their descendants were destined to own Canaan. To leave now would be to threaten the future that God had promised and that he had worked so diligently to build. If Isaac was not there to defend his rights, invaders might claim the land. Or worse, Isaac might be tempted to stay in Mesopotamia. After all, it was a beautiful, highly civilized country with many appealing luxuries.

But Abraham did not want to cut all ties to his old family. He knew that his brother Nahor had produced many children. If Isaac married a woman from within his family network and could convince her to live in Canaan, then Abraham could retain his bonds to the brother he had not seen for years without losing his stake in the Promised Land. In addition, Isaac's new bride would help him stave off any temptation to merge into Canaanite culture. Together, they could preserve their distinctive identity as members of Abraham's tribe. It was fine for his family to live near the Canaanites, to mingle and chat and bargain with them, but they must always retain their difference from their neighbors.

Some may criticize Abraham for not wanting Isaac to marry a native woman. Did he think his family was superior to the Canaanites? Was he being uncharitable? But such critiques miss the uniqueness of Abraham's maneuver. Abraham was grappling with a very "modern" situation: how do strangers live in close proximity when they do not share customs or beliefs? Most tribal leaders in the ancient world chose to settle conflicts with others through violence or else avoided strangers altogether.

Abraham's strategy of coexistence without full assimilation was a pragmatic solution to the problem of foreign cultures dwelling side by side. His ideas still have a crucial application today, as his principles enable people to live together without having to surrender their identities or incur bloodshed. Indeed, it is this policy that is at least partially responsible for the famous longevity of Jewish religion and culture. As Rabbi Harold Kushner writes, "Much of Jewish history has seen the majority of Jews living as 'resident aliens' in the midst of other nations."[11]

To help Eliezer understand the significance of his mission, Abraham decided to tell him about the Lord's revelations: "[God] promised me on oath," Abraham told his servant, "saying, I will assign this land to your offspring" (24:7). Eliezer did not have to worry about choosing the right woman, Abraham explained, as God would send an angel to Mesopotamia before he got there, and this angel would do the difficult work of locating her. Once the angel found the right woman, though, she must be willing to travel to Canaan. If she refused to leave her father's home, Eliezer should leave her behind and return to Abraham. "Do not take my son back there," he exclaimed, repeating his previous order (24:8). The import of this command is underlined by the fact that these are Abraham's last words in the Bible.

To Abraham, then, Isaac's residency in Canaan was even more important than his marriage. During these last months of his life, it was the continuation of his legacy in the Promised Land that dominated the patriarch's thinking. Fortunately, Eliezer understood his master's preoccupation and agreed to all of Abraham's terms. So, after he had "put his hand under the thigh of his master," he gathered ten camels and other rich gifts and set forth for Aramnaharaim, where Nahor, Abraham's brother, lived.[12]

After many days of travel (although there is an alternative version of the story that says it only took him three hours because God was so eager to solve the problem of the brideless Isaac), Eliezer arrived outside the city walls. The trip had been long, hot, and dusty, and as he brought the camels to the well, the young women of the city came to draw water. Immediately, Eliezer gave notice to God that he was not going to wait for an angel to arrive to point out the perfect maiden. Instead, he declared that he had a plan and petitioned God for assistance, saying, "O God of my master Abraham, grant me good fortune this day, and deal graciously with my master Abraham" (24:12).

While the girls began the laborious process of drawing water,

Eliezer explained his idea to God: "Let the maiden to whom I say, 'Please lower your jar that I may drink,' and who replies, 'Drink and I will also water your camels'—let her be the one whom You have decreed for your servant Isaac" (24:14).

This is the first time in the Bible that anyone had prayed to God for aid in solving a problem.[13] Neither Abraham nor Sarah had asked for guidance in Egypt or Gerar. They had not even sought God's help with Sarah's barrenness. Hagar had wept, but she had not directly petitioned God. Now a simple servant in Abraham's household turned to the divine with a personal outcry. Perhaps because this was such a departure from the past, the servant's words have occasioned both criticism and respect from readers of the Bible. Some think he was too demanding and argue that one should not request a miracle or a sign, but should leave such mystical affairs to God's discretion. Others believe his prayer demonstrated the man's worthiness and piety—fitting attributes for someone so important to the well-being of his master's family.[14]

In this case, though his exchange was not as intimate as Hagar's, Eliezer was confident enough to have an independent relationship with his master's God. In addition, the test he had devised demonstrated that he was a compassionate and sensitive person, as he understood that the traumatized Isaac needed a woman who would look after him with kindness and generosity. After all, he could have created a very different sort of contest, based on beauty or wit.[15]

A moment later, a young and "very beautiful" woman came walking down the path to the well, balancing a clay jug on her shoulder. When she had finished filling her jar with water, the servant approached her, dusty from his travels, and implored her for a drink. Without any hesitation, in fact, "quickly," she offered him the jar, treating him with respect and addressing him as "lord," despite his humble appearance (24:19). This was generous behavior on her part, as drawing water was difficult and sweaty labor. The wells of the ancient world were neither tidy nor efficient like those of rural England and America. Instead, they were often little more than fortified holes dug deep into the sandy ground. You tied a rope around your jar or bucket, dropped it into the water, and sloshed it around until it felt full. Then you had to drag it back up without the benefit of a pulley, pitting your weight and strength against gravity.

Yet this young woman did not begrudge Eliezer a drop. When he had finished drinking, the girl noticed the tired camels kneeling by the walls of the town. She took pity on them, too, saying, "I will also draw for your camels, until they finish drinking" (24:19).

The man was astonished. Was it possible that this young woman was Isaac's prospective bride? Had God already answered his prayer? Taking no note of the servant's stunned silence, she emptied her jar into a trough for the camels and then watered all of them—an extraordinary task, since, for all this young woman's eagerness, it would have taken hours of hard labor to draw enough water for ten thirsty camels.[16] Yet the girl did not complain, nor did she appear to struggle. Not only was she kind, she was also strong and efficient, essential qualities for the sort of life Isaac's wife would lead on the frontier in Canaan.

The last test was her family's identity. Eliezer did not want his master's son to link himself to an inferior clan. But this last qualification seemed too much to ask, so the servant "stood gazing at her, silently wondering whether the Lord had made his errand successful or not" (24:21). At length, when the camels were done lapping in the trough, he stepped forward and presented her with some pieces of heavy gold jewelry: a nose ring and two armbands that weighed ten shekels, or about two pounds (24:22).

This was a lot of wealth for someone to have on hand, let alone to bestow on an unknown young woman, no matter how helpful she had been. But the maiden was not startled. Nor did she refuse, as she might have if this were a modern parable. Instead, she demonstrated a boldness the Bible holds up as a model, accepting the jewelry as though it were her due. Does this mean that she was acquisitive or scheming? Not in Biblical terms. Her cheerful acceptance of Eliezer's gold is presented as further evidence that she is the right choice for Isaac.

The text goes even further by implying that she may have realized Eliezer was a rich man. He had arrived in her city with ten laden camels, a sign of remarkable wealth. Thus, perhaps she was not simply an innocent girl who took pity on a stranger. Perhaps she had attempted to charm this wealthy man in hopes of a reward. In the ancient world, such strategic forethought was an asset, as it was important for a wife to contribute to the family's financial success. If this young woman could intuit that Eliezer was a man worth pleasing, then she was canny enough to help Isaac increase his holdings.

Eliezer, encouraged by her willingness to take his master's gifts, asked the question that was weighing on him.[17] "Pray tell me, he said, whose daughter are you?"

Now the young woman revealed the miraculous truth. "I am the daughter of Bethuel, the son of Milcah, whom she bore to Nahor." Her name was Rebecca, and she was the granddaughter of Abraham's brother (24:24). It was clearly not a coincidence that the young woman who had assisted Eliezer was the grandniece of Abraham. God had brought her to the spring.

Her qualifications to be Isaac's bride were now complete. The man "bowed low [to God] and said, 'Blessed be the Lord, my master's God, who has not withheld His steadfast faithfulness from my master. For I have been guided on my errand by the Lord, to the house of my master's kinsmen'" (24:27).

All that lay between the servant and success was the consent of the bride and her family. He could only hope that the gold jewelry that now glittered on Rebecca's arm and in her nose would help this process along. As politely as he could manage, he asked this self-assured young woman if there would be room for him, his men, and his camels to stay overnight.

Rebecca answered generously, demonstrating the kind of hospitality that was so important in the Bible's world. "There is plenty of straw and feed at home, and also room to spend the night," she declared. Then she "ran" home to tell her family all that had happened. Sure enough, when her brother Laban caught sight of the beautiful bracelets that adorned his sister he hastened to the well to find this wealthy stranger. "Come," Laban said when he found Eliezer. "Why do you remain outside, when I have made ready the house and a place for the camels?" (24:25–31).

The servant followed Laban back to the family's home and with great formality told them who he was and the nature of his errand. As he told the story, he made it clear that he was serving not only his master, Abraham, but also the Lord.[18] It was God, he declared, "who led me . . . to get the daughter of my master's brother for his son" (24:48).

Laban and his father, Bethuel, were suitably impressed. Despite his dirty feet and sweaty clothing, Eliezer was a messenger on behalf of the divine. Besides, the gold he had given Rebecca demonstrated that Abraham had indeed become wealthy. So, when Eliezer requested Rebecca's hand in marriage for Isaac, they replied, "The matter was decreed by the Lord . . . Here is Rebecca before you; take her and go, and let her be a wife to your master's son, as the Lord has spoken" (24:50). It would be foolish to spurn the advances of such a rich man.

Again, Eliezer "bowed low" in gratitude, not to the two men, but to the Lord. Everything was going so smoothly; God had surely been watching over him. However, the next morning, he ran into his first snarl. "Give me leave to go to my master," he said to Bethuel. But Rebecca's family protested. There were elaborate leave-taking rituals that had not been completed. Rebecca's mother was not yet ready to part with her daughter. Understandably, she wanted a little more time to prepare for this separation.

Up until now, Rebecca had not had any say in the matter, as she was "only" a woman. The men in her life were in charge of her fate. But Eliezer remained so adamant that at last Laban and Bethuel did something unusual. Without any fanfare, they said, "Let us call the girl and ask for her reply" (24:57).

Although some argue that this was the custom in this part of the world and therefore not particularly significant, never before in the Bible had a woman been asked for her opinion about the direction of her future.[19] It is unclear why Rebecca's father and brother took this step. One argument is that Rebecca, like Sarah, was in fact the next in line to be a Mesopotamian priestess, in which case the men in her family would defer to her wishes.[20] Another, more straightforward explanation is that they actually cared about Rebecca's opinion. Was she ready to leave? If so, they would listen to her wishes.

This moment is one of the central reasons the religious leaders of both Judaism and early Christianity believed that a woman needed to give her consent before she married.[21]

When her brother and father asked her what she wanted to do, in front of the stranger and her large extended family, Rebecca boldly said, "I will [go]" (24:58). It is safe to assume this was not what her relatives had expected to hear. Although they were eager to marry her to a wealthy man, they had clearly not been ready to say good-bye this abruptly. Now they were stuck; they would have to allow her to have her way.

Already, it was clear that this young woman was unique. Most girls her age would have been loath to leave their families and set forth into the unknown. But, like her future father-in-law, Rebecca revealed herself to be ready for the great adventure that lay ahead.

For Rebecca's mother, this farewell was like a death. In fact, when Rebecca waved good-bye, it was the last time she saw any member of her family. Like Abraham, she had received the command to leave her father's home and her native land, so she went. But in one regard she had outdone her father-in-law: not only had she obeyed God's wishes, but she had also articulated her intentions to those she would leave behind. When Abraham had received God's order, he had simply started walking without making any formal announcement of his purposes. His father never had the chance to say good-bye.

Bethuel and Laban, on the other hand, had the opportunity to give Rebecca their blessing, declaring:

May you grow
Into thousands of myriads;
May your offspring seize
The gates of their foes. (24:60)

Interestingly, these words are still recited in a traditional ceremony known as "the veiling of the bride" that occurs before a Jewish bride enters the synagogue to make her wedding vows.[22]

Rebecca's declaration to her parents and older brother demonstrated that she was precisely the right woman to continue Abraham and Sarah's legacy. She had all the energy and initiative Isaac seemed to lack. More important, she was not afraid to strike out into the wilderness, an essential quality for those who were part of God's dream for the future.

CHAPTER THIRTY-TWO

COMING HOME

Eliezer did not hesitate once they left Mesopotamia. He led his party straight into untamed lands with no apparent fear of getting lost or of supplies running out. The other servants and Rebecca trailed along behind him without asking any questions. The way was hot and steep—this was to be expected—but as they wandered deeper into the wilderness, his followers must have wondered if the servant knew what he was doing. The man marched forward as though God was his guide, although some among the party must have harbored their doubts. Perhaps the man was deluded. Perhaps he was being controlled by an evil spirit.

The strange thing is that the question of Eliezer's reliability has never really been put to rest. Over the centuries there have been unpleasant rumors about the man. Some muttered that he wanted Isaac to marry his own daughter and did everything in his power to sabotage Abraham's mission. Others whispered that he dishonored Rebecca on the way to find Isaac.[1]

The basis for this last rumor is the awkward wording of the text "Then Rebecca and her maids arose, mounted the camels, and followed the man. So, the servant took Rebecca and went his way"

(Gen. 24:61). Why, the sages wondered, was there a need for this last sentence? It only seems to muddle the order of events. Shouldn't it come before Rebecca arising and mounting the camels? As David Klinghoffer notes, "The biblical text alludes to something dark.... The Hebrew words normally translated as 'and the servant took Rebecca' . . . could also mean 'and the servant consummated a sexual relationship with Rebecca.'"[2]

Yet, even if Eliezer had attempted rape, it is hard to imagine the bold Rebecca remaining silent. Surely, she would have screamed for help and fought the loss of her virginity. Thus it seems more likely that Eliezer was a contributor to Isaac's good fortune rather than a scoundrel scheming to seize the young woman for himself. Indeed, his uncanny success in finding Rebecca points to an important theme in this story and in the Bible in general — the theme of the loyal servant or messenger.

In Hebrew, the word *malachi* means "messenger," but it can also mean "angel," as angels are God's messengers. Although the Bible depicts Eliezer as a human messenger rather than a divine one, his ability to do exactly the right thing suggests he was close to God.

Like Hagar's, his interaction with the divine took place at a well, and although God did not speak to him directly, Rebecca's sudden appearance was evidence of His involvement. It is possible, therefore, that if Abraham had not relied on Eliezer, Isaac might never have found the right wife. Although this dependence on a servant to perform such significant duties might seem contradictory to the modern reader, it was not unusual in the world of the Bible. Male servants could be influential in their own right. Their masters often relied on their judgment and gave them some level of autonomy.[3] Eliezer himself was probably allowed to own property and slaves.

The importance of servants in furthering Abraham's lineage is reinforced by the tale of Ishmael. As we have seen, without Hagar's resourcefulness and courage, the boy might never have been born, or he might have died in the desert. That both servants were responsible for the creation of Abraham's descendants emphasizes the fact that Abraham and Sarah were only two characters in a more complicated story. Master, mistress, male servant, female servant—all were essential for building a strong foundation for the future.

The ancient rabbis took note of Eliezer's abilities and featured him in their stories as an example of a virtuous trickster. In one such tale, Eliezer is beaten up by Sodomites until he bleeds, but when he goes to a Sodomite judge, the judge rules that Eliezer should pay the perpetrators for making him bleed. Unfazed, Eliezer picked up a stone, "wounded the judge with it, and said: 'Pay the fee you owe me for bleeding to [those who wounded me]; as for my own money, it will remain in its place.'" In another story, Eliezer tricks the Sodomites into feeding him even though it was considered a crime to feed a hungry stranger in Sodom.[4]

Just how extraordinary Eliezer was became evident when, after a short period in the desert—the legends again say only three hours—he led his party over a hill and they saw a solitary figure walking in the fields. The servant had completed his mission with ease and perfection. Quickly, Rebecca climbed down from her camel to ask Eliezer who the man might be, and Eliezer said, "My master," indicating that Isaac had replaced Abraham as the patriarch now that Eliezer had brought him back a wife.

Isaac hastened toward them just as his father used to rush to greet visitors. Sheep and cattle grazed quietly in fields that stretched to the horizon. Although the Bible is not clear about the precise location of this spot, it does tell us that Isaac had just come from Beer-la'hai-roi. Isaac may not have been aware of the story of Hagar's first revelation in the desert, but the reader will remember that the name Beer-la'hai-roi was based on Hagar's name for God, "He who I have seen and gone on living" or "He that lives and sees me." Clearly, the Bible wants to remind the reader of Hagar right at this climactic moment in Isaac's story. Why?

Isaac had more in common with Hagar than he could possibly suspect. To begin with, Isaac and Hagar had both endured nearly fatal experiences because of Abraham. Both were ultimately saved from death by God. Far from being opponents, therefore, the son of the covenant and the mother of Ishmael were linked, and the two peoples they would help create, the Arabs and the Israelites (or the Muslims and the Jews), were related not just because they had the same father, but because both lineages were born out of suffering that was redeemed by God. Interestingly, Isaac and Rebecca would settle in Beer-la'hai-roi after Abraham's death, reinforcing the relationship between the son of Sarah and the mother of Ishmael.[5]

Isaac, who had been out inspecting his flocks—or praying, as the early Jewish thinkers argued—little suspected that the dust that rose up along the horizon announced the arrival of his father's servant and his future bride.[6] But as he hurried toward the caravan under the enormous desert sky, it would have been understandable if Isaac felt God's presence. Perhaps this is why the ancient rabbis said it was Isaac who invented *mincha,* the afternoon prayer service still chanted by modern Jews.[7]

When at last Isaac had drawn close enough to greet everyone, Rebecca did not lift her hand, smile, or try to please him. Instead, she immediately "took her veil and covered herself," transforming herself from a beautiful, forthright young woman to a mysterious maiden (24:65). After her direct manner with the servant at the spring, this sudden shyness seemed out of character.

Some explain her behavior as a sudden attack of propriety and consider her veiling as the appropriate display of modesty for a bride of the ancient world. Others say that she was suffering from shyness. One legend has a different explanation, declaring that an angel had just told her that she "was destined to be the mother of the godless Esau . . . and trembling, she fell from the camel and inflicted an injury upon herself."[8]

However, Rebecca had not appeared particularly retiring back in Mesopotamia. She had willingly talked to a strange man, received gifts of gold, and rebelled against her mother's wishes in order to launch herself into a new life. Although meeting her new husband was certainly more overwhelming than speaking to Eliezer, it also seems likely that Rebecca had a plan.

No other woman in the Bible had hidden her face when she met her husband, at least not that we know about. Indeed, until now, the initial meeting between man and wife had not been deemed worthy of reporting. Thus Rebecca initiated not only a tradition but a way of thinking about marriage that was entirely new. Ever since, brides have traditionally worn a veil during their marriage ceremonies, evoking this moment of meeting between Rebecca and Isaac.

The instant Isaac recognized his father's servant, he must have wondered about the identity of this cloaked female. Perhaps he and his father had discussed Eliezer's mission to Mesopotamia. It is likely he knew Abraham wanted him to marry. But in case Abraham had not warned his son about his matchmaking ideas, Eliezer took matters into his own hands and explained "all the things that he had done" (24:66). Isaac did not protest, although he could discern nothing about his prospective bride. She remained silent while the servant told his story, but it was impossible to ignore her presence, a dark bundled shape who did not appear particularly eager to greet him.

Rebecca, on the other hand, could easily observe Isaac, forming her own judgments about her prospective groom before Isaac could do the same with her. While Rebecca enjoyed the luxury of being the first to inspect her partner, she was also whetting Isaac's appetite. Certainly, it was both worrisome and exciting to meet a veiled woman. Would she be ugly? Was it too much to hope for beauty?

The moment his conversation with the servant was over, Isaac did not hesitate. Although they had not spoken a word, he "brought [Rebecca] into the tent of his mother Sarah, and took Rebecca as his wife" (24:67). Thus, the first act between Isaac and Rebecca was sex. There was no intermediate period of courtship, no long engagement, and certainly no ceremony. Instead, the two plunged straight into each other's arms.

Perhaps Rebecca sensed that this was the kind of closeness

Isaac needed after all he had been through. If so, she was right, as after they had sex, he "loved her" and at last "found comfort after his mother's death" (24:67). This is the first time the word "love" is used in the Bible to describe the relationship between man and wife. As we have seen, the only other time the word had been used was right before Moriah, when God had described Isaac as the son whom Abraham loved.[9] Thus, unlike the somewhat ambiguous union between Abraham and Sarah, the Bible makes it plain that this would be a close marriage, one where the husband, at least, cared deeply for the wife.

But it is not so clear whether Rebecca loved Isaac. The Bible does not answer this question, leaving the reader to wonder what she felt. Although Isaac probably believed that his new wife possessed the maidenly reserve the veil implied, the veil was only the first example of how Rebecca would hide herself and her real intentions from her husband. Over the years, Rebecca would reveal herself to be wily, maneuvering her husband into giving his blessing to her favorite son, Jacob, by teaching the boy how to disguise himself as his brother. In an interesting twist, in the next generation, Rebecca's brother Laban would use a bridal veil to trick Rebecca and Isaac's son into marrying the wrong girl. Clearly, Rebecca came from a family well versed in disguise. Thanks to Laban's mischief, there is a Jewish tradition of making sure the groom can discern the face of his future wife through the veil so that he marries the right woman.

Yet God had specifically chosen Rebecca as the bride for Abraham's son. Thus it is difficult to impute any evil to her intentions. As with Sarah, God had His reasons for wanting this woman to marry the next patriarch. Perhaps He based His reasoning on her ability to conceal her true intentions, as this was the central skill she would pass on to Jacob, the father of the Jewish people. After all, disguise was an essential survival strategy to use when threatened by more powerful enemies. Even Abraham and Sarah had employed it in their intrigues with Pharaoh and Abimelech, suggesting that this kind of covert behavior was sanctioned by God.

Still, despite God's apparent approval of Rebecca, readers of this story have continued to worry about her character. In response, many legends have sprung up to defend Rebecca's purity. One such story featured Abraham advising his son to "take the young woman into the tent and remove her hymen with your finger. If her maidenhood is intact, behold by the Mighty One she is yours."[10] Rebecca agreed to this humiliating plan and was found to be a virgin. Her virginity was not surprising, according to Rashi, who added a soothing tone to the consternation about Isaac's bride, arguing that the Bible declared that not only was she "a virgin," but "no man had ever known her." To Rashi, this repetition meant that she had abstained not only from vaginal intercourse, but also all other sexual activities, such as anal and oral sex.[11]

That there is any debate about Rebecca's virginity introduces an interesting parallel to her mother-in-law. As with Sarah, it is not always clear that Rebecca slept only with her husband. First, there were the rumors about Eliezer. Later in Rebecca's life, the king of Gerar, Abimelech (whether it is the same Abimelech or his son is unclear), would desire her, just as foreign rulers had once wanted Sarah. Isaac would deal with this confrontation just as his father had: by lying and saying that Rebecca was his sister (26:7).

As with Sarah in the earlier story, Rebecca would ostensibly escape being raped by the king, yet her fidelity to her husband would be an ongoing question. Did Abimelech touch her? Did she fight him off? Teubal argues that she was the next in line of the matriarchal priestesses and, like Sarah, had a responsibility to have ceremonial intercourse with rulers to test their fertility and their virtue.[12] But the more conventional hypothesis is that these threats to her chastity were meant to represent her preciousness to Isaac as well as her desirability to other men.

Still, whatever questions there have been about Rebecca's character, the moment she slept with Isaac, it was obvious that Isaac had no doubts. Furthermore, by making love in his mother's tent, he had taken over Abraham's role, and Rebecca had assumed Sarah's.

One Midrash says, "As long as Sarah lived, a cloud [of glory] hovered over the entrance to her tent. After she died, the cloud disappeared. But when Rebecca came, the cloud returned."[13] As the potential parents of the new generation, Rebecca and Isaac were the ones now answerable to God.

With true wisdom, Abraham stayed clear of his son and daughter-in-law once they had assumed the mantle of leadership. If he had attempted to live with them, it would have been too easy for people to defer to his judgment out of sheer force of habit. It was time for Isaac and Rebecca to bear the burden of God's legacy.

CHAPTER THIRTY-THREE

HINNENI

Abraham may have been free to do what he liked now that his
son had married. But it seems odd he did not greet Rebecca
when she arrived in Canaan. Why wouldn't he want to meet the
new member of his family? Where was he?

It turns out he *was* with his family, but a different family from
the one we know. After burying Sarah, the old man promptly married someone else. Her name was Keturah, and she gave birth to a
baby and then five more, all of whom survived infancy to grow into
healthy adults.

At last, Abraham was "contented" (Gen. 25:8). Keturah had
undoubtedly made him happy by giving him a large brood of
children. But there was something mysterious about her identity,
as her name has little precedent in the Bible. The word is related
to the Hebrew word for "spicy" and could well be derived from the
Egyptian, particularly as the Egyptians were famous for their perfumed oils.[1]

This confusion about her origins caused some of the early rabbis
to argue that she was actually Hagar in disguise, since her name
evoked Egypt, Hagar's home. To support their claim, they point
out that the Bible says Abraham only had one concubine, not two,

suggesting that Keturah was not a new partner, but rather the same woman Abraham had been with before.[2] Although it is true that Ishmael is not listed as one of Keturah's offspring, the rabbis felt that the real identity of Abraham's second wife could not be written directly into the Bible as this would have bolstered any claims Ishmael had to be Abraham's primary heir. Rashi, on the other hand, had no fears about proclaiming that Keturah was Hagar. He explained that Isaac had been at Beer-la'hai-roi right before he met Rebecca because he had gone to fetch Hagar for his father to "take her again as his wife."[3]

Despite its speculative nature, the idea that Keturah was actually Hagar has persisted, painting a love story between Abraham and his second wife that is almost unparalleled. It is as though Tristan and Isolde were reunited, or Romeo came back from the dead to marry a still living Juliet, although in the case of Abraham and Hagar, the reunited lovers were quite elderly. Abraham would have been at least 140 years old and Hagar was probably over seventy-five.

If Hagar and Abraham's estrangement was ultimately healed, this would mean that her children would at last be gathered under one roof with their father. Furthermore, if Hagar's exile was only temporary, then those Christians and Jews who have characterized Muslims as Abraham's cast-off children must rethink their position. A reunited Hagar and Abraham would remind readers that Jews, Muslims, and Christians all share in Abraham's inheritance. In addition, for those who condemn Abraham for exiling Hagar and Ishmael in the first place, her return offers Abraham a chance at redemption. He can end his life in peace with his second wife rather than racked with guilt about her fate in the desert.

The Bible says that the aging father took care of his new offspring, generously providing them with money and "gifts" (25:6). Isaac, on the other hand, would have to suffer under the yoke of God's commandments, and his relationship with Abraham would remain complicated and unresolved. Meanwhile, Ishmael flourished, creating a family in the desert near Egypt or Mecca, depending on whether you are reading the Jewish or Muslim version of the tale.

Once he had passed the baton to Sarah's son and enjoyed the "blessings" of the last chapter of his life, Abraham, too, had to face death. The Midrash says that God sent the angel Michael to tell Abraham that his life was over. But in a shocking display of self-assertion, Abraham resisted this announcement and refused to go with Michael to heaven.[4]

Abraham's rebellion is puzzling. Perhaps the ancient storytellers had at last found an acceptable outlet for the contrariness that seemed to be at the core of this man's soul. Or perhaps after years of struggles, he had finally found happiness on earth and was loath to leave it. Whatever the reason, according to these early commentators, Abraham asked God to allow him to see "the creatures that the Lord has created on heaven and earth" before he died. God consented, so Michael swept Abraham up into the sky where he could look down on the entire planet. From his heavenly vantage point, he saw all sorts of evils. People were stealing and murdering. Husbands and wives routinely betrayed their spouses. Aghast at the sinful nature of human beings, Abraham asked God to destroy all sinners. God did as Abraham wished, and the earth swallowed up the wrongdoers.[5]

Distressed at Abraham's lack of compassion, God told Michael to show him "the place of judgment of all souls." When Abraham saw how narrow the gate was for prospective souls to pass through, he felt guilty and begged God to forgive him for his self-righteousness and restore life to those he had condemned. God agreed, saying, "Abraham, I have hearkened to thy prayer, and I forgive thee thy sin, and those whom thou thinkest that I destroyed, I have called up and brought them into life by My exceeding kindness." Abraham, having learned a valuable lesson about mercy and humility, assumed his position in heaven, operating as a kind of mediator between God and sinners, often asking God to act with compassion.[6]

Although this Midrash is usually included in the compilations of legends about Abraham, it does not appear anywhere in the hadith and is not widely known in either Jewish or Christian congregations. The story appears to be based on several events in the Bible: Abraham's intercession on the part of the Sodomites and his vision of the stars when God tells him how numerous his offspring will be (15:5). In the Sodom story, Abraham's role is to plead for God's justice. In the Midrash, by the end of the story, he emerges as the mediator between God and humankind. In the star story, God granted the patriarch a glimpse of how infinite his descendants would be. In the Midrash, God grants Abraham a god's-eye view of all humanity.

Although this story demonstrates an important characteristic about Abraham—his commitment to justice—what makes it particularly interesting is the insight it gives us into early Jewish views of the afterlife and the parallels with developing Christian ideas.

In the first and second centuries after the destruction of the Temple in 70 C.E., both early Christians (who still thought of themselves primarily as Jews) and Jews who had not accepted the new Messiah scrambled to shape new religious identities for themselves. The results share some fascinating parallels. First, like Abraham, Christ is a savior who intercedes on behalf of others. Second, he lives on after death and is seated in heaven near his "Father." Of course, there are many differences between the two emerging traditions, yet this story suggests that, like Christ, no heavenly transformation could make Abraham forget his humanity or his time living in this world. Even in death, he does not die.

Intriguing though this tale is, the Biblical version has a simpler account of Abraham's death that is potentially more important to the modern world. When they heard that Abraham had died, Isaac and Ishmael, who had not seen each other since Ishmael's exile, traveled to Hebron to bury their father (25:9). The Bible does not add any details to this account, but, brief though the story is, it shows the two men had no quarrel with each other or with the other's branch of the family. Indeed, Isaac continued to dwell near Hagar's oasis, suggesting a stronger alliance with her than with his father. And Ishmael evinced no concerns about burying Abraham with Sarah, even though his own mother, whether she was now called Hagar or Keturah, still lived and might have wanted the spot for herself.

In the Bible's version, then, Abraham's final act—death—inspired reconciliation. When his two sons arrived to pay tribute to their father, they had to cooperate in order to bury him in the tomb he had purchased from the Hittites. That the brothers accomplished this task without argument is a hopeful moment in the Bible. Too often, the descendants of both sons have used the story of Ishmael's expulsion as an excuse for enmity. But Abraham's burial is an important emblem of fraternal unity, and the Bible underlines its importance by repeating a similar theme a generation later. When Isaac died, his quarreling sons put aside their disagreements and buried him next to his father and mother (35:29). At least in death, these three were reunited.

Accordingly, despite the trials that Abraham endured and the difficulties he had inflicted on his sons, his death achieved a happy ending of sorts. However, his story was not quite over: the Bible ends its account of his life with the cryptic sentence "He was gathered to his people" (25:7). Abraham's "people," Laban and Bethuel, were back in Mesopotamia worshipping idols. Nahor presumably had died. Abraham's sons were not yet dead. So it is not entirely clear whom the Bible meant.

The early Christians solved this dilemma by saying that Abraham's "people" were members of the eternal community of the faithful. Their purpose was to assert Christian claims of primacy by extending Abraham's legacy to include those who were not ethnically descended from the Israelites.[7] As we have seen, Paul argues that those who believe in Jesus are the real children of Sarah and the true inheritors of God's covenant. He writes, "If you are Christ's, then you are Abraham's seed, heirs according to promise" (Gal. 3:29). However, the Bible implies that Abraham was not and never could be the founder of only one faith.[8] Logically, if the faithful were

Abraham's "people," then his descendants were not only Christians, but also pious individuals of the other monotheistic faiths—Jews and Muslims. What linked his followers, therefore, was not ethnicity but a reverence for God, even if each group worshipped Him according to its own traditions.

To those who regard Abraham as their spiritual father, the harmony between Isaac and Ishmael at their father's burial can be seen as a message. If these two brothers could come together, then perhaps battling Jews, Christians, and Muslims can put down their swords as well. As one commentator in a Jewish prayer book writes, "Can not [the reconciliation of the sons] be a model for the descendants of Ishmael and Isaac, contemporary Arabs and Israeli Jews, to find grounds for forgiveness and reconciliation?"[9]

Despite the optimism of such appeals, though, there was one crucial reconciliation that did not occur. Sarah and Abraham had never resolved their conflicts. Naturally, there are many stories that attempt to heal this breach. For example, one legend says that many centuries after the death of Abraham, a distinguished rabbi came to Hebron on a pilgrimage to the tomb of the patriarch and matriarch. But when he found the burial cave, the ghost of Abraham's servant Eliezer suddenly appeared, blocking the entrance so that the rabbi could not go in to pay his respects. The rabbi's curiosity was immediately sparked. "What is Abraham doing?" he asked Eliezer.

"He is lying in Sarah's arms, and she is gazing at his head," Eliezer responded. The rabbi was satisfied with this answer, and so, apparently, were all those who read or heard this odd story, although the modern reader can't help but be perplexed.[10]

Interpreters theorize that Eliezer's answer was meant to suggest that Abraham and Sarah's relationship had not ended when they died. In fact, it implies that both characters continued on as ghosts or superhuman figures who had spent centuries working on their marriage. Thus, by the time the rabbi arrived at their grave, they had at long last resolved their disputes. Sarah expressed her admiration of her husband's intellect by staring at his head. Abraham expressed his dependence on her by allowing her to hold him tightly for eternity.[11]

Over time, more legends about the tomb have emerged. Isaac and Rebecca are reputed to be buried there, as is their son Jacob and his wife Leah (Rachel was buried elsewhere when she died in childbirth). As a result, the grave has become a powerful symbol for marriage as well as for reconciliation. The irony, however, is that it has also been at the center of history's bloodiest and most hate-filled religious battles.

With admirable prescience, King Herod understood the controversy that would surround Hebron. Two thousand years ago he built a giant wall to surround the spot where he believed the famous couples were buried. Like the Temple walls the king had erected in Jerusalem, the enclosure was constructed of enormous stones in order to keep the sacred ground safe from enemy attacks.

For six hundred years his strategy worked and the site was left alone. But Herod's enormous protective walls were a reminder of the dangers that loomed. Eventually, the tomb became one of the most contested sites in the holy wars waged by Jews, Christians, and Muslims.

Byzantine Christians were the first to build a structure over the site of the tombs, placing a simple church there in the sixth century. But this quiet place of worship did not last long. In the seventh century, Muslims invaded the city and converted the church into a mosque. Jews and Christians were still allowed to visit the shrine, and Jews built a synagogue nearby. There was even a Jewish kitchen on the site that provided food for "all pilgrims rich and poor," creating a tradition called "the table of Abraham."[12]

When European Crusaders poured into the land in 1099, they drove Muslims out of Hebron and erected crosses and altars in the mosque and synagogue, changing both structures into one large church. They also forced out the Jews who lived nearby, although they still allowed Jewish pilgrims to enter the site. In 1165 Maimonides recalled visiting Hebron, writing that he went "to kiss the graves of my forefathers in the Cave of Machpelah."[13] The victory for Christianity was short-lived, as less than a hundred years later, the Muslims reclaimed the site. They converted the church back into a mosque, calling it the Ibrahimi (Abraham's) Mosque and burning the Christian artifacts. However, they did allow Jews and Christians to enter the structure and pray.

This enlightened policy did not endure. By 1300 Jews and Christians were only allowed to climb the first seven steps of the entrance, and this remained true for more than seven hundred years. Pilgrims still flocked to Hebron, however, where they found a small crack in Herod's wall that allowed them to glimpse what lay on the other side. But the animosity among the followers of the different faiths could only intensify as, for centuries, Jews and Christians watched Muslims enter the precincts to pray, while they were reduced to peering through a hole.

In 1967, Israeli forces captured Hebron, placing it under their jurisdiction. For centuries, reports of supernatural events had circulated about the Machpelah.[14] Moshe Dayan, the famous general of the conquering Israeli army, was so consumed by these stories that one of the first things he did after his victory was try to find a way into the underground caves. But the two existing entrances had been sealed for centuries. The first one, located near Abraham's memorial (erected by Muslims in the ninth century), has a protective grating. The other is blocked by a large flat stone on which Muslim pilgrims unroll their mats to pray.

Finally, Dayan found a space between the paving stones in the floor of the mosque. Now he needed someone who was small enough and brave enough to shimmy through the crack to the subterranean cave. Enter twelve-year-old Michal Arbel. She slid down a rope, disappearing into the dank underground room beneath the mosque. However, when Dayan drew her back up, eager to hear what she had to say, she had disappointing news: the chamber contained nothing but three stone markers with Arabic verses from the Koran.[15]

Even though the cave was empty, Abraham's legacy is still contested. In 1994, the Jewish settler Baruch Goldstein walked into the mosque dressed in his army uniform and shot Muslims at prayer, killing 26 and injuring 125 others. This violence occasioned a furious Arab backlash against the Jewish presence in Hebron, and, as part of the Arab-Israeli peace process, the Wye River Accords gave control of most of the site back to Muslims in 1995.

Currently, Jews and Christians are allowed to pray in the courtyard outside the mosque, but guards are posted to make sure no one gets hurt. As a result, there has been no more bloodshed inside the walls of the enclosure, but the hatred continues. In the nearby Jewish settlement of Kiryat Arba, a memorial to Goldstein has been erected. Although the Israeli government has outlawed its presence and destroyed it several times, the settlers insist on rebuilding it.[16] To these men and women, Goldstein is a hero who tried to reclaim one of Judaism's holiest sites. Both Israelis and Palestinians worry about plots to blow up the Machpelah or to destroy Muslims or Jews. Tourists are discouraged from visiting not only the sacred location, but also the town itself.

I have never been to the Machpelah, but I have heard a rumor that now and then a strange wind seeps up from the caves through the cracks in the floor of the mosque.[17] This seems fitting, since wind is supposed to be a sign of what the French call a *revenant*, a spirit that has come back from the dead to speak to the living. If these are the spirits of Abraham and Sarah, then what, one wonders, are they trying to say? Do they condemn us? Perhaps they are praying. Or maybe Abraham is simply saying, "*Hinneni*. Here I am." As for Hagar, her voice could never be heard in Hebron. But perhaps if one went on hajj, or pilgrimage to Mecca, one could hear an echo of her saying, "I am the one who saw God and went on living."

ACKNOWLEDGMENTS

My father died halfway through the writing of this book. The sorrow of that event and the understanding of the complexities that shape a father's legacy have informed these pages.

My mother is my most loyal fan. Without her, I would never have begun my own journey of faith. I am deeply grateful to her. I am also grateful to my son, Brooks Richon, for his patience and love. In many ways I wrote this book to help him understand the complexities of his family's heritage.

My dear friends Johanna Chao Kreilick and Laila Goodman have been my advisers and supporters for many, many years. Carolyn Cooke is always a source of inspiration. More recently, Phoebe Potts and Gab Watling have delighted me with their humor, intelligence, and creativity. I am grateful for the friendship of these women.

My indefatigable and brilliant editor, Asya Muchnick, read the manuscript cover to cover many times, often in the dead of night. No writer could ask for a better or smarter reader. My champion agent, Brettne Bloom, who is friend, adviser, first reader, and so much more, helped shape the book from cloudy impulse to full realization. I am also the fortunate beneficiary of the sage advice of Jill Kneerim and Ike Williams.

Naomi Konecky, Alex Edwards, Chris Stodolski, Glenn Berntson, Jeff Marshall, Barry Moir, Casey Moir, and Gretchen Putnam provided generous love and much practical help. Mark Konecky was an astute early reader of the manuscript; the moms of my son's friends offered rides, snacks, and playdates at a moment's notice, particularly Stephanie Williams and Ruth Rich, mother of Ben. My cousin Michael Janeway is an invaluable guide to the ups and downs of the writing business. My father's brother, Nick Gordon, and his wife, Estelle, my brothers, sisters, and their children have cheered me on from the inception of this project to its finish. I am particularly grateful to my sister Helen. Her knowledge of both Christianity and Judaism is truly remarkable. Finally, Geoff Richon's love and support have been a crucial part of my growth as a writer. He has believed in my work since the beginning.

Jon Levenson, Vanessa Ochs, Howard Schwartz, Myron Geller, Samuel Barth, and Arthur Waskow kindly read chapters, corrected errors, and gave valuable suggestions. The mistakes that remain are mine. For help with Jewish sources and translations, I turned to Jacob Pinnolis and Myron Geller. My teachers Elie Wiesel and Myron Geller have taught me the importance of religious identity. I am grateful for the wisdom they have shared with me.

My colleagues at Endicott College are a gold mine of knowledge and generosity. I am especially grateful to Willie Young, Todd Wemmer, Betty Roland, Dan Sklar, Mark Herlihy, and Peter Eden. I am also grateful to Susan Koso for finding me in the first place. I would not have been able to write this book without the support of Vice President/Dean of the Undergraduate College Laura Rossi-Le, and President Dick Wylie. No writer could work for a more generous institution.

I was very fortunate to have such a strong team at Little, Brown: Alexis Schaitkin, Val Russo, Carolyn O'Keefe, and Peggy Freudenthal. I am also grateful to Lucinda Dyer for her expertise in publicity, and Rose Daniels for her web design.

Finally, Paul Fisher's grace, irony, kindness, patience, and wit have been an almost daily part of my life since our days in Cambridge, almost thirty years ago. I dedicate this book to him in gratitude for our friendship. Together, we have forged our writing lives.

SOME DEFINITIONS

AKEDAH: The story of the "binding" of Isaac.

BERESHIT: The first word of the Bible in Hebrew. Also the Hebrew title of the opening book of the Bible, known as Genesis in English.

GEMARA: The extensive rabbinic commentaries, explanations, and discussions on Mishnah that form part of the Talmud.

GENESIS RABBAH: The collection of Midrash based on Genesis. It is thought that "Rabbah" comes from the third word of the opening passage, "Rabbi Oshaya Rabbah." Oshaya Rabbah was the son of R. Judah the Prince, and the book was originally called Bereshit of Rabbi Oshaya Rabbah. As additional midrashic collections were made over centuries to encompass the entire corpus of Biblical texts used liturgically in the synagogue, the name was changed to Midrash Rabbah.

HADITH: The collection of Islamic stories, traditions, and commentary on the Koran.

IBN EZRA: Rabbi Abraham Ibn Ezra, Spanish commentator on the Bible, c. 1089–1164.

KAABA: The sacred place of worship for Muslims. Located in Mecca.

KABBALAH: The medieval Jewish tradition of mysticism and esoteric study.

LEKH LEKHA: Hebrew words that mean "Go forth." Also, a portion of the Torah (Gen. 12:1–17:27).

MACHPELAH: The famous burial site in Hebron where Abraham, Sarah, Isaac, Rebecca, Jacob, and Leah are supposed to be buried.

MAIMONIDES: Rabbi Moses ben Maimon; Spanish, 1135–1204. Also known by his acronym, Rambam.

MIDRASH: A Jewish method of Biblical exegesis. Also refers to the interpretations themselves. Hence, "a Midrash" is a story from the collections of interpretation of the Bible. Often, these collections are named for the parts of the Bible they comment on: e.g., Genesis Rabbah, Exodus Rabbah, Sifre Devarim (on Deuteronomy). Midrash can be homiletic narratives (aggadah) or legal expositions (halakhah).

MISHNAH: The first official collection of rabbinic law, although earlier versions existed. Based on the Oral Torah, it includes rabbinical sayings, case studies, and legal codes. According to tradition, it was recorded around 200 C.E. With Gemara, Mishnah forms the basis of the Talmud.

NACHMANIDES: Rabbi Moses ben Nachman; Spanish, 1194–1270. Also known by his acronym, Ramban.

ORAL TORAH: The "second" Torah that Moses received from God, transmitted in an unbroken chain to the rabbis who recorded it in the Talmud and Midrash.

PIRKE AVOT: A collection of rabbinic ethics that serves as an introduction to the Mishnah, establishing the line of authority from Sinai down to Rabbi Judah Hanasi, editor of the Mishnah.

TALMUD: The collection of rabbinical commentaries on the law and traditions, consisting of Mishnah (law) and Gemara (discussion and extension of Mishnah). Two different Talmuds exist, the Babylonian Talmud (c. 500 C.E.) and the Jerusalem Talmud (c. 400 C.E.).

TORAH: The first five books of the Bible: Genesis, Exodus, Leviticus, Numbers, and Deuteronomy (also known as the Pentateuch).

Notes

Frequently cited sources have been abbreviated as follows:

B. Bat.   *Baba Batra* (Talmud). *The Talmud of the Land of Israel*, vol. 30: *Baba Batra.* Edited and translated by Jacob Neusner. Chicago Studies in the History of Judaism. Chicago: University of Chicago Press, 1984.

Ber.   *Berachot* (Talmud). *The Talmud of the Land of Israel*, vol. 1. Edited by Jacob Neusner. Translated by Tzvee Zahavy. Chicago Studies in the History of Judaism. Chicago: University of Chicago Press, 1990.

B. Ber.   *Berachot* (Babylonian Talmud). *Soncino Babylonian Talmud.* Tractate *Berakoth.* Edited and translated by Rabbi Dr. Isidore Epstein. London: Soncino, 1978.

Etz Hayim   *Etz Hayim Torah and Commentary.* English translation, Jewish Publication Society, 1985, 1999. The Rabbinical Assembly the United Synagogue of Conservative Judaism. Jewish Publication Society, 2001.

Gen. R.   *Genesis Rabbah.* Edited by Jacob Neusner. Tampa: University of South Florida, 1985.

M. Hag.   *Hagigah* (Mishnah Talmud). *Soncino Babylonian Talmud.* Trac-
            tates *Taanith, Megillah Hagigah* (Hebrew–English Edition of the
            Babylonian Talmud Seder Moed). Edited and translated by
            Rabbi Dr. Isidore Epstein. London: Soncino, 1967.

Ned.   *Nedarim* (Talmud). *The Talmud of the Land of Israel,*
            vol. 23: *Nedarim.* Edited and translated by Jacob Neusner.
            Chicago Studies in the History of Judaism. Chicago:
            University of Chicago Press, 1985.

Pirqe R. El. *Pirqe de-Rabbi Eliezer.* Translated by Gerald Friedlander. Skokie,
            IL: Publisher's Row/Varda Books, 2008.

Rosh Has.   *Rosh Hashana* (Talmud). *The Talmud of the Land of Israel,* vol 16:
            Rosh Hashanah. Edited by Jacob Neusner. Translated by Edward
            A. Goldman. Chicago Studies in the History of Judaism. Chi-
            cago: University of Chicago Press, 1988.

Sanh.   *Sanhedrin* (Talmud). *The Talmud of the Land of Israel,* vol. 31:
            Sandhedrin and *Makkot.* Chicago Studies in the History of Juda-
            ism. Chicago: University of Chicago Press, 1984.

Sefer   Maimonides. *Sefer Hamitzvot. The Commandments: Sefer Ha Mitz-*
Hamitzvot   *voth of Maimonides.* Translated by Charles B. Chavel. London:
            Soncino, 1967.

Sforno   Obadiah ben Jacob Sforno. *Sforno: Commentary on the Torah,* vol.
            1. Translated by Raphael Pelcovitz. Brooklyn: Artscroll/Meso-
            rah Publications, 1989.

Sabb.   *Shabbat* (Talmud). *The Talmud of the Land of Israel,* vol 11:
            Shabbat. Chicago Studies in the History of Judaism. Chicago:
            University of Chicago Press, 1991.

Tos. Hag.   *Hagigah* (Tosefta Talmud). *The Talmud of the Land of Israel,*
            vol. 20: *Hagigah.* Translated from the Hebrew with
            a new introduction by Jacob Neusner. Chicago:
            University of Chicago Press, 1986.

Zebah   *Zevachim* (Talmud). *The Talmud of the Land of Israel,* vol. 16: *Rosh
            Hashanah.* Edited by Jacob Neusner. Translated by Edward A.
            Goldman. Chicago Studies in the History of Judaism. Chicago:
            University of Chicago Press, 1988.

INTRODUCTION

1. "President Mahmoud Ahmadinejad's address to an international religious conference in Tehran, August 18, 2007," *Iran's President Mahmoud Ahmadinejad in His Own Words, Anti-Defamation League,* 2009, http://www.adl.org/main_International_Affairs/ahmadinejad_words.htm?Multi_page_sections-sHeading_4 (April 20, 2009).

2. Joan Chittister, OSB, Murshid Saaid Shakur Chishti, Rabbi Arthur Waskow. *The Tent of Abraham: Stories of Hope and Peace for Jews, Christians, and Muslims,* (Boston: Beacon Press, 2006). As Rabbi Arthur Waskow writes, "One of the most important teachings of [the] rabbis was that the Torah was written not in black ink on white parchment but in black fire on white fire and that the white fire, the 'blank' spaces, were waiting in every generation to be read anew" (29).

3. There are, of course, notable exceptions to this oversight. For instance Bruce Feiler attempts to look at the patriarch from the three perspectives of Judaism, Christianity, and Islam. See *Abraham: A Journey to the Heart of Three Faiths,* (New York: Doubleday, 2002). Another important example is *The Tent of Abraham.* In this book, three religious leaders from the Jewish, Muslim, and Christian faiths explore and retell this story, emphasizing the lessons of reconciliation that are to be found here. Joan Chittister, OSB, Murshid Saadi Shakur Chishti, Rabbi Arthur Waskow. *The Tent of Abraham: Stories of Hope and Peace for Jews, Christians, and Muslims.* (Boston: Beacon Press, 2006).

4. "No Religion Is an Island," in *Moral Grandeur and Spiritual Audacity,* edited by Susannah Heschel (New York: Farrar, Strauss, 1996), 237.

CHAPTER 1: Beginnings

1. Piotr Michalowski, *Lamentation over the Destruction of Sumer and Ur* (Winona Lake, IN: Eisenbrauns, 1989), lines 64–65. See Michalowski Chapter 4 for full version of lament. Also available at http://etcsl.orinst.ox.ac.uk/cgi-bin/etcsl.cgi?text=t.2.2.2&charenc=j#.

2. Contemporary archaeologists have actually found no evidence to corroborate the Biblical tradition that Abraham came from Ur. One of the most prominent, William Dever, has proposed that Abram and his little band were not Mesopotamian at all but were actually disenchanted Canaanites who fled their overlords and moved inland to start their own colony in the interior of Canaan. Thus, there was still a flight from an old world to a new one, but the journey was much shorter. See William G. Dever, *Who Were the Early Israelites and Where Did They Come From?* (Grand Rapids, MI: Eerdmans Publishing Co., 2003), 176–77.

3. Michael Roaf, *Cultural Atlas of Mesopotamia and the Ancient Near East* (New York: Equinox, 1990), 20; Harriet E. W. Crawford, *Dilmun and its Gulf Neighbours* (Cambridge: Cambridge University Press, 1998), 5, 8.

4. Roaf, *Atlas,* 101.

5. Ibid., 105.

6. Ibid., 81–83; David Klinghoffer, *The Discovery of God: Abraham and the Birth of Monotheism* (New York: Doubleday, 2003), 6.

7. Roland de Vaux, *Ancient Israel,* vol. 2, *Religious Institutions,* 2nd ed. (New York: McGraw Hill, 1965), 433.

8. D. Winton Thomas, ed., *Documents from Old Testament Times* (New York: Harper Torchbooks, 1958), 12. In his introduction, Thomas writes that the essential element of the religion is "the story of . . . the battle between [the gods] Marduk and Tiamat, and the creation of man in a god-ordered universe," 3. In fact, in the *Enuman elish,* the epic poem that describes these battles, Marduk only decides to create humanity to spare his enemies, the vanquished gods, from having to serve as slaves to their conquerors. Nahum Sarna also argues that the God of the Hebrew Scriptures has an inherently more positive relationship to His creation and that, therefore, humankind is able to look to God for "assurances." He writes, "One of [Genesis's] seemingly naïve features is God's pleasure at his own artistry. . . . But this naivete of idiom cloaks a profundity of thought that marks off the mood of Hebrew civilization from that of Mesopotamia in a most revolutionary manner. . . . A strong streak of optimism has displaced the acute awareness of insecurity." Nahum Sarna, *Understanding Genesis: The Heritage of Biblical Israel,* 5th ed. (New York: Jewish Theological Seminary of America, 1966; New York: Schocken Books, 1978), 18. Citations are to the Schocken edition. See also Klinghoffer, *Discovery,* 7.

9. Roaf, *Atlas,* 85–86, 92–93. Some contemporary scholars dispute Woolley's theories that human sacrifice was an essential element of the religious rites of Ur. Roland de Vaux writes, "Human sacrifices . . . were so exceptional that one hesitates to call them true sacrifices" (*Ancient Israel,* 441). However, the majority of commentators support the idea that the land of Abraham and Sarah's birth was dominated by an oppressive atmosphere of blood and terror. Sarna writes, "The ever present pall of anxiety that hung over Mesopotamian life is the measure of the failure of its civilization, religiously speaking" (*Understanding Genesis,* 101). See chapter 2, note 9, below, and chapter 28, for further discussion of the prevalence (or lack thereof) of human sacrifice in the ancient Near East. Finally, like most of ancient Mesopotamian culture, the specific tradition that created these tombs remains a mystery. Some scholars argue that these are not the graves of kings but were dedicated entirely to some unknown religious ritual. See also Karen L. Wilson, "Treasures from the Royal Tombs of Ur," *The Oriental Institute News and Notes* 167, Fall 2000, http://oi.uchicago.edu/research/pubs/nn/fa100_wilson.html (April 21, 2009).

10. Karen Armstrong, *A History of God,* 2nd ed. (New York: Ballantine, 1994), 14.

11. James Kugel, *The God of Old: Inside the Lost World of the Bible* (New York: Free Press, 2003), 84.

12. Klinghoffer, *Discovery,* 11; H.W.F. Saggs, *The Greatness That Was Babylon: A Survey of the Ancient Civilizations of the Tigris-Euphrates Valley* (New York: Praeger, 1962), 310.

13. Kugel writes, "Thus this craftsman could not be the one who made this statue—he had no hands" (*God of Old,* 85).

14. The source is the Book of Jubilees (12:1–20), a non-canonical Jewish text from the second century B.C.E.

15. According to Klinghoffer, Augustine was troubled by the idea that Terah believed in the Mesopotamian deities, and instead argued that he was a monotheist and passed this belief on to his son (*Discovery,* 11). As late as 1835, there were those who defended Abram's early faith. Joseph Smith, the founder of the Mormons, claimed to have come into possession of a mysterious text from Egypt written in Abram's own hand that recorded his early belief in God as well as his persecution by the priests and rulers of the time. In this document, known as the Book of Abraham, the youthful Abraham says:

    > And as they lifted up their hands upon me, that they might offer me up and take away my life, behold, I lifted up my voice unto the Lord my God, and the Lord hearkened and heard, and he filled me with the vision of the Almighty, and the angel of his presence stood by me, and immediately unloosed my bands (1:15).

16. Thus, the Midrash rejects his earlier identity as a simple Mesopotamian (Abram) and refers to him exclusively as Abraham, the name God gives him much later as a sign of His covenant.

17. Adapted from Louis Ginzberg, *Legends of the Jews,* 6th ed. (Philadelphia: Jewish Publication Society, 1992), 87–88. The Talmud identifies Abraham's mother as Amatlai, daughter of Karnivo. Klinghoffer writes that this name is "built on the Aramaic root *amatla,* meaning a plausible reason for contradicting a statement" (*Discovery,* 12–13).

18. Klinghoffer recounts his journey to this famous site, writing, "The entrance today is guarded by a one-eyed Muslim in robes who, when I was there, scowled as I purchased a ticket and removed my shoes to enter. Inside is a grotto with water pooled some distance below ground level, barred against entry and almost invisible in the dark" (*Discovery,* 3).

19. Ginzberg, *Legends,* 88.

20. *Pirqe R. El.* 26; Klinghoffer, *Discovery,* 2.

21. Ginzberg, *Legends,* 88–89.

22. Karen Armstrong, *In the Beginning: A New Interpretation of Genesis* (New York: Ballantine, 1996), 58.

23. Ginzberg, *Legends,* 94.

24. Ibid. See also *Genesis Rabbah,* 60–61. For the Koran's version, see Surahs 6:74 and 21:51–71.
25. Ginzberg, *Legends,* 88.
26. Ibid., 92–93.

CHAPTER 2: *Lekh Lekha*

1. Miroslav Volf, *Exclusion and Embrace* (Nashville: Abingdon Press, 1996), 39.
2. As we have already seen, William Dever argues that this tale of departure from Mesopotamia has no archaeological or historical basis. He theorizes that the early Israelites were disenchanted Canaanites who left the coast and moved inland to start their own way of life and culture (see *Early Israelites,* Ch. 11). However, even if Dever's point is correct, the premise of *lekh lekha* remains the same. God tells Abraham to leave his familiar surroundings and set forth for a new world and a new life.
3. *Etz Hayim,* 70n1.
4. Joseph Campbell, *Myths to Live By* (New York: Viking, 1972), 65.
5. Sarna writes, "Could not the ancestral soil of Mesopotamia have witnessed the birth of Israel? The answer to this question may perhaps be sought in the very nature of Mesopotamian civilization as contrasted with the destiny of the nation yet to emerge. The land between the Tigris and Euphrates rivers was already heir to a tradition of hoary antiquity by the time [Abraham] arrived on the scene . . . it was not a situation that would be likely to encourage a challenge to its basic conservatism" (*Understanding Genesis,* 101).
6. Klinghoffer gives a full account of his visit there. He also supplies the population of the ancient community of Haran (see *Discovery,* 30). For a description of Haran's role as an "important" center of trade, see *Etz Hayim,* 62n31.
7. This is the traditional theory with which Sarna disagrees. However, it is the story people have believed for centuries. Sarna writes, "All over the ancient world masses were on the march, radically altering ethnic and political patterns. Viewed against this broader background, the attachment of Terah and his family to the migratory stream of Semites wending their way from East to West was hardly more than a trivial incident. Yet to biblical historiotophy it became a stirring event of universal significance . . . " (*Understanding Genesis,* 100). If one adheres to the principle that Abraham's family really did come from Mesopotamia and were not indigenous to Canaan, then the corollary assumption is that the tribe was probably of Amorite origin and, therefore, participated in the "invasions" of Ur and other Mesopotamian cities at the beginning of the second millennium B.C.E. Klinghoffer provides an evocative description of the movements of the period: "A century or so before Abraham's birth, Sumerian civilization was transformed by the influence of Semitic invaders from the Syrian desert, called Amorites or Martu, meaning 'Westerners'" (*Discovery,* 9). In further support of this thesis, see

Roaf, *Atlas*, 103; Roland de Vaux, *Ancient Israel*, vol. 1, *Social Institutions*, 2nd ed. (New York: McGraw Hill, 1965), 321ff.

8. Klinghoffer writes, "Haran was a center of worship for the moon god Sin and Terach's name has lunar associations. So do the names of Abram's wife, Sarai, and sister-in-law Milcah" (*Discovery*, 10). See also Umberto Cassuto, *A Commentary on the Book of Genesis*, trans. Israel Abraham (Jerusalem: Magnes, 1964), 298. Also Paul Johnson, *A History of the Jews* (New York: Harper and Row, 1987), 16.

9. Whether the Mesopotamians practiced human sacrifice is a matter of debate. Sarna writes, "throughout the ancient Near East, though animal sacrifice was normal, official religions fostered the idea that there were occasions when the gods could be conciliated only by the offering of the fruit of the human womb, the most precious thing that this life affords. Even in Israel this monstrous idea was not entirely eradicated from the popular consciousness until the Babylonian Exile" (*Understanding Genesis*, 159). However, Roland de Vaux discounts such arguments, writing, "Often enough, these theories [about human sacrifice] are based upon wrong translations of certain texts, and the way in which the texts are then combined leaves much to be desired" (*Ancient Israel*, vol. 2, 434). See chapters 1 and 28 for further discussion of this topic.

10. Hammer, *Etz Hayim*, 58n11. In a recent online discussion of the meaning of the Tower of Babel story, Rabbi Ismar Schorsch, the chancellor of the Jewish Theological Seminary, concurs with Hammer. He writes, "God is less accessible in a man-made world. Surrounded by monuments of our own ingenuity, we grow deaf to the echoes of eternity. In the biblical tale, God's voice is conspicuously absent. In the face of human arrogance, God withdraws to the most remote corner of the cosmos. Hence the desire to storm the heavens." "Accessing God in a Man-Made World," *My Jewish Learning*, http://www.myjewishlearning.com/texts/Weekly_Torah_Commentary/noah_jts.htm (January 9, 2009).

11. It is no accident that Abram and Sarai have served as models for converts as well as emigrants. After living through the religious civil war that tore apart his country, Croatian theologian Miroslav Volf looked to Abraham as a model of hope. Volf writes, "Children of Abraham can 'depart' from their culture without having to leave it." In other words, for those who are raised to hate others, particularly on the basis of religion, as in Croatia, a country divided between Muslims, Roman Catholics, and Orthodox Christians, Abraham's openness to change is what is most important about *lekh lekha*. Abraham's willingness to turn his life upside down in response to God's command represented the sort of revolution Volf hoped could happen to the religious extremists in his country. "Departure is no longer a spatial category; it can take place within the cultural space one inhabits." He argues that for the devout, departures are an essential aspect of one's spiritual journey. "Without a departure," he writes, no "new beginnings" can happen. Therefore, journeys can be internal and figurative as well as literal (*Exclusion & Embrace*, 49).

CHAPTER 3: Hebrews

1. The list of exchanges and messages between Mesopotamia and Canaan is extensive. For example, Abraham sends his servant to find a wife for Isaac in Mesopotamia. Rebecca sends her son Jacob to her brother Laban in Mesopotamia. A Mesopotamian messenger finds Abraham to tell him that his brother died. Clearly, there could have been contact between Abram and his father if either one had really wanted to be in touch.

2. Rashi on Gen. 11:32

3. Ibid.

4. Isa. 41:8; Jewish "friend of God," Ginzberg, *Legends,* 86. For Muslim "friend of God," Ibn Kathir, *Stories of the Prophets* (New York: Dar-us-Salam, 2003), 131. Maimonides writes that Abraham inspired humanity to love God, *Sefer Hamitzvot,* positive commandment no. 3. Klinghoffer discusses this topic in *Discovery,* 32.

5. See Klinghoffer, *Discovery,* 31 and 52, for a full discussion of Abram's followers, *"asu,"* and the theories of Maimonides and the Sefer Hayashar.

6. "To an Israelite, this great river needed no further description" (*Etz Hayim,* 15n14).

7. Roaf, *Atlas,* 51, 123.

8. The Midrash actually suggests three explanations for the term "Hebrew." According to *Etz Hayim,* "One connects the term . . . with Eber, grandson of Noah, who is mentioned in Gen. 10:24 and 11:4. Another derives it from the Hebrew word *eiver* (beyond), that is 'the one from beyond [the river Euphrates].' The third alludes to Abram's non-conformism: 'All the world was on one side (*eiver*) and he on the other side'" (79n13).

9. This description of their appearance is based on the Beni Hasan mural, a tomb painting from ancient Egypt that depicted Semitic traders. See Klinghoffer, *Discovery,* 67.

10. Ross Burns, *Damascus: A History* (New York: Routledge, 2007), xix. See also Ayman Haykal, "Damascus in History," *Damascus Online,* 2000. http://www.damascusonline.com/damascus.htm (October 19, 2008).

11. Sarna argues that although there is some evidence that camels were known during Abram's lifetime, they did not become the principal mode of transportation until the twelfth century (*Understanding Genesis,* 105).

12. Ibid.

13. Many centuries later, Nachmanides, a medieval Jewish sage, said that Abram traveled from town to town waiting for God to say, "Wait, stop here; this is your new home" (on Gen. 12:1). See also Klinghoffer, *Discovery,* 53.

14. Klinghoffer, *Discovery,* 53.

15. James Pritchard, ed., *Ancient Near Eastern Texts Relating to the Old Testament* (Princeton, NJ: Princeton University Press, 1969), 19. Cited in Klinghoffer, *Discovery,* 53.

CHAPTER 4: Sacrifices

1. Jonathan N. Tubb, *Canaanites* (London: University of Oklahoma Press, 1998), 15. Of course, Dever's hypothesis that the Israelites are actually descendants of Canaanites precludes any such "discovery" of Canaanites in the land. Instead, Dever says that when the Israelites fled the coastal Canaanites, their overlords, in order to establish an independent culture safe from oppression, they developed a complicated web of stories to distance themselves from their real origins. See Dever, *Early Israelites,* chapter 10.

2. Tubb, *Canaanites,* 15.

3. Rashi on Gen 12:7: "They [the Canaanites] were gradually conquering the land of Israel from the descendants of Shem, for it had fallen to the share of Shem when Noah apportioned the earth among his sons. . . . For this reason the Lord said to Abram (v.7) 'to thy seed will I give this land'—I will in some future time return it to thy children who are descendants of Shem."

4. Again, Dever's theory that the Israelites were actually Canaanites traveling inland to start their own society does not contradict this narrative, but actually reinforces it. In either case, the Israelites chose to live apart from the dominant culture on the western coast. See Dever, *Early Israelites,* chapter 10.

5. Further adding to the tension is that Shechem is famous for being the gravesite of Joseph, Abraham's great-great-grandson. Describing the violence that often occurs there, Isabel Kershner writes, "In 1996, six Israeli soldiers were killed there in a wave of riots by the Palestinian police and militants throughout the West Bank. The second Palestinian uprising broke out in September 2000, and the tomb was the scene of a battle in which 18 Palestinians and an Israeli border policeman were killed; the policeman was left to bleed to death inside." "Pilgrimage to Roots of Faith and Strife," *New York Times,* October 24, 2008, A5.

6. Many recent scholars argue that the ancient Israelites did not conceive of God as a single entity and were, in fact, polytheistic. Even more interesting is the hypothesis that God had a wife. As Mark Smith writes, "At the top of the Judean pantheon stands the divine couple, Yahweh and Asherah." *The Origins of Biblical Monotheism: Israel's Polytheistic Background and the Ugaritic Texts* (New York: Oxford University Press, 2001), 47. See also notes 9 and 10.

7. See Savina Teubal, *Sarah the Priestess: The First Matriarch of Genesis* (Athens: Ohio University Press, 1984). She argues that it was actually Sarai's status as a high priestess that led the tribe to these groves. She writes, "Mamre at Hebron was chosen by Abram as the residence of Sarah" (28). Dever writes about Israelite religion in general, rather than Abram in particular, saying, "The more we learn about official religion and especially about popular or folk religion in the entire biblical period, the more we see that it is an outgrowth of Canaanite religion, no matter how much Yahwism eventually transformed it later. . . . The Israelite sacrificial system goes back to

Canaanite culture. Even the liturgical calendar has a Canaanite and agricultural basis" (*Early Israel*, 199–200).

8. Tubb, *Canaanites*, 14.

9. Ibid., 65–69.

10. Ibid., 67–68. Dever and others argue that these were not all Canaanite statues, but were actually Israelite representations of Asherah, Yahweh's wife. For the archaeological perspective on this topic, see William Dever, *Did God Have a Wife? Archaeology and Folk Religion in Ancient Israel* (Grand Rapids, MI: Eerdmans Publishing Co., 2005). He writes, "I was the first to argue for a 'cult of Asherah' in ancient Israel (1984), based on the newer *archaeological* evidence. That was heresy twenty years ago, but now it is so taken for granted that most biblical scholars have forgotten where the idea originated" (79). For a comprehensive study of the scholarship on Asherah, see Judith M. Hadley, *The Cult of Asherah in Ancient Israel and Judah: Evidence for a Hebrew Goddess* (Cambridge: Cambridge University Press, 2000). See also Diana Edelman, *The Triumph of Elohim: From Yahwisms to Judaisms* (Grand Rapids: Eerdmans Publishing Co., 1996); Richard E. Friedman, *The Bible with Sources Revealed* (New York: HarperOne, 2005).

11. Tubb, *Canaanites*, 67–68. Tubb endorses the theory that the Israelites soon adopted Asherah as their own. He writes, "It is clear from the large number of terracotta figurines of Asherah . . . found at sites in Israel and Judah that these female deities continued to be worshipped throughout the Iron Age, and a series of early eighth-century B.C. inscriptions found at the site of Kuntillet 'Ajrud in Sinai imply that Asherah was seen as Yahweh's consort. . . . It is also important to realize that these stories [of the gods and goddesses] represent the literary heritage of Canaan, a heritage in which Israel, as a sub-polity of Canaan shared" (75).

12. Ibid., 74.

13. W. C. Graham and H. G. May, *Culture and Conscience* (Chicago: University of Chicago Press, 1936), 77 ff.; J. Finegan, *Light from the Ancient Past* (Princeton, NJ: Princeton University Press, 1959), 148; E. Anati, *Palestine Before the Hebrews* (London: Jonathan Cape, 1963), 427; Sarna, *Understanding Genesis*, 158.

14. See note 10.

15. Tubb, *Canaanites*, 74.

CHAPTER 5: Beautiful Woman

1. Rashi on Gen. 12:10: "[This was] in order to test him [Avram] whether he will question the words of G-d who had told him to go to the Land of Canaan and now is forcing him to leave it." Rashi bases this argument on *Pirqe R. El.*, 26.

2. Mark Twain, *Innocents Abroad* (New York: Signet, 1966), 351.

3. Nelson Glueck, *Rivers in the Desert: A History of the Negev* (New York: Farrar,

Straus & Cuddahy, 1959), 88. See also, "The Age of Abraham in the Negev," BA 18:2–9. Cited in Klinghoffer, *Discovery,* 67.

4. Klinghoffer, *Discovery,* 66.

5. According to Klinghoffer, there were seven wells: Ain Quadeis, Ain el-Qudeirat, Bir Auja, Bir Birein, Bir Reseisyah, Bir Hafir, Ain Mureifiq. Ibid., 66–67.

6. Ibid., 67.

7. Rashi on Gen. 12:11. He cites the Midrash, writing, "Until now he had not been aware [of her beauty] due to the modesty of both of them. But, now, he became aware of her due to this event." Rashi offers another traditional explanation for Abram's sudden acknowledgment of Sarai's beauty, from *Gen. R.* 40: "It is usual that due to the hardship of travel a person becomes uncomely, but [Sarai] had retained her beauty." But, Rashi says that "the real sense of this text is 'Behold I now realize [that] the time has come to be concerned over your beauty. I have known for a long time that you are beautiful. But, now we will be coming amongst black and repulsive people, brothers of the Kushim, who are not accustomed to [seeing] a beautiful woman.'"

8. This passage is from the *Genesis Apocryphon,* a Midrash on the Abraham story that was discovered in the Dead Sea Scrolls. Geza Vermes, *The Complete Dead Sea Scrolls in English* (London: Penguin, 1998), 454. Cited in Klinghoffer, *Discovery,* 25–26.

9. Klinghoffer, *Discovery,* 67. The Beni Hasan mural was discovered in an ancient Egyptian tomb on the Nile. The tombs are from the Middle Kingdom, c. 1991–1786 B.C.E. and thus represent what Abram's band might have looked like.

10. John Wilson, *The Culture of Ancient Egypt* (Chicago: University of Chicago Press, 1951), 258. Cited in Klinghoffer, *Discovery,* 67–68.

11. The Biblical scholar E. A. Speiser has written that in the ancient world it was considered honorable to have married a sister, and thus, Abram was trying to bolster his image in front of Pharaoh. However, recent scholarship has disproved this theory, arguing that in fact the idea of marriage to a sister was a sign of low social stature. See E. A. Speiser, *A New Translation with Introduction and Commentary* (New York: Doubleday, 1964), 91 ff; Herschel Shanks, "The Patriarchs' Wives as Sisters: Is the Anchor Bible Wrong?" *BARev* 1, no. 3 (1975): 22–26. Klinghoffer analyzes the history of this debate in *Discovery,* 75. In addition, this incident has been used to help date the period of the patriarchs. Speiser argued that the evidence of wife/sister relationships in other archeological finds, places the patriarchal period in the first half of the second millennium. But by the 1960s, many scholars criticized this theory. For a further discussion of this issue, see Iain Provan, V. Phelps Long, Tremper Longman, eds., *A Biblical History of Israel* (Louisville, KY: Westminster John Knox Press, 2003), 113–15.

12. Jack Miles, *God: A Biography* (New York: Vintage Books, 1996), 49. He writes, "Abram gives his wife to Pharaoh to act out his displeasure with the Lord.

Against the Lord's wishes, Abram is giving offspring to Pharaoh by giving Sarai to Pharaoh."

13. Teubal outlines her argument, writing, "I give evidence to show that Sarah was a 'priestess' whose intimate relationship with the supernatural made her privy to the mysteries of religions and endowed her with the power of the office that went with it. I also suggest that the particular office held by Sarah was the most elevated in rank and status, the most sacred and most revered – a position comparable to that of women known as *en* and *naditu* who belonged to religious orders in the ancient Mesopotamian region of Sumer"(*Sarah the Priestess,* xv).

14. *Etz Hayim,* 72n10. "'Abram went down to Egypt.' He lowered himself to the moral level of that society. Even an Abraham is not immune to the influence of his surroundings. In a setting of danger and depravity, he can be vulnerable to fear and tempted to deceive others to save himself."

15. *Book of Abraham* 2:22–25.

16. Nachmanides writes, "Know that our father Abraham inadvertently committed a great sin by placing his virtuous wife in a compromising situation because of his fear of being killed. He should have trusted in God" (*Etz Hayim,* 73n13).

17. Two important exceptions are the medieval commentators Maimonides and Nachmanides. Both comment on Abram's sins in this episode. See Klinghoffer, *Discovery,* 70–71, for an overview of these viewpoints.

CHAPTER 6: Rape in the Palace

1. Ginzberg, *Legends,* 100–101.

2. Ibid.

3. Quoted in Klinghoffer, *Discovery,* 66.

4. J.E.M. White, *Everyday Life in Ancient Egypt* (New York: Dover Publications, 1963), 32–39; 113–28. These descriptions are based on White's account of the Egyptians and life in the Pharaoh's palace.

5. Ibid., 113–28.

6. Rosalie David, *Handbook to Life in Ancient Egypt* (New York: Oxford University Press, 1998), 182.

7. White, *Everyday Life,* 94–95; 169–70.

8. Ibid., 100.

9. David, *Handbook,* 328.

10. David, *Handbook,* 120–21. White, *Everyday Life,* 131.

11. White, *Everyday Life,* 94–95.

12. *Gen. R.,* 62. "Hagar was the daughter of the Pharaoh who captured Sarah, and on restoring her to Abraham he presented Sarah with Hagar as her maid."

13. In a contemporary Midrash, Rabbi Phyllis Berman writes, "[Sarai] looked around for a friend and quickly found another young woman, who only weeks before had herself been added to the collection of Pharaoh's women.... So

Sarai and Hagar, both far from home, uncertain when they'd be released or what would happen until then . . . became immediate and intimate friends." Chittister, Chishti, and Waskow, *Tent,* 210.

14. Historically speaking, the laws in the Torah that make adultery a capital offense for the woman come later in the development of Israelite culture. But they reflect ancient codes. For instance, adultery was punishable by death by Babylonian law although the husband had the right to spare his offending wife. "The Law Code of Hammurabi," in D. Winton Thomas, ed., *Documents from Old Testament Times,* 2nd ed. (New York: Harper Torchbooks, 1961), 31, 36.

15. White, *Everyday Life,* 185.

16. Ibid., 189.

17. The Egyptologist Ruth Antelme writes that for the Egyptians, the Pharaoh's "public embraces, caresses, and kisses are a demonstration of the divine sexual unity rediscovered." Ruth Antelme and Stephane Rossini, *Sacred Sexuality in Ancient Egypt* (Rochester, Vermont: Inner Traditions, 2001), 99.

18. *Gen. R.* 60:5. Quoted in Klinghoffer, *Discovery,* 121.

19. Rashi on Gen. 12:17.

20. Harold Bloom, *The Book of J* (New York: Vintage, 1991), 200.

21. Phyllis Trible, "Ominous Beginnings for a Promise of Blessing," in *Hagar, Sarah, and Their Children: Jewish, Christian, and Muslim Perspectives,* ed. Phyllis Trible and Letty Russell (Louisville, KY: Westminster John Knox Press, 2006), 33–70. Trible writes, "Most translations drop the term *word* to give the meaning 'on account of' or 'because of Sarai.' An alternative keeps the phrase 'because of the deed [or matter] concerning Sarai.' Both renderings present Sarai as the object of divine solicitude. But a third translation stays close to the Hebrew: 'because of the word of Sarai.' In contrast to the other choices, it presents Sarai not just as object but as subject with speech (even if the text does not give her particular word). . . . This third translation may suggest that from the beginning Sarai did not assent to Abram's plan, though she was unable to thwart it" (36–37). Fokkelien Van-Dijk-Hemmes supports this theory, writing that the Hebrew phrase could also be translated as "because of the word of Sarah." "Sarai's Exile: A Gender-Motivated Reading of Genesis 12.10–13.2," in Brenner, *A Feminist Companion to Genesis,* 231.

22. "Settling at Beer-lahai-roi," in *Daughters of Abraham: Feminist Thought in Judaism, Christianity, and Islam,* eds. Yvonne Yazbeck Haddad and John L. Esposito. (Gainesville: University of Florida Press, 2001), 22.

23. Rashi on Gen. 12:17; Ginzberg, *Legends,* 102.

24. Ginzberg, *Legends,* 100.

25. As Amy-Jill Levine writes, "Perhaps it is religious conservatism that prevents the suggestion that Sarah, tired of infertility in infertile Canaan, and tired of Abraham's perfunctory attitude toward her, actually appreciated her time amid the fleshpots of Egypt." "Settling at Beer-lahai-roi," in *Daughters of Abraham,* 22.

26. Ginzberg, *Legends,* 101.
27. An alternate interpretation, however, suggests that Hagar and Sarai remained each other's closest allies and supporters. See Rabbi Phyllis Berman, "Why Hagar Left," in Chittister, Chishti, and Waskow, *Tent,* 207–18.

CHAPTER 7: War

1. Trible, "Ominous Beginnings," 37.
2. Nachmanides on Gen. 12:10. Cited in Klinghoffer, *Discovery,* 66. See also *Jewish Study Bible.* Abram's sins were: "not trusting in God's protection, leaving the promised land, and subjecting his righteous wife to the possibility of sexual victimization. This, Nachmanides remarks, will be the cause of his descendants' painful exile in Egypt," 31n.
3. Jack Miles argues that after the initial creation, God decided that he wanted to reclaim His control over human fertility. He writes that the Abraham story introduces this struggle: "In Genesis 12 and the remaining chapters of the book of Genesis, we see the deity . . . in an ongoing struggle with mankind over control of human fertility" (*God,* 47–48).
4. Ibid.
5. Rashi on Gen. 13:10–11. Rashi cites the Midrashic tradition that says this choice was "to Lot's discredit" because Lot chose Sodom precisely because the people there "were addicted to lewdness" (*Gen. R.* 41). Rashi cites another damning Midrashic explanation: since Lot had to travel from east to west to get to Sodom, "he traveled away from the Originator of the Universe"(*Gen. R.* 41).
6. Al-A'raf 7:80–84; An-Naml 27:54–58; Al-'Ankabut 29:28–31.
7. Rashi on Gen. 13:11. *Gen. R.* 41.
8. Nelson Glueck, "The Age of Abraham in the Negev," *BA* 18: 7–8. Cited in Klinghoffer, *Discovery,* 86.
9. *Gen. R.* 42:7.
10. Ibid., 42:5.

CHAPTER 8: Dinner with Jesus

1. See David Klinghoffer, *Discovery,* 98–99, for a more complete discussion of reading this passage as the results of an editing decision, rather than for its symbolic content.
2. Klinghoffer offers a clear explanation of the Christian position on Melchizedek: "The author of the New Testament's Letter to the Hebrews uses the mysterious figure [Melchizedek] to prove that God has rejected the Jewish priesthood descended from Moses' brother, Aaron. Abram represents that outmoded cultic system, whereas Melchizedek stands in relation to Christ" (*Discovery,* 97).
3. According to the Bible, the Israelites were descended from the twelve sons

of Jacob. During the Exodus, the descendants of Levi, Jacob's third son, were the ones who remained loyal to God. As a result, they became anointed as the priestly tribe, the ones responsible for the ritual life of the community, tending the Ark of the Covenant in the desert and the Temple, once it was built in Jerusalem. After the destruction of the Second Temple in 70 C.E., the Levites could no longer fulfill their responsibilities. Into the breach stepped the rabbis, and, in fact, modern Judaism is a result of the adaptation that followed. In small houses of learning (synagogues), the rabbis taught and interpreted the lessons of the Torah and the Oral Torah. Thus, it became these men, rather than the Levites, who carried forward the religious life of the Jewish people. However, it is still a matter of pride for Jewish families to claim descent from Levi.

4. The Letter to the Hebrews emphasizes Melchizedek's lack of lineage: "Without father, without mother, without genealogy, having neither beginning of days nor end of life, but made like the Son of god, he remains a priest perpetually" (Heb 7:1–3).

5. On the website biblestudy.org with over 3 million yearly visitors, minister Jim Bowen declares that Melchizedek was indeed Jesus Christ. In his essay "Did Abraham Ever Have Dinner with Jesus?" he argues that Melchizedek's appearance in Abram's story is evidence that Jesus was alive when the patriarch walked the earth. Therefore, Jews cannot claim historical precedence over Christians. In support of this, he cites Jesus's words "Before Abraham was, I Am" (John 8:58). Accordingly, Melchizedek "became the Son of God and the fulfillment of the . . . promise of Genesis 49:10." "Who Was Melchizedek?" *Bible Study* 2009, www.biblestudy.org/basicart/whomelcz.html (January 15, 2009).

6. Klinghoffer, *Discovery*, 99.

7. Ibid., 97.

8. Ginzberg, *Legends*, 304–5. Klinghoffer also tells this story in *Discovery*, 98.

CHAPTER 9: Silences

1. Augustine, *On Christian Doctrine*, trans. by D.W. Robertson (New York: Prentice Hall, 1958), Book III, 27:38.

2. *Sanh.* 34b.

3. Augustine, *On Christian Doctrine*, Book III, 5:9.

4. According to Caroline Walker Bynum, one reason for this interpretive silence is that male writers and biographers tend to view the lives of women as liminal. But she argues, "Women's lives are not liminal to women." See *Essays on Gender and the Human Body in Medieval Religion* (New York: Zone, 1991), 48–49. In the last few decades, many feminist scholars have sought to fill in the gaps. In his overview of this trend, John L. Esposito writes that feminist interpreters of all three monotheistic traditions have attempted "to recover the 'lost voices' of women in past centuries who served as leaders

and who contributed to the development of religion and spirituality. They engage in scriptural studies and a new exegesis that often asks new questions and often finds fresh answers" (*Daughters of Abraham*, 4).

5. Sarna, *Understanding Genesis*, 128.

6. Bruce Metzer and Michael Coogan, eds., *The Oxford Companion to the Bible* (New York: Oxford University Press, 1993), s.v. "women."

7. Ibid.

8. Ibid., s.v. "clothing."

9. Ibid.

10. *Gen. R.* 39:14.

CHAPTER 10: Trembling before God

1. Dietrich Bonhoeffer, quoted by Maria von Wedemeyer-Weller, "The Other Letters from Prison," in *Letters and Papers from Prison*, 3rd edition, Eberhard Bethge, ed. and trans., (New York: Collier Books, 1971), 419.

2. "High Star," in *How I Pray: People of Different Religions Share With Us That Most Sacred and Intimate Act of Faith*, Jim Castelli, ed. (New York: Random House, 1994), 70; Rabbi Joseph B. Soloveitchik, "Adam and Eve," in *Family Redeemed: Essays on Family Relationships*, David Shatz and Joel B. Wolowelsky, eds. (New York: Toras HoRav Foundation, 2000), 3–30. Soloveitchik writes, "Loneliness is a spiritual human situation. It is both an inspiring as well as destructive experience. . . . It is only man-persona [the man who has entered into relationship with God] — introspective, meditating, and experiencing estrangement from nature — who is lonely" (16). Thus, according to Soloveichik, only when one has experienced the contradictions of being human and realized that one is a part of God and alienated forever from God, can one embark on the pilgrimage of faith.

3. Admittedly the Bible is not precise about when God spoke to Abram since this moment in Abram's story was meant to be outside of ordinary time and separated from Abram's usual life. In every other scene the Bible specifies the location and the time of the episodes in the patriarch's life. But the word, "*ahar*" which introduces this episode, implies that Abram's vision began "immediately" after the Melchizedek episode and Abram's refusal to take riches from the king of Sodom. This would make sense as both episodes prepared Abram for the harrowing experience that lay ahead. See Rashi on Gen. 15:1 for a more complete explanation.

4. He uses the Latin words: "*mysterium terribile et fascinans.*" Rudolph Otto, *The Idea of the Holy, an Inquiry into the Non-rational Factor in the Idea of the Divine and Its Relation to the Rational*, trans. John W. Harvey (Oxford: Oxford University Press, 1923), 29–30.

5. *Ned.* 38a; *Shabb.* 92a. Maimonides, *Mishneh Torah, Hilchot yesodei HaTorah*, 7:1–4. Quoted in Klinghoffer, *Discovery*, 47–48. See also Klinghoffer's extensive discussion of prophecy and the identity of the prophet, 47–49.

6. Rashi on Gen. 15:1.

7. Sarna, *Understanding Genesis,* 121. After pondering these words, Rashi wrote that *"maggen Avraham"*—the name of the prayer uses the name God gives Abram later in the story—was yet more divine reassurance for Abram's fear of the kings' revenge. Rashi supported this idea with the fact that the word *maggen,* or shield, comes from the same root as *miggin,* the word Melchizedek used to invoke God's deliverance when he blessed Abram. Rashi on Gen. 15:1.

8. Klinghoffer, *Discovery,* 48.

9. Maimonides, *Mishneh Torah, Hilchot Yesodei HaTorah,* 7:1–4.

10. Ibid. Also, Klinghoffer, *Discovery,* 48. My description of the prophet's experience is based on Klinghoffer's more thorough analysis.

11. William James, *The Varieties of Religious Experience* (1902; reprint, New York: Collier Books, 1961), 300.

12. Abraham Heschel, *The Prophets* (1962; reprint, New York: HarperCollins, 2001), 30–31.

13. Sarna argues that it would have been strange if Abram had not adopted a son. That men like Abram valued children above almost all else is made clear by the sheer number of adoption contracts that have been excavated in the famous archaeological site Nuzi. Almost always, these contracts provide for the contingency of a son being born after the adoption, in which case the adoptee has to cede priority. *Understanding Genesis,* 123.

14. Hayyim of Tzantz, quoted in *Etz Hayim,* 83n.

15. Pierre Hadot, *Philosophy as a Way of Life: Spiritual Exercises from Socrates to Foucault* (Wiley-Blackwell, 1995).

16. *Memoiren einer Idealistin,* 1900. Quoted in William James, *Varieties of Religious Experience,* 311.

17. Ralph Waldo Emerson, "Circles," in *Essays* (New York: Macmillan, 1899), 252.

18. Augustine wrote to God, "You were within and I was in the external world and sought you there, and in my unlovely state I plunged into those lovely created things which you made. You were with me, and I was not with you. The lovely things kept me far from you, though if they did not have their existence in you, they had no existence at all." *Confessions* 1.1, trans. Henry Chadwick (Oxford: Oxford University Press, 1991), 3. Quoted in Armstrong, *History,* 121; David Brewster, ed., *Memoirs of the Life, Writings, and Discoveries of Sir Isaac Newton,* vol. 2 (London and Edinburgh, 1855), chap. 27. Newton famously remarked, "I seem to have been only like a boy playing on the seashore . . . whilst the great ocean of truth lay all undiscovered before me." *Never at Rest: A Biography of Isaac Newton,* ed. Richard S. Westfall (Cambridge: Cambridge Paperback Library, 1980), 863.

19. Rashi on Gen. 15:6. Also see Klinghoffer, *Discovery,* 107, for his analysis of Rashi.

20. Kenneth L. Vaux, *Jew, Christian, Muslim: Faithful Unification or Fateful Trifurcation?* (Eugene, OR: Wipf and Stock, 2003), 46–47.

CHAPTER 11: Covenant of the Parts

1. Sarna, *Understanding Genesis,* 127.
2. Rashi on Gen. 15:8.
3. Rashi writes that the heifer was in place of the bull that was sacrificed when "the correct interpretation of a precept was unknown to the leaders of the nation" (Rashi on Gen. 15:9–10).
4. Ibid. Rashi writes, "he [Abram] therefore divided the animals indicating that other nations will gradually perish . . . but 'the birds split he not' suggesting thereby that Israel will live forever." Interestingly, Rashi based this commentary on the ancient writings of *Pirqe R. El.,* 28.
5. *Etz Hayim,* 84 n.
6. There is, however, an alternate interpretation of this text that says there were actually no birds of prey. According to a medieval Yemenite Jewish version of the *Midrash Ha-Gadol,* Abraham had actually cut the birds for the ritual in half and "when Abraham laid the halves of the pieces over against each other, they became alive and flew away, this being God's way of demonstrating to him the doctrine of Resurrection of the Dead" (on Gen 15:11). Although the tale is absent from the mainstream Jewish tradition, according to the scholar Eliezer Siegal, it recurs in the Arabic translation of the Bible by the tenth-century scholar Rabbi Saadiah Gaon. Gaon interpreted "the Hebrew phrase *vayashev otam Avram,* normally rendered as "Abram drove [the birds] away," as "Abraham brought them back to life." Siegal argues that this interpretative tradition not only points to an early interest among Jewish scholars in the doctrine of resurrection, but also illustrates an important intersection between Islam and Judaism, as the first version of a story about Abraham and resurrection seems to be from the Koran: "And when Abraham said: 'Lord show me how you will revive the dead,' He said, 'What, do you not yet believe?' Said he, 'Yea, but that my heart may be quieted.' He said, 'Then take four birds, and take them close to yourself; then put a part of them on every mountain; then call them, and they will come to you in haste; and know that God is mighty, wise'" (Koran 2:260). Eliezer Siegal, "Abraham Our Father—and Theirs: Christianity and Islam Share a Reverence for Judaism's Patriarch," *My Jewish Learning,* 2009, http://www.myjewishlearning.com/history_community/Ancient/TheStoryTO/Patriarchs/Abraham/AbrahamOthers.htm (April 10, 2008).
7. Nachmanides on Gen. 12:10. Quoted in Klinghoffer, *Discovery,* 77.
8. Sarna, *Understanding Genesis,* 124.
9. Sarna makes this point about the extraordinary nature of Israel's inheritance. He writes, "This amazing explanation means that the displacement of the native population of Canaan by Israel was not to be accounted for on grounds of divine favoritism or superior military prowess on the part of the invading Israelites. . . . The pre-Israelite inhabitants of Canaan had been doomed by their own corruption." See *Understanding Genesis,* 124–25.

CHAPTER 12: Sarai's Proposition

1. Although there are arguments that Sarai is simply following the rules of the Biblical period (see notes 2 and 3 in this chapter), there is also the possibility that her proposal is truly unconventional, in which case her words initiate another important transition in Abram's life. In her comparative study of Gilgamesh and the Biblical story of David, Susan Ackerman argues that women often prompt men's transition away from normal time and structured social conventions into the realm of an in-between, liminal arena, what she calls a "movement in and out of liminal time and space." See *When Heroes Love: The Ambiguity of Eros in the Stories of Gilgamesh and David* (New York: Columbia University Press, 2005), 147.

2. Sarai's own granddaughter-in-law Rachel, who also had difficulty bearing children, would use her handmaidens to have babies by her husband, claiming the children as her own.

3. The evidence for Sarna's argument comes from the clay tablets that were dug up at the archeological site of Nuzi. He writes, "One legal contract between a husband, Shennima, and a wife, Kelim-ninu, declares: 'If Kelim-ninu does not bear [offspring], Kelim-ninu shall acquire a woman . . . as wife for Shennima, and Kelim-ninu may not send the offspring away'" (*Understanding Genesis,* 128). For further analysis of the Nuzi laws, see Klinghoffer, *Discovery,* 123.

4. The most famous examples are Isaac and Rebecca (24:67), Jacob and Rachel (29:11), and Hannah and her husband (Samuel 1:4).

5. "With the first person suffix followed by a particle [*hinneh*] is used often in the prophets as a statement of what God will do." Robert L. Harris, ed., *Theological Wordbook of the Old Testament* (Chicago: The Moody Bible Institute, 1980), 220–21.

6. Josephus, *Complete Works,* trans. Syvert Havercamp (New York: Bigelow, Brown & Co., Inc.), 35.

7. Although the dominant story in Islam is that Sarai was a jealous wife, there is also a tradition of seeing Sarai as unselfish. For the traditional version, see John L. Esposito, *What Everyone Needs to Know About Islam* (Oxford: Oxford University Press, 2002), 5. For the selfless Sarah, see one of the most frequently visited websites devoted to Islam, islamiCity.com: "Time went by and no children were born to Sarah. She realized she was sterile. She accepted her fate and submitted to the will of Allah. Ibrahim and Sarah moved to Egypt where the king gave Sarah a woman to be her servant. The woman's name was Hajar. Sarah was seeing Ibrahim' s hair getting white, and it grieved her to see his chance of having any child slipping away. She offered Hajar her servant as a wife to her husband, and prayed Allah to bless Hajar and Ibrahim with a child. And so came Ismail, a baby boy born to Hajar. How unselfish Sarah was! For her, the need to have an offspring who would carry the Message after Ibrahim was greater than her pride. Fourteen years later Allah rewarded Sarah with a son, Ishaq in spite of her old age."

"Prophet Ibrahim: The Father of the Prophets," *Human Assistance & Development International (HADI)*, 2009, http://www.islamicity.com/Mosque/ ibrahim.htm (June 3, 2008).

8. Tikva Frymer-Kensky, *Reading the Women of the Bible* (New York: Schocken Books, 2002), 232.

CHAPTER 13: Do with Her as You Will

1. Jon Levenson writes, "If [Abram's] acceptance of Sarai's suggestion is not owing to a loss of faith, why has he not resorted to surrogate motherhood earlier, or taken a second wife? If the answer is his sensitivity to Sarai, then why has he been valuing this over his role in the providential drama? Is this sensitivity not also a manifestation of a lack of commitment to the God who set him on this journey?" Levenson also cites Joel Rosenberg's comparison of this story to the story of the garden of Eden, writing, "The problem is not men's obeying their wives, but men and women's acting against God's wishes." *The Death and Resurrection of the Beloved Son* (New Haven: Yale University Press, 1993), 91. Jack Miles, on the other hand, argues that Sarai is the rebellious one here. He writes that she says it is God who has made her barren and it is no fault of her own. Thus, "She sends Abram to her Egyptian servant girl, Hagar, angrily, in defiance of the Lord, rather as Abram earlier sent her to Pharaoh" (*God*, 51).

2. Levenson writes, "In defense of Abram and Sarai against the charge of faithlessness, however, it must be noted not only that the matriarch of the promised progeny has never been indicated, but also that the Hebrew Bible does not generally support an equation of faith with passivity. Even on the shore of the Sea of Reeds, Israel is not only enjoined to hold their peace, but also in the very next verse, 'to go forward' (Exod 14:15)—not to wait quietistically for YHWH to rescue them" (*Beloved Son*, 92).

3. Joseph Smith, *Doctrines & Covenants*, 132:34–35, 37. Smith goes on to say, "Abraham received concubines, and they bore him children; and it was accounted unto him for righteousness, because they were given unto him, and he abode in my law; as Isaac also and Jacob ... and because they did none other things than that which they were commanded, they have entered into their exaltation, according to the promises, and sit upon thrones, and are not angels but are gods."

4. Fawn Brodie writes, "Probably no one will ever know exactly how many women Joseph Smith married." However, she estimates the number of wives at forty-eight. *No Man Knows My History: The Life of Joseph Smith*, 2nd ed. (New York: Vintage, 1995), 328.

5. Wade Goodwyn, Howard Berkes and Amy Walters, "Warren Jeffs and the FLDS," *National Public Radio*, May 3, 2005, http://www.npr.org/templates/ story/story.php?storyId=4629320 (January 22, 2009).

6. *Gen. R.* 45:3.

7. Ginzberg, *Legends*, 108.

8. This is Klinghoffer's observation. *Discovery*, 121.

9. Rashi bases his argument on *Gen. R.* 45. See Rashi on Gen. 16:3.

10. Rashi on Gen. 16:4. For a similar account, see Ginzberg, *Legends*, 109.

11. Ibid.

12. *Gen. R.* 45:5. "A midrash sees in Sarai's behavior an object lesson in the dangers of litigiousness: Had she not been so single-mindedly and insensitively preoccupied in demanding justice for herself, her life span would have equaled Abram's. Instead, whereas he lived to 175, she died at 127" (25:7, 23:1) (*Gen. R.* 45:5). Adele Berlin and Marc Brettler, eds., *The Jewish Study Bible* (New York: Oxford University Press, 2004), 36n16.5–6. Rashi writes that she is also talking to Hagar, arguing, that it was "as though Sarah turned to Hagar saying, 'May God judge between me and thee'" (on Gen 16:5). See Klinghoffer, *Discovery*, 128–29, for a thorough analysis of the Talmud's response to Sarai's words. Interestingly, none of the commentary speculates on forty-eight, the number of years cut from her life.

13. For an overview of this interpretive stance, see Klinghoffer, *Discovery*, 128.

14. Frymer-Kensky, *Reading the Women*, 228, cites the host's words when he offers his daughter and the Levite's concubine to the angry crowd (Judg. 19:22–26).

15. Ibid., 229.

16. Rashi on Gen. 16:5.

17. *Gen. R.*, 45:6. Klinghoffer explains that Sarai's "humiliation" of Hagar is unacceptable because it is "the sin of working a slave in such a way that his or her slave status is made known to all. Deriving this from a verse in Leviticus, Rashi gives the example of one who orders his servant to 'carry his belongings behind him to the bathhouse'" (*Discovery*, 129).

18. Klinghoffer writes, "Though Sarai's intent was pedagogical, her purpose being to encourage Hagar to repent of her bad attitude, it is not the place of one human being to impose a Yom Kippur on her fellow. That right is reserved to God alone" (*Discovery*, 129).

19. Frymer-Kensky, *Reading the Women*, 223.

20. Quoted in *Etz Hayim*, 87n6.

CHAPTER 14: Hagar and the Wilderness

1. The Bible does not say Hagar's escape took place at night. Commentators make this assumption to explain why no one stopped her.

2. According to most Islamic thinkers, "Prophecy has come to an end, so no one can imitate Mohammed in his role as messenger." See William C. Chittick, *The Sufi Path of Knowledge* (New York: State University of New York Press, 1989), 310. For Christian beliefs about prophecy, *The Oxford Companion to the Bible* states, "When the New Testament canon was completed . . . emphasis shifted to the interpretation of existing revelation. Sporadically throughout the history of Christianity, there have been those who claimed to have personal revelations. The orthodox churches have always tested these by and

subordinated them to scripture. The Roman Catholic church has allowed that new revelation also exists in the form of church tradition and is as binding as scripture, while Protestants consider the Bible to be the sole authority." S. v. "Revelation."

3. Moses, Jesus, and Elijah would each have to spend time alone in the desert.

4. *Etz Hayim,* 86n1.

5. The full passage from Exodus: "Now when they came to Marah, they could not drink the waters of Marah, for they were bitter. Therefore the name of it was called Marah. And the people complained against Moses, saying, 'What shall we drink?' So he cried out to the Lord, and the Lord showed him a tree. When he cast it into the waters, the waters were made sweet" (Ex. 15:22–25).

6. The location of Hagar's well was first mentioned by Eusebius, but it is unclear where it actually was. Morris Jastrow, Jr., "Beer Lahai Ro'I," *Jewish Encyclopedia Online,* 2002, http://www.jewishencyclopedia.com/view.jsp?art id=519&letter=B&search=Beer%20Lahai%20Ro%E2%80%99I (June 3, 2008).

7. Rashi on Gen. 20:7. See Psalm 52 for an example of the prophetic equation between the divine and water: "As a deer longs for flowing streams/ I long for you, O God./ My soul thirsts for God, the living God" (Psalms 52:1–3). If men of God failed at their task of finding water, God stepped in, leading them to a spring, or sending messengers with supplies. For instance, an angel delivered water to Elijah during his sojourn in Shur (1 Kings 19:67).

CHAPTER 15: The Well

1. For a comprehensive catalogue of how Hagar has been viewed by African American theologians and writers, see Delores S. Williams, "Hagar in African American Biblical Appropriation." In *Hagar, Sarah, and Their Children,* 171–84. She writes, "For more than two hundred years, African Americans have appropriated the biblical figure Hagar" (171).

2. Phyllis Trible, *Texts of Terror: Literary-Feminist Readings of Biblical Narratives* (Philadelphia: Fortress Press, 1978), 28.

3. George E. Ganss, ed. *Ignatius of Loyola: Spiritual Exercises and Selected Works* (New York: Paulist Press, 1991), 247.

4. *Zen Flesh Zen Bones: A Collection of Zen and Pre-Zen Writings,* eds. Paul Reps and Nyogen Senzai (Boston: Tuttle Publishing, 1998 rep. 1957), 96–97.

5. See Frymer-Kensky, *Reading the Women,* 230, for this reading of God's address to Hagar.

6. Devora Steinmetz, *From Father to Son: Kinship, Conflict, and Continuity in Genesis* (Louisville, KY: Westminster John Knox Press, 1991), 76–78. She writes, "Hagar has rejected both the suffering of the present and the promise of the future" (77).

7. Frymer-Kensky, *Reading the Women,* 233.

8. Deuteronomy 23:15–16; Frymer-Kensky, *Reading the Women,* 230. Frymer-Kensky points out that Biblical law conflicted with Near Eastern laws about slavery.

9. Elsa Tamez and B. Yeager, "The Women Who Complicated the History of Salvation," in John S. Pobee and Barbel von Wartenberg-Potter, eds., *New Eyes for Reading* (Geneva: World Council of Churches, 1986), 14. Also see Alice Bellis, *Helpmates, Harlots, and Heroes: Women's Stories in the Hebrew Bible* (Louisville, KY: Westminster John Knox Press, 1994), 76. Again, Rashi insists that Hagar miscarried the first baby and thus had to return. He writes, "This explains what the angel said to Hagar, 'behold, thou wilt conceive'; but had she not already conceived and yet he announces to her that she would conceive? This therefore informs us that she miscarried in this, her first conception" (on Gen. 16:5).

10. For the conflict between Jewish and Muslim commentators, see Klinghoffer, *Discovery,* 134–35. Also Rashi on Gen. 16:12.

11. See Klinghoffer's angel discussion, *Discovery,* 132. Also see Moshe Chayim Luzzato, *The Way of God,* Aryeh Kaplan, trans. (NewYork: Feldheim, 1988), 75.

CHAPTER 16: A Second Concubine

1. I am indebted to Frymer-Kensky for my understanding of the concubine's story (*Reading the Women,* 119–38). Because the Judges story also contains a link to a famous moment in the future life of Lot, it is easy to overlook the link between Hagar and the Judges concubine.

2. Frymer-Kensky points out this parallel in *Reading the Women,* 125.

3. The Judges story has not always been seen in a negative light. Rather, it served as a precedent for those who wanted to promote the concept of a holy war. In defense of the English Civil War (1642–51), John Milton argued that the bloodiness of the English wars was justified, just as the Benjaminite battles had been necessary to avenge the concubine. "All Israel saw that without much shedding of blood she could not avenge the outrage and murder of the Levite's wife; did they think that for this reason they must hold their peace, avoid civil war however fierce, or allow the death of a single poor woman to go unpunished?" John Milton, *Eikonoklastes* (London, 1649), in *The Complete Prose Works of John Milton,* vol. III, Don M. Wolfe, ed. (New Haven, CT: Yale University Press, 1962).

4. Tradition holds that the book of Judges was written by Samuel sometime around 1000 B.C.E. during the reign of Saul. However, a theory called the Documentary Hypothesis suggests that the Book of Judges was not written by one author, but was compiled by a Biblical redactor. One suggestion is that the Levite story was written during the reign of King David (1010–970 B.C.E.). Its anti-Benjaminite sentiment is typical of that time, as the king before David was Saul, a Benjaminite. See Richard F. Friedman, *Who Wrote the Bible?* (New York: Simon and Schuster, 1987), 123, 130–31. The story of the Sabine women was recorded many centuries after the Bible story. However, both events could well have occurred within a few centuries of each other, as the traditional founding date of Rome is 753 B.C.E.

CHAPTER 17: Naming God

1. *Etz Hayim,* 88n.
2. Ibid.
3. Ibid.
4. "The Cloud of Unknowing," in *Visions of God,* Karen Armstrong, ed. (New York: Bantam, 1994), 62.
5. Abraham Heschel, *The Prophets* (New York: Harper Collins, 2001 rep. 1962), 5–6.
6. In an attempt to reverse this trend, recent feminist scholarship has focused on Hagar. But the lack of material on Hagar may simply be because there is no argument about her legitimacy as a foremother. As Hibba Abugideiri writes, "Her near absence from Islamic texts is not necessarily because of her sex; rather, it comes from the lack of dispute surrounding her significance in Islam." "Hagar: A Historical Model for 'Gender Jihad'" in *Daughters of Abraham,* 81.

CHAPTER 18: Ishmael

1. Even two thousand or so years after the period of the matriarchs, women were still at great risk during labor. Amy Wordelman writes, "Women often died from either childbirth or disease. High infant and high maternal mortality rates made childbirth a constant arena of danger and grief in women's lives." "Everyday Life in the Period of The New Testament" in Carol Newsome and Sharon Ringe, eds., *The Women's Bible Commentary* (Louisville, KY: Westminster John Knox Press, 1992), 395.
2. Miriam Vamosh, *Food at the Time of the Bible* (Herzlia, Israel: Palphot Ltd., 2007), s.vv. "Nard," and "Sage," 76–77.
3. Howard Eilberg-Schwartz theorizes that the story of the virgin birth ushered in a new attitude toward masculinity and fatherhood. He argues that God's replacement as the Father of Jesus undermines the importance of the human father and forever alters the relationship men have to their own sexuality. He writes, "For if the religious role of masculinity was no longer to continue the lineage of the fathers, then the male organ of generation would begin to lose the positive value it once had." *God's Phallus and Other Problems for Men and Monotheism* (Boston: Beacon Press, 1994), 235.
4. Bruce Metzger and Michael D. Coogan, eds., *The Oxford Companion to the Bible,* s.v. "Women."
5. Rashi on Gen. 16:12. He writes that Ishmael was "one who loves the open spaces to hunt wild animals" and cites Gen. 21:20 as his evidence for this point: "And [Ishmael] dwelt in the wilderness and became an archer."

CHAPTER 19: El Shaddai

1. *Jewish Study Bible,* 36n1. "El Shaddai is believed to have originally meant 'God, the One of the Mountain' and thus to have expressed the association

of a deity with his mountain abode well known in Canaanite literature (cf. the "Lord, him of Sinai in Judg. 5.5). In the Priestly conception, the four-letter name translated as Lord was disclosed only in the time of Moses (Exod 6.2–3) and El Shaddai was the name by which God revealed Himself to the patriarchs." For "raw power," see Miles, *God*, 51. On the other hand, Rashi interprets "Shaddai" as a derivative of the Hebrew word, "*dai*," meaning "enough" or "sufficient." Thus, when God introduces Himself as El Shaddai, He is saying, "I am all that you need, Abraham" (Rashi on 17:1). Finally, there are some scholars who have proposed that the title could imply a feminine nurturing deity, as Shaddaim could also mean breasted, or mothering god. These writers argue that this is the name of God that is often used in conjunction with fertility blessings and point to three instances in Genesis, "May El Shaddai ... make you fruitful and increase your numbers (Gen. 28:3); "I am El Shaddai: be fruitful and increase in number (Gen. 35:11); and "By El Shaddai who will bless you with blessings of heaven above, blessings of the deep that lies beneath, blessings of the breasts [shadayim] and of the womb [racham]" (Gen. 49:25). See Harriet Lutzky, "Shadday as a Goddess Epithet," *Vetus Testamentum* 48 (1998): 15–36. See Also W. F. Albright, "The Names Shaddai and Abram," *Journal of Biblical Literature* 54 (1935): 173–210.

2. *Etz Hayim*, 89n.

3. Rashi writes, "Abram fell upon his face through fear of the shechinah [the holy presence], because before he was circumcised he did not have the strength to stand on his feet whilst the Holy Spirit stood over him" (on Gen. 17:3).

4. On change from Abram to Avraham being the change to "father of multitudes," *Etz Hayim*, 90n. The rabbinic text, *Mekh Yitro* argues, "The letter hei, representing the name of God, is added both to [Sarai's] name and to Abram's name, as a reward for their pious behavior. To do good deeds is to link our name with the name of God" (*Etz Hayim*, 91n15).

5. Sarna, *Understanding Genesis*, 131.

6. These pragmatic accounts may well derive from Herodotus's observation that the Egyptians believed in circumcision "for the sake of cleanliness, considering it better to be clean than comely" (Histories, II: 36f., 104, quoted in Sarna, *Understanding Genesis*, 131). Philo, the first-century Jewish writer who dedicated himself to finding philosophically sound reasons for Jewish religious practices, argued that circumcision promoted health and fertility. But by the Middle Ages, Maimonides understood circumcision solely as a matter of faith. Anthropologists have argued that circumcision derived from the Israelite need for a distinguishing mark from their Babylonian conquerors in the sixth century. Later Jews clung to this ritual as a way to differentiate themselves from Gentiles. Still, the assumption of "many later commentators" that "circumcision was a health measure—a surgery mainly aimed at disease" fails to offer a true explanation for its origins. (David L. Gollaher, *Circumcision: A History of the World's Most Controversial Surgery* [New York: Basic Books, 2000]. On Philo, see p. 13; on Maimonides, see p. 20;

on "health measure," see p. 4.) The modern idea that circumcision provides health benefits is primarily derived from late nineteenth-century medical theory. In 1910, the *Encyclopedia Britannica* explained circumcision as a surgery "commonly prescribed for purely medical reasons" (11th edition, vol. 6, s.v. "Circumcision"). Currently, however, there is no longer medical consensus about the procedure.

7. In Romans 4:12, Paul writes, "He received the sign of circumcision, a seal of the righteousness of the faith, which he had being yet uncircumcised." See also Romans 2:29.

8. Howard Eilberg-Schwartz, *God's Phallus and Other Problems for Men and Monotheism* (Boston: Beacon Press, 1994). In an overview of Freudian theory, he writes, "For Freud and his followers, religion reflects and repeats the experience of having a father ... it is the boy's oedipal struggles, his feelings of love, hate, and competition toward his father, that are projected onto the heavenly father" (14–15).

9. *Discovery,* 149.

10. Klinghoffer cites Maimonides (Rambam) in his extensive discussion of circumcision. He writes, "Rambam adds that when the foreskin is amputated, sexual pleasure for the man is diminished. The membrane of the glans penis is left exposed to the wide world, with the consequence that a degree of sensitivity is lost" (*Discovery,* 149). See also Maimonides, *The Guide for the Perplexed,* trans. M. Friedlander (reprint New York: Dover, 1956), 378.

CHAPTER 20: Sarah and God

1. Rashi writes that Sarai means "a princess to me and not to others," whereas Sarah has a more "general sense," in that she shall be princess over all. Rashi on Gen. 17:15.

2. *Ber.* 13; *Gen. R.* xivii, 1. See also *Jewish Encyclopedia,* 2002, s.v. "Sarah."

3. J. F. McLaughlin and Judah David Eisenstein, "Names of God," *Jewish Encyclopedia.com,* s. v. http://www.jewishencyclopedia.com/view.jsp?artid=52&letter=N&search=names%20of%20god (February 10, 2008). Rabbi Arthur Waskow writes that the divine name YHWH can be "spoken with no vowels—Yyyyhhhhwwwwhhhh—and heard simply as a breathing sound, thus 'Breath of Life, or Breathing Spirit of the World.' " Chittister, Chishti, and Waskow, *Tent,* 6.

4. Matis Weinberg, *Frameworks — Genesis* (Boston: The Foundation for Jewish Publications, 1999), 86. As part of his discussion on Abraham's laughter, Weinberg cites Maimonides. He goes on to say that, according to the ancient Jewish commentators, God's proclamation was truly miraculous, not just because Sarah was so old, but because they believed that she lacked a uterus altogether. Klinghoffer also mentions this legend in *Discovery.* He writes, "The third-century A.D. sage Rabbi Ami received the scandalous tradition that Abram and Sarai were 'of doubtful sex [*tumtummin*]'" (28).

5. Rashi on Gen. 17:17.

6. As Tikva Frymer-Kensky writes, "Instead of seeing the [descendants of Ishmael] as an unsocialized element within its boundaries or as demonic opponents of God's will, or even as people who have to be expelled or tamed, Genesis integrates Ishmael into Israel's self-understanding as its God-approved alter ego. For Ishmael is in many respects the polar opposite of Israel, and a nation that often found itself marginal, exploited, and on the brink of destruction may have appreciated Ishmael's destiny of utter freedom" (*Reading the Women*, 237).

7. Rashi on Gen. 16:12

8. *Etz Hayim*, 89n5. "In the Bible a change of name is of major significance. It symbolizes the transformation of character and destiny."

9. As Klinghoffer explains, Nachmanides writes that it was Abraham's passivity that helped create the strife between Hagar and Sarai (*Discovery*, 129). Nachmanides argued that both Abram and Sarai behaved so badly in the case of Hagar that the Jews have suffered "all manners of affliction" at the hands of the Arabic people. Quoted in Klinghoffer, *Discovery*, 127. See Nachmanides on Gen. 16:6.

10. Rashi helps create the tradition of contempt for Ishmael. He writes that Abraham hated Ishmael because the boy "had taken to degenerate ways" (on Gen. 21:14).

11. Levenson, *Beloved Son*. Christian supercessionism, Levenson argues, is necessarily preoccupied with the tale of Abraham. He writes, "[Supercessionists'] very effort to dispossess the community of the Torah bears eloquent and enduring witness to the indispensability of the Torah to the early Church and to the thoroughly intertextual, indeed midrashic character of the most basic elements of the Christian message—a point with which most Christians, even most New Testament scholars, have failed to reckon" (229–30).

CHAPTER 21: God the Father

1. It is also likely that God was announcing He would no longer tolerate any vestiges of polytheism; there could be only one God, and the remnants of other divines and semi-divines would have to be stamped out.

2. Marvin H. Pope, *El in the Ugaritic Texts* (Leiden: Brill, 1955), 38–39, quoted in Eilberg-Schwartz, *God's Phallus*, 108.

3. Eilberg-Schwartz, *God's Phallus*, 78, 108.

4. Kugel, *God of Old*, 104.

5. Ibid., 106.

6. See James Kugel's discussion of the "appearances" of the divine in *God of Old*, 99–107. Kugel discusses the "moment of confusion" in ch. 2, 5–36.

7. For examples of Biblical characters seeing God, see Exodus: "Then Moses, Aaron, Nadab, Abihu, and seventy elders of Israel ascended and they saw the God of Israel: under His feet there was the likeness of a pavement of sapphire, like the very sky for purity; Yet he did not raise His hand against the leaders of the Israelites; they beheld God and they ate and drank" (Ex. 24:9–11).

Or the full text of Ezekiel's vision: "From what appeared as His loins up, I saw a gleam as of amber—what looked like fire encased in a frame; and from what appeared as His loins down, I saw what looked like fire. There was a radiance all about him. Like the appearance of the bow which shines in the clouds on a day of rain, such was the appearance of the semblance of the Presence of the Lord" (Ezek. 1:27–28). Also, the prophets Amos (9:1), Isaiah (6:1–2), Micaiah (1 Kings 22:19), and Daniel (7:9–11)—and there are many more examples—include descriptions of God's body in their accounts of their divine encounters. Although it is possible to say that the prophets are simply using figurative language to explain their visions, the story in Exodus is an explicit depiction of God's form.

8. *M. Hag.* 2:1; *Tos. Hag.* 2:1, quoted in Eilberg-Schwartz, *God's Phallus,* 176. Scholars should not "expound upon . . . [Ezekiel's vision] before one, unless he was a sage [and] understands his own knowledge." Clearly, Ezekiel's vision was too easy for students to misunderstand. Therefore, according to the Talmud, this passage could only be taught one-on-one, rather than to groups of students, lest the students were tempted to interpret Ezekiel's vision literally. See Klinghoffer, *Discovery,* 131, for a more complete discussion of this topic. See also *Chagigah* 11b. Maimonides writes, "You know very well how difficult it is for men to form a notion of anything immaterial and entirely devoid of corporeality, except after considerable training" (Maimonides, *Guide,* 66, quoted in Klinghoffer, *Discovery,* 131).

9. Frank Moore Cross, *Canaanite Myth and Hebrew Epic* (Cambridge: Harvard University Press, 1973), 23. Quoted in Eilberg-Schwartz, *God's Phallus,* 86.

10. Eilberg-Schwartz writes, "An Israelite male who gazed at God was like Ham, who looked at his naked father" (*God's Phallus,* 97). Furthermore, he points out that exposure and shame are often linked in the Bible. *God's Phallus,* 88.

11. This is the central question in Eilberg-Schwartz's work. He writes, "The question I want to ask is not whether Jews really believed God had a body, but why, when they imagined God in a human form, that form was so carefully veiled and why it was veiled in the particular way it was. This question remains relevant whether the images are taken literally or figuratively" (*God's Phallus,* 75). For further elucidation of this question, see *God's Phallus,* 97.

12. William Butler Yeats, "Leda and The Swan," in M. L. Rosenthal, ed, *Selected Poems and Three Plays of William Butler Yeats,* 3rd ed. (New York: Collier Books, 1986), 121.

13. Eilberg-Schwartz writes, "Where Hamor [Dinah's rapist] did violence to Dinah's genitals, Jacob's sons do violence to the Hivites by getting them to injure their own genitals. The rape has been reversed. In other words, circumcision is an eminently appropriate way of unmanning the Hivites and preparing to murder them" (*God's Phallus,* 157).

14. Eilberg-Schwartz, *God's Phallus,* 172.

15. *Genesis Rabbah* 46:4.

16. Brother Antoninus (William O. Everson), *The Crooked Lines of God* (Detroit:

University of Detroit Press, 1959), 86–87, quoted in Eilberg-Schwartz, *God's Phallus*, 137.

CHAPTER 22: Circumcision

1. *Theological Word Book of the Old Testament* (Chicago: The Moody Bible Institute, 1980), s. v. *"arel."* This adjective "became a word of contempt, used particularly with reference to the Philistines who did not practice circumcision.... This term was associated with moral and spiritual uncleanness ... as well as with organs that did not function properly.... Circumcision was a spiritual act as well. Egypt, Edom, Ammon, Moab—and Judah!—all practiced circumcision of the penis, but not the heart.... Hence Israel was commanded to circumcise the foreskin of the heart."

2. Karen Armstrong writes, "When P[the priestly source] described the institution of circumcision, a practice which acquired a new religious importance in the sixth century, BCE, he made it clear that Abraham and his son Ishmael, who was thirteen years old at the time, were circumcised on the same day ... Regarded as the cousins of Israel, Ishmael and his descendants were still regarded as honorary members of the covenant in P's time" (*Beginning*, 67).

3. As Nahum Sarna writes, "The Bible shifted its performance [of circumcision] from puberty to the eighth day of birth, a radical distinction from well-nigh universal practice which not only marks the distinction between Isaac and Ishmael, but even more importantly establishes another essential differentiation of the biblical institution of circumcision from its contemporary pagan counterpart" (*Understanding Genesis*, 132). The reason for the eighth day seems to be related to the injunction from Leviticus that all creatures, whether human or animal, are deemed unclean until they are eight days old (Lev. 22:27).

4. Rashi on Gen. 18:1

5. Ibid.

6. Ibid. Rashi cites *Babe Mezia* 86b.

7. *Etz Hayim*, 99n.

8. Rashi writes that God was aware that his chosen one was sad not to be enacting his role as host, so he immediately brought the three visitors to his tent. Rashi on Gen. 18:1.

9. *Etz Hayim*, 99n. BT *Shab*, 127a, quoted in *Etz Hayim*, 99n.

10. *Etz Hayim*, 99n.

11. Rashi on Gen. 18:7–8.

12. Klinghoffer writes, "According to Ishmael's Islamic descendants this item can be found today among other Muslim relics, such as beard hairs of the prophet, Muhammed, in the treasury room of the great Ottoman palace, Topkapi, in Istanbul. I saw it myself: a stoneware vessel, prominently labeled, that looked somewhat less than the 3,700 years old it would have to be if it were authentic" (*Discovery*, 159).

13. For Ishmael's piety, "We imposed a duty upon Abraham and Ishmael, (saying): Purify My house for those who ... meditate therein and those who bow down and prostrate themselves (in worship)." Koran 2:125. For Ishmael's blunders, see Carol Delaney, *Abraham on Trial* (Princeton, NJ: Princeton University Press, 1998), 177.

14. For the cornerstone story, see Ibn Kathir, *Stories of the Prophets*, trans. Rashad Ahmad Azami (New York: Dar-us-Salam, 2003), 177. For another version of the same story, see Delaney, *Abraham on Trial*, 177.

15. *Pirqe R. El.*, 36.

16. Ginzberg, *Legends*, 137.

17. *Pirqe R. El.*, 36. Also, Ginzberg, *Legends*, 137.

18. Of course this was not a kosher meal, as eating milk and meat together would not be forbidden until the time of Moses. The scholars explain this aberration on Abraham's part by saying the men were angels and therefore did not really eat the food and by reminding us that the law had yet to be made. *Etz Hayim*, 100–101n8. Muslim commentators see this story as an example of one of the mistakes in the Torah. "The People of the Book hold that he brought to them a roasted calf, bread, curd and milk, and they all ate (Genesis 18). But this is not true. It is said that they were pretending that they were eating, but the food just disappeared in the horizon." Kathir, *Stories of the Prophets*, 170.

19. *Etz Hayim*, 101n12. However, Klinghoffer has a different interpretation. He writes, "The obscure Hebrew word ednah, which, following Rashi, I have translated as 'clear, lustrous skin,' shares a three-letter root with the word 'Eden,' where the primordial Garden lay from which Adam and Eve were expelled." *Discovery*, 164.

20. *Gen. R.*, 48:18. *Etz Hayim*, 102n18.

CHAPTER 23: The Debate

1. Sarna writes, "there is a very good case for placing the lost cities to the south of the Lisan ... that tongue-shaped peninsula that juts into the middle of the Dead Sea" (*Understanding Genesis*, 139).

2. *Jewish Study Bible*, 16:33n.

3. Ginzberg, *Legends*, 115.

4. "A Rabbinic tradition maintains that Abraham instituted the morning service (Shaharit), interpreting the verse to mean that he prayed when he rose early to face God" (*B. Ber.* 26a quoted in *Etz Hayim*, 102n22).

5. *Etz Hayim*, 104n.

6. Ibid., 103n.

7. Klinghoffer, *Discovery*, 170. For more rabbinical descriptions of the land's beauty, see *Sanh.* 109a; *Midrash Rabah* Leviticus 5:2; *Midrash Rabah* Numbers 9:24.

8. Klinghoffer, *Discovery*, 170–171. *Etz Hayim*, 107n. See also David Graves and Jane Graves, "Sodom and Gomorrah," *The Scroll: Multimedia Study Bible*, 1995, http://www.abu.nb.ca/ecm/topics/arch5.htm (November 7, 2007).

9. D. Neev & K. O. Emery, *The Destruction of Sodom, Gomorrah, and Jericho: Geological, Climatological, and Archaeological Background* (New York: Oxford University Press, 1995), 13–14, 33, 37; G. M. Harris and A. P. Beardow, "The Destruction of Sodom and Gomorrah: A Geological Perspective," *Quarterly Journal of Engineering Geology* 28 (1995): 360.

10. H. Shanks, "Have Sodom and Gomorrah Been Found?" *BARev* 6, no.5 (1980): 26–36.

11. Walter E. Rast and R. Thomas Schaub, "Sites," *Expedition to the Dead Sea Plain,* http://www.nd.edu/~edsp/index.html (October 27, 2006). See also Meredith Chesson, "Libraries of the Dead: Early Bronze Age Charnel Houses and Social Identity at Urban Bab edh-Dhra', Jordan," *Journal of Anthropological Archaeology* 18 (1999): 137–64. Meredith Chesson, "Embodied Memories of Place and People: Death and Society in an Early Urban Community," *Social Memory, Identity and Death: Ethnographic and Archaeological Perspectives on Mortuary Rituals,* ed. Meredith S. Chesson, Archaeological Publications of the American Anthropological Association Publication Series, vol. 10 (Arlington, VA: American Anthropological Association, 2001), 100–113.

12. *Etz Hayim,* 105n.

13. Ibid.

14. There is some confusion about how many daughters Lot actually had. According to the *Jewish Study Bible,* "Since Lot's two daughters mentioned in v.8 are unmarried, these sons-in-law are either engaged to them (so the Vulgate and Rashi say) or married to two other daughters, who die in the conflagration along with their husbands" (19:14n).

15. Ginzberg, *Legends,* 118.

16. To Islamic thinkers, Lot's weaknesses as they are portrayed in the Bible are "a mistake due to distortion of the text." According to Muslim tradition, Lot invited the Sodomites to marry his daughters in order to instruct them in proper sexual behavior. Lot wanted the Sodomites to stop their homosexual ways because he was a prophet: "Lot called [the Sodomites] to heed Allah's Command and to worship Him alone" (Kathir, *Prophets,* 208, 196). See chapter 25 for a more complete discussion of the conflict between Jewish/Christian and Muslim interpretations.

17. *Etz Hayim,* 108n.

18. Rashi on Gen. 19:17.

CHAPTER 24: Gerar and a Cave

1. It is not entirely clear what gods the Zoarites worshipped except that they did not bow down to Abraham's God. In the Midrash, the inhabitants of Zoar, Sodom, and Gomorrah are often depicted as sun and moon worshippers. Ginzberg, *Legends,* 118.

2. Rashi on Gen. 20:1.

3. *Strong's Hebrew Bible Dictionary,* Bible Software by johnhurt.com, 2001, http://www.htmlbible.com/sacrednamebiblecom/kjvstrongs/STRHEB16.htm. (November 14, 2006), s.vv. "1601 (Go'ah)" to "1700 (dibrah)," *Etz Hayim,* 110n.

4. In the 1920s archaeologists began the process of digging at Tell Gemmeh, eight miles south of Gaza, believing that this was the site of ancient Gerar. The archaeologist W. M. Flinders Petrie writes, "That this mound of Tell Gemmeh is the site of the ancient Gerar is indicated by the name of the district El Jura around it, and by the name of a daughter-town Umm Jerar, entirely of Roman age, at a couple of miles down the stream." *Gerar* (London: London Office of School of Archaeology, 1928), 2.

5. It is interesting to note that many scholars believe that a third repetition of this tale, the story in which Isaac claims his wife Rebecca is his sister, is the original one of the three. Gerhard Von Rad writes that the Isaac story is "especially ancient" and almost exclusively consists of material from J, the oldest source of the Bible: "These Isaac traditions were written down essentially in their ancient version, without being harmonized with the subsequent large composition of the patriarchal stories." John Marks, trans. *Genesis: A Commentary* (Philadelphia: The Westminster Press, 1956), 265.

6. Devora Steinmetz writes that the repeated events in the Abraham story follow a pattern that represents Abraham's spiritual growth. She suggests that the birth of Ishmael is a turning point of his life. Before Ishmael, he focused on the welfare of Sarai and Lot, his Mesopotamian family. After Ishmael was born, he lost his focus on his first wife and his Mesopotamian family, and it does not return until the birth of Isaac. *From Father to Son*, 63 ff.

7. The Documentary Hypothesis holds that the repeated events in the Abraham story are doublets that represent the different authors of the Bible, in this case J and E. The Abimelech story is attributed to E, as "the emphasis lies on points of law and ethics and on the motivation of the protagonists, and the moral and psychological situation is much more complex than in . . . the parallel narratives [which are attributed to J]." *Jewish Study Bible*, 42n20. According to Richard Elliott Friedman, after the united empire of David divided into the northern and southern kingdoms, Israel and Judah (933 B.C.E.), tensions necessarily arose. If one looks carefully at the repeated passages in the Bible, one can see that one set of passages reflects the interests of Judah and the other reflects the interests of the north. Based on their names for God and the clues they left behind, "the author of J came from Judah and the author of E came from Israel" (*Who Wrote The Bible?*, 61).

8. Miles writes that those critics who subscribe to the Documentary Hypothesis "resist assigning meaning" to the repeated incidents as they see these "doublets" as almost an "accidental inclusion" in the Bible. *God*, 58.

9. Ibid.

10. See Klinghoffer, *Discovery*, for a full description of what Gerar might have been like during Abraham's visit, 186–90.

11. Teubal, *Sarah the Priestess*, 96–109. For this evidence, see especially 119–20, although the entire book constructs this argument.

12. Ibid., 110–22.

13. Ibid., 110–11.

CHAPTER 25: Incest

1. White, *Everyday Life*, 114.
2. *Etz Hayim*, 109nn37–38.
3. Ibid.
4. "And his people [the Sodomites]came unto him [Lot], running towards him — and before then they used to commit abominations — He said: O my people! Here are my daughters! They are purer for you. Beware of Allah, and degrade me not in (the person of) my guests. Is there not among you any upright man?" (Koran 11:78. See also 15:71).
5. According to Muslims, the stories that recount Lot's failings are only a few of the examples of the Torah's mistakes, which God sent Mohammed to rectify. As John Esposito writes, "Muslims believe that over time the original revelations to Moses and Jesus became corrupted. The Old Testament is seen as a mixture of God's revelation and human fabrication. The same is true for the New Testament and what Muslims see as Christianity's development of 'new' and erroneous doctrines such as that Jesus is the Son of God and that Jesus' death redeemed and atoned for humankind's original sin" (*Islam*, 76).
6. According to the Midrash, "To silence those who asked significantly, 'Can one a hundred years old beget a son?' God commanded the angel who has charge over the embryos, to give them form and shape, that he fashion Isaac precisely according to the model of Abraham, so that all seeing Isaac might exclaim, 'Abraham begot Isaac'" (Ginzberg, *Legends*, 121).
7. Rashi writes, "[God] had already remembered her before he healed Abimelech." On Gen. 21:1.
8. Teubal, *Sarah*, 110–32.

CHAPTER 26: Laughter

1. Ginzberg, *Legends*, 121.
2. Ibid., 121–22. *Etz Hayim*, 113–14n7. The commentators write, "A tradition suggests that all those who convert to Judaism are the descendants of those children nursed by Sarah."
3. *Gen. R.* 53:11. *Etz Hayim*, 114n9.
4. On "playing Isaac," see Robert Alter, *The Five Books of Moses* (New York: Norton, 2004), 163n9. *Yitzhak* is the future tense of the verb "to laugh." It means "will laugh." *Etz Hayim*, 114n, n9.
5. Teubal, *Sarah the Priestess*, 32–33.
6. Sarna writes, "What Sarah demanded was that Hagar and her son be given their freedom, thereby renouncing all claim to a share of the family estate. This being the case, the entire episode can be seen as having taken place according to the social custom and legal procedure of the times" (*Understanding Genesis*, 156). However, Sarna goes on to argue that this was not the whole story as God intervenes to support Sarah. He says, "A story that began as a reflection of ancient Near Eastern socio-legal convention has

been transformed in the Bible into a situation involving moral dilemmas and God's long range purposes" (*Understanding Genesis,* 157).

7. Chittister, Chishti, and Waskow, *Tent,* 217.

8. Ibid., 207.

9. *Pirqe R. El.* 30:67a, quoted in *Etz Hayim,* 114n11. "This banishment of Abraham's firstborn son and the child's mother was the hardest of his many trials."

10. According to Phyllis Trible, God's words "shift" His promise of descendants away from Hagar to Abraham. She will no longer be the founder of a people as He had promised at the well. Now, Ishmael's sons will be Abraham's, not hers. *Texts,* 22. However, the concluding verses of Hagar and Ishmael's story—"And his mother found him a wife" (21:21)—suggest that Hagar considered herself Ishmael's sole parent and the founder of the nation that would grow through his children and grandchildren.

11. There is some question about the meaning of the verb in this passage. Levenson writes, "For it is unclear in the structure of the verse whether 'the child' is the object of 'gave' . . . (along with 'some bread and a skin of water' understood) or of 'placed'" (*Beloved Son,* 104). However, *Etz Hayim* writes that the verb refers only the bread and water as "Ishmael could hardly have been carried by his mother" (114n14).

12. Levenson gives an overview of this confusion, explaining, "The simplest solution is the documentary one: the teenaged Ishmael is a product of P, a later source than the one reporting the episode of his near-death, which is almost universally attributed to E" (*Beloved Son,* 105).

13. Jewish tradition has another way of reading this story. Rashi offers an explanation that cuts through the confusion of Ishmael's age. He cites a Midrash that says "Sarah had cast an evil eye upon [Ishmael], so that a fever seized him and he could not walk (*Gen. R.* 53)" (on Gen. 21: 14).

CHAPTER 27: Exile

1. Jewish tradition has another version of this episode where Hagar's piety drains away from her the farther she goes from Abraham. Before long, she starts to worship idols. *Pirqe R. El.,* 30. Rashi writes that "she wandered" means "she reverted to the idol-worship of her father's house" (on 21: 14).

2. As Herbert Basser writes, "Tears are supposed to be answered in Jewish tradition; important passages in the literary tradition tell us that tears are more efficacious than prayer." "Weeping in Jewish Sources," in *Holy Tears: Weeping in the Religious Imagination,* Kimberly Christine Patton and John Stratton Hawley, eds. (Princeton, NJ: Princeton University Press, 2005), 180.

3. *Etz Hayim* cites Mendel of Worca, writing, "But we never read that Ishmael cried aloud! Thus, we learn that God can hear the silent cries of the anguished heart, even when no words are uttered" (115n17). Rashi concurs, "From this we may infer that the prayer of a sick person is more effective than the prayer offered by others for him and that it is more readily accepted

(Gen. R. 53)" (on Gen. 21:17). However, both commentators ignore the fact that although God may have heard Ishmael's silent cry, he speaks to Hagar.

4. Esposito, *Islam*, 23.

5. Reuven Firestone, *Journeys in Holy Lands: The Evolution of the Abraham-Ishmael Legends in Islamic Exegesis* (Albany: State University of New York Press, 1990), 63–68.

6. Kathir, *Prophets*, 160.

7. Ibid., 161.

8. Ibid., 162.

9. Ibid.

10. Esposito, *Islam*, 22.

11. Kathir, *Prophets*, 162.

12. Ibid.

13. Ibid.

14. The Midrash also says that Hagar chose Ishmael's wife. "Hagar had come from Egypt, and to Egypt she returned, to choose a wife for her sons" (Ginzberg, *Legends*, 123). As Sharon Pace Jeansonne points out, "Hagar demonstrates her strength and independence by selecting a wife for her son from among her own people." *The Women of Genesis: From Sarah to Potiphar's Wife* (Minneapolis: Fortress Press, 1990), 4.

15. Adapted from Ginzberg, *Legends*, 124. For the hadith, see Kathir, *Prophets*, 234.

16. Ibid.

17. Ginzberg, *Legends*, 125.

18. Trible, *Texts*, 28.

19. Ginzberg, *Legends*, 123.

20. Kathir, *Prophets*, 162.

21. *Etz Hayim*, 116n31.

22. Hagar has been an inspiration for modern Muslim women who seek to integrate feminist principles, Islamic legal codes, and worship practices. As Hibba Abugideri writes, "Just as Hagar's faith inspired her to struggle to establish God's will in a pagan patriarchal society, so does the faith of these women inspire them to embark upon a jihad of gender aimed at correcting the misogynist ideas and behaviors that plague Muslim communities today. As Hagar's struggles were accepted by the Almighty and were consequently enshrined within the Islamic ritual of hajj, their struggles produce an equally noteworthy result by creating a female role in the scriptural and legal interpretive process of how to worship." See Hibba Abugideri, "Hagar: A Historical Model for 'Gender Jihad,'" in *Daughters of Abraham*, 99–100.

CHAPTER 28: Mount Moriah

1. Elie Wiesel, *Messengers of God* (New York: Touchstone, 1976), 71.

2. Klinghoffer makes this point in *Discovery*, 238.

3. Kathir, *Prophets*. He writes, "There are many Muslim scholars who followed

this opinion that it was Isaac who was offered in sacrifice. They perhaps took this opinion from Ka'b Al Ahbar, or from Judaic sources." However, the idea that the favorite son was Isaac has now become a source of tension between Judaism and Islam. Kathir argues that the Jewish sources have been "tampered with" in order to "take away this honour from Arabs," (166).

4. Even the verb God uses, "take" has an urgency that is invisible to English readers. In the Hebrew there is an untranslated particle (na) attached to the verb that gives God's imperative an extra emphasis. *Etz Hayim,* 118n2.

5. As we shall see in the next chapters of this book, God does communicate to Abraham once more on Mount Moriah. Although these final words can also be seen as a kind of commandment, the two central commandments seem to be the order to leave Ur and the order to sacrifice his son, as God uses the same language in each. The commandments on Mount Moriah are emendations of the initial order.

6. *Gen. R.* 55:7. Levenson, *Beloved Son,* 127.

7. Levenson, *Beloved Son,* 72–74. Levenson cites and discounts the reasons for Abel's status as the favored son that theologians and scholars have listed over the years: Cain was a tiller of fields and God preferred shepherds like Abel; Cain's offering was less appealing than Abel's; Cain had worked less diligently to prepare his offering than Abel. These arguments, Levenson says, miss the real point of the story, which is that God's reasons were hidden from human logic. The boys were equals as they approached the altar to make their sacrifice and remained so until God chose. Levenson quotes Claus Westermann, who writes, "Both [Cain and Abel] recognize the giver in their gifts and therefore both are linked with the power which is the source of the blessing. Now inequality enters in; it has its origin in the regard of God. Blessing or its absence depends on the regard of God. It is a misunderstanding in the real meaning to look for the reason for the inequality of God's regard. The narrator wants to say that in the last analysis there is something inexplicable in the origin of this inequality." Westermann, *Genesis 1-11* (Minneapolis: Augsburg, 1984), 297.

8. Levenson writes, "Though this biblical term [*yahid*], in its masculine and feminine forms, occurs only twelve times, it is suggestively prominent in stories of child sacrifices. The aqeda terms Isaac as Abraham's *yahid* on no fewer than three occasions (Gen 22:2, 12, 16) and Jephthah's daughter is the *yehida* of her father (Judg 11:34). Amos delivers an oracle in which God threatens to make the earth 'mourn as for an only child' (*ke'ebel yahid*) (Amos 8:10), and Jeremiah, employing the same phrase (which he may well have gotten from Amos), issues this macabre summons:

> *My poor people,*
> *Put on sackcloth,*
> *And strew dust on yourselves!*
> *Mourn as for an only child (ebel yahid);*
> *Wail bitterly,*
> *For suddenly the destroyer*
> *Is coming upon us.* (Jer. 6:26)

Levenson adds that the term *yahid* might be related to Canaanite practices. He cites Eusebius's account (based on a history written by an earlier Phoenician priest) that records the God-king El's sacrifice of his beloved son. The name of this son is either Iedoud or Ieoud. Levenson writes that the latter is "most likely the Phoenician equivalent of the biblical Hebrew word *yahid*" (*Beloved Son*, 27-28).

9. Although the laws of Exodus are given to Moses after Abraham's death, it is highly possible that the law of Exod. 22 was written around the same time as this tale. Levenson, personal communication to author, September 21, 2008. He writes, "In the Hebrew Bible, as elsewhere in the cultural world in which it was composed, law often articulates a theological and moral ideal; it does not always stipulate a practice that all can reasonably be expected to undertake. The theology underlying Exod. 22:28 is that first-born sons, like the male first-born of animals and the first fruits of the soil, belong to YHWH; they are not the father's, to do with as he sees fit" (*Beloved Son*, 15–16).

10. On the "highly suggestive" connection, Levenson, personal communication to author, September 21, 2008. On the Jephtha story, Levenson writes, "Whereas the rabbis, however, saw Jephthah's vow as invalid, the Bible seems not to fault him for honoring it once it was uttered. In fact, both he and his daughter are portrayed as devoutly upholding YHWH's law that 'if a man makes a vow to the Lord . . . he must carry out all that has crossed his lips' (Num. 30:3). 'I have uttered a vow to the Lord and I cannot retract,' Jephthah, grief-stricken, tells his doomed daughter. 'Father,' she poignantly replies, 'you have uttered a vow to the Lord: do to me as you have vowed, seeing that the Lord has vindicated you against your enemies, the Ammonites' (Judg. 11:35–36)" (*Beloved Son*, 16).

11. Levenson, *Beloved Son*, 19. The stone pillar was found in a neo-Phoenician settlement in southern Spain called Pozo Moro.

12. Shalom Spiegel, *The Last Trial* (New York: Behrman House, 1967), 64. Quoted in Levenson, *Beloved Son*, 12.

13. *Etz Hayim*, 118n1.

14. Søren Kierkegaard, *Fear and Trembling* (1843; reprint, Garden City, NY: Doubleday, 1954), 46–47. Also quoted in Levenson, *Beloved Son*, 130.

15. *Etz Hayim*, 117n1.

16. Levenson, personal communication to author, September 21, 2008.

17. 2 Chr. 3:1, in Levenson, *Beloved Son*, 114.

18. John Skinner writes, "All attempts to explain the name and identify the place have been futile." *A Critical and Exegetical Commentary on Genesis* (Edinburgh: T. & T. Clark, 1969), 328. Other scholars argue that the identification of Moriah with Jerusalem is meant to "enhance the prestige of that city as the sole authorized center of the Jewish cult." Jacob J. Finkelstein, "The Bible, Archaeology, and History: Have the Excavations Corroborated Scripture?" *Commentary* 28 (1959): 347.

19. *Gen. R.* 56:8; Jub. 17: 15–16; Levenson, *Beloved Son*, 133. The age thirty-seven comes from the Midrash. The logic is that immediately after the story of the

sacrifice of Isaac, known as the Akedah, the Bible jumps to Sarah's death at the age of one hundred twenty-seven. The rabbis decided that this leap in the text meant that she died because of the Akedah and so the two events must have happened concurrently. If Sarah had Isaac when she was ninety and died at one hundred twenty-seven, then Isaac must have been thirty-seven at the time of the Akedah. However, Levenson cites other Midrash that calculate Isaac's age as twenty-six (*Gen. R.* 56:8), and another tradition that predates the rabbis where Isaac is fifteen (Jub. 17:15–16). *Beloved Son,* 133.

20. On mysticism, Klinghoffer, *Discovery,* 233. On the Bible's use of three days as a formula for a long journey, *Etz Hayim,* 119n4.
21. Ginzberg, *Legends,* 130. This is my paraphrase.
22. Rashi on Gen 22:4.
23. Rashi on Gen 22:5. Also in Levenson, *Beloved Son,* 130.
24. Levenson points out the parallels between the loss of the two sons. See *Beloved Son,* 132.
25. *Gen. R.* 56:3.
26. Shalom Spiegel. *The Last Trial: On the Legends and Lore of the Command to Offer Isaac as a Sacrifice,* trans. Judah Godlin (Woodstock, VT: Jewish Lights, 1993, rep.), 152.
27. Levenson, *Beloved Son,* 134.
28. Kierkegaard, *Fear,* 46–47.
29. "Abraham reasoned that God was able to raise even from the dead and he received Isaac back as a symbol" (Heb. 11:17-19).

CHAPTER 29: The Beloved Son

1. Ginzberg, *Legends,* 135.
2. Levenson, *Beloved Son.* For Biblical tradition of sacrifice, 30. For Isaac as the only Biblical example, 135.
3. Ginzberg, *Legends,* 132. This is my paraphrase.
4. Terence Freithem and others, eds., *The New Interpreters Bible,* Vol. 1, *General and Old Testament Articles: Genesis, Exodus, and Leviticus* (Nashville: Abingdon, 1994), 497. The Bible scholar Walter Brueggemann writes that the Akedah "is not a game with God; God genuinely does not know.... The flow of the narrative accomplishes something in the awareness of God. He did not know. Now he knows." *Genesis: Interpretation: A Bible Commentary for Teaching and Preaching* (Louisville, KY: Westminster John Knox Press, 1982), 187. For commentary on God's foreknowledge, or lack thereof, see Terence E. Fretheim, *The Suffering of God: An Old Testament Perspective* (Augsburg: Fortress Publishers, 1984), 45–59.
5. Miles, *God,* 59.
6. Ginzberg, *Legends,* 135.
7. Ibid., 133–34.
8. Levenson writes, "As an etiology of the redemption of the first-born son

through the death of the sheep, however, the aqedah is, it seems to me, most ineffective. For although Abraham does indeed spot and then sacrifice a ram just after hearing the gruesome command rescinded (Gen 22:13), he is never actually commanded to offer the animal, as he was commanded to sacrifice his only beloved son, Isaac. And so, in fact, so far as we know, Israelite tradition never explained the substitution of the sheep for the first-born son by reference to the aqedah; it was the tenth plague upon Egypt that served that role, with the paschal lamb spelling the difference between life and death for the Israelite first-born males (Exodus 12–13)" (*Beloved Son*, 13).

9. This paraphrase is from *Etz Hayim*, 121n19.

10. There have been a few problems translating this phrase, *Adonai-yireh*. The central issue is that it is not immediately clear who or what the subject is. The Septuagint (the Greek translation of the Hebrew Scripture that dates from sometime between the third and first centuries B.C.E.) solves the problem by saying the phrase means, "on the mount the Lord appears." But according to the prominent Jewish scholar Reuven Hammer, the best paraphrase of Abraham's speech is "the high point where I saw God." *Etz Hayim*, 121n14.

11. Kathir, *Prophets*, 165–66. This account, including the dialogue, is my paraphrase.

12. See Levenson, *Beloved Son*, 200. He writes, "Jesus' gory death was not a negation of God's love . . . , but a manifestation of it, evidence that Jesus was the beloved son first prefigured in Isaac."

13. Levenson, *Beloved Son*, 216.

14. Paul's assertions of Christianity's Abrahamic pedigree stemmed from his ambitions for Christianity. Steeped as he was in Jewish Scripture, he believed he needed to show that Jesus, not Isaac, was the true son of God's promise so that Christians could be its real inheritors. As Jon Levenson explains, "Jesus supplants Isaac in Paul's theology, and the Church, the Jews" (*Beloved Son*, 220).

15. Paul preached to the Galatians, the small gentile community he hoped to convert to the worship of Christ, "if you thus belong to Christ, you are the 'issue' of Abraham, and so heirs by promise." He went on to retell the story of Hagar and Sarah, concluding, "the two women stand for two covenants. The one bearing children into slavery is the covenant that comes from Mount Sinai: that is Hagar. Sinai is a mountain in Arabia and it represents the Jerusalem of today, for she and her children are in slavery. But the heavenly Jerusalem is the free woman; she is our mother. . . . And you, my brothers, like Isaac, are children of God's promise . . . what does Scripture say? 'Drive out the slave-woman and her son, for the son of the slave shall not share the inheritance with the free woman's son.' You see, then, my brothers, we are no slave-woman's children; our mother is the free woman. Christ set us free, to be free men" (3:29; 4:24–31). In one sweeping move, then, Paul equated Jews with Hagar, and Christians with Sarah. Sinai, where Moses received the commandments, becomes synonymous with slavery and bondage to

the law, whereas an idealized "heavenly" Jerusalem becomes the emblem of Christ. If Christians were now children of Sarah, Jews were now sons of Hagar. Hence, later Christian theologians tend to castigate Jewish enslavement to "law." *Beloved Son*, 219. For a fuller explanation of Paul's formulations, see also 214–16.

CHAPTER 30: The Death of Sarah

1. Ginzberg, *Legends*, 135.
2. *Ber. abb.* 62b.
3. Ibid.
4. *Zevachim* 62a. Rashi on Gen. 22:19. Spiegel, *The Last Trial*, 33–37. Klinghoffer points out these traditions in *Discovery*, 239–40.
5. Ginzberg, *Legends*, 135. This is my paraphrase. Wiesel also recounts it in *Messengers*, 92–93.
6. Ibid.
7. Ibid., 134.
8. Ibid., 128.
9. Ibid.
10. Klinghoffer writes that Satan is often a stand in for our own doubts. See *Discovery*, 235. Wiesel writes, "Through [the Midrash], internal conflicts become tangible, visible.... Satan personifies the doubt Abraham had to have in order to remain human" (*Messengers*, 86).
11. *Messengers*, 74.
12. Ibid., 83.
13. *Etz Hayim*, 121n19.
14. Rashi is the first to make this point. Rashi on Gen 23. Klinghoffer writes, "there is only one logical route from Jerusalem, the site of Mt. Moriah, to Beersheba: the road called Derech Ephratah, the Way to Ephrat. Proceeding south-southwest, it passes more or less in a straight line through Bethlehem, then Hebron, then Beersheba. Either Abraham took the Derech Ephratah and slipped through Hebron without Sarah's noticing, or he took some other, much more roundabout path so as to avoid Hebron and Sarah completely" (*Discovery*, 248). Trible, "Ominous Beginnings," 54.
15. Arthur Strimling, "Sarah Sees," *Living Text: The Journal of the Institute of Contemporary Midrash* 8 (2000): 13–15.
16. Ginzberg, *Legends*, 136.
17. Ibid.
18. Ibid.
19. Ibid., 137.
20. Klinghoffer, *Discovery*, 249.
21. Ibid., 249–50.
22. *Rosh Hashana* 16b. Also cited in Klinghoffer, *Discovery*, 250.
23. Wiesel, *Messengers*, 94.
24. Ginzberg, *Legends*, 137.

25. This poem, "Aishet Chayl," concludes the Book of Proverbs. Klinghoffer writes, "Customarily this hymn . . . is sung by a Jewish husband to his wife on their wedding day, on his knees, and again each Sabbath evening for the rest of their lives" (*Discovery*, 251). See Chapter 9 for a longer quote from this poem.
26. *Gen. R.* 58:6. Actually, in this text it is the angel of death who appears to Abraham, not Satan, but the Talmud links these two figures in *B. Bat.* 16a. See Klinghoffer, *Discovery*, 251.
27. Klinghoffer, *Discovery*, 251.

CHAPTER 31: Burial and Mission

1. See Klinghoffer, *Discovery*, 252, for a full description of the site.
2. Klinghoffer cites the Talmud's discussion of the laws of betrothal in the tractate *Kiddushin*, which begins with "the statement that the very first law of betrothal is crystallized in Abraham's purchase of the Machpelah" (*Discovery*, 257).
3. Ibid.
4. See *Sarah the Priestess*, 99. Teubal lists five traits that are "characteristic of a priestess."
    1. Sarah's choice of residence at the terebinth of Mamre;
    2. her childlessness;
    3. the episodes with Pharaoh and Abimelech;
    4. the supernatural conception of Isaac;
    5. Sarah's burial in the cave of Machpelah.
5. Ginzberg, *Legends*, 138.
6. Ibid., 139.
7. Wiesel makes this point. *Messengers*, 83.
8. Ginzberg, *Legends*, 136.
9. Ibid., 139–42.
10. Ibid., 140.
11. *Etz Hayim*, 128nn10–16.
12. The Septuagint took the second word of the place name, Aram-naharaim, "to mean 'two rivers,' and so arose the name 'Mesopotamia': literally, the land 'between the two rivers'" (*Etz Hayim*, 132n10). Klinghoffer writes that we know that it was Haran, the same place Abram and Sarai left all those years ago, because this is where Laban, Rebecca's brother, was said to have lived (*Discovery*, 267).
13. *Etz Hayim*, 132n12.
14. *Etz Hayim*, 132n12ff. The commentator writes, "Some of the Sages criticize the servant for his prayer. Conceivably, an unsuitable young woman might have come along to offer him water. Furthermore, although miracles do happen, a person may not demand a miracle. Others see the content of the prayer as a brilliantly intuitive realization . . . "
15. Jewish scholars tend to see Rebecca's "distinguishing characteristic" as kindness. In *Etz Hayim*, the commentator writes, "Abraham and Sarah, for

all of their pioneering religious achievements, were sometimes insensitive to members of their own household. Rebecca's kindness and generosity may have been what was needed to correct those family dynamics" (133n16).

16. As one scholar writes, "A single camel . . . requires at least 25 gallons of water to regain the weight it loses in the course of a long journey. It takes a camel about ten minutes to drink this amount of water" (*Etz Hayim*, 133n14).

17. Rashi views the servant's action as "expression of faith in God's response to his prayer" on 24:22. Many commentators, however, say that the order of events here is different than how the servant will later retell the story. The rabbis cite Gen. 24:47, saying that the servant did not give her jewelry until he knew her name and what family she belonged to (*Etz Hayim*, 134n22).

18. Regarding the servant's lengthy recap of the story, the commentator of *Etz Hayim* writes, "This type of repetition, which has its origins in orally transmitted literature, is characteristic of ancient Near Eastern epics and is found in various kinds of biblical prose narrative" (135n34).

19. Klinghoffer writes, "in line with the regional custom of the period, a woman had the right to answer such a proposal herself" (*Discovery*, 273).

20. Teubal argues that the silence of Rebecca's father Bethuel illustrates that the family is essentially matrilineal. She writes, "Bethuel is represented as being alive but virtually without authority. His inconsequential position is particularly apparent because Rebecca's mother plays such a prominent part in her daughter's betrothal." She argues that the authorities are Laban and the unnamed mother, a typical characteristic of matrilineal society. However, Teubal does not take into account the mother's lack of name, an anonymity that would seem to argue against the point that the mother is the most significant player in the story. *Sarah the Priestess*, 62.

21. *Etz Hayim*, 137nn57, 60.

22. *Etz Hayim*, 137n60.

CHAPTER 32: Coming Home

1. Klinghoffer, *Discovery*, 273.

2. Ibid.

3. Ibid., 273.

4. Hayim Nahman Bialik and Yehoshua Hana Ravnitzky, eds., *The Book of Legends, Sefer Ha-Aggadah*, William Braude, trans. (New York: Schocken Books, 1992), 36–37.

5. Amy-Jill Levine also makes this observation, writing, "The son of Sarah moves to the site named by Hagar; the sons of Ishmael, 'from Havilah to Shur' (Gen. 25:18), are neighbors. The relationship between the families is not one of enmity but apparently one of peace." She also points out the marriage of Esau and Ishmael's daughter, Mahalath, citing Gen. 28:9: "Esau went to Ishmael and took Mahalath, daughter of Abraham's son Ishmael, and sister of Nebaioth, to be his wife in addition to the wives he had." "Settling at Beer-lahi-roi," in *Abraham's Daughters*, 25.

6. The verb that describes Isaac's action is unclear. The commentator in *Etz Hayim* writes, "The Talmud takes the word to mean 'praying.' Rebecca saw Isaac praying and was impressed by the piety of her future husband" (138n63). But Von Rad writes, "Isaac's activity in v. 63 immediately prior to the meeting is not clear; the verb is not translatable," *Genesis*, 254.

7. For Minhah, *Etz Hayim*, 138n63.

8. Ginzberg, *Legends*, 142.

9. *Etz Hayim*, 138n67.

10. Klinghoffer, *Discovery*, 275.

11. Kinghoffer writes that Rashi means "that she was innocent of every kind of intercourse, vaginal, oral, and anal" (275).

12. Teubal writes, "Sarah and Rebecca's association with Pharaoh and Abimelech has been attributed to their beauty (Gen. 12:11, 14, and 26:7); in reality the two women participated in significant international interactions with the kings on the order of political alliances.... the matriarchs Sarah, Rebecca, and Rachel were associated in an important way with a religious order.... I will refer to the women as 'priestesses' ... [who] were highly regarded in their office as *en* during a ceremony known as the Sacred Marriage (*hieros gamos*) in which they were looked upon as the Goddess incarnate" (*Sarah the Priestess*, 68, 71).

13. Bialik, *Book of Legends*, 43.

CHAPTER 33: *Hinneni*

1. Emil Hirsch and M. Seligsohn state, "She is identified in the Midrash (Gen. R. lxi., quoted also by Rashi) and in the Palestinian Targumim with Hagar, who was the first concubine of Abraham.... In Gen. xxv. 5 the Midrash (l.c.) reads the term 'ha-pillagshim' (= 'the concubines') without the yod, which is the sign of the plural, explaining that there was only one concubine, as Hagar and Keturah were one person. Still it seems that such was not the opinion of the Talmudic doctors; for the children of Ishmael and the children of Keturah are kept distinct in the story of their complaints against the Jews before Alexander the Macedonian (*Sanh.*, 91a)." "Keturah," *Jewish Encyclopedia Online*, 2002, http://www.jewishencyclopedia.com/view .jsp?artid=190&letter=K (December 18, 2006).

2. This theory is not limited to the ancient rabbis. Rabbi Arthur Waskow writes, "Over the years, Abraham had been visiting [Hagar] in disguise, to make sure she and her son were well cared for. At last they were reunited, and the last loose thread in his adventurous life neatly, sweetly tied." Chittister, Chishti, and Waskow, *Tent*, 16.

3. Rashi is probably the commentator who made famous this idea that Keturah is Hagar. He writes, "This is Hagar. She was named Keturah because her deeds were as beautiful (sweet) as incense (Ketoreth)" (on Gen. 24:25). See also *Gen. R.* 61. There is another tradition that says Hagar is called Keturah because Keturah is a pun on the word "sealed and knotted." Hence, as Rashi

says, "she tied up her opening, from the day she left Abraham, she did not couple with any man" (on Gen. 24:25). However, there are many commentators who disagree with this tradition, including Maimonides, Nachmanides, and Ibn Ezra. For Isaac's trip to fetch Hagar: Rashi on Gen. 24:62.

4. Ginzberg, *Legends,* 143–44.

5. Ibid., 145.

6. Ibid., 146.

7. Klinghoffer writes, "The commentator Sforno notes the difficulty in reading this verse as other than a pious and meaningless cliché. If he really was 'gathered to his people,' what people do we mean? His family was buried not in the Machpelah, but back in Haran. And they were all pagans. Is it not an insult to Abraham to suggest that he joined them in their eternal reward? The early Christians ... argued that Abraham's true 'people,' his authentic 'seed' was not defined by blood, including the blood of the ethnic group called Jews, but was rather the community of the faithful of all races. In this view, the definition of Abraham's 'people' transcends blood" (*Discovery,* 281–82). See also Sforno on Gen. 25:8.

8. See also Klinghoffer, *Discovery,* 282. He cites the writer of Hebrews to make this same point.

9. *Etz Hayim,* 140n9.

10. Klinghoffer tells this story in *Discovery,* 258–59. The original version is in *B. Bat.* 58a.

11. This is Klinghoffer's interpretation. See *Discovery,* 258.

12. Amy Singer, *Constructing Ottoman Beneficence: An Imperial Soup Kitchen in Jerusalem* (New York: SUNY Press, 2002), 148.

13. In Herbert Davidson, *Moses Maimonides: The Man and His Works* (New York: Oxford University Press, 2005), 30. However, Davidson cautions the reader against putting too much stock in the details of Maimonides's Hebron visit. He argues that it is true that Maimonides went to Palestine, but the details of his visit are unclear as neither of the sources that tell us this story, nor the quote itself, are particularly reliable.

14. Klinghoffer, *Discovery,* 290–91.

15. Moshe Dayan, *Living with the Bible* (New York: William Morrow, 1978), 48.

16. Joel Greenberg, "Israel Destroys Shrine to Mosque Gunman," *New York Times,* December 30, 1999, A6.

17. Klinghoffer writes, "One Islamic story tells of a man who on entering the cave fell paralyzed to the floor. Another recounts the experience of Ali of Heart, who in 1192 descended and felt the breeze gusting about that others have reported. ... Christians, during their periods of control, have descended and brought back detailed description of what lies beneath. In 1119 a monk felt an unexpected breeze blowing from a crack in the flagstones near Isaac's cenotaph" (*Discovery,* 290–91).

BIBLIOGRAPHY

Abugideri, Hibba. "Hagar: A Historical Model for 'Gender Jihad.'" In *Daughters of Abraham: Feminist Thought in Judaism, Christianity, and Islam*. Edited by Yvonne Yazbeck Haddad and John Esposito. Gainesville: University Press of Florida, 2001.

Ackerman, Susan. *When Heroes Love: The Ambiguity of Eros in the Stories of Gilgamesh and David*. New York: Columbia University Press, 2005.

Aharoni, Yohanan. "The Land of Gerar." *Israel Exploration Journal* 6 (1956): 26–32.

Aharoni, Yohanan, et al. *The Macmillan Bible Atlas*. 3d ed. New York: Macmillan, 1993.

Albright, W.F. *Archaeology and the Religion of Israel*. Baltimore: Johns Hopkins University Press, 1946.

———. *From the Stone Age to Christianity: Monotheism and the Historical Process*. Baltimore: Johns Hopkins University Press, 1957.

———. *The Biblical Period from Abraham to Ezra*. New York: Harper and Row, 1963.

———. "The Names Shaddai and Abram." *Journal of Biblical Literature* 54, 1935, 173–210.

———. *Yahweh and the Gods of Canaan*. London: Athlone Press, 1968.

Alter, Robert. *The Five Books of Moses, A Translation with Commentary*. New York: Norton, 2004.

Anati, Emmanuel. *Palestine Before the Hebrews*. London: Jonathan Cape, 1963.

Antelme, Ruth, and Stephane Rossini. *Sacred Sexuality in Ancient Egypt*. Rochester, VT: Inner Traditions, 2001.

Armstrong, Karen. *A History of God*, 2d ed. New York: Ballantine, 1994.

————. *In the Beginning: A New Interpretation of Genesis.* New York: Ballantine, 1996.

————. *Jerusalem: One City: Three Faiths.* New York: Ballantine, 1996.

Armstrong, Karen, ed. *Visions of God.* New York: Bantam, 1994.

Auerbach, Eric. *Mimesis: The Representation of Reality in Western Literature.* Princeton, NJ: Princeton University Press, 1953.

Augustine. *Confessions.* Translated by Henry Chadwick. Oxford: Oxford University Press, 1991.

————. *On Christian Doctrine.* Translated by D.W. Robertson. New York: Prentice Hall, 1958.

————. *The City of God.* Translated by Marcus Dods. New York: Modern Library, 1950.

Bach, Alice. *Women in the Hebrew Bible: A Reader.* New York: Routledge, 1999.

Bakan, David. *And They Took Themselves Wives.* San Francisco: Harper and Row, 1979.

Bakhos, Carol. *Ismael on the Border: Rabbinic Portrayals of the First Arab.* Albany, NY: SUNY Press, 2006.

Bammel, E. "Christian Origins in Tradition." *New Testament Studies* 13 (1967): 317–35.

Baskin, Judith. *Midrashic Women: Formations of the Feminine in Rabbinic Literature.* Hanover and London: Brandeis University Press, 1997.

Basser, Herbert. "Weeping in Jewish Sources." In *Holy Tears: Weeping in the Religious Imagination.* Edited by Kimberly Christine Patton and John Stratton Hawley. Princeton, NJ: Princeton University Press, 2005.

Bellis, Alice Ogden. *Helpmates, Harlots, and Heroes: Women's Stories in the Hebrew Bible.* Louisville, KY: Westminster John Knox Press, 1994.

Berlin, Adele, and Marc Brettler, eds. *The Jewish Study Bible.* New York: Oxford University Press, 2004.

Berman, Chaim, and Michael Weitzman. *Ebla: A Revelation in Archaeology.* New York: New York Times Book Co., 1979.

Berner, Leila Gal. "Hearing Hannah's Voice: The Jewish Feminist Challenge and Ritual Innovation," in *Daughters of Abraham: Feminist thought in Judaism, Christianity, and Islam.* Edited by Yvonne Haddad and John Esposito. Gainesville: University Press of Florida, 2002.

Biale, David. *Eros and the Jews: From Biblical Israel to Contemporary America.* New York: Basic, 1992.

Bialik, Hayim Nahman, and Yehoshua Hana Ravnitzky, eds. *The Book of Legends, Sefer Ha-Aggadah.* Translated by William Braude. New York: Schocken Books, 1992.

Bird, Phyllis A. *Missing Persons and Mistaken Identities: Women and Gender in Ancient Israel.* Minneapolis: Augsburg Fortress, 1917.

Bloom, Harold. *The Book of J.* New York: Vintage, 1991.

Bonhoeffer, Dietrich. Quoted by Maria von Wedemeyer-Weller. "The Other Letters from Prison." In *Letters and Papers from Prison,* 3d ed. Edited and translated by Eberhard Bethge. New York: Collier Books, 1971.

Borgman, Paul. *Genesis: The Story We Haven't Heard*. Downer's Grove, IL: Inter-Varsity Press, 2001.

Bowen, Jim. "Who Was Melchizedek?" *BibleStudy.org*, 2009, www.biblestudy .org/basicart/whomelcz.html (January 15, 2009).

Brewster, David, ed. *Memoirs of the Life, Writings, and Discoveries of Sir Isaac Newton*. Vol. 2. London and Edinburgh: 1855.

Bright, John. *A History of Israel*. 2d ed. Philadelphia: Westminster Press, 1972.

Brodie, Fawn. *No Man Knows My History: The Life of Joseph Smith*. 2d ed. New York: Vintage, 1995.

Brother Antoninus [William O. Everson]. *The Crooked Lines of God*. Detroit: University of Detroit Press, 1959.

Brueggemann, Walter. *Genesis: Interpretation: A Bible commentary for Teaching and Preaching*. Louisville, KY: Westminster John Knox Press, 1982.

Burrow, M. *The Basis of Israelite Marriage*. New Haven: American Oriental Series, 1939.

Bushman, Richard. *Rough Stone Rolling: A Cultural Biography of Mormonism's Founder*. New York: Knopf, 2005.

Butler, Judith. *Gender Trouble: Feminism and the Subversion of Identity*. New York: Routledge, 1990.

Bynum, Caroline Walker. *Fragmentation and Redemption: Essays on Gender and the Human Body in Medieval Religion*. New York: Zone Books, 1991.

Cahill, Thomas. *The Gifts of the Jews*. New York: Doubleday, 1998.

Campbell, Joseph. *Myths to Live By*. New York: Viking, 1972.

Caputo, John D. *Against Ethics: Contributions to a Poetics of Oblication with Constant Reference to Deconstruction*. Bloomington: Indiana University Press, 1993.

Cassuto, Umberto. *A Commentary on the Book of Genesis*. Translated by Israel Abraham. Jerusalem: Magnes, 1964.

———. *The Goddess of Anath*. Translated by Israel Abraham. Jerusalem: Magnes, 1971.

Castelli, Jim, ed. *How I Pray: People of Different Religions Share With Us That Most Sacred and Intimate Act of Faith*. New York: Random House, 1994.

Charry, Ellen T. "Christian Jews and the Law." *Modern Theology* 11, no.2 (1995): 185–93.

Chesson, Meredith. "Embodied Memories of Place and People: Death and Society in an Early Urban Community." In *Social Memory, Identity and Death: Ethnographic and Archaeological Perspectives on Mortuary Rituals*. Edited by Meredith S. Chesson. Archaeological Publications of the American Anthropological Association Publication Series, vol. 10. Arlington, VA: American Anthropological Association, 2001.

———. "Libraries of the Dead: Early Bronze Age Charnel Houses and Social Identity at Urban Babe dh-Dhra', Jordan." *Journal of Anthropological Archaeology* 18 (1999): 137–64.

Chittister, Joan, Murshid Chishti, Arthur Waskow. *The Tent of Abraham: Stories of Hope and Peace for Jews, Christians, and Muslims*. Boston: Beacon Press, 2006.

Chodorow, Nancy. *The Reproduction of Mothering: Psychoanalysis and the Sociology of Gender*. Berkeley: University of California Press, 1978.

Christie, Agatha. *An Autobiography.* London: Collins, 1977.

Cohen, Shaye. *Josephus in Galilee and Rome: His Vita and Development as a Historian.* Leiden: E. J. Brill, 1979.

————. *The Beginnings of Jewishness.* Berkeley: University of California Press, 1999.

————. *From the Maccabees to the Mishnah.* Philadelphia: Westminster Press, 1989.

Coote, R.B. *Early Israel: A New Horizon.* Minneapolis: Fortress, 1990.

Craigie, P. *The Problem of War in the Old Testament.* Grand Rapids: Eerdmans Publishing Co., 1978.

Crawford, Harriet E.W. *Dilmun and its Gulf Neighbours.* Cambridge: Cambridge University Press, 1998.

Cross, Frank Moore. *Canaanite Myth and Hebrew Epic.* Cambridge, MA: Harvard University Press, 1973.

Darr, Katheryn Pfisterer. *Far More Precious than Jewels: Perspectives on Biblical Women.* Louisville, KY: Westminster John Knox Press, 1991.

David, Rosalie. *Handbook to Life in Ancient Egypt.* New York: Oxford University Press, 1998.

Davies, P.R. "In Search of 'Ancient Israel.'" *Journal for the Study of the Old Testament Supplement Series* 148 (1992).

Dayan, Moshe. *Living with the Bible.* New York: William Morrow, 1978.

Delaney, Carol. *Abraham on Trial.* Princeton, NJ: Princeton University Press, 1998.

Del Mastro, M.L. *All the Women of the Bible.* Edison, NJ: Castle Books, 2004.

Dever, William G. *Did God Have A Wife? Archaeology and Folk Religion in Ancient Israel.* Grand Rapids: Eerdmans Publishing Co., 2005.

————. "The Identity of Early Israel: A Rejoinder to Keith W. Whitelam." *Journal for the Study of the Old Testament* 72 (1996): 3–24.

————. *Who Were the Early Israelites and Where Did They Come From?* Grand Rapids: Eerdmans Publishing Co., 2003.

Diakonoff, Igor M. "On the Structure of Old Babylonian Society." In *Ancient Mesopotamia.* Moscow: Nauka Publishing House, 1969.

Donahue, J. "Geological Reconstruction of Numeira." *Bulletin of the American Schools of Oriental Research* 255 (1984): 83–88.

Donahue, J., B. Peer, and R.T. Schaub. "The Southeastern Dead Sea Plain: Changing Shorelines and Their Impact on Settlement Patterns Through Historical Periods." In *Studies in the History and Archaeology of Jordan,* vol. 4. Edited by Adnan Hadidi. Jordan: Department of Antiquities, 1992.

Driver, G.R., and J.C. Miles. *The Babylonian Laws: The Translation and Commentary,* vols. 1 and 2. London: Oxford University Press, 1955.

Dunn, James. *The Theology of Paul the Apostle.* Grand Rapids: Eerdmans Publishing Co., 2006.

Edelman, Diana. *The Triumph of Elohim: From Yahwisms to Judaisms.* Grand Rapids: Eerdmans Publishing Co., 1996.

Eilberg-Schwartz, Howard. *God's Phallus and Other Problems for Men and Monotheism.* Boston: Beacon Press, 1994.

————. *The Savage in Judaism: An Anthropology of Israelite Religion and Ancient Judaism*. Bloomington: Indiana University Press, 1990.

Eisen, Chaim. "Unmasking Avraham's Slave: A Midrashic Analysis of Eliezer." In *The 1991 Book of Jewish Thought*. Edited by Chaim Eisen and Moshe Sosevsky. New York: Orthodox Union/Yeshivat Ohr Yerushalayim, 1993.

Eisenman, Robert. *James The Brother of Jesus: The Key to Unlocking the Secrets of Early Christianity and the Dead Sea Scrolls*. New York: Penguin, 1997.

Eliade, Mircea. *The Myth of the Eternal Return*. Translated by Willard R. Trask. 1954 Reprint. Princeton, NJ: Princeton University Press, 1974.

————. *Rites and Symbols of Initiation: The Mysteries of Birth and Rebirth*. New York: Harper and Row, 1958.

Emerson, Ralph Waldo. "Circles." In *Essays*. New York: Macmillan, 1899.

Engelsman, Joan Chamberlain. *The Feminine Dimension of the Divine*. Philadelphia: Westminster Press, 1979.

Esposito, John L. *What Everyone Needs to Know About Islam*. Oxford: Oxford University Press, 2002.

————. *Abraham: A Journey to the Center of Three Faiths*. New York: William Morrow, 2002.

Feiler, Bruce. *Walking the Bible: A Journey by Land Through the Five Books of Moses*. New York: William Morrow, 2001.

Finegan, J. *Light From the Ancient Past*. Princeton, NJ: Princeton University Press, 1959.

Finkelstein, Israel, and Neal Asher Silberman. *The Bible Unearthed: Archaeology's New Vision of Ancient Israel and the Origins of Its Sacred Texts*. New York: Free Press, 2001.

Finkelstein, Jacob J. "The Bible, Archaeology, and History: Have the Excavations Corroborated Scripture?" *Commentary* 28 (1959): 341–49.

Finkelstein, Louis. *Akiba: Scholar, Saint, and Martyr*. New York: Atheneum, 1975.

Firestone, Reuven. *Journeys in Holy Lands: The Evolution of the Abraham-Ishmael Legends in Islamic Exegesis*. Albany: State University of New York Press, 1990.

Fishbane, Michael. *Text and Texture: Close Readings of Selected Biblical Texts*. New York: Schocken, 1964.

Ford, David and Graham Stanton, eds: *Reading Texts, Seeking Wisdom: Scripture and Theology*. Grand Rapids: Eerdmans Publishing Co., 2004.

Frankiel, Tamar. *The Voice of Sarah: Feminine Spirituality and Traditional Judaism*. New York: Harper Collins, 1990.

Free, Joseph P. "Abraham's Camels." *Journal of Near Eastern Studies* 3: 187–93.

Freedman, David. "A New Approach to the Nuzi Sistership Contract." *The Journal of the Ancient Near Eastern Society of Columbia University* 2 (1970): 77–85.

Fretheim, Terence. *The Suffering of God: An Old Testament Perspective*. Minneapolis: Augsburg Fortress Publishers, 1984.

Friedman, Richard E. *The Bible with Sources Revealed*. New York: HarperOne, 2005.

————. *Who Wrote the Bible?* New York: Simon and Schuster, 1987.

Fritz, V. and P.R. Davies, eds. "The Origins of the Ancient Israelite States."

Journal for the Study of the Old Testament Supplement Series 228. Sheffield: Sheffield Academic, 1996.

Fröhlich, B., and D.J. Ortner. "Excavations of the Early Bronze Age Cemetery at Babe dh-Dhra' Jordan, 1981: A Preliminary Report." *Annual of the Department of Antiquities of Jordan* 26 (1982): 249–65, LXV–LXXIV.

Frymer-Kensky, Tivka. *Reading the Women of the Bible.* New York: Schocken Books, 2002.

Ganss, George E., ed. *Ignatius of Loyola: Spiritual Exercises and Selected Works.* New York: Paulist Press, 1991.

Ginzberg, Louis. *Legends of the Jews* 6th ed. Philadelphia: Jewish Publication Society, 1992.

Glueck, Nelson. *Rivers in the Desert: A History of the Negev.* New York: Farrar, Straus & Cuddahy, 1959.

Goldenberg, Naomi. *Returning Words to Flesh: Feminism, Psychoanalysis, and the Resurrection of the Body.* Boston: Beacon Press, 1990.

Gollaher, David L. *Circumcision: A History of the World's Most Controversial Surgery.* New York: Basic Books, 2000.

Goodwyn, Wade, Howard Berkes, and Amy Walters. "Warren Jeffs and the FLDS." National Public Radio. May 3, 2005. http://www.npr.org/templates/story/story.php?storyId=4629320 (January 22, 2009).

Gordis, Daniel. *Does the World Need the Jews? Rethinking Chosenness and American Jewish Identity.* New York: Scribners, 1997.

Gordon, Cyrus. *The Common Background of Greek and Hebrew Civilizations.* New York: W. W. Norton, 1965.

Gordon, Cyrus, and Gary A. Rendsburg. *The Bible and the Ancient Near East.* New York: Norton, 1997.

Gorenberg, Gershom. *The End of Days: Fundamentalism and the Struggle for the Temple Mount.* New York: Free Press, 2000.

Gottwald, N.K. *The Tribes of Yahweh: A Sociology of the Religion of Liberated Israel, 1250–1050 B.C.E.* Maryknoll, NY: Orbis Books, 1979.

Graham, W. C., and H. G. May. *Culture and Conscience.* Chicago: University of Chicago Press, 1936.

Graves, David, and Jane Graves. "Soddom and Gomorrah." *The Scroll: Multimedia Study Bible.* 1995 http://www.abu.nb.ca/ecm/topics/arch5.htm (November 7, 2007).

Graves, Robert, and Raphael Patai. *Hebrew Myths: The Book of Genesis.* Garden City, NJ: Doubleday & Co., 1964.

Gray, John. *Archaeology and the Old Testament World.* New York: Harper and Row, 1962.

———. *The Canaanites.* New York: Frederick A. Praeger, 1964.

Green, Arthur. "Bride, Spouse, Daughter: Images of the Feminine in Classical Jewish Sources." In *On Being a Jewish Feminist.* Edited by Susannah Heschel. New York: Schocken, 1983: 254–57.

Gross, Rita. "Steps Toward Feminine Imagery of Deity in Jewish Theology." In

On Being a Jewish Feminist. Edited by Susannah Heschel. New York: Schocken, 1983: 234–47.

Gunn, James. *Jesus Remembered: Christianity in the Making,* vol. 1. Grand Rapids: Eerdmans Publishing Co., 2003.

Haddad, Yvonne Yazbeck, and John L. Esposito, eds. *Daughters of Abraham: Feminist thought in Judaism, Christianity, and Islam,* Gainesville: University Press of Florida, 2001.

Hadley, Judith M. *The Cult of Ashera in Ancient Israel and Judah: Evidence for a Hebrew Goddess.* Cambridge: Cambridge University Press, 2000.

Hadot, Pierre. *Philosophy as a Way of Life: Spiritual Exercises from Socrates to Foucault.* Wiley-Blackwell, 1995.

Harlan, Jack R. "The Garden of the Lord: A Plausible Reconstruction of the Natural Resources of Southern Jordan in Early Bronze Age." *Paleorient* 8 (1982): 71–78.

Harland, J. Penrose. "Sodom and Gomorrah." In *The Biblical Archaeologist Reader,* vol. 1. Garden City, NJ: Anchor, 1961.

Harris, G.M., and A.P. Beardow. "The Destruction of Sodom and Gomorrah: A Geological Perspective." *Quarterly Journal of Engineering Geology* 28 (1995): 360.

Harris, Rivkah. "The Case of Three Marriage Contracts." *Journal of Near Eastern Studies* 33 (1974): 4.

Harris, Robert L., ed. *Theological Wordbook of the Old Testament.* Chicago: The Moody Bible Institute, 1980.

Heidel, Alexander. *The Gilgamesh Epic and Old Testament Parallels.* Chicago: University of Chicago Press, 1965.

Heschel, Abraham. *God in Search of Man: A Philosophy of Judaism.* New York: Noonday, 1955.

———. *Moral Grandeur and Spiritual Audacity.* Edited by Susannah Heschel. New York: Farrar, Strauss & Giroux, 1997.

———. *The Prophets.* 1962. Reprint. New York: HarperCollins, 2001.

Heschel, Susannah. "Anti-Judaism in Christian Feminist Theology." *Tikkun* 5, no. 3 (1990): 26–49.

"High Star." In *How I Pray: People of Different Religions Share With Us That Most Sacred and Intimate Act of Faith.* Edited by Jim Castelli. New York: Random House, 1994.

Hogarth, David G., ed. *Authority and Archaeology: Sacred and Profane: Essays on the Relation of Monuments to Biblical and Classical Literature.* London: John Murray, 1899.

Hooke, S. H. *Babylonian and Assyrian Religion.* Norman: University of Oklahoma Press, 1963.

———. *Myth, Ritual and Kingship.* Oxford: Clarendon Press, 1958.

Hooker, Morna. *From Adam to Christ: Essays on Paul.* Eugene, OR: Wipf & Stock, 2008.

———. *The Signs of a Prophet.* Harrisburg, PA: Trinity Press International, 1997.

Horbury, William. *Jews and Christians in Contact and Controversy.* Scholar's edition. Edinburgh: T.&T. Clark, 1998.

Houten, Christina van. "The Rape of the Concubine." *Perspectives* 12, no. 8 (1997): 12–14.

Human Assistance & Development International. "Prophet Ibrahim: The Father of the Prophets." *IslamiCity.com,* 2009, http://www.islamicity.com/Mosque/ibrahim.htm (June 3, 2008).

The Interpreter's Bible. New York: Abingdon-Cokesbury Press, 1951.

Jacobsen, Thorkil. *The Treasures of Darkness: A History of Mesopotamian Religion.* New Haven, CT: Yale University Press, 1976.

James, E. O. *The Ancient Gods: The History and Diffusion of Religion in the Ancient Near Eastern Mediterranean.* New York: G. P. Putnam's Sons, 1960.

James, William. *The Varieties of Religious Experience.* 1902. Reprint. New York: Collier Books, 1961.

Jastrow, Morris, Jr. "Beer Lahai Ro'I." *Jewish Encyclopedia Online,* 2002, http://www.jewishencyclopedia.com/view.jsp?artid=519&letter=B&search=Beer%20Lahai%20Ro%E2%80%99I (June 3, 2008).

Jeansonne, Sharon Pace. *The Women of Genesis: From Sarah to Potiphar's Wife.* Minneapolis: Fortress Press, 1990.

Johnson, Elizabeth A. *She Who Is: The Mystery of God in Feminist Theological Discourse.* New York: Crossroad, 1993.

Johnson, Paul. *A History of the Jews.* New York: Harper and Row, 1987.

Jonte-Pace, Diane. "Object Relations Theory, Mothering, and Religion: Toward a Feminist Psychology of Religion." *Horizons* 14, no. 2 (1987): 310–27.

Josephus. *Complete Works of Josephus. A New and Revised Edition.* Based on Havercamp's translation. New York: Bigelow, Brown & Co., 1925.

Josephus. *The Jewish War.* London: Penguin, 1981.

Kallai, Z. "The Twelve-Tribe Systems of Israel." *Vetus Testamentus* 47 (1997): 53–90.

Kaplan, Arych. *Sefer Yetzirah: The Book of Creation.* York Beach, ME: Samuel Weiser, 1997.

Kardimon, Samson. "Adoption as a Remedy for Infertility in the Period of the Patriarchs." *Journal of Semitic Studies* 3 (1958): 123–26.

Kathir, Ibn. *Stories of the Prophets.* Translated by Rashad Ahmad Azami. Riyadh: Dar-us-Salaam Publications, 2003.

Katz, Claire Elise. *Levinas, Judaism, and the Feminine: The Silent Footsteps of Rebecca.* Bloomington: Indiana University Press, 2003.

Kenyon, Kathleen. *Archaeology in the Holy Land.* New York: Norton, 1979.

Kershner, Isabel. "Pilgrimage to Roots of Faith and Strife." *New York Times,* October 24, 2008.

Kierkegaard, Søren. *Fear and Trembling.* 1843. Reprint. Garden City, NY: Doubleday, 1954.

Klinghoffer, David. *The Discovery of God: Abraham and the Birth of Monotheism.* New York: Doubleday, 2003.

———. *Why the Jews Rejected Jesus: The Turning Point in Western History.* New York: Doubleday, 2005.

Kohler, Ludwig. *Hebrew Man.* Translated by Peter R. Ackroyd. New York: Abingdon Press, 1953.

Kramer, Samuel Noah. "Poets and Psalmists: Goddesses and Theologians." In *The Legacy of Sumer.* Edited by Denise Schmandt-Basserat. Malibu, CA: Udena Publications, 1976.

———. "Sumerian Literature, A General Survey." In *The Bible and the Ancient Near East.* Edited by G. E. Wright. New York: Anchor Books, 1965.

———. "Shulgi of Ur: A Royal Hymn and a Divine Blessing." *The Seventy-Fifth Anniversary Volume of the Jewish Quarterly Review* (1967): 396–480.

———. *The Sacred Marriage Rite: Aspects of Faith, Myth and Ritual in Ancient Sumer.* Bloomington: Indiana University Press, 1969.

———. *The Sumerians: Their History, Culture and Character.* Chicago: University of Chicago Press, 1963.

Kugel, James. *The Bible as It Was.* Cambridge, MA: Harvard University Press, 1997.

———. *The God of Old: Inside the Lost World of the Bible.* New York: Free Press, 2003.

Lapp, N. "Who is This That Comes from Edom?" In *Scripture and Other Artifacts: Essays on the Bible and Archaeology in Honor of Philip J. King.* Edited by M.D. Coogan, J.C. Exum, and L.E. Stager. Louisville, KY: Westminster John Knox Press, 1994: 216–29.

Lapsley, Jacqueline. *Whispering the Word: Hearing Women's Stories in the Old Testament.* Louisville, KY: Westminster John Knox Press, 2005.

Lehmann, Manfred R. "Abraham's Purchase of Machpelah and Hittite Law." *Bulletin of the American Schools of Oriental Research* 129 (1953): 15–18.

Levenson, Jon. *Creation and the Persistence of Evil: The Jewish Drama of Divine Omnipotence.* New York: Harper and Row, 1988.

———. *The Death and Resurrection of the Beloved Son.* New Haven, CT: Yale University Press, 1993.

Levinas, Emmanuel. *Otherwise than Being, or Beyond Essence.* Translated by Alphonso Lingis. Pittsburgh: Duqueshe University Press, 1998.

Levine, Amy-Jill. "Settling at Beer-lahi-roi," in *Daughters of Abraham: Feminist Thought in Judaism, Christianity, and Islam.* Edited by Yvonne Yazbeck Haddad and John Esposito. Gainesville: University Press of Florida, 2001.

Lind, M. *Yahweh is a Warrior: The Theology of Warfare in Ancient Israel.* Scottsdale, PA: Herald, 1980.

Lipton, Diana. *Revisions of the Night: Politics and Promises in the Patriarchal Dreams of Genesis.* Sheffield: Sheffield Academic Press, 1999.

Liverani, M. "The Amorites." In *Peoples of Old Testament Times.* Edited by D. J. Wiseman. Oxford: Oxford University Press, 1978.

Lutzky, Harrlet. "Shadday as a Goddess Epithet." *Venus Testamentum* 48, 1998: 15–36.

Luzzato, Moshe Chayim. *The Way of God.* Translated by Aryeh Kaplan. New York: Feldheim, 1988.

Maimonides. *The Guide for the Perplexed.* Translated by M. Friedlander. Reprint. New York: Dover, 1956.

Matthews, Victor H. "The Wells of Gerar." *Biblical Archaeologist* 49 (1986): 118–26.

McNeil, W. H., and J. W. Sedlar, eds. *The Ancient Near East.* London: Oxford University Press, 1968.

Metzger, Bruce, and Michael Coogan, eds. *The Oxford Companion to the Bible.* New York: Oxford University Press, 1993.

Meyers, Carol. *Discovering Eve: Ancient Israelite Women in Context.* Oxford: Oxford University Press, 1988.

Michalowski, Piotr. *Lamentation over the Destruction of Sumer and Ur.* Winona Lake, IN: Eisenbrauns, 1989.

Miles, Jack. *Christ: A Crisis in the Life of God.* New York: Knopf, 2001.

———. *God: A Biography.* New York: Vintage Books, 1996.

Miller, Nancy. "Patriarchal Burial Site Explored for First Time in 700 Years." *The Biblical Archaeological Review* 9, no. 3 (1985): 26–43.

Miller, P. D. *The Divine Warrior in Early Israel.* Cambridge: Harvard University, 1973.

Milne, Pamela J. "Toward Feminist Companionship: The Future of Feminist Biblical Studies and Feminism." In *A Feminist Companion to Reading the Bible: Approaches, Methods and Strategies.* Edited by Athalya Brenner and Carole Fontaine. Sheffield: Sheffield Academic Press, 1997.

Milton, John. "Eikonoklastes (London, 1649)." In *The Complete Prose Works of John Milton,* vol. 3. Edited by Don M. Wolfe. New Haven, CT: Yale University Press, 1962.

Moberly, R. "The Earliest Commentary on the Akedah." *Vetus Testamentum* 38 (1998): 302–3.

Moberly, Walter. *The Bible, Theology, and Faith: A Study of Abraham and Jesus:* Cambridge: Cambridge University Press, 2000.

Motzvafi-Haller, Pnina, and others. "About Hagar." In *Hagar: Studies in Culture, Polity and Identities* 7, no.3, 2007, http://hsf.bgu.ac.il/hagar/about.aspx (January 28, 2009).

Mullner, Ilse. "Lethal Differences: Sexual Violence as Violence Against Others in Judges 19." In *Judges.* Edited by Athalya Brenner. FCB 2/4. Sheffield: Sheffield Academic Press, 1999: 126–42.

Nasr, Seyyed. *The Heart of Islam: Enduring Values for Humanity.* New York: Harper Collins, 2002.

———. *Islam: Religion, History, and Civilization.* New York: Harper Collins, 2003.

Neev, D., and K.O. Emery. *The Destruction of Sodom, Gomorrah, and Jericho: Geological, Climatological, and Archaeological Background.* New York: Oxford University Press, 1995.

The New Interpreter's Bible, vol. 1. New York: Abingdom Press, 1994.

Newsome, Carol, and Sharon Ringe, eds. *The Women's Bible Commentary*. Louisville, KY: Westminster John Knox Press, 1992.

Niditch, S. *Ancient Israelite Religion*. Oxford: Oxford University Press, 1997.

———. "The 'Sodomite' Theme in Judges 19–20: Family, Community, and Social Disintegration." *Catholic Biblical Quarterly* 44 (1982): 365–78.

———. *War in the Hebrew Bible: A Study in the Ethics of Violence*. New York: Orbis, 1992.

Noth, Martin. *A History of Pentateuchal Traditions*. Translated by Bernhard Anderson. Chicago: Scholars, 1981.

Nunnally-Cox, Janice. *Foremothers: Women of the Bible*. San Francisco: Harper & Row, 1981.

Ochs, Carol. *Behind the Sex of God: Toward a New Consciousness Transcending Matriarchy and Patriarchy*. Boston: Beacon Press, 1977.

Ochs, Vanessa. *Sarah Laughed*. New York: McGraw Hill, 2005.

Ochshorn, Judith. *The Female Experience and the Nature of the Divine*. Bloomington: Indiana University Press, 1981.

Ortner, D. J. "A Preliminary Report on the Human Remains from the Bab edh-Dhra' Cemetery." In "The Southeastern Dead Sea Plain Expedition: An Interim Report of the 1977 Season". *Annual of the American Schools of Oriental Research,* vol. 46. Edited by W.E. Rast and R.T. Schaub. Cambridge, MA: American Schools of Oriental Research, 1981: 119–32.

———. "Disease and Mortality in the Early Bronze People of Bab edh-Dhra', Jordan," *American Journal of Physical Anthropology* 51 (1979): 589–97.

Osiek, Carolyn. "The Feminist and the Bible: Hermeneutical Alternatives." In *Feminist Perspectives on Biblical Scholarship*. Edited by Adela Yarbro Collins, 93–106. SBLBSNA 10. Chico, CA: Scholars Press, 1985.

Otto, Rudolph. *The Idea of the Holy, an Inquiry into the Non-rational Factor in the Idea of the Divine and Its Relation to the Rational*. Translated by John W. Harvey. Oxford: Oxford University Press, 1923.

Otwell, J. H. *And Sarah laughed: The Status of Women in the Old Testament*. Philadelphia: Westminster Press, 1977.

Pagels, Elaine. *The Gnostic Gospels*. New York: Vintage, 1981.

———. *The Origin of Satan*. New York: Random House, 1995.

Pardes, Ilana. *Countertraditions in the Bible: A Feminist Approach*. Cambridge, MA: Harvard University Press, 1992.

Parrot, Andre. *Abraham and His Times*. Translated by James H. Farley. Philadelphia: Fortress Press, 1968.

Patai, Raphael. *Gates to the Old City: A Book of Jewish Legends*. New York: Avon Books, 1980.

———. *Sex and Family in the Bible and the Middle East*. Garden City, NJ: Doubleday & Co., 1982.

Patton, Kimberley Christine, and John Stratton Hawley, eds. *Holy Tears: Weeping in the Religious Imagination*. Princeton, NJ: Princeton University Press, 2005.

Pelikan, Jaroslav. *Whose Bible Is It? A History of Scripture Through the Ages*. New York: Viking, 2005.

Peters, F. E. *The Children of Abraham: Judaism, Christianity, Islam*. Princeton, NJ: Princeton University Press, 2004.

Petrie, W.M. Flinders. *Gerar*. London: London Office of School of Archaeology, 1928.

Plaskow, Judith. *Standing Again at Sinai*. New York: Harper and Row, 1990.

Pope, Marvin H. *El in the Ugaritic Texts*. Leiden: Brill, 1955.

Pritchard, James, ed. *Ancient Near Eastern Texts Relating to the Old Testament*. Princeton, NJ: Princeton University Press, 1969.

Provan, Iain, V. Philips Long, and Tremper Longman, eds. *A Biblical History of Israel*. Louisville, KY: Westminster John Knox Press, 2003.

Rad, Gerhard von. *Genesis: A Commentary*. Translated by John H. Marks. Philadelphia: Westminster Press, 1972.

———. *Holy War in Ancient Israel*. Grand Rapids: Eerdmans Publishing Co., 1991.

Ramsey, G. W. *The Quest for the Historical Israel*. Atlanta: John Knox, 1981.

Rast, W. E. "Bab edh-Dhra'." In *Anchor Dictionary of the Bible*, vol.1. Edited by David Noel Freedman. New York: Doubleday, 1993.

———. "Bronze Age Cities along the Dead Sea." *Archaeology* 40, no. 1 (1987): 42–49.

———. "Early Bronze Age State Formation in the Southeast Dead Sea Plain, Jordan." In *Studies in the Archaeology of Israel and Neighboring Lands in Memory of Douglas L. Esse*. Edited by S.R. Wolff. *Oriental Institute of the University of Chicago, Studies in Ancient Oriental Civilization*, No. 59. Chicago: Oriental Institute, University of Chicago, 2001: 519–34.

———. "Society and Mortuary Customs at Bab edh-Dhra'." In *Archaeology, History and Culture in Palestine and the Near East, Essays in Memory of Albert E. Glock*. Edited by T. Kapitan. Atlanta: Scholars Press, 1999.

Rast, Walter E., and R. Thomas Schaub. "Sites." *Expedition to the Dead Sea Plain*, 2009, http://www.nd.edu/~edsp/index.html (October 27, 2006).

Reuther, Rosemary. *Sexism and God-Talk: Toward a Feminist Theology*. Boston: Beacon Press, 1983.

Ringgren, Helmer. *Israelite Religion*. Translated by David E. Green. Philadelphia: Fortress, 1966.

Roaf, Michael. *Cultural Atlas of Mesopotamia and the Ancient Near East*. New York: Equinox, 1990.

Roberts, J. J. M. "Does God Lie? Divine Deceit as a Theological Problem in Israelite Prophetic Literature." In *The Bible and the Ancient Near East: Collected Essays*. Winona Lake, IN: Eisenbraum, 2002.

Robinson, James, ed. *The Nag Hammadi Library*. San Francisco: Harper and Row, 1981 (Brill, 1978).

Rohl, David. *Pharaohs and Kings: A Biblical Quest*. New York: Crown, 1995.

Rohrlich-Leavitt, Ruby. "Women in Transition: Crete and Sumer." In *Becoming Visible: Women in European History*. Edited by Renate Bridenthal and Claudia Koonz. Boston: Houghton Mifflin Co., 1977.

Roop, Eugene. *Genesis*. Nappanee, IN: Evangel Publishing House, 1987.

Rosenberg, David. *Abraham: The First Historical Biography.* New York: Basic Books, 2006.

Rubinkiewicz, R. "Apocalypse of Abraham: A Translation with Introduction." In *The Old Testament Pseudepigrapha,* vol.1. Edited by James H. Charlesworth. Garden City, NJ: Doubleday, 1983.

Sacks, Jonathan. *A Letter in the Scroll.* New York: Free Press, 2000.

Safi, Omid. *Progressive Muslims: On Justice, Gender and Pluralism,* Oxford: One World, 2003.

Saggs, H.W.F. *The Greatness That Was Babylon: A Survey of the Ancient Civilizations of the Tigris-Euphrates Valley.* New York: Praeger, 1962.

Sakenfeld, Katharine Doob. *Just Wives? Stories of Power and Survival in the Old Testament and Today.* Louisville, KY: Westminster John Knox Press, 2003.

———. *The Meaning of Hesed in the Hebrew Bible: A New Inquiry.* HSM 17. Missoula, MT: Scholars Press, 1978.

Sarna, Nahum. "Abraham in History." *The Biblical Archaeology Review* 3, no. 12 (1977): 5–9.

———. *Understanding Genesis: The World of the Bible in the Light of History.* The Heritage of Biblical Israel, vol. 1. 5th ed. New York: Schocken, 1978. First published 1966 by Jewish Theological Seminary of America.

Sasson, Jack M. "Circumcision in the Ancient Near East." *Journal of Biblical Literature* 85 (1966): 473–76.

Schaub, R.T. "An Early Bronze IV Tomb from Bab edh-Dhra'." *Bulletin of the American Schools of Oriental Research* 210 (1973): 2–19.

———. "Feifa and Khanazir." In "Archaeology in Jordan," *American Journal of Archaeology* 95 (1991): 254–55.

———. "Patterns of Burial at Bab edh-Dhra'." *Annual of the American Schools of Oriental Research* 46 (1981): 45–68.

———. "Southeast Dead Sea Plain." In *The Oxford Encyclopedia of Archaeology In the Near East,* vol. 5. Edited by Eric M. Meyers. New York: Oxford University Press, 1997.

Schiffman, Lawrence. *From Text to Tradition: A History of Second Temple and Rabbinic Judaism.* Hoboken, NJ: Ktav Publishing House, Inc., 1991.

Scholem, Gershom G. *Jewish Gnosticism, Merkabah Mysticism, and Talmudic Tradition.* New York: Jewish Theological Seminary of America, 1960.

Schorsch, Ismar. "Accessing God in a Man-Made World." *MyJewishLearning.com,* http://www.myjewishlearning.com/texts/Weekly_Torah_Commentary/noah_jts.htm (January 9, 2009).

Schottrof, Luise, Silvia Schroer, and Marie-Theres Walker. *Feminist Interpretation: the Bible in Women's Perspective.* Minneapolis: Fortress Press, 1998.

Schroeder, Gerald. *The Science of God: The Convergence of Scientific and Biblical Wisdom.* New York: Free Press, 1997.

Seibert, Ilse. *Women in the Ancient Near East.* Leipzig: Edition Leipzig, 1974.

Shanks, Hershel. "Have Sodom and Gomorrah Been Found?" *The Biblical Archaeology Review* 6, no.5 (1980): 26–36.

———. *The Mystery and Meaning of the Dead Sea Scrolls.* New York: Vintage, 1999.

———. "The Patriarchs' Wives as Sisters: Is the Anchor Bible Wrong?" *The Biblical Archaeology Review* 1, no. 3 (1975): 22–26.

Sheridan, Mark, ed. *Ancient Christian Commentary of Scripture: Genesis 12–50.* Downers Grove, IL: InterVarsity Press, 2002.

Siegal, Eliezer. "Abraham Our Father—and Theirs: Christianity and Islam share a reverence for Judaism's patriarch." *MyJewishLearning.com*, http://www.myjewishlearning.com/history_community/Ancient/TheStoryTO/Patriarchs/Abraham/AbrahamOthers.htm (April 10, 2008).

Siker, Jeffrey S. *Disinheriting the Jews: Abraham in Christian Controversy.* Louisville, KY: Westminster John Knox Press, 1991.

Simpson, V. "Genesis." In *The Interpreter's Bible,* vol. 1. New York: Abingdon-Cokesbury Press, 1951.

Singer, Amy. *Constructing Ottoman Beneficence: An Imperial Soup Kitchen in Jerusalem.* New York: SUNY Press, 2002.

Skinner, John. *A Critical and Exegetical Commentary on Genesis.* 1910 Reprint, Edinbugh: T. & T. Clark, 1969.

Smith, Mark. *The Origins of Biblical Monotheism: Israel's Polytheistic Background and the Ugaritic Texts.* New York: Oxford University Press, 2001.

Soloveitchik, Joseph B. "Adam and Eve." In *Family Redeemed: Essays on Family Relationships.* Edited by David Shatz and Joel B. Wolowelsky. New York: Toras HoRav Foundation, 2000.

Speiser, Ephraim A. *Genesis: A New Translation with Introduction and Commentary.* New York: Doubleday, 1964.

———. "The Wife-Sister Motif in the Patriarchal Narratives." In *Biblical and Other Studies.* Edited by A. Altman. Cambridge, MA: Harvard University Press, 1963.

Spiegel, Shalom. *The Last Trial: On the Legends and Lore of the Command to Offer Isaac as a Sacrifice.* Translated by Judah Goldin. New York: Behrman House, 1967.

———. *The Last Trial: On the Legends and Lore of the Command to Offer Isaac as a Sacrifice.* Translated by Judah Goldin. Reprint. Woodstock, VT: Jewish Lights, 1993.

Steinberg, Naomi. *Kinship and Marriage in Genesis: A Household Economics Perspective.* Minneapolis: Fortress Press, 1993.

Steinmetz, Devora. *From Father to Son: Kinship, Conflict, and Continuity in Genesis.* Louisville, KY: Westminster John Knox Press, 1991.

Stern, David. *Parables in Midrash.* Cambridge, MA: Harvard University Press, 1991.

Strimling, Arthur. "Sarah Sees." *Living Text: The Journal of the Institute of Contemporary Midrash* 8 (2000): 13–15.

Swindler, Leonard. *Biblical Affirmations of Woman.* Philadelphia: The Westminster Press, 1979.

Tamez, Elsa, and B. Year. "The Women Who Complicated the History of Salvation." In *New Eyes for Reading.* By John S. Pobee. Edited by Barbel von Wartenberg-Potter. Geneva: World Council of Churches, 1986.

Tannen, Deborah. *Gender and Discourse.* New York: Oxford University Press, 1994.

Teubal, Savina. *Sarah the Priestess: The First Matriarch of Genesis.* Athens: Ohio University Press, 1984.

Theological Word Book of The Old Testament. Chicago: The Moody Bible Institute, 1980.

Thomas, D. Winton, ed. *Documents from Old Testament Times,* 2d ed. New York: Harper Torchbooks, 1961.

Thompsett, Fredrica Harris. *Living With History,* vol. 5, *The New Church's Teaching Series.* Cambridge: Cowley Publications, 1999.

Thompson, John L. *Writing the Wrongs: Women of the Old Testament Among Biblical Commentators from Philo through the Reformation.* Oxford: Oxford University Press, 2001.

Thompson, Thomas. L. "Early History of the Israelite People: from the Written and Archaeological Sources." *Studies in the History of the Ancient Near East* 4. Leiden: E. J. Brill, 1992.

———. *The Historicity of the Patriarchal Narratives.* Berlin: de Gruyter, 1974.

Toperoff, Shlomo, ed. *Avot: A Comprehensive Commentary on the Ethics of the Fathers.* Northvale, NJ: Jason Aronson Inc, 1997.

Towner, W. Sibley. *Genesis.* Louisville, KY: Westminster John Knox Press, 1989.

Trible, Phyllis. *God and the Rhetoric of Sexuality.* Philadelphia: Fortress Press, 1989.

———. *Texts of Terror: Literary-Feminist Readings of Biblical Narratives.* Philadelphia: Fortress Press, 1984.

Trible, Phyllis, and Letty Russell, eds. *Hagar, Sarah, and Their Children: Jewish, Christian and Muslim Perspectives.* Louisville, KY: Westminster Press John Knox Press, 2006.

Tubb, Jonathan N. *Canaanites.* Norman: University of Oklahoma Press, 1998.

Twain, Mark. *Innocents Abroad.* New York: Signet, 1966.

Twersky, Isadore, ed. *A Maimonides Reader.* West Orange, NJ: Behrman House, 1972.

Vamosh, Miriam. *Food at the Time of the Bible.* Herzlia, Israel: Palphot Ltd., 2007.

Van Buren, Elizabeth Douglas. "The Sacred Marriage in Early Times in Mesopotamia." *Orientalia* 13, no. 4 (1944): 1–72.

Van-Dijk-Hemmes, Fokkelien. "Sarai's Exile: A Gender-Motivated Reading of Genesis 12:10–13:2," in *A Feminist Companion to Genesis.* Edited by Athalya Brenner. Sheffield: Sheffield Academic Press, 1993.

Van Seters, Jan. "The Problem of Childlessness in Near Eastern Law and the Patriarchs of Israel." *Journal of Biblical Literature* 87 (1968): 401–408.

Vaux, Kenneth L. *Jew, Christian, Muslim: Faithful Unification or Fateful Trifurcation?* Eugene, OR: Wipf and Stock, 2003.

Vaux, Roland de. *Ancient Israel.* Vol. 1, *Social Institutions,* 2d ed. New York: McGraw Hill, 1965.

———. *Ancient Israel.* Vol. 2, *Religious Institutions.* 2d ed. New York: McGraw Hill, 1965.

————. *The Early History of Israel: To the Exodus and the Covenant of Sinai*. Translated by David Smith. London: Daron, Longman & Todd, 1978.

Volf, Miroslav. *Exclusion & Embrace*. Nashville: Abingdon Press, 1996.

Wadud, Amina. *Qur'an and Woman: Rereading the Sacred Text from a Woman's Perspective*. NY: Oxford University Press, 1999.

Webb, Stephen H. *The Gifting God: A Trinitarian Ethics of Excess*. New York: Oxford University Press, 1996.

Weems, Renita J. "The Hebrew Women Are Not Like the Egyptian Women: The Ideology of Race, Gender, and Sexual Reproduction in Exodus 1." *Semeia* 59 (1992): 25–34.

Wegner, Judith Romney. *Chattel or Person? The Status of Women in the Mishnah*. New York: Oxford University Press, 1988.

Weinberg, Matis. *Frameworks: Bereishit-Genesis, Parashot II–XII*. Boston: The Foundation for Jewish Publications, 1999.

Westermann, Claus. *Genesis 1–11: A Commentary*. Translated by John J. Scullion. Minneapolis: Augsburg, 1984.

————. *Genesis 12–36: A Commentary*. Translated by John J. Scullion. Minneapolis: Augsburg, 1985.

Westphal, Merold. *Suspicion and Faith: The Religious Uses of Modern Atheism*. Grand Rapids: Eerdmans Publishing Co., 1993.

White, J.E.M. *Ancient Egypt: Its Culture and History*. New York: Dover Publications, 1970.

————. *Everyday Life in Ancient Egypt*. New York: Dover Publications, 1963.

Whitelam, K. W. "The Identity of Early Israel: The Realignment and Transformation of Late Bronze-Iron Age Palestine." *Journal for the Study of the Old Testament* 63 (1994): 57–87.

Wiesel, Elie. *Messengers of God*. New York: Touchstone, 1976.

Williams, J. G. *The Bible, Violence, and the Sacred. Liberation from the Myths of Sanctioned Violence*. San Francisco: Harper & Row, 1991.

Williamson, Ronald. *Jews in the Hellenistic World: Philo*. Cambridge, MA: Harvard University Press, 1989.

Wilson, John A. *The Culture of Ancient Egypt*. Chicago: University of Chicago Press, 1951.

Wilson, Karen L. "Treasures from the Royal Tombs of Ur." *The Oriental Institute*, Fall 2000, http://oi.uchicago.edu/research/pubs/nn/fal00_wilson.html (April 21, 2009).

Wintermute, O.S. "Jubilees: A New Translation and Introduction." In *The Old Testament Pseudepigrapha*, vol. 2. Edited by James H. Charlesworth. New York: Doubleday, 1985.

Wiseman, D. J. "Abraham Reassessed." In *Essays on the Patriarchal Narratives*. Edited by A. R. Millard and D. J. Wiseman. Winona Lake, IN: Eisenbrauns, 1983.

Wolkstein, Diane, and Samuel Noah Kramer. *Inanna, Queen of Heaven and Earth: Her Stories and Hymns from Sumer*. New York: Harper and Row, 1983.

Woolley, C. Leonard. *The Sumerians*. 1928, New York: Norton, 1965 Reprint.

Wright, Ernest G. *Biblical Archaeology*. Philadelphia: Westminster Press, 1962.

Yeats, William Butler. "Leda the Swan." In *Selected Poems and Three Plays of William Butler Yeats*. 3d ed. Edited by M.L. Rosenthal. New York: Collier Books, 1986.

Zornberg, Aviva. *The Beginning of Desire: Reflections on Genesis*. New York: Image, 1995.

ABOUT THE AUTHOR

CHARLOTTE GORDON graduated from Harvard College and received a Master's in Creative Writing and a PhD in History and Literature from Boston University. She has published two books of poetry and, most recently, the biography *Mistress Bradstreet,* which was a Massachusetts Book Award Honor Book. From 1999 to 2001, she taught at Boston University's School of Theology and the University Professors Program. Currently, she is an assistant professor of English at Endicott College. She lives in Gloucester, Massachusetts. Charlottegordonhome.com.